Gender Relations in an Indonesian Society

Verhandelingen van het Koninklijk Instituut voor Taal-, Land- en Volkenkunde

VOLUME 303

The titles published in this series are listed at *brill.com/vki*

Gender Relations in an Indonesian Society

Bugis Practices of Sexuality and Marriage

By

Nurul Ilmi Idrus

TUTA SUB AEGIDE PALLAS · 1683 ·

BRILL

LEIDEN | BOSTON

The realization of this publication was made possible by the support of KITLV (Royal Netherlands Institute of Southeast Asian and Caribbean Studies).

Cover illustrations: Left: Bugis couple in traditional wedding costume (photograph by Studio Spectrum Foto). Top right: Bugis Cosmic House (photograph by Alvian Ikram). Bottom right: Happily married couple (photograph by Mariani Nordin).

Library of Congress Cataloging-in-Publication Data

Names: Idrus, Nurul Ilmi, author.
Title: Gender relations in an Indonesian society : Bugis practices of sexuality and marriage / by Nurul Ilmi Idrus.
Other titles: Verhandelingen van het Koninklijk Instituut voor Taal-, Land- en Volkenkunde ; 303.
Description: Leiden ; Boston : Brill, 2016 | Series: Verhandelingen van het Koninklijk Instituut voor Taal-, Land- en Volkenkunde ; 303 | Includes bibliographical references and index.
Identifiers: LCCN 2015047444 (print) | LCCN 2015048552 (ebook) | ISBN 9789004311305 (hardback : alk. paper) | ISBN 9789004311947 (e-book) | ISBN 9789004311947 (E-book)
Subjects: LCSH: Marriage customs and rites--Indonesia--Sulawesi Selatan. | Bugis (Malay people)--Marriage customs and rites. | Sex role--Indonesia--Sulawesi Selatan. | Sulawesi Selatan (Indonesia)--Social life and customs. | Customary law--Indonesia--Sulawesi Selatan.
Classification: LCC GT2780.A3 I37 2016 (print) | LCC GT2780.A3 (ebook) | DDC 306.8109598--dc23
LC record available at http://lccn.loc.gov/2015047444

Want or need Open Access? Brill Open offers you the choice to make your research freely accessible online in exchange for a publication charge. Review your various options on brill.com/brill-open.

Typeface for the Latin, Greek, and Cyrillic scripts: "Brill". See and download: brill.com/brill-typeface.

ISSN 1572-1892
ISBN 978-90-04-31130-5 (hardback)
ISBN 978-90-04-31194-7 (e-book)

This book is printed on acid-free paper and produced in a sustainable manner.

Printed by Printforce, the Netherlands

Contents

Preface

In the text, terms in languages other than English are rendered in *italics*. Each is followed by an indication of its language and then by an English gloss of its meaning, or vice versa. Most of these words are Bugis (B.), or Indonesian (I.), but some are Arabic (A.) and Makassar (M.). Where many terms from one language, usually Bugis, are used in quick succession, only the first is identified.

Like other Austronesian languages, Bugis employs a wide variety of affixes, especially prefixes. It is often easier to recognise basic meanings and cognates by stripping off these affixes. For example, *madduta* (B. to delegate) from *ma-* and the noun duta (delegation); *mabbainé* (to marry) from *ma-* and *bainé* (woman).

There is no agreed form of rendering the glottal stop, which has an important role in Bugis. I use q, but others use an apostrophe (') or (k), especially in final position. A glottal stop before certain consonants is written as a double consonant. It also omits inter-vocalic glides, though these are commonly shown; thus *ia*, not *iya* and *ua*, not *uwa*. As is now usual, I render the pepet as 'e' and the strong vowel as 'é'; thus *maringngerrang* and *maéga*.

In addition, *tau* and *to* are two different words of similar meaning to describe person. Thus *to*, not *tau*. The title, such as *Pak* (for *Bapak*), *Ibu*, or *Hajj* is written in italics.

Except for the names of well-known figures and individuals names in newspaper, all personal names are pseudonyms. All place names are real.

Acknowledgements

In the name of Allah, Most Gracious, Most Merciful

The completion of this book is based on the extensive help of many people. I would like to thank the following people:

The people of Kulo, especially my host and his family for kindly allowing me to stay in their house and become part of their family before, during and after the research, who made Kulo a home rather than a field site. I thank Muhlis Hadrawi for his kindness in transliterating selected *lontaraq* for my thesis and for his on-going dialogue through email. To former and current *camat* of Kecamatan Kulo, *Bapak* Ahmad Yasin and *Bapak* Nurdin Rahman, and staff at Kantor Desa who provided me with access to their primary data from Kantor Kecamatan and Kantor Desa Kulo. I owe many thanks to the judges and staff at the Pengadilan Agama Sidrap, particularly to *Bapak* Akhiru for his time in discussing the nature of court hearings in the Pengadilan Agama Sidrap, the Head of KUA/PPN, Kecamatan Panca Rijang, Sidrap, and *Bapak* H. Abdul Azis for discussion of marriage registration; and also to *Bapak* Sama, *Ibu* Naima and *Ibu* Mawaddah for their time to provide assistance to update my data during my occasional visits after the initial fieldwork.

In Makassar, I am grateful to Ibu Syarifah Nuraeni, one of the judges in the Pengadilan Agama Makassar, Bapak H. Abdillah Yusuf and his staff, Ibu Husnang of BP4 (Badan Penasihat Perkawinan, Perselisihan dan Perceraian) Makassar. The late Christina Joseph, the director of LBH-P2I (Law Service for Indonesian Women's Empowerment) and her staff for their valuable discussion on women and law, and commitment to supporting women who are the victims of violence in both domestic and public spheres. Christina Joseph passed away on St Valentines Day, 14 February 2003. This research was made possible with the financial support of AusAid, and the field research grant from the Department of Anthropology, Research School of Pacific and Asian Studies, the Australian National University.

In particular, my deepest gratitude goes to my *punggawa* Prof. Kathryn M. Robinson who acted not only as a supervisor, but also a mother and a friend who has given both academic and moral support in patient, supportive and constructive directions. She came to visit me in Makassar when I did my fieldwork and turned my frustrated moments into challenging encouragement by her advisory and profitable strategies. When I came back from the field, she patiently read my chunk chapters and conference papers to improve them into something readable and presentable. I am grateful also to my advisers: Prof. Em. Campbell Macknight who is not just an adviser, but also my Bugis 'dictionarist' and La Galigo 'consultant,' Prof. Virginia M. Hooker who always encouraged me to keep going and reminded me to stay healthy and finally gave me the title as 'Bugis sex expert' just a few days before I completed my thesis. To Prof. Gavin W. Jones and Prof. Em. Terry Hall, thanks for their valuable demographic advise and discussion.

I am particularly grateful to my examiners, Prof. Lyn Parker and Prof. Tom Boellstorff for their valuable comments and encouragement for the publication of the book. My sincere thanks go to Dr. Linda R. Bennett and Dr. Sharyn Graham Davies for their time to comment on the first draft of some chapters of the book as well as to Prof. Tom Boellstorff for his particular critical remark in the introductory chapter of the book; to Sita van Bemmelen and the publisher's two anonymous reviewers for their detailed review of all chapters of the book. I am also indebted to Amelia D. Ihsan and Andrew Gebhardt for their help in the technical and grammatical revision of the book respectively. I would also thank those who allowed me to use their personal images to be presented in this book; and my thankfulness goes to the editors Rosemarijn Hoefte and Henk Schulte Nordholt (*KITLV*, Leiden) as well as the staff of Brill, especially Nienke Brienen-Molenaar, who made it possible for the manucript to be finally published.

To my *to masiri'*: my parents (M. Idrus Nurdin and St. Rasyidah Noor), my *pangngulu bola* (Muhammad Firda), and my *anaq oroané* (Fadel Fuady Firda) for their outstanding support during my study and upon the completion of this book. I am indebted to so many people in Sidrap and Makassar, I ask for forgiveness for not mentioning all the names in this book.

Parts of Chapter 2 were developed from '*Siri'*, Gender, and Sexuality among the Bugis in South Sulawesi', *Antropologi Indonesia*, 76 (2005): pp. 43–54. Parts of Chapter 3 were developed from 'Behind the Notion of *Siala*: Marriage, *Adat* and Islam among the Bugis in South Sulawesi', http://wwwsshe.murdoch.edu.au/intersections/issue10/idrus.html (2004). Parts of Chapter 5 were developed from 'Seksualitas dan Reproduksi di Masyarakat Bugis: Antara Mitos dan Pragmatisme', *Jurnal Perempuan*, 54 (2007): pp. 125–140. 'Islam, Marriage and Gender Relations in Bugis Lontaraq: A Critical Analysis of Lontaraq Daramatasia', in Susanne Schröter (ed), *Gender and Islam in Southeast Asia: Women's Rights Movements, Religious Resurgence and Local Traditions*. Leiden: Brill (2013): pp. 95–110.

Parts of Chapter 6 were developed from 'It's the Matter of a Piece of Paper: Between Legitimation and Legalisation of Marriage and Divorce in Bugis Society', http://intersections.anu.edu.au/issue19/idrus.htm (2006); 'Bugis Marriage: State

Laws, Islam and Local Practice', in Gavin W. Jones, Terrence H. Hull and Masnah Mohammad (eds), *Changing Marriage Patterns in Southeast Asia: Economic and Sociocultural Dimensions*. London: Routledge (2011): pp. 99–116; and 'Dissolution of Marriage: Gender, State and Islam in Contemporary Bugis Society in South Sulawesi, Indonesia', http://intersections.anu.edu.au/issue30/idrus.htm (2012).

Makassar, 15 February 2015

List of Maps, Tables, Plates, and Diagrams

Maps

Table

Plates

Diagrams

Maps

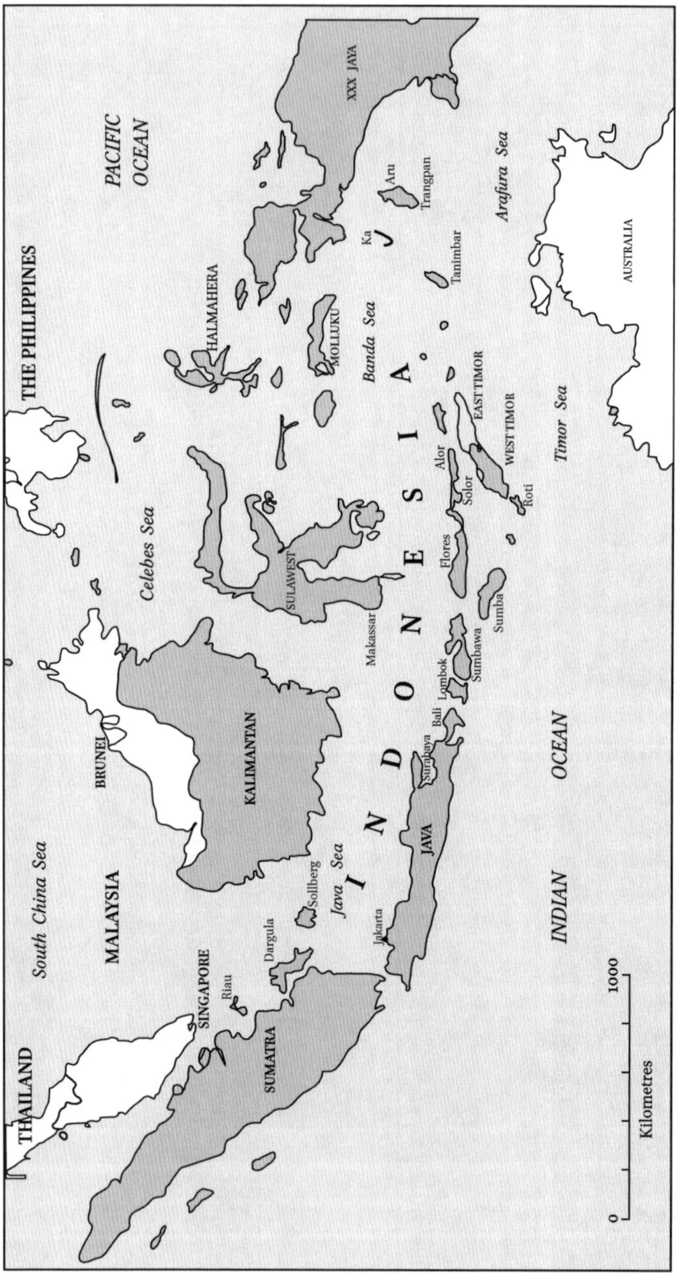

MAP 1.1 *Indonesia*

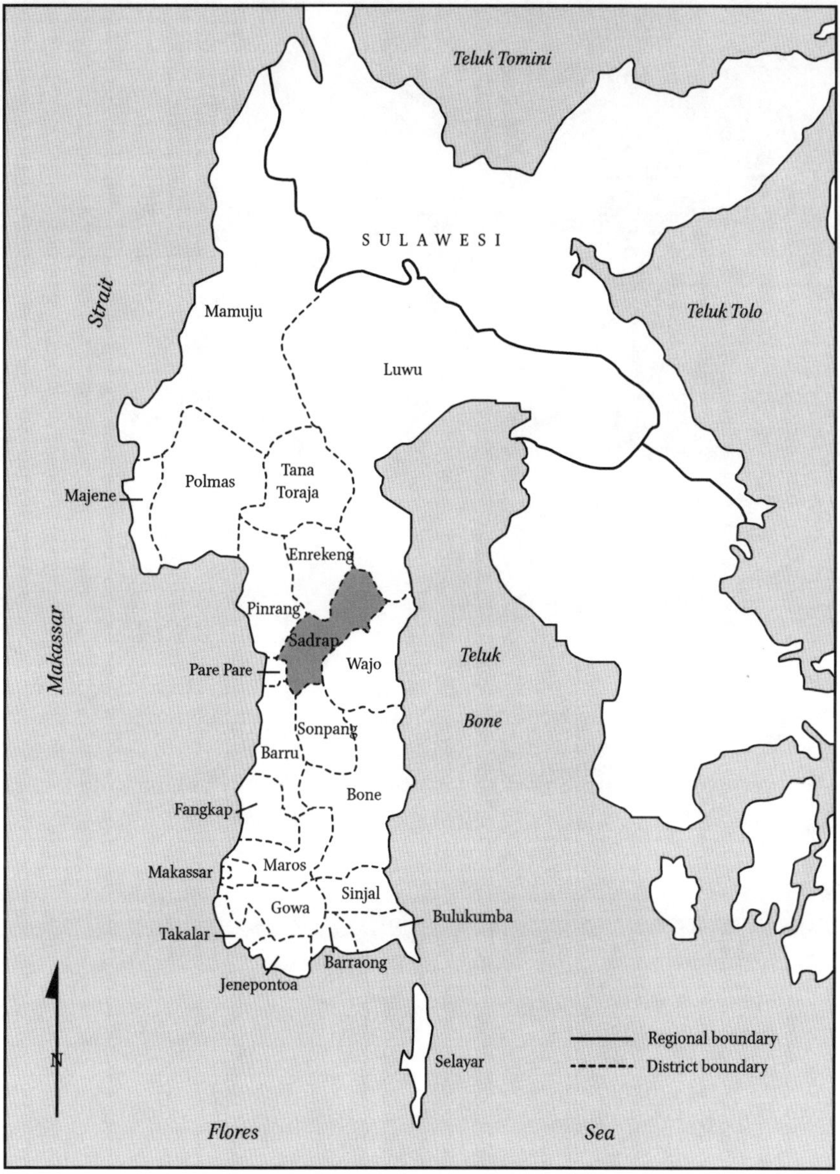

MAP 1.2 *South Sulawesi by Regencies*

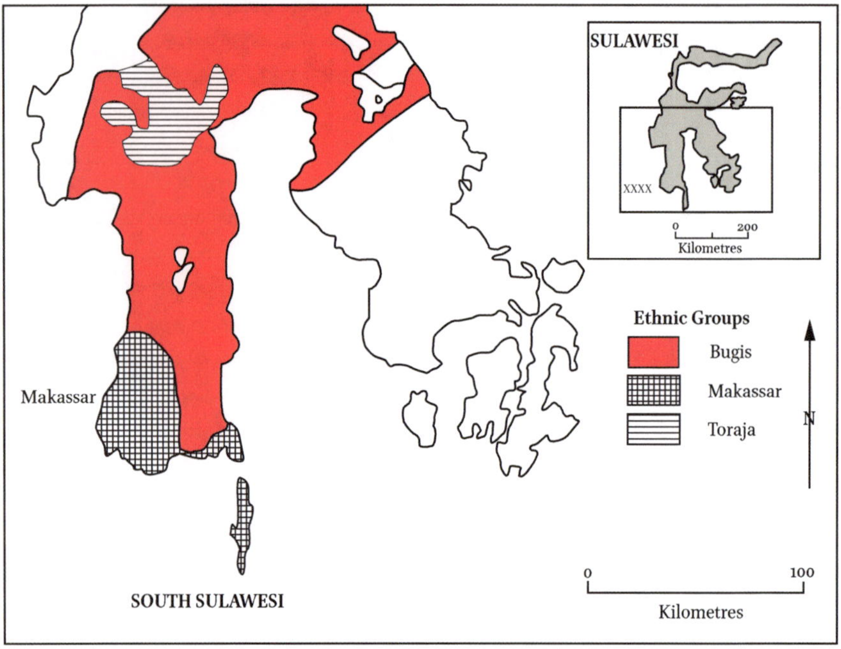

MAP 1.3 *South Sulawesi by Ethnic Groups*

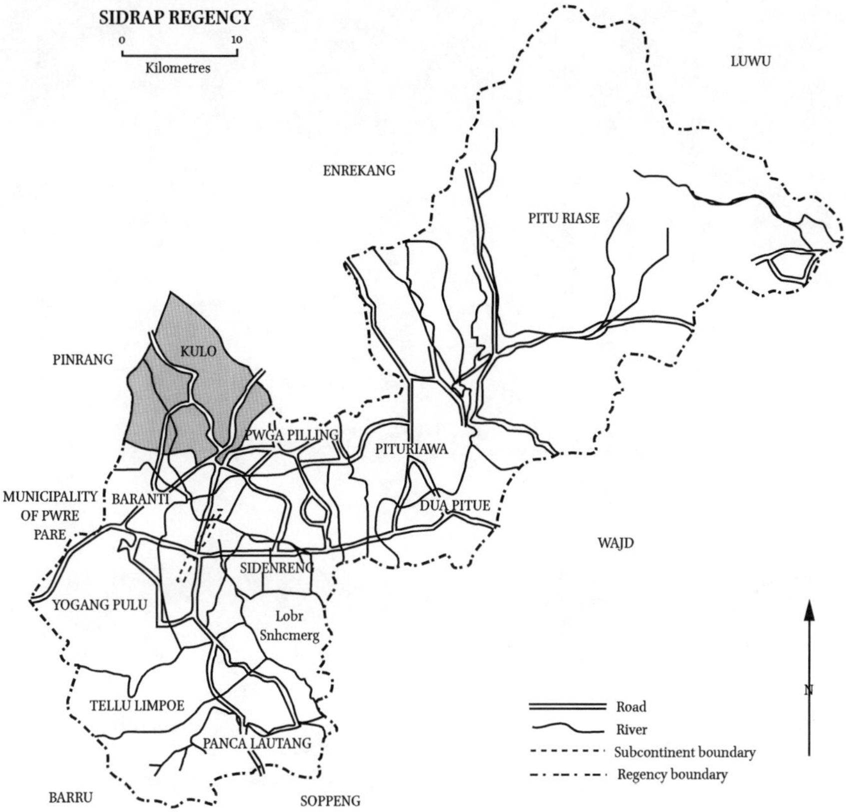

MAP 1.4 *Sidrap Regency and Subdistricts*

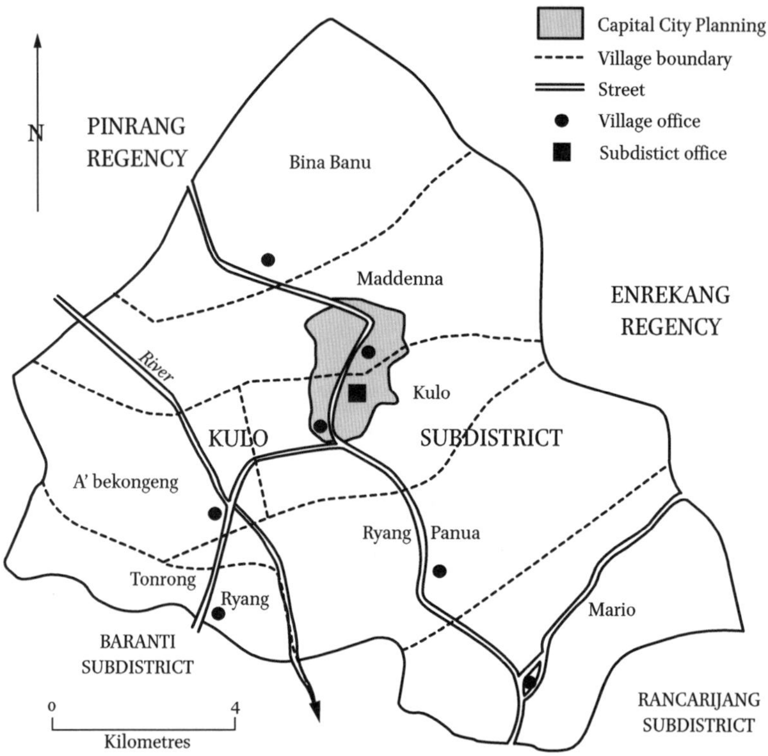

MAP 1.5 *Kulo Subdistrict and Villages*

Abbreviations

BPS	Badan Pusat Statistik (Central Bureau of Statistics)
BP4	Badan Penasehat Perkawinan, Perselisihan dan Perceraian (Institute for Marriage Disputes and Divorce Counselling)
EP2V	Economic, Psychological, Emotional, and Political Violence
FGD	Focus Group Discussion
FPMP	Forum Pemerhati Masalah Perempuan (Women's Forum)
GBHN	Garis-Garis Besar Haluan Negara (Guidelines for State Policy)
KHI	Kompilasi Hukum Islam (Compilation of Islamic Law)
KKN	Kuliah Kerja Nyata (university-sponsored community service program)
KUA	Kantor Urusan Agama (Religious Affairs Office)
LBH-P2I	Lembaga Bantuan Hukum untuk Peberdayaan Perempuan Indonesia (Law Service for Indonesian Women Environment)
LBP2	Lembaga Bantuan Perlindungan Perempuan (Institution for Women Protection Service)
LP	Lembaga Pemasyarakatan (Detention Centre)
NATO	No Action Talking Only
NGO	Non-government Organisation
P3N	Pedoman Pegawai Pencatat Nikah (Guidelines for Marriage Registrar)
P3N & P3N	Pedoman Pegawai Pencatat Nikah dan Pembantu Pegawai Pencatat Nikah (Guidelines for Marriage Registrar and Assistant)
PKK	Pemberdayaan Kesejahteraan Keluarga (Family Welfare Empowerment)
PP	Peraturan Pemerintah (State Regulation)
PPN	Pegawai Pencatat Nikah (Marriage Registrar)
PV	Physical Violence
RAN-PKTP	Rencana Aksi Nasional-Pemberantasan Kekerasan Terhadap Perempuan (National Action Plan on the Elimination of Violence against Women)
SD	Sekolah Dasar (Primary School)
SMP	Sekolah Menengah Pertama (Lower Secondary School)
SMU	Sekolah Menengah Umum (Upper Secondary School)
SV	Sexual Violence
WHO	World Health Organisation

CHAPTER 1

Introduction

> It becomes essential to know a great deal more about the way in which a field anthropologist went about his task: how well he knew the language, whether he lived among the people as a prince or a beggar or like an 'ordinary' person, who were his friends and who told him what, when and why, and what if anything he did about the things he was told.
>
> MAX GLUCKMAN 1969:XXII

Native Anthropology: Studying One's Own Culture

'What are you studying?' a fellow student asked me.

'I am studying Bugis culture, my own culture', I said.

'What?' he hissed. 'That is cheating', he continued.

'Why?' I asked him.

'Because you already know everything about your culture'.

This was a conversation I had one day in the printing room of the Anthropology Department, at the Australian National University. I felt discouraged. But then, I asked myself: 'Do I know everything about my culture?'

I realized during my fieldwork how wrong was his judgment of people who study their own culture. I found that the more I learnt about my culture, the more I realized how little I knew about it, or had known only passively. I am in agreement with Okely (1996)—a feminist anthropologist—who argues in her book *Own or Other Culture* that an anthropologist's own culture may become another culture when he/she is doing fieldwork in his/her own country.

The practices and meanings of ethnography have undergone a significant shift 'through a series of transformations whose impetus can be traced to the 1960s' (Bunzl 2005:188), including debates over colonialism and conflict. These debates were accompanied by the increasing presence of women, people of color, non-Westerners, and queer persons as ethnographers. The varied positions of these persons as 'native' ethnographers (Haniff 1985; Abu-Lughod 1991), particularly if they studied communities to which they in some sense belonged, troubled the distinction between Self and Other pivotal to classic assumptions about ethnographic research. The relational distance between researcher and subject, the belief in standing somehow neutrally 'outside of'

 | DOI 10.1163/9789004311947_002

one's fieldsite, became problematized, offering the opportunity to reconsider principles of ethnographic research, including the possibility of 'studying up' to explore 'those who shape attitudes and actually control institutional structures' in one's own society (Nader 1969:284). From the 1970s through the 1990s, these varied shifts contributed to a rethinking of the practices of writing and representation that are at the core of ethnography as textual product (e.g., Geertz 1983; Clifford and Marcus 1986; Visweswaran 1994; Behar and Gordon 1995). While a detailed discussion of these developments lies beyond the scope of this short history, as will be seen throughout this book, these interventions influenced our own thinking in various ways.

Starting my fieldwork was an excited moment, not just because it was conducted in South Sulawesi, my home province, where I could meet my family, but also because this was my first ethnographic experience. My chosen community did not realize what my research was actually about, at least in the beginning of the study during the period when I was still establishing rapport with people. Total honesty as the best strategy for fieldwork suggested by Sjafri in her study of hamlet in Cisaat village (Aida Sjafri 1991:74) was not an appropriate strategy for my study, an ethnography of marriage which included domestic violence.

Why did I choose to write an ethnography of Bugis marriage? Previously I researched sexual violence within marriage in Bugis society in South Sulawesi (Nurul Ilmi Idrus 1999, 2001 and Nurul Ilmi Idrus and Bennett 2003). The results of this earlier study on intimate partner violence provided a comprehensive understanding of how and why Bugis women are violated by their husbands. The findings of this study, however, left an impression that all Bugis men are violent. I often heard people—men as well as women—discuss my findings in a negative manner. Comments varied from denial of violence in Bugis marriages, to the notion that Bugis men are not violent, to a concern that the study findings exaggerated the facts. I took these responses as a challenge to do further research for my PhD that would contextualize my earlier findings. I had in mind a study of violence against women in conjugal relationships in Bugis society.

The first three months of my fieldwork were frustrating because I focused my attention solely on domestic violence. Then, I took a step back to look more broadly at gender relations and marriage in Bugis society. But to get a comprehensive understanding of gender relations in marriage, the ethnography includes how girls and boys are brought up, how they engage in courtship, how men and women interact in the house and in public, how gendered socialization affects marital life, and how people deal with marriage, divorce and reconciliation.

My focus shifted to an ethnographic account of marriage, with a discussion of domestic violence in the broader context of marital relations. I have focused on specific Bugis practices concerning gender, sexuality and marriage which covers the journey from single status to marriage, based on the ideologies and practices associated with adat, Islam and the modern state, aspects of Bugis society which influence each other, though they do not necessarily result in harmony. This thesis is an ethnography of Bugis marriage, examining cultural specificities of social and sexual relations between men and women.

Personal Connection to the Village

I began fieldwork in South Sulawesi in December 1999. With the help of my husband, all the matters related to obtaining an official research permit went well. My husband and I spent two days in Makassar and a day in Pangkajene Sidenreng—the capital city of Sidenreng Rappang (Sidrap) Regency—to get my research permit.

I hoped that finding accommodation in the village would not be a problem as I had already had a close contact with a family—the Bakris—as the eldest daughter was a close friend of mine. To find out whether the family would allow me to stay in their house, we visited the village. Driven by my husband and accompanied by my son, the three of us tried to find the house we had only visited once in 1997 when the eldest daughter of *Pak* Bakri[1] was married. Although they had moved, it was not difficult to find them because *Pak* Bakri was the principal of a primary school close by and well-known in the village. We were worried, however, when we found no one there except for *Pak* Bakri's son from his second marriage, whom we had never met before. I was told that his stepmother, *Ibu* Darma, and youngest stepbrother were visiting their family in Malaysia. That was not good news. If *Ibu* Darma was not there, it was almost impossible for me to live in the house because she was the only woman and my presence without her in the house would not be appropriate and would become a potential subject of gossip in the village. Therefore, I would have to find another place to stay. But I finally decided to write a letter stating my purpose and seeking *Ibu* Darma's help. I returned to Makassar in a state of uncertainty about my accommodation.

1 *Bapak* (or *pak*) literally means father and is the title for married men. The term *bapak* pairs with *ibu* (or *bu*) meaning mother, an inclusive title for married women. But *bapak/ibu* can also be applied to single men/women because of their status, for example, as teachers, or to show respect.

A few days after the first visit, Ati—the youngest daughter of *Pak* Bakri who was studying in Makassar—came to visit to inform me that I was welcome to stay with her family in Desa (I. Village) Maddenra, Kecamatan (Subdistrict) Kulo during my fieldwork, but I had to wait until her mother came back from Malaysia a week later. I stayed in Kulo for a period of thirteen months from December 1999 to January 2001. Additionally, following the period of formal fieldwork, on a number of occasions when I was on holiday or at a conference in Indonesia, I visited Kulo and the Religious Court (Pengadilan Agama), for the purpose of cross-checking my existing data.

The Journey to the Village

To get to Sidrap from Makassar—the capital city of South Sulawesi—one has to pass through four regencies (Maros, Pangkep, Barru and Pare-Pare, see Map 1.2). There are three possible types of transportation: *panter* (local term for the most popular inter-regency transportation), bus and personal car. My favourite was *panter*. Despite the fact that *panter* is smaller than a bus, it is more popular not only because it is faster than the bus (people say it's not *panter* if it's not speeding), but also because the atmosphere is more friendly.

In a *panter*, the passengers—consisting of eight to ten people including the driver—talk about current local and national, events. These events varied from gossip about who was going to get married, divorced, or perform the pilgrimage to Mecca to the mounting price of basic needs or how incapable Gus Dur (Abdurrahman Wahid) was as the president of Indonesia because of his blindness.

One's personal life may become public during these journeys. For example, once on the way to Sidrap, I heard a female passenger in her early fifties—who was a neighbour and a regular customer (I. *langganan*) of the driver—ask him about his personal life. Overhearing the conversation, I found out that the driver was divorced from his wife because of the interference of his mother-in-law. His wife had been urged by her mother to file for a divorce even though her husband wanted to stay married. Although the problem was not quite clear, he proclaimed that the marriage could still be saved, especially because they had two children. His wife's family, however, forced a divorce.

On another journey, I heard a merchant woman discuss how she managed to save money to perform the pilgrimage to Mecca. She said: 'If one is honest, one's livelihood will also be a blessing' (B. *nakko malempuq itu taué, mabbarakkaq toi tu dalléqna*). She expressed the belief that one should have balance inside and outside of one's body because such balance affects one's spiritual life. I assumed that she was talking about the balance of inner and outer worlds (I. *lahir* and *bathin*). She went on to say that if one is involved in business, it is not merely about economic life, but also morality. Rudnyckyj (2009:183) terms this as 'market Islam', which is 'designed to merge Muslim religious practice and capitalist ethics'. Accordingly, it forms effective self-management by making 'people better from the inside' and 'breaking the boundaries', in this context, the boundary between 'religion and work'.

I listened to such conversations for the length of the journey from Makassar to a village type eatery between Pangkep and Barru, where the driver usually stopped briefly to have lunch. There are lots of eatery around, but each driver usually stopped at a particular eatery where he had a 'deal' with the owner; the driver could eat there for free because the majority of the passengers usually ate at the same eatery.

The journey from the eating place to the destination was a bit lonely because passengers got sleepy. If I could not sleep, I could still enjoy the view of the fresh green rice fields (I. *sawah*), or traditional and modified stilt-houses (*rumah panggung*) and the standard white paint of the bamboo fences all along the right and the left hand sides of the road. One by one the passengers arrived at their destinations. I was usually the last passenger as my destination was in the central market of Rappang, the last stop for the *panter* (see Map 1.2).

From Rappang to Kulo—the subdistrict where I conducted my fieldwork—there was only one possible type of public transportation, *pété-pété* (a term for a local mini bus in South Sulawesi), which circulates between seven in the morning and five in the afternoon. I always had to make sure I arrived before five, otherwise I had to spend the night in Rappang and continue the short journey the following morning. Even though one of *Pak* Bakri's relatives in Rappang offered to let me spend the night if I happened to miss the local transportation, whenever I left Kulo, for example to go to Pangkajenene Sidenreng—the capital city of Sidrap—to attend a court hearing at the Religious Court (I. Pengadilan Agama) or observing people in the market, I made sure to arrive before five.

Kulo: The People and the Village

Kulo[2] is one of the districts in Sidrap, and consists of seven villages: Desa Mario, Desa Rijang Panua, Desa Kulo, Desa Abbokongeng, Desa Maddenra, and Desa Bina Baru. Kulo has a population of 12,653 consisting of 6,251 (49%)

2 Sidrap consists of eleven districts, namely Panca Lautang, Tellu Limpoe, Watang Pulu, Baranti, Panca Rijang, Kulo, Maritengngae, Watang Sidenreng, Pitu Riawa, Dua Pitue, Pitu

males and 6,402 (51%) females (Kulo District in Figures 2014). Kulo subdistrict is adjacent to Enrekang Regency to the North, Baranti subdistrict to the South, Panca Rijang subdistrict to the East, and Pinrang Regency to the West (see Map 1.5) and is located about 200 kilometres from Makassar,[3] the capital city of South Sulawesi. Makassar has 1,408,072 inhabitants, consisting of 695,955 (49%) males and 712,117 (51%) females (Makassar in Figures 2014), a population that is heterogenous compared to other regions in South Sulawesi. People from other regencies migrate to the city to find jobs, children come to pursue their higher education. The journey to Makassar took at least four hours by *panter*. More than once, however, I heard that people in Kulo in particular, and Sidrap in general, considered it is easier to get to Jakarta—the capital city of Indonesia—than to Makassar. This is not only because Pare-Pare harbour is very close to Sidrap (see Map 1.2), but also because people considered it is more fascinating to go to Jakarta in Java than to go to Makassar in Sulawesi.

In South Sulawesi, nearly 90% of populations are Muslims (Sensus Penduduk-2010 [2011a]). Although there are no statistics on religion from either the village office (I. Kantor Desa) or district office (Kantor Kecamatan, see Plate 1.1),

PLATE 1.1 *Kulo district office*

Riase with total of population 283,307 comprising 138,126 men (49%) and 145,181 women (51%) (Sidenreng Rappang in Figures 2014) (see Map 1.4).

3 Makassar consists of fourteen districts, namely Mariso, Mamajang, Tamalate, Rappocini, Makassar, Ujung Pandang, Wajo, Bontoala, Ujung Tanah, Tallo, Panakkukang, Manggala, Biringkanaya, and Tamalanrea.

I was told by the official staff of the Kantor Kecamatan that everyone in Kulo was Muslim, and this is strengthened by the statistics on Kulo district which shows that no other religion except Islam. In Sidrap, 91.75% of population are Muslims (Sidenreng Rappang in Figures 2014).

A population of more than eight million residents of South Sulawesi comprise a variety of ethnic groups. Consequently, when I am talking about the Bugis, people who are not familiar with this ethnic group, both foreign and Indonesian scholars, usually respond with a question: 'Who are the Bugis?'.

The native populace in South Sulawesi is made up of four ethnic groups: Bugis (*To-Ugiq*), Makassar (*To-Mangkasaq*), Toraja (*To-Raja*), and Mandar (*To-Menreq*).[4] The Bugis represents 45% of the population of South Sulawesi (Sensus Penduduk-2010 [2011a]).[5]

In spite of ethnic boundaries, members of each ethnic group are found across all regions, especially in urban areas. But there are regencies which have mixed dominant ethnic groups (underlined below), such as Maros, Pangkep and Makassar which consist of *To Ugiq* and *To Mangkasaq*; and Polmas which is a mixture of *To Menreq*, *To Ugiq* and *To Raja* (see Mattulada 1995: Table III, 476).

Based on geographical area, persons of Bugis ehnicity mainly live in 15 out of 24 regencies in South Sulawesi: Polmas, Luwu, Enrekang, Pinrang, Sidrap, Pare-Pare, Wajo, Soppeng, Barru, Bone, Pangkep, Maros, Makassar, Sinjai, Bulukumba (see Map 1.2 and 1.3).[6] *To Mangkasaq* reside in Pangkep, Maros, Makassar, Gowa, Takalar, Jeneponto, Bantaeng, and Selayar. *To Menreq* inhabit Polmas, Majene and Mamuju ; and *To Raja* are in Tana Toraja. Since 2003, however, five new regencies have been added to South Sulawesi, namely Luwu Utara, Luwu Timur, Palopo, Mamuju Utara, and Mamasa. Later in 2004, a number of regencies was separated from South Sulawesi, they were Polmas (which was divided into two regencies, Polman and Mamasa), Mejene, Mamuju and Mamuju Utara. Since then, these five regencies are united and become a new province, called West Sulawesi.

In Kulo, almost 100% of the population is Bugis. I knew that a Javanese family who could speak 'Bugis-Jawa' (a Javanese influenced dialect of Bugis) lived there for years, and had opened a small food stall for local people. *Bakso*

4 In Makassarese, they are called *To Bugisiq*, *To Mangkasaraq*, *To Raja*, and *To Mandaraq*.

5 Population Census 2010 only include Bugis and Makassar in its classification of population by ethnic group in Indonesia.

6 South Sulawesi comprises twenty four regencies, namely Selayar, Bulukumba, Bantaeng, Jeneponto, Takalar, Gowa, Sinjai, Maros, Pangkep, Barru, Bone, Soppeng, Wajo, Sidrap, Pinrang, Enrekang, Luwu, Tana Toraja, Luwu Utara, Luwu Timur, Toraja Utara, Makassar, Pare-Pare, and Palopo with a population of 8,342,047 consisting of 4.071,434 (49%) males and 4,270,613 (51%) females (Sulawesi Selatan in Figures 2014) (see Map 1.2).

PLATE 1.2 *Kulo wet rice fields*

(I. meat ball soup) and *gado-gado* (salad eaten with peanut sauce) had become their main menu at a good price. There, I could meet people and talk with them while we ate. The more frequently I came, the more friends I had; and the more familiar I became to the local people, the more people invited me to come to their houses, young as well as older people.

Kulo's economy is predominantly based on agriculture, with cocoa and rice being the main crops (see Plate 1.2). Seeking a better life, many people have left their village to make a living. Many migrate to Malaysia, legally or illegally, or to other parts of Indonesia.[7] This is not a new phenomenon; Bugis in particular have long been known for their mobility as the result of high competition in social life related to the hierarchical nature of Bugis society (Pelras 1996:4–5).[8] There is a Bugis philosophy related to this: 'Wherever there are many fruits, there one should go searching' (*tégi-tégi maéga bua-bua, kogitu lao massappaq*) (see Acciaioli 1989:267), and female labour migrants have become more common among the Bugis in South Sulawesi (Nurul Ilmi Idrus 2008a).

7 This phenomenon increased after the monetary crisis hit Indonesia in 1997. For example, overseas workers processed by the Ministry of Labour indicate that there was a 12 percent increase in labourers entering Malaysia between 1997/1998 and 1998/1999 (Hugo 2002:160).

8 See, for example, Lineton (1975) for the history of Bugis emigration.

Family Involvement and Social Acceptance

My background as a Bugis woman did not automatically facilitate easy rapport with the community and had become my personal and intellectual dilemmas (see Narayan 1993:682). In the beginning, people would just stare at me in response to my smiling greetings. One morning, I went to the Kulo subdistrict office in order to find some local statistical data. I was greeted cynically by the young official of the Kantor Kecamatan when I told him the aim of my work. He asked me a number of questions one after the other:

- '*Dari mana?*' (I. Where are you from?),
- '*Mahasiswa* KKN *ya?*' (You are a KKN student, aren't you?),[9]
- '*Mau apa?*' (What do you want?).

I kept smiling and answered all his questions politely while wondering if I looked 'young' enough to be a KKN student, in consequence of my small stature, or if my appearance was too casual.

He continued to ask about my university. When he knew that I studied in Australia, he became more polite and friendly and expressed shame at his earlier response. Most importantly, he helped me to get some statistics on the region. While I made my notes, he kept questioning me: Why did I choose to study in Australia and not in Indonesia since I am married. How did Australians treat me? Why did my husband let me study in Australia, far away from home, while I left him in Indonesia? Why did I come to stay in Kulo, while my husband and my son were in Makassar? Who cooked and cleaned the house while I was away? Who took care of my son? He asked lots of questions concerning my personal life.

When I went home, everybody in the house—*Ibu* Bakri,[10] her son, and her father—was curious to know what I had done in the subdistrict office. As I told of my experience, *Ibu* Bakri and her son responded that it was because *Ibu* Ilmi looked like an ordinary college student (I. *mahasiswa*) wearing a T-shirt and jeans. They suggested the official thought that *Ibu* Ilmi was 'nobody', to account for his lack of respect. Since I had arrived in Kulo with a notion of the simplicity (*kesederhanaan*) of village life, I had decided to dress as plainly as I could, so I would not be considered an outsider. Hastrup point

9 KKN (*Kuliah Kerja Nyata*) is an obligatory rural social action internship for advanced university students whose age ranges between 20 and 25 years.

10 *Ibu* Bakri (the wife of *Pak* Bakri) and *Ibu* Darma are two different names of the same person that I use interchangeably in the chapters.

out that 'ethnographers learn to think, feel and often even behave like a native' (Hastrup 1995:146). I had miscalculated in my dress during my office visit, however, I came to understand the importance of my appearance in social interaction in the village.

In the afternoon when *Pak* Bakri went home, *Ibu* Darma told him about my experience in the subdistrict office. *Pak* Bakri felt that he had been shamed (B. *ripakasiriq*) by the unwelcome reception of the official at the subdistrict office in Kulo. In response, he not only talked to Pak Camat (the head of subdistrict) about his inferior's attitude, but also announced my presence in the village mosque. He testified to the purpose of my stay and said I was not to be considered as mere 'guest' of the village, but as a part of the community. This introduction was, however, not equivalent to establishing rapport or being accepted as a researcher who was staying with *Pak* Bakri's family. But it was because 'a person cannot live in a household and remain *to laing* (B. outsider) because it would be intolerable for the household' (Errington 1989:149). This indicates that once an individual is accepted in a family, his/her *to laing* status is transformed to *tennia to laing* (not outsider). Therefore, *Pak* Bakri's response was a result of his responsibility to protect me from being offended by someone else, as I had 'lost' my *to laing* status in his family. The announcement of my presence in the village by a respected person like *Pak* Bakri was the best 'ticket' for me to study the community, otherwise unwelcome responses could have influenced my research (Fetterman 1989:43) even though my fieldwork was conducted in my own society (see, for example, Aida Sjafri 1991 and Bhachu 1991).

The presence of my husband and my son on the second visit helped me to establish my status as a married woman and a mother of a six-year old son. This presence not only helped me to introduce 'who I was' to the people, but also my marital status. This, I realized later, protected them from feeling insecure as there had been two cases of adultery concerning two unmarried female students who had conducted KKN in the village, and two married men (see the case of *Ibu* Warnidah in Chapter 3). Therefore, a lack of clarity surrounding my marital status could have affected the success of my research in its early stages, particularly with other married women concerned about their husbands' fidelity. Married women in the village seemed to be more secure with 'new comer' married women rather than single ones.

From the collection of fieldwork experiences from female Asian and African researchers who studied their own culture, Panini (1991:5) argues that it is easier to establish rapport between local women and a married researcher than between local women and an unmarried researcher in view of the fact that they share the 'traditional patriarchal notion of a woman as a wife and as a mother'. My fieldwork experience confirmed this view, not only because I shared womanly interests, but also because I developed social attachments with women. The kitchen is a woman's domain. In Bugis culture, once a person is allowed to enter the kitchen, it indicates that she/he is accepted in the family. Despite the fact that I could enter someone's family kitchen, most families preferred me to sit in the living room or on the veranda so that they could show respect to their 'guest'. As Panini (1991:8) argues the researcher cannot be an insider in every moment of their encounter in the community. The difference between insider and outsider may become ambiguous for the researcher in different circumstances (see, for example, Masliana Bangun 1991, Bennett 2002). For example, in spite of the fact I recruited a local field assistant who was a male insider, women were reluctant to talk about their marital circumstances if men were around. This was the case when I came to *Ibu* Halimah's house for an interview (see her story in Chapter 4). She asked my assistant—Farhan—who is her second cousin (B. *sappokkadua*) to leave when the informal interview was conducted (see below). Although Farhan was already familiar with *Ibu* Halimah's marital problem, she felt uncomfortable talking about it with me, even if in front of her male insider.

But dealing with young girls in the village was entertaining. When I approached them, they would tease each other, asking questions such as: Who has a boyfriend? or Who is going to have a secret date? These questions were spurred by the topics of discussion of the focus group (see below). But such conversations rarely happened when boys were around. In a private space, a girl would talk about her boyfriend without being afraid that I would tell her relatives or other people, which indicated that these young girls had built trust in me.[11] Even though they called me *Ibu*, because of my age difference and marital status, they considered me a friend. They said I was too 'young' to be a mother. I guessed what they meant was I was too small because I am only 1.54 metres tall.

In the initial part of my study, the *ibu-ibu* (I. mothers) were always curious about my son and my husband who stayed in Makassar. They questioned how the two could handle their daily life without me or vice versa. But, at the same time people also envied me and the happiness I got from the relationship with my husband and my son. What they said was, to some extent, true. It was not easy to leave my family behind when I had to do my research in the village. My husband became a 'local single parent' as well as a house-husband during my fieldwork. He took all the domestic 'responsibilities' I left, though with the help of my part-time maid. I could not deny that I felt guilty whenever I wanted to go to the village. My son once asked me: 'Why do you spend

11 See Chapter 2 for detailed discussion on courtship.

most of your time in Sidrap?', 'what is so good about the place?'. His questions were not only related to his curiosity about my interest in the village and the community, but also because he had had a bad experience when he accompanied me once to the village during his school vacation. He could not stand the crowds of mosquitoes, especially at night, and he also could not take a bath in an open space. Hence, every time I wanted to leave for Kulo, he would warn me: 'Mum, do not let mosquitoes bite you', or 'tie your sarong carefully when you take a bath'. These comments reflected his fear of my being away from home. He was afraid that I would become sick because of mosquito bites or my sarong would drop when I took a bath and people would see me naked.

In my mid-term review at the Australian National University, I was asked why I choose a young man instead of a young woman as my research assistant. This was actually not a perfect choice since I would have preferred a woman. Instead of Ati, *Pak* Bakri's daughter (24), Farhan (20), *Pak* Bakri's son and Ati's younger brother, gave me assistance because Ati had moved away to pursue her education in Makassar. *Pak* Bakri had other daughters from his second marriage, but they lived with their mother in Rappang (ten kilometres away from Kulo), coming to Kulo to visit when they needed, for example, money from their father. Choosing one of them as my assistant would have been difficult because it might have affected my relationship with *Ibu* Bakri, as there was usually tension between *Ibu* Bakri and her stepchildren. It was much easier for me to have Farhan as my assistant not just because he lived with *Pak* Bakri in the same house as me, but also because I could talk in a more natural way about, for example, prospective informants or what was going on in the village, without setting a time with him since he was at home and without work. Fortunately, there was never any anxiety about being a subject of gossip because of my researcher-assistant relationship with Farhan during my fieldwork. This was probably because I was older than him, and also because I was known as an older 'sister' of Farhan, and as a 'sister' he had to protect me from any offensive behaviour by others which might result in *siriq,* not only for my self, but also to the Bakris (*siriq* is discussed at length in Chapter 2).

Style of Communication in the Field

The language of everyday communication in Kulo was Bugis.[12] In primary (SD) and lower secondary schools (SMP), students and teachers spoke to each other outside the classroom in Bugis. This was also the case in local offices, e.g.

12 See Frieberg and Frieberg (1985) for details on languages and dialects in South Sulawesi; Grimes and Grimes (1987) discuss the geographical dialects of Bugis.

Kantor Desa or Kantor Kecamatan. In teaching, the teachers used a mixed language (I. *bahasa gado-gado*), a combination between Bahasa Bugis and Bahasa Indonesia[13] to their students as the language of instruction. Both the teachers and the students used pure Bahasa Indonesia only when they read text books. Thus, their Bugis was more fluent than their Bahasa Indonesia. Once children entered upper secondary school (SMU) in Rappang, however, Bahasa Indonesia was the language of instruction in the classroom.

Even though I could speak the local language, people preferred to speak Bahasa Indonesia with me as much as they could, especially young people. This was to indicate that their geographical residence was not necessarily synonymous with isolation and was also a way to express the fluency of their Bahasa Indonesia. But, they said: '*Déqna ullé ribaluq Ibu* Ilmi, *apaq maccai mabbasa ugiq*' (B. *Ibu* Ilmi cannot be 'sold' because she can speak Bugis). 'Sold' in this sense indicates that they could not talk about me in Bahasa Bugis because I could understand them. This was quite important since they also occasionally used mixed language when they spoke about me to the elders, as they said: '*mabbicara gado-gado kiq sibawa Ibu* Ilmi' (we speak mixed language with *Ibu* Ilmi). Using *bahasa gado-gado* helped them to express what they wanted to say to me when they could not express it in Bahasa Indonesia.[14] But elders or *ibu-ibu* usually spoke solely in Bahasa Bugis with me. An example of mixed language is: *tidak masiriq, tidak* is Bahasa Indonesia for not and *masiriq* is Bugis for becoming ashamed. In purc Bahasa Indonesia, it becomes *tidak malu* or *déqna masiriq* in pure Bahasa Bugis.

International labour migration to Malaysia (Sabah) also plays an important role in shaping another *bahasa gado-gado* style of communication among people in Kulo. This is the integration between Bahasa Indonesia, Bahasa Melayu and English with a Malaysian accent. For example, when the Bakris held a wedding party for their son, members of their family came from Malaysia to attend. Their attendance indicated their success after leaving the village in making their living (B. *massompeq*). There is a Bugis maxim associated with this: 'leaving bald headed, returning with luxuriant hair' (*makkeluq peppéko mulao mabbulu rombéko lésu*) (Muhammad Sikki et al. 1998:11), meaning that one must not return without success. They came with lots of presents for the

13 The term *bahasa gado-gado* describes the mixture of the language. *Gado-gado* is a type of food that consists of various vegetables (boiled potato, been sprouts, long beans, and cabbage) plus fried tofu and tempeh, eaten with chips and peanut sauce. Thus, this mixture serves as a metaphor for mixed language.

14 See Bennett's (2002:49–51) discussion on language and cultural style of communication in the field. She used the term *bahasa campur* to refer to the mixture of local slang, words from other regional languages and English terms.

family (shampoo, milk, chocolate powder), wore luxurious attire (for example, national Malaysian women's attire) and jewellery, spoke in *bahasa gado-gado* with a Malaysian accent amongst themselves and with other people in the village. This appearance and style of talking were significant in displaying their 'modern' life style for social status[15] as successful *passompeq* (migrant or wanderer).[16] Their attendance was also important for the status of the host. The people who could respond in a similar *bahasa gado-gado* would also gain status from the conversation, by showing they could participate in the 'modern' way of life. An example of this kind of *bahasa gado-gado* is '*budak itu tidak pakai* slipper-*nya*' (that kid didn't put on his slipper). *Budak* is *Melayu* for kid; *itu* (that), *tidak* (not), *pakai* (put on), *nya* (his) are Bahasa Indonesia, and slipper is English. I had an interview with an informant who responded with Malaysian influenced *bahasa gado-gado* (see the story of *Ibu* Warnidah in Chapter 3).

Whatever language my interlocutors preferred to use to communicate with me, I could understand what they said. This is central to ethnographic research because the ability to speak the field language may affect the recounting of the spoken materials (Ellen 1984:75). Ellen concludes her section on the 'Preparation of Fieldwork' by stating that 'trying to talk in others' terms is a surrender of one's own otherness, and generally respected as such', as he came to realize the great importance of conversation in the findings of ethnographic fieldwork (Ellen 1984:187).

Research Participants and Data Collection

Although my research focused on marriage, my core research participants were not limited to couples or married women. They varied on the basis of marital status, age group, educational level, and employment status. In addition to this, residence of the participants was also not limited to Kulo. I intended to explore the process of life from early socialization to marriage in both rural and urban areas. Therefore, interviewing unmarried men and

15 For discussion on displaying status through demonstrating fluency in a foreign language (e.g. English) in other Indonesian cities, see Iwu D. Utomo (1997), Beazley (1998), and Bennett (2002).

16 From the story I was told and from the pictures I was shown of people who migrated from Kulo to Malaysia, I assume that their Bugis-ness was awakened when the Bugis became a diaspora community, transplanted from Kulo to contemporary Malaysia where they were forced to think about their ethnic identity for life survival.

women was as crucial as interviewing married men and women, though I did not set out to recruit particular numbers of sex and age groups.

In Bugis society, women must maintain social distance from men. This affected my potential involvement with male participants. My engagement of a male research assistant was crucial to my ability to interview men while observing local etiquette.

It was also evident that there was a distance among age groups: youth, adults, and elders. When the three age groups were present at the same time, for instance, when we gathered together at the *pos ronda* (I. guard station) during *agustusan* (a celebration of the national independence day in August) and we watched a group walking competition, it was clear to me that young women were more inhibited when elders were there. Married women seemed to be more flexible in talking to other older women in public space of *pos ronda*. Even though *Pak* Bakri had left the house together with his family and myself to join in the celebration of *agustusan*, he did not join us at the *pos ronda*, instead sitting with another man on the veranda of a nearby house.

Spradley (1979:3) defines ethnography, as 'learning from people' by participant observation as a strategy for both listening to people and watching them in natural settings. Ellen, however, extends this to include the study of written documents including the accounts of other observers (Ellen 1984:8). Emerson et al. (2011:1) points out the core ethnographic research which involves two interconnected activities: firsthand daily participation (participant observation) and the production of written accounts from such participations.

A combination of data collection methods was used in my study: interviews, participant observation and focus groups became the primary data collection methods. In addition, I consulted many kinds of written materials and, of course, the previous ethnographic literatures. This triangulation of methods was particularly important in order to find a 'complete' picture of the ethnography of marriage in Bugis society.

My initial simple methods were 'watching' and 'listening',[17] as I thought this was the best way to 'learn from people', but I took notes and filled in my diary regularly. I was usually teased by my assistant that I was writing a 'teenage diary'. With the exception of my informants in jail, people were reluctant to be tape recorded.

As soon as I got to Kulo, or even on the way to Kulo, I started to watch what people were doing, and listen to people. Then, I spoke to them, and interviewed them informally (Spradley 1979). But when it came to face-to-face interaction between me and my informants, for example when I talked to *Ibu* Bakri about

17 See, for example, Siapno (1997) for the nature of her fieldwork in Aceh.

her husband's polygamous marriage in the past, she realized that she had been 'interviewed', though in a relaxed atmosphere and of course not in her husband's presence. As she told me: '*nawawancarainaq Ibu* Ilmi' (B. *Ibu* Ilmi is interviewing me). In fact, she became one of my primary informants during my fieldwork not only because I stayed with her, but also because her personal life is particularly important to my study.

Another example is *Ibu* Warnidah, whom I happened to meet when she came from Malaysia to visit her family in Kulo for a few weeks. One afternoon, she came to 'my house' to see *Ibu* Bakri (her cousin), and asked *Ibu* Bakri about me and what I was doing in Kulo. After realizing the subject of my research, she enthusiastically invited me to come to her house and to talk about her husband's infidelity (see her story in Chapter 3). To me, such an invitation was as if she had asked me: *Ibu* Ilmi, come and interview me; both of us realized that an interview was occurring. *Ibu* Warnidah was not the only person who sought me for an interview. Through this, I developed individual case studies which allowed me to see the uniqueness of each case as individual experience. Thus, my interviews were conducted in a variety of ways depending on how people reacted to me and how I stimulated people to talk.

Focus group discussion (FGD) was one among other methods used in addition to participant observation and individual interviews. This contributed a different perspective by determining the topic and gaining data from group interactions (Morton 1997:6). Topics included perceptions of the younger generation on ideal age of marriage, ideal partners, the ideal number of children a couple should have and how these are different from the perceptions of older generations. Though some opinions were predictable, information on a wide range of topics can be 'quick and easy' to obtain through focus groups (Morton 1997:13).

The focus groups in my research were conducted with informality because formal approaches tended to make participants uncomfortable and lessen their interest, as they were afraid of being unable to answer the questions asked of them.

The members of focus groups consisted of males and females whose age ranged between 16 to 20, with educational status varying from SMU (upper secondary) to undergraduates. Because my goal was to explore their perceptions on the subjects mentioned above in a natural group discussion, I initially led the discussion on a broader topic (marriage), then let my assistant guide them to speak without much guidance from me, or at least to minimise my involvement in the group discussion. But, the discussion was controlled to some extent to produce more structured results and the participants found a relaxed and free atmosphere to express their views without being interrupted by the instruction of the facilitator. With six as a minimal number of participants in the group (Morton 1997:43), the discussion went well in terms of enthusiasm in responding to the topic and sharing their views with each other. In response to one of the sub-topics in FGD, a girl, for example, teased other participants about their 'ideal partner', and then another girl teased other girls about their ideal age of marriage, without embarrassing each other. But the following day, the topic discussed became public. The mother of a girl who had participated in the discussion told people that one girl expected her prospective husband to be employed (B. *urané engkaé jama-jamanna*), and that another girl wanted to have a husband who already had a house (*urané engkaé bolana*). Then, I realized that it would not be possible to discuss sensitive topics (such as virginity) using this method.[18]

Another valuable source of information was discussion of Muslim ideas with community figures, such as *pak desa* (I. village headman), *kepala sekolah* (principal) in Kulo, judges in Sidrap and Makassar Religious Courts (Pengadilan Agama) regarding the application of the Qur'an and popular Hadith.[19] With these same figures, I also discussed local adat concerning expected behaviours of unmarried as well as married men and women, relationships between men and women, marriage and its consequences.

Judges in the Religious Court became a valuable source of information on divorce and reconciliation. I attended court hearings numerous times, between December 1999 and February 2000 in Makassar, and between May and December 2000 in Sidrap. During this period, I was able to discuss with several judges what I had observed during the court hearings, including discussion of legal matters.

Local newspapers (Berita Kota Makassar, Fajar), the national newspaper (Kompas), tabloids and popular Bugis songs and poetry were extra source of information for my study. Newspapers and tabloids were meaningful sources of information on what was going on locally and nationally. Inspired by the TVRI program on *lagu-lagu daerah* (indigenous songs, mostly Bugis songs) in the afternoon before the time for sunset prayer, I collected a number of cassettes from local markets in Sidrap and Pare-Pare and shops in Makassar, as many of the lyrics of Bugis popular songs stigmatise women.

---

18 Although topics related to sexuality are discussed in FGD by single sex participants, see, for example, Bennett (2002) in her study of maidenhood in Lombok, and Nurul Ilmi Idrus (2006b) on female same-sex relationship in Makassar.

19 Hadith is the tradition of the Prophet. Those reports from the first generations of Muslims regarding the words and actions of the Prophet Muhammmad, judged as genuine, constitute a second scripture in Islam, ancillary to the Qur'an (Federspiel 1995:70).

While my fieldwork in the research site ended in 2000, the ethnography continues (see Fetterman 2010:10) to date, though, in a more of what Madden calls as 'step-in-step-out ethnography' (Madden 2013:80).

Lontaraq, La Galigo and Bugis Cosmology

As well as ethnographic techniques, I have also relied upon Bugis written sources, mostly known as *lontaraq*. This term, which literally refers to the leaves of the *lontar* palm once used to write on, has come to signify both the manuscript corpus of traditional Bugis literature (now almost exclusively on paper) and several varieties of South Sulawesi script. By far the most important of these scripts is the 'four-sided script' (B. *ukiq sulapaq eppaq*) normally used for Bugis. Tol has given a good illustrated account of the various scripts used in South Sulawesi (Tol 1996), and other chapters in the same volume provide the wider context of local written traditions across the archipelago (Kumar and McGlynn 1996).

Lontaraq contain Bugis oral and literary traditions which I have cited throughout the chapters. *Lontaraq* cited here vary from a number of wise sayings, aphorisms, advice to correct behaviour passed on from local people (particularly elders) to young people. I have used mainly the microfilm collections held in Arsip Nasional Wilayah Makassar (I. National Archives Makassar Branch), the Australian National University library, and from published texts written by Bugis scholars. Although *lontaraq* are not read by the majority of young people, some of their content has been orally passed on from older generations and used as guides in the everyday life of the Bugis. The *lontaraq* cited in this thesis show the significance of *lontaraq* in the everyday life of the Bugis since they have entered into oral tradition (e.g. sayings, aphorisms, advice). The *lontaraq* show not just the weight of tradition, but also the ways Islamic discourse are mixed up in local discourses which sacralize the content of *lontaraq*.

It remains uncertain when the written tradition in South Sulawesi began. Caldwell (1988) has edited a number of Bugis texts dealing with the period between 1300 and 1600 AD, that is three centuries before the official adoption of Islam. Some sources, such as *Lontaraq Purukani* (Roll 41/No.9 in the collections of Arsip National Wilayah Makassar), describe the coming of the New Religion, called *assellengeng* (B. Islam). As Mukhlis notes in his catalogue of this collection, this suggests that the tradition of writing predates the arrival of Islam in South Sulawesi (Mukhlis 1994:2–3). The point is further confirmed by the Indic nature of the script.

Drawing on knowledge of the method of producing written tradition, Macknight (1993:29–30) suggests that the production of manuscripts is by 'creation and copying'. In my experience, this seems to be the case because some content in one *lontaraq* includes similar content of another *lontaraq*. Some oral tradition (such as sayings, advice etc.) are also found in certain manuscripts. In fact, the oral and the written sources of Bugis tradition are complementary to each other. In contemporary South Sulawesi, the *lontaraq* script is taught in primary public schools and classified as Bahasa Daerah (I. regional language). This teaching of the script, however, does little except enable students to read the simple textbook produced for this purpose. The young are not stimulated to create new works of Bugis literature using the script or even to read widely in existing manuscripts. At best, such teaching prepares an audience for oral performances of traditional literary material.

Bugis literature is exceptional in terms of both quality and quantity. In particular, there is the very extensive cycle of stories known as La Galigo. Its production is both oral and written, but its consumption is aural (Macknight 1993:30).[20] A single episode of La Galigo consists of hundreds of pages (Macknight 1993:26), some of it has been transliterated and translated into Bahasa Indonesia.

The language used in La Galigo is quite different from the everyday language of the Bugis (Macknight, 1993; Muhammad Salim and Fachruddin Ambo Enre 1995:2 and 2000:2), and the text falls into segments, each consisting of five (or occasionally four) syllables (Fachruddin Ambo Enre 1983:107–13; Macknight 1993:26). Considering that the La Galigo epic has sacred value for the Bugis, it has been used as a guide for social conduct (Mattulada 1995:10). The discussion below is an overview of Bugis cosmology derived from La Galigo.

Drawing on Bugis cosmology, Mattulada (1998:106) divides the social strata of Bugis into three levels: upper level (those descended from the upper world), middle level (lesser nobles and officials); and lower level [*To Maradeka* (freemen) or *To Tebbeq* (commoners)].[21] Lineton (1975:191) makes up a practical distinction based on the degree of 'blood' of people in Wajo where she conducted her study into *Anaq Mattola* (B. pure blooded royalty), the *Arung* (chiefs of the tiny princedoms), the *T*[*o*] *Décéng* (good people), the *T*[*o*] *Maradéka* (free commoners), and *Ata* (slaves). In the study of the polity of the Tae people

20 For an analysis of the production and consumption of both written and oral tradition in the Malay world, see Sweeney (1980 and 1987).

21 In reference to the social stratum in the ancient kingdom of Bone, Mattulada (1995:26–7) classifies people into *anakarung* (B. noble people), *to maradeka* (free people), and *ata* (slaves).

in Luwu, Errington (1989:96) indicates three divisions of rank: the *To Malebbiq* (big or better people), the *To Samaq* ([regular] people), and the *Ata* (slaves). Pelras (1996:105–6) contrasts this caste-like division and absolute power described in the La Galigo texts with socio-political innovations in the early historical texts which involved contractual partnership between the rulers and the local community in which rights and duties are reciprocal, though the people's security and prosperity are still most important. But Pelras came to realize that the power of the ruler is borrowed from the divine ruler and extended to the people of the land. From this point of view, these three dimensions (the divine ruler, the ruler of the land, and the people of the land) also reflect the idea of cosmological socio-political power.

Contemporary Bugis society does not manifest these social divisions found in La Galigo. The stratum of *ata* no longer exists, and people are also ranked on their personal achievement rather than ascribed status alone. However, my book aims to show the significance of this historical epic to Bugis gender, sexuality and marriage.

New Order Development Ideology: Dharma Wanita, the PKK Movement and the Family Planning Programme

While, as noted above, I pay attention to how Bugis traditions shape gender, sexuality, and marriage, I am equally concerned to show how contemporary ideologies of the Indonesian state also have a significant influence. This study is based on ethnographic work in a single society, whilst the issues of courtship, marriage and divorce have been significantly influenced by Indonesian national policies and practices.

Indonesia's transformation from the leadership of Sukarno to that of Suharto resulted in a dramatic transformation from radical nationalism to national development (Robinson 1989:21). This change has also affected women's lives on the basis of New Order development ideology. Sexuality, marriage and family have become pivotal means of the New Order's effort to modernize the nation through, for example, Dharma Wanita (Women's Duties), Family Welfare Movement (Pembinaan Kesejahteraan Keluarga, hereafter PKK), and the Family Planning Programme, aspects of which have been criticised by both Western[22] and Indonesian scholars.[23]

---

22 See, for example, Robinson (1987, 1989, 1994, 1998a, 1996), Sullivan (1983, 1994), Djajadiningrat-Nieuwenhuis (1987), and Manderson (1983).

23 See, for example, Julia I. Suryakusuma (1987), Istiadah (1995), Mansour Fakih (1996), and Saraswati Sunindyo (1993).

The family principle (I. *kekeluargaan*) is a basic principle of the development ideology of the New Order. The state is articulated as the family, with Suharto as the father of development (*Bapak Pembangunan*). While there is no strong notion of the mother of development (*ibu pembangunan*), *ibu* (mother) is used as a mediator to reach the power. Julia I. Suryakusuma expresses this ideology in a single term: '*bapak-ibuism*' (father-motherism) (Julia I. Suryakusuma 1996:102). Hence, mothers (*ibu-ibu*), in this sense wives, are organized to support the development of the nation through state sponsored organizations.

Dharma Wanita, an organization for wives of civil servants whose membership is compulsory, was formed in 1974 under the leadership of the First Lady of Indonesia, *Ibu* Tien Suharto, and coordinated by the Ministry of Women's Affairs. Given that the women's leadership positions in this organization are based on their husbands' hierarchical rank in bureaucracy, women's personal achievements are not taken into account.[24] This reflects the 'shadow authority' of women in this organization, or what Julia I. Suryakusuma (2000) calls 'artificial power', since it is solely borrowed from the state through women's husbands.

Accordingly, if the head of Dharma Wanita cannot perform her tasks because of her lack of skill to do so, the members of Dharma Wanita and their husbands make sarcastic jokes about it. In such cases, an inferior is usually asked to perform various tasks on her behalf (for example, leading the monthly meeting). The authority of the head of Dharma Wanita towards her inferiors, however, remains powerful, as if her words are absolute. It is not rare to hear the members of Dharma Wanita complain about activities in which they are reluctant to become involved, but have no courage to refuse, afraid such reluctance may affect their husbands' careers.

The official Indonesian state development ideology of a 'good wife' and 'good mother' is based on Panca Dharma Wanita (I. women's five principal duties): as appendages and companions to their husbands, procreators of the nation, mothers and educators of children, housekeepers, and members of Indonesian society.[25]

These principles reinforce the notion Julia I. Suryakusuma (1987) calls 'state *ibuism*' to describe how the New Order idealizes a domesticated, dependent wife and mother whose self-sacrifice is accentuated not only for her husband, but also for the family and the nation. Women are called upon to sacrifice

24 See, for example, Gerke (1992), Wieringa (1992), Saraswati Sunindyo (1993), Robinson (1994), Julia I. Suryakusuma (1996).

25 See Robinson (2009, 1998), Saraswati Sunindyo (1993, 1996), Julia I. Suryakusuma (2004, 1996, 1987), Istiadah (1995), and Sullivan (1983, 1994), Gerke (1993).

themselves in the interest of a male-dominated household which is designed to support government policies. The concept of *kemitrasejajaran* (I. equal gender partnership) was introduced in the last few years of Suharto's government, as stated in the 1998 Guidelines of State Policy (*Garis-Garis Besar Haluan Negara*, GBHN). Even though the concept of *kemitrasejajaran* reflects gender equity, the operationalization of the concept is based on the dominant model of the New Order, which only accepts what the state considers as appropriate to Indonesian social values (Robinson 2009 and 1998b). Julia I. Suryakusuma (2012) argues that despite the fact Suharto regime has fallen, 'state *ibuism*', the concept which she coins over twenty years, is still relevant in contemporary Indonesia.

The politics of gender differences in the New Order is reflected in the goals of the state through Dharma Wanita, summarized by Saraswati Sunindyo as follows:

> By founding this women's organisation, the government aimed to strengthen national unity, secure the loyalty of government employees, increase political stability, concentrate all the energy of civil service on assisting the economic development plan, and encourage the wives of government employees to support their husbands' careers and responsibilities. The goals of Dharma Wanita are to give guidance in promoting and strengthening women's consciousness and responsibility towards the nation; promote the channelling of 'sisterly' feeling under one unified national banner; and mobilize all wives' organisations in serving the nation.
>
> SARASWATI SUNINDYO 1993:135

This set of goals bears strong political and ideological objectives. It became a vital weapon for the New Order to control the nation through Dharma Wanita. Women were lulled by various expressions, such as the queen of the household (I. *ratu rumah tangga*) or the pillar of the state (*wanita sebagai tiang negara*) which was only lip service and was actually created systematically to subjugate women through an institutional movement by the state.

As Suharto stepped down in the reform period, some changes occurred which were intended to democratize Dharma Wanita. In the Musayawarah Nasional Luar Biasa (Munaslub) Dharma Wanita in 1999, Shinta Nuriah, the primary advisor of Dharma Wanita, suggested to change the name of this organization to Dharma Wanita Persatuan (DWP) to adjust with the name of the cabinet under the presidency of Abdurrahman Wahid, namely, Kabinet Persatuan Nasional. Despite this change, the practice of Dharma Wanita remained essentially the same. The wife of the head of the office is no longer automatically the leader of Dharma Wanita for that office, but she is the adviser (I. *penasehat*). The *penasehat* is the one who gives advice to her inferiors. In many cases, the advice is not something that may be considered, but it is absolute. Of course, the members of Dharma Wanita are afraid to oppose the advice given by the *penasehat* because, as it was during the New Order, to do so could threaten their husbands' careers. But, changing the system of leadership in Dharma Wanita is not easy because it has been going on for almost forty years now.

While Dharma Wanita was set up for and dominated by the urban, elite women, PKK's members are village women. Both organizations are coordinated through the Department of Home Affairs. Accordingly, Dharma Wanita is the primary connector between the state and urban women, and PKK is the connector between the state and village women. Thus, these two women's organizations are set up on the basis of structured divisions between elite urban and rural women.

Sullivan (1983) notes that despite the fact that PKK is a 'non-political movement,' it is a combination of 'male theory and female practice.' This is because most of the theorists of PKK are men, but their targets are women, whose activities centre on 'female interests' in order to modernize the nation. The 'ideology of natural patriarchal authority in the family and women's subordinate status' is spread through this women's group (Robinson 1998b:209). Its principles and practice are taught in primary and secondary schools as a compulsory subject also called PKK,[26] so that children can learn from their early socialization.[27] In her book on *Gender, Islam and Democracy in Indonesia*, Robinson (2009) demonstrates how gender relations have become the target of politics and have been gradually transformed on a vast scale.

Wieringa (1993:30) portrays PKK as a movement which strengthens 'women's gender subordination' through activities that fully support the government programme.[28] This programme focuses on the ideology of motherhood to promote the role of women in nurturing the welfare and health of the family. Saraswati Sunindyo (1996:136) claims that the encouragement of

---

26 PKK stands for *Pendidikan Kesejahteraan Keluarga* (Family Welfare Education). But in the new curriculum of the reform era, this subject has been substituted by KTK (*Kerajinan Tangan dan Kesenian* [Handicraft and Art]).

27 For further discussions of women's organisations under the New Order, see Sullivan (1983, 1994), Robinson (1994) and Julia I. Suryakusuma (1996).

28 This national programme does not have a uniform effect in terms of various systems of gender relations. See Sullivan (1983, 1994) for a discussion of the local replication to PKK in Yogyakarta.

a 'functional' role within the sexual division of labour in the family and the society is hidden behind the promoted role of women in development.

While the intervention of the state in public life is clearly reflected in PKK and its activities, state intervention in domestic life can be seen in the national Family Planning programme to control the fecundity of women's bodies (see also Plate 1.3 for other intervention). This programme has been used to reduce population growth since women are seen as the cause of the baby boom in Indonesia. Its success is based on statistical calculations of the acceptance by women of using contraception, rather than decline in population growth measured by the census. In fact, it is also a strategy for disciplining women in their domestic roles.

The New Order development policy on fertility decline has transformed the private matter of reproduction and its prevention into a public matter through the family planning program (Robinson 2009, 1989:22; Brenner 1998:227). An ideal marriage is described as a husband and a wife with two children, with the slogan 'two children are enough' (I. *dua anak cukup*). The ideology is reflected in the campaign of family planning in Indonesia during the New Order which illustrates a man, a woman and two children with the slogan 'small, happy and prosperous family' (I. *keluarga kecil, bahagia dan sejahtera*).[29] The government controls the number of children for civil servants by, for example, denying a subsidy to the third child. But the Indonesian Family Planning campaign of 'two children are enough' is no longer uniform, at least for Balinese. For example, a Balinese woman activist—Dr. Luh Ketut Suryani—advocated a contradictory idea that two are no longer enough in a Seminar on 'Women's Reproductive Health Within Balinese Culture and Custom'. This idea of increasing the population of Balinese and protecting Balinese identity and Hindu religion is completely against the ideology of modernising the nation of the New Order.[30]

Despite the fact that Khofifah Indar Parawansa—the Ministry of Women's Empowerment—period in the cabinet finished (less than two years) before her plans were fully implemented, following the end of Abdurrahman Wahid's (Gusdur) presidency, there existed a number of significant change. Among others, following the change of name, from the Ministry of Women's Affairs to the Ministry of Women's Empowerment which aims to reconstruct women's role in the family, the society and the state. In addition, the term *pembinaan* (I. guidance from above) in PKK was transformed to

29 See, for example, Pausacker (2001:92–4) in her discussion on the advertisement of family planning in Indonesia; and Brenner (1998:225–9) in her analysis on a government-sponsored campaign to promote family planning in Laweyan (Java).

30 For detailed discussion on this, see Bellows (2003).

PLATE 1.3 *The heart of* PKK

pemberdayaan (empowerment) by integrating the spirit of gender awareness through which women is seen as *mitra sejajar* (equal partner) rather than solely as *pendamping suami* (husband's companion). Another significant change was the inclusiveness of husband in the family planning (*keluarga berencana*, KB) program, while in the New Order, women are the main target of KB.

In her era of ministry, Gusdur also responded the result of Beijing Conference by establishing National Development Program (Program Pembangunan Nasional, Propenas 2000–2004) to encourage gender justice in national development, followed by the issuance of presidential instruction No. 9/2000 on gender mainstreaming in development.

The State Laws and Regulations on Marriage and Divorce in Indonesia

I have mentioned some state regulations associated with marriage and divorce in this book. These include the Marriage Law No.1/1974, the Implementation Regulation No.9/1975, *Kompilasi Hukum Islam* and the State Regulation No.10/1983. They may be described as follows:

The Marriage Law No.1/1974 and its Implementation Regulation No.9/1975

Following the tension between the state and Islam (and local traditions) in the early days of the New Order as to whether or not the state should intervene in family matters, a secular Marriage Law was introduced (Robinson 2000:146) on 2 January 1974.[31] The implementation of the Marriage Law was regulated under State Regulation (*Peraturan Pemerintah*) No. 9/1975.

Arso Sosroatmojo and Wasit Aulawi (1978) point out that the fundamental principle of the Marriage Law 1974 is to ensure that marriage is voluntary, includes family involvement, restricts divorce and polygyny, that bride and groom are mature and to improve women's status. In addition, Nani Soewondo (1977) notes that the 1974 Marriage Law is aimed to protect women from marriage against their will and give them the same rights as their husbands to

31 See Blackburn and Bessell (1997) for details on the struggle between women's organisations and religious organisations, and between women's organisations and the parliament between the 1950s and 1960s on debates of draft legislation on marriage, and the period preceding the adoption of the 1974 legislation.

initiate divorce. However, many people have questioned whether the legislation really protects women. Are they really treated as equal with men?

The foundations and pre-requisites for marriage, the legality of marriage and its registration are subjects covered in the Marriage Law of 1974. It legislates the minimum age of marriage (16 for females and 19 for males), annulment, marital agreement, the rights and duties of husband and wife, common property in marriage, termination of marriage, polygyny, status of children, rights and duties between parents and children, custody, and mixed-marriage. Furthermore, PP No.9/1975 covers registration of marriage, procedures for marriage and divorce, annulment, the waiting period for divorcees and remarriage for widows, polygyny and penalties resulting from any offence related to marriage and divorce. Thus, the PP No.9/1975 clarifies the implementation of the Marriage Law.

Regardless of the fact that the Marriage Law (Chapter VI, 31:1) states that husband and wife have equal rights and position in the household, it states that the husband is the *kepala keluarga* (I. head of the family) and the wife is the *ibu rumah tangga* (housewife) (article 31:3) indicating inequality between the two, as if the former is superior to the latter. One may argue that it is impossible to have two leaders in the family, as it is in the state, because the members may confuse which direction to follow in the family, as in the state. In this sense, the state is seen as the family, and the terms *kepala rumah tangga* and *ibu rumah tangga* are based on structural relationship which promotes the idea of strong paternalism (see Robinson 2009; Julia I. Suryakusuma 2004 and 1996; Saraswati Sunindyo 1998).

Even if the principal foundation of the Marriage Law is based on monogamy, polygyny is permitted for Muslims under certain circumstances. These circumstances emphasise the wife's duties and neglect her rights. Take for example, Chapter VIII:41a of the Implementation Regulation which states that polygyny is allowed under the following circumstances: if the wife cannot perform her duties as a wife, if the wife is handicapped or suffers from disease which cannot be cured, and if the wife cannot bear a child.

It is stated in the 1974 Marriage Law (Chapter I:1) that marriage is the union of outer and inner worlds (I. *ikatan lahir dan bathin*) between a man and a woman, which indicates that the husband and the wife are 'two-in-one.' Therefore, if one cannot perform her/his duties, the other party should help, not just consider her/his duties and neglect her/his rights. If one suffers from a disease, the other party would also suffer, and not take another wife/husband. And if they did not have offspring, it is not necessarily that one is responsible and the other is not. Marrying another woman does not solve the problem, especially if the husband is the one who is infertile. Therefore, these circumstances contradict another chapter in the Marriage Law (Chapter VI, 34:1) which states that the husband must protect his wife and provide for household needs to the best of his abilities. I would argue, however, that the legitimate circumstances for polygyny are based on an assumption of inequality between husband and wife since the question of 'who can treat each of one's wives and children in the same manner?' is always a matter of concern, in particular how to measure it?

Kompilasi Hukum Islam (KHI) *No. 1/1991*

Kompilasi Hukum Islam (I. Compilation of Islamic Law) is specific to Indonesia, but its principles follow the universal conception of Islamic law (Abdurrahman 1992). It is based on the social condition of the necessity of law for Indonesian Muslims and on *fiqh* (A. study of Islamic law), interviews with Islamic scholars, the jurisdiction of the Religious Court (I. Pengadilan Agama), comparative study of law with other [Islamic] countries, and discussion on materials of law for the Religious Court (Abdurrahman 1992:36–7).

Since there are various views about what is regarded to be Islamic law and how to carry it out, KHI is considered as the mediator. Thus, KHI is a compilation of various perspectives and is used as a guide or precedent for judges in the implementation of Islamic Law in the Religious Court. It contains a series of regulations which explain local norms of social interaction, and normative dimensions of functional interpretations of Islam. These stimulate the compilation of the necessity of law, social demand, and the anticipation from Indonesian scholars that KHI is a written Islamic regulation produced on the basis of social conditions of Indonesian society (A. Gani Abdullah 1994:61–2). Therefore, the application of KHI itself aims to mediate between religion (Islam) and local norms throughout the archipelago, and is used as a guide for judges of the Religious Court in solving problems associated with marriage, inheritance and property. This coherence was produced under Presidential Instruction No.1/1991 (Robinson 2001:29).[32]

KHI consists of three books: each book concerned with a different subject. Book I is about marriage, Book II concerns inheritance, and Book III deals with property. The first book consists of 170 articles, the second comprises 44 articles and the third contains 15 articles. Thus, KHI as a whole includes 229 articles. With more articles related to marriage, the production of KHI focuses more on marriage than on inheritance and property laws.

32 See Bowen's (1993) discussion on the ways Gayo people articulate older forms of knowledge and practice within broader political and religious cultural spheres.

KHI associated with the marriage law deals with making a proposal, essential principles (A. *rukun*) and pre-requisites (*syarat*) of marriage, bridewealth, prohibition of marriage, marital agreement, marriage with premarital pregnancy, polygyny, prevention and cancellation of marriage, rights and duties of husband and wife, common property in marriage, child-rearing, custody of children, termination of marriage and mourning period.

In his book *Kompilasi Hukum Islam di Indonesia*, Abdurrahman (1992)—a lecturer in law at the Mulawarman University—criticises the content of the KHI. For example, he thought that some terms in the compilation were not clarified (e.g. *isbath nikah, qabla-al-dukhul, ijab-kabul*), and the use of the words *kawin* and *nikah*. However, he also found some contradiction as well as overlapping material in the Marriage Law No. 1/1974 and in PP No. 9/1975.

However, apart from its shortcomings, KHI gives a new look, though it has been in force for more than 20 years, to the implementation of Islamic law in solving problems associated with marriage, inheritance and property rights in Indonesia by considering existing local values of the society. This is due to the fact that Indonesia consists of various cultures, and when one talks about culture, one cannot separate it from religion. But the criticism mentioned above should be considered as significant input to improve the content of KHI in the future. The implementation of KHI in the courts is discussed in Chapter 6.

Siti Musdah Mulia—a feminist liberal Islamic scholar—criticized KHI not just in terms of demanding its level of regulation from a presidential instruction to a higher level of law (*undang-undang*), but also a number of article in KHI is discriminative toward women and lacks of spirit of protection toward children (islamlib.com 2003). In 2004, she and her Team called Tim Penyusun CLD-KHI challenged the government to revise KHI by suggesting counter legal draft (CLD) of KHI. The Minister of Religion—Said Agiel Al Munawah not just rejected the idea, but also strongly warned this team not to make such effort under the name of Department of Religion. In fact, in the 2007 International Women's Day, Siti Musdah Mulia got an International Women of Courage from the Ministry of External Affairs award, handed by Condoleezza Rice in Washington for her brave effort to make significant changes in Islamic law.

The State Regulation No. 10/1983

In addition to the 1974 Marriage Law and the State Regulation No.9/1975 (PP9), another regulation related to marriage has been promulgated, Peraturan Pemerintah No. 10/1983, popularly known as PP10. This regulation was produced to control the family lives of civil servants, and deals with marriage, divorce and sexual behaviour among civil servants (Robinson 1994, Julia I. Suryakusuma 1996).

PP10 concerns the registration of marriage, permission for marriage and divorce, salary splitting arrangements following a divorce, and extramarital sexual relationships of civil servants. The circumstances of polygyny have been discussed earlier in the Marriage Law section.

In reference to permission for polygyny and divorce based on PP10, article 7 (2) states that permission for divorce for a civil servant cannot be granted if the given reason is that the wife is handicapped or sick, which makes her unable to perform her duties, while article 10 (2b) determines that the permission for polygyny can be granted if the wife is subject to any of the three circumstances stated in the 1974 Marriage Law (Chapter VIII:41a, as mentioned earlier). In this view, the wife faces a dilemma because of these two articles, since the husband can say: 'If you don't want to have a co-wife, then I will divorce you' (I. *kalau tidak mau dimadu, ya dicerai saja*). Thus, the protection of the wife by her husband and the equality between husband and wife stated in the 1974 Marriage Law do not exist in reality.

PP10 was produced on the basis of a request from Dharma Wanita to protect the wives of civil servants from any extramarital affairs of their husbands, which might lead them to take second wives and mistresses (Julia I. Suryakusuma 1996:103).[33] Taking into account that civil servants are to be the models for the rest of society, this regulation is aimed at disciplining civil servants.

Yet, if the PP10 was expected to be a *senjata pamungkas* (I. ultimate fatal weapon) for the members of Dharma Wanita, it might rebound on them (Julia I. Suryakusuma 1996:109), or became *senjata makan tuan*. It literally means that a 'gun' which eats its owner, and gun being PP10 and 'its owner' is the members of Dharma Wanita. Why? Even though Dharma Wanita was the initiator of PP10, the authority of its members is as no more than a 'pressure group' since the law itself does not give any legal status for Dharma Wanita to act on any problems related to divorce or plural marriages of male civil servants. Besides, no statement in PP10 regulates persistent infidelity. Thus PP10 has become a boomerang for the members of Dharma Wanita (Julia I. Suryakusuma 1996:109).

33 Though there have been a number cases of infidelity of civil servants, the extramarital relations of a high-ranking official of the cabinet secretariat—Dewanto—became the climax for the demand of *Dharma Wanita* members to regulate the family life of civil servants (Julia I. Suryakusuma 1996:103). This case was publicly exposed by the media after the report of Rahmini—the second secret wife—because of an attempted murder (Saraswati Sunindyo 1996).

Take for example, article 15 (1), which states that a civil servant is prohibited from living together with another woman/man without a legal marital union. This is followed by article 2, which states that the civil servant will be admonished (I. *ditegur*) by his superior if the superior happens to identify any extramarital sexual relationship of the inferior. This is tricky. If an extramarital sexual relationship is secret, or at least, is 'considered to be secret', then it does not matter. Thus, one may assume that as long as the relationship remains secret, it is all right. In fact, there is no single article in the PP10 which regulates this, except being reproved by his/her superior (see Chapter VII for a discussion on the sexual infidelity of a civil servant in Makassar).

There is rumour frequently uttered in regard to PP10 that when *Ibu* Tien—the wife of President Suharto—died, PP10 was no longer in effect. This countered the previous rumour that the establishment of PP10 was a reflection of *Ibu* Tien's anxiety about polygyny. There was also an issue that PP10 would be abolished when Khofifah Indar Parawansa was the Ministry of Women Empowerment. But, she calmly responded by stating that the existing of PP10 does not make any difference to the life of the wives of civil servant. Until the end of her power to the present, PP10 is still existed and polygyny among civil servant is continued to be practised, as requirements for polygyny under the Marriage Law and PP10 can easily be speculated.

Previous Research

In the preface of her monograph *Bugis Weddings*, Millar (1989:xi–xii) notes a number of studies on the Bugis during the 1970s and early 1980s conducted by both foreign as well as Bugis-Makassar scholars, including Pelras, Lineton, Millar, Errington, Andaya, Sutherland, Harvey, Mattulada, Patunru and Abidin.[34] This interest continued in the second half of the 1980s onward, as seen from the number of more recent publications on South Sulawesi, and on Bugis in particular.

Ethnographic Studies of Gender and Sexuality in South Sulawesi

As a reaction to feminist approaches in the 1970s, gender and sexuality emerge as a separate topic of anthropological research. In 1980, such topic continues to be a marginalized phenomenon and (if any) it includes under

34 For reference, see Millar (1989, Bibliography).

'family life' (Pelras 1996:39–40). In her article on *The Invention of Bugis Gender*, Millar notes:

> ...gender relations in society are almost entirely subordinate to a cultural preoccupation with hierarchical social location. Social location is an attribute of each individual and has far less to do with gender than with individual characteristics distributed without reference to gender.
>
> MILLAR 1983:477

From this point of view, Millar argues that for the Bugis, gender is second to social location. However, Davies (2006) raises a question: Is gender subordinate to status as an organisational principle in Bugis society? Her finding shows how males and females should adhere to the clear ideals of femininity and masculinity in the everyday life of the Bugis, she comes to a conclusion that gender is not subordinate to social status, but is a central part of Bugis social life. My book strengthens Davies' argument.

On his book *Kinship, Status and Gender*, Chabot (1996) notes on the interconnectedness among the aspect of gender, status and kinship in Makassar society, one of the ethnic groups in South Sulawesi. Despite it was published more than forty years after his extensive fieldwork, the book contains what Rössler and Rötger-Rössler phrase it as 'the essentials of Makassar social life'.

In the second half of 1990s onward, the study of gender and sexuality in South Sulawesi attracted more attention of researchers'. Andaya (2000:27) asserts that the study of the 'third gender' is still in infancy in Southeast Asia. Speaking on South Sulawesi, Pelras (1996:165) remarks that:

> One cannot conclude a discussion of gender among the Bugis without reference to the existence and importance of an, as it were, third gender, the *calabai*, and less well-known fourth gender one, the *calalai*.'

'Numbering' the category of gender is, however, problematical as it leads to the rigid category of gender, while *calabai, calalai,* and *bissu* are binary in their category, each uses a separate unique aspect of gender. Interpreting phenomena like *calabai, calalai,* and *bissu* as third, fourth, or fifth genders is in my view problematic because it can lead us to reify notions of 'female' and 'male'.

In his work on *bissu*—whose origin is linked to the androgynous character of female moon diety—of South Sulawesi, Andaya claims that his category of *bissu* as the third gender is 'to indicate another space, not between a society's dominant paradigm of male/female sex, masculine/feminine gender, but outside of it' (Andaya 2000:29), and therefore *bissu* is placed in a separate 'third' gender category.

Following Pelras' category of gender, Davies (2010) explores the nature of gender diversity in Indonesia and examines the place of such subjectivities in relation to theories of gender, gender diversity and sexuality. Drawing from the third sex/gender theory, the terms 'third gender' may be problematical, if not, overemployed and poorly defined (Boellstorff 2004a:161). In society where more than three sex/gender categories like Bugis, Herdt (1994:19–20) who recognizes the possible multiple gender in a given society, uses 'thirdness' heuristically.

In the Bugis context, however, where there are *calalai, calabai* and *bissu* (Pelras 1996, Andaya 2000 and Davies 2007 and 2010), Andaya (2000) categorizes *bissu* as the 'third gender' category, Davies (2001, 2007, 2010) classifies *bissu* as being 'the fifth gender.' This raises a significant question: who has the authority to categorize who comes first (as the third gender), who comes later (the forth gender) and so on, while all three (*calalai, calabai* and *bissu*) have the combination that transcend dualism. For example, Boellstorff (2004a:161) argues that '*waria* are not a 'third gender' but a male femininity.'

An outstanding piece of ethnographic work is *Gay Archipelago* of Boellstorff (2005), whose research setting included Makassar of South Sulawesi, examines the history of homosexuality in Indonesia and how gay and lesbian identities are lived in Indonesian everyday life. With triangulation of field methods in his ethnographic research, Boellstorff not merely explores love, desire, and romance of gay men and lesbian women, but he also looks at the roles of mass media, the state, and marriage in gay and lesbian identities.

While global queer studies focus mainly on urban area of study, Wieringa et al. (2009) produce a collection of articles which includes working class and transgender females whose voices unheard or rather neglected. The chapters reveal how community participate in and respond to global political and queer movement in Asia, the struggles towards the state gender regime and religious fundamentalist in the national level. One of the chapters of Davies' (2009) ethnographic base study which deals with *calalai* subjectivities of the Bugis in South Sulawesi examines the notions of ideal Bugis masculinity and femininity; the influence of local and national ideologies and Islamic discourses on gender ideals of the Bugis; and ways in which *calalai* engage and rework dominant gender discourses.

In Indonesia, when speaking about homosexuality, people commonly associate these as part of western culture, and deviant behaviour, as well as homophobic (Nurul Ilmi Idrus 2008b, Boellstorff 2004b). While Indonesia is assumed to be 'tolerant culture', because gay, lesbian, and transgendered persons are respected as shamans or performers, the reality is more complex (Boellstorff 2006:158). However, Boellstorff claims that only elites jet-set of gay and lesbian Indonesia who get benefit from globalisation, make contact, and share with western gay and lesbian. The idea 'to become' *gay* and *lesbi* is, however, not originated from one's ethnic group or local tradition, even though it historically shows that outside ideas may be localized (Boellstorff 2006:3). Boellstorff (2005) notes that for many gay and *lesbi* Indonesians, their subjectivities are developed at a national level and they feel themselves part of a gay world (*dunia gay*) that supercedes ethnolocality. At this point, Boellstorff makes a point that a critique of ethnolocality opens up a space where we can imagine new geographies of identification and provide ourselves to better respond to an already globalized world (Boellstorff 2002:38). Their homosexuality as socially assumed deviant behaviour makes them susceptible towards violence (Nurul Ilmi Idrus 2008b, Boellstorff 2004b) and strong social stigma, especially when one of them gets involved in a criminal act (Nurul Ilmi Idrus 2009b). In turn, Peletz's (2009) unprecedented study on gender pluralism offered an ethnographic account of the politics of transgender and same-sex identities in Southeast Asia and in diaspora. He explores the question of 'pluralism' in the context of tolerance and legitimacy to gender diversity.

In South Sulawesi (as well as in other area of Indonesia), people commonly view that being gay and lesbian is associated with their 'environment', and therefore it can be easy for them 'to go back' to their nature. In my own earlier work (2006) on gender identity among lesbians in South Sulawesi I indicate that:

> 'Becoming' a lesbian can be 'in-between' congenital (nature) and acquired (culture), given that the boundary between the two is blurred. The fact that hunter-congenital and lines-acquired cannot be rigidly dichotomised since one 'become a *lesbi*' because s/he has a capability to be a *lesbi*, but she may also learn it from hir/her culture or environment. Though there is a tendency that most hunters are congenital and most lines are acquired.
>
> NURUL ILMI IDRUS 2006B:18–9

This contributes to the understanding that 'becoming' lesbian cannot be understood in terms of dichotomy of nature and culture, but it lies in between these two oppositions.

In his book *Coincidence of Desire*, Boellstorff (2007) undermines more traditional notions of linear, hierarchical time that structure a range of hegemonic dualities, including male–female and modern-traditional. His visit to Indonesia

for over a decade, as an anthropologist explored gender and sexuality and as an activist involved in HIV prevention work, Boellstorff provides several in-depth case studies, primarily concerning the lives of Indonesian men who term themselves *gay*, which include Makassar of South Sulawesi as his field site. His work contributes to the 'coincide' between queer studies and anthropology, and how these two fields of studies might enrich both fields. Based on her extensive ethnographic research, Davies (2010) examines the lives and roles of variously gender subjectivities in everyday life, and analyses the place of such subjectivities in association with theories of gender, gender diversity and sexuality.

Whereas existing ethnographic studies on gender and/or sexuality in South Sulawesi concentrate more on the nature of gender diversity (Davies 2010, 2009 and 2007, Andaya 2000), gay and lesbian identities (Boellstorff 2004c, 2005; Nurul Ilmi Idrus 2006b), and whilst two manuscript-based studies deal with sexual norms with heavy Islamic influence (Muhlis Hadrawi and Anwar Ibrahim 1999; and Muhlis Hadrawi 2009), and contributing to the understanding of ideal Bugis sex norms, my book is focused on gender and sexuality among heterosexual beings with the use of rich written tradition, the narrative of everyday life with a number of case studies.

Ethographic Studies on Marriage in Indonesia

A number of ethnographic studies dealing with marriage in Indonesian have been carried out. A pioneer of ethnographic study on kinship and socialization of the Javanese was H. Geertz (1961) on *The Javanese Family*. Geertz makes an important contribution to the understanding of the value of the Javanese family through an examination of kinship in Javanese life cycles, including marriage, from its arrangement, selection of mate, courtship, wedding rituals, divorce and property division to the transition after the first month of marriage.

Both Boon's (1977) and Hobart's (1980) studies focusing on kinship structures of Bali, though Boon dealt more on historical framework. These two studies provide insight into how family is operated on the basis of structuralist tradition and how marriage is occurred. While previous ethnographic studies of Bali tended to be more structuralist in nature, Jennaway (1996) in her *Sweet Breath and Bitter Honey* centres more on women's sexuality and fecundity in the context of marriage. Jennaway examines women's emotional realities in marriage through their individual stories.

Brenner's (1998) outstanding ethnographic study on *Domestication of Desire* among urban Javanese merchants looks at the domestic sphere of the market place as much women's domain as the private space of the household. Brenner explores the ambivalence between women's self-control and their control over the money among female Javanese traders. Brenner found the market as a component of the domestic sphere and as a site of feminine authority associated with the production and conservation of wealth.

The study of gender in island Southeast Asia requires an understanding of the local system of power and prestige, and how gender is mapped on these ideas (Errington 1990). A number of studies identifies Indonesian women's relative financial autonomy portrayed several decade earlier (H. Geertz 1961 and Jay 1969). However, ethnographic studies in 1990s by Brenner (1998), Sullivan (1994), and Wolf (1992) indicated that women's control over household finances did not necessarily offer them higher status within the family. However, participation of single women in the economy had an effect on their marital autonomy (Wolf 1992, Handcock 2000, Nurul Ilmi Idrus 2008a). Women's economic participation tends to marry later or gives them a bargain position to negotiate their single status (Bennett 2008; Nurul Ilmi Idrus 2008; Wolf 1992), though a single status for working daughter is relatively not an option (Augustina Situmorang 2011).

Blackwood's (2000) *Webs of Power*, Krier's (2000) *The Marital Project* and Sanday's (2002) *Women at the Center* deal with the complexity of power relations within Minangkabau. By focusing on marriage as an exchange of men among Minangkabau, Krier identifies the notion of marriage as a strategic project. Blackwood focuses more on female dominance in Minangkabau's contemporary matriarchy, and Sanday explores how national and global discourse have significant impact on women's lives.

In her introductory chapter on her ethnographic study of maidenhood in Lombok, Bennett (2002:1) states:

> Maidenhood is a journey, beginning when girls surrender their childhood at menarche and culminating in their arrival at the adult destination of marriage and motherhood.
>
> BENNETT 1989:XI–XII

This implies the journey and the dynamic life of women from maidenhood to the marriage life. In her book *Women, Islam and Modernity*, Bennett (2005b) highlights the processes of social and sexual development of young Muslim women in Lombok, by exploring their experiences of womanhood. She focuses on the dialectics of desire by examining maidenhood identity, desire and modernity in Mataram. She criticises the development policies from the New Order and post-Suharto eras in regard to single women's sexuality and reproductive health, arguing that individual identities and exercising personal autonomy not merely belong to married, but also to unmarried women.

Nina Nurmila's (2009) piece of work, *Women, Islam and Everyday Life*, focuses on women's experiences in polygynous marriage. It examines the competing interpretation of the Qur'an verses the controversies among Muslims, and the strategies in dealing with it. Applying contextual approach in her analysis, she not only criticised the literal interpretation of the Qur'an in regard to polygyny,[35] but also challenge for the abolition of it, as it has become the source of injustice to women as well as children. Her argument is based on the understanding that the Qur'an is divine, but its interpretation is human, hence it opens for speculation and debatable.[36] My unique contribution in the present book is the examination of polygyny in the context of illegal marriage (*kawin liar*, literally 'wild marriage') and marital violence, dissolution of marriage, and how women exercise agency in dealing with them.

Nakamura (1981:137), criticising research conducted by western social scientists on Javanese divorce, such as Prins (1951), H. Geertz (1961) and Lev (1972), concludes that they come to understand the Javanese divorce behaviour in terms of their own culture which is, according to Nakamura, based on a misunderstanding of the implementation of Islamic law. I question this. It is not that western social scientists were wrong in terms of their interpretation of Javanese behaviour regarding divorce, although I disagree with the term 'not real' Muslims, according to Nakamura, used by a number of westerners who have studied Javanese divorce (1981:137), as this problematizes the dichotomy between 'real' and 'not real' Muslims. Indeed, they have shown a significant correlation between how Javanese culture and Islamic law come together in dealing with divorce, an aspect that was not taken into account in Nakamura's study, despite the fact she claims that the dissolution of marriage in Kotagede is based on the Qur'an, Islamic Law, custom and tradition (Nakamura 1981:35).

In Sidrap, where the majority of the population (91.75%) are Muslims (Sidenreng Rappang in Figures 2014), local norms significantly influence how people deal with marriage, divorce and reconciliation. Such correlations may be invisible on the surface without studying the cultural background of a certain society. Therefore, it is not a matter of whether or not Javanese are 'real' Muslims or whether or not western social scientists studying Javanese divorce behaviour misunderstood the implementation of Islamic law, but the study conducted by Prins, Geertz and Lev (above) which considers the coherence between culture and religion can lead to these sorts of justifications. Thus, it is not just about the 'ideal' (based on religion), but it is also about the 'practice' of divorce.

---

35 Despite the term polygamy is not commonly use in everyday language, I use the term polygyny consistently since it is more specialized and specific.

36 For the debate on polygamy, see, for example, Van Doorn-Harder (2013), Nurul Ilmi Idrus (2006a), Abdul Halim Soebahar et al. (2005).

Another criticism by Nakamura about western social scientists is their 'externalist approach' to the study of religion. She argues that they should have studied the nature of religious faith in the life of an individual through an 'ethical approach' (Nakamura 1981:160). However, she herself studied the dissolution of marriage through courts and other related institutions rather than ethnographic research, thus largely neglecting local discourse and individual practice. It is difficult, if not impossible, to study the nature of religious faith without addressing the everyday social practice.

While in her study of dissolution of marriage in Kotagede, Central Java, Nakamura (1981) solely focuses on courts and related institutions, my contribution to the study of divorce is the discussion on the local discourse and individual practice (including the practice of *cerai liar*, literally 'wild divorce'), aspects that are rather largely neglected in Nakamura's study.

Ethnograhic Research on Marriage in South Sulawesi

Part of Robinson's (1986) ethnographic study on the political economy of development in Soroako dealt with marriage. Robinson explores the impact of economic development in social relations among Soroakans (who also include Bugis people), by examining forms of marriage, ideas of romantic love, marriage stability, and status in relation to marriage. This study shows the Soroakan adoption of Bugis adat in their daily activities and how the mining company has impacted on the social relationship of the surrounding community as the result of the development of political economy in Soroako, including their marital relation.

Röttger-Rössler's (2000) examines some aspects of gender and authority in Makassar society. She found that right, obligations, and the scope of authority are not dominated by men, but must be evenly distributed between men and women, and that responsibility is shared between the sexes in this society.

Most recent ethnographic studies on marriage in Indonesia have tended to deal with issues such as courtship and entry into marriage (Bennett 2005), marital violence (Nurul Ilmi Idrus 2001 and Nurul Ilmi Idrus and Bennett 2003), and women's experience of polygyny (Nina Nurmila 2009). Platt (2010, 2012) deals with a more comprehensive view of marriage and gender relations in contemporary Lombok through women's narrative and individual experience. Platt contribution to the study of marriage is the discussion on the issue of extramarital relation (*pacaran lagi*) among Sasak ethnic group indigenous to Lombok. She conceptualized a wide range of marital experiences as occurring across a marital continuum, not necessarily as a linier process.

To date, there is merely one ethnographic study related to marriage among the Bugis in South Sulawesi which was conducted in the 1980s by Susan Millar, and is closely related to my own work. Millar's Bugis weddings explores the practical operation of weddings based on the fundamental principle of differential status on the basis of birth (ascribed status) as opposed to achieved status in modern South Sulawesi. This ethnographic account shows the significance of Bugis weddings in making manifest one's social location; kinship in relation to the practical operation of weddings, and marriage procedures.

Errington's *Meaning of Power* (1989) examines the polity of the Kingdom of Luwu and Millar's *Bugis Weddings* are notable for their almost complete neglect of matters Islamic, the latter provides thick description on different weddings from different status groups, and alludes to the distinction between registered and unregistered marriage.

In spite of the fact that my study builds on all these previous studies, I also make a unique contribution. My book shows how Islam and adat are intertwined and cannot be separated in the everyday life of the Bugis (M.B. Hooker 2002), though there is a high degree of variability in the way they are practiced across archipelago. I explore the construction of gender identities for single people and gender relations in marriage in Bugis society. In doing so, I examine the fundamental concept of *siriq* and its relation to gender socialization, sexuality between the sexes, and sex within marriage. Matters such as shameful marriages, divorce and reconciliation in relation to adat and state law which highlight the tension between the state and Islam; and how women exercise agency in the realm of illegal marriage, marital violence and how women deal with it are also examined. These aspects have become my pivotal concerns in this book. I use textual analysis of traditional manuscripts and incorporation of oral traditions, aspect that in many previous ethnographic research is rather neglected, which in fact is reflected in the Bugis life.

I also consider how Bugis cultural specificities are affected by the national ideology of contemporary Indonesia. This approach is based on the idea that, in addressing marriage and marital conflicts among the Bugis, it is not enough to just look at specific features of local cultures as elements in discrete closed systems since the combination of local culture and Indonesian nation state underlies the dynamics of everyday life as observed in the field.

As the above review of my sources and materials shows, these are both numerous and diverse. They make possible a richness of discussion not often available even for other Indonesian societies and rare in wider context.

Whenever possible, I have sought to support the discussion of particular points with different kinds of evidence.

My aim is to present an interpretation of Bugis social and sexual experience by connecting gendered values, marriage and marital violence using a well established tradition of analysis to provide an understanding of gender relations of contemporary Bugis society through an ethnography of marriage.

CHAPTER 2

Siriq, Gender and Sexuality

> Everybody knows that men and women are different. But behind this knowledge lies a certain uneasiness: How different are they? What is the extent of the difference? What significance does it have for the way male and female behave and are treated in society.
>
> OAKLEY 1972:9

Introduction

Jolly and Manderson (1997:1) argue that neither the study of sexuality nor the study of gender has allowed us to come down on the side of either biological essentialism or cultural construction. Errington (1990:11) formulates this dualism into 'biology' and 'culture.' She argues for a relationship between the two rather than taking one side or the other. She states:

> The most basic and obvious importance of embodiment for culture and vice versa is that we are born biologically unfinished and require human culture in order to develop into humans.
>
> ERRINGTON 1990:11

In applying this understanding to gendered social practices, Errington writes 'bodies and cultures interact and form each other, and interpretation of the nature and functions and capacities of the body differ in different cultures' (Errington 1990:14). Thus, gender is not something one is born with, but it is a social practice of human life.

This chapter examines cultural specificities of the notion of gender and sexuality in relation to the concept *siriq* in Bugis society. I first discuss *siriq* as a defining part of Bugis identity and how *siriq* is manifested in gender-specific ways. Thus, I explore how Bugis notions of gender and sexuality are influenced by customary ideals derived from written traditions, as well as popular sayings and advice, and draw upon a number of case studies. The chapter aims to explain Bugis concepts of the masculine and the feminine in relation to *siriq* and sexuality as well as to explore gender in social encounters, in both private and public spaces. The chapter contributes to the understanding of how

 | DOI 10.1163/9789004311947_003

customary law (I. adat, B. *adeq*) and ethnic identity shape gender differences, and accordingly how men and women are treated differently in Bugis culture.

Siriq, To Masiriq and Gender

Siriq, which may be defined as 'shame' or 'honour', has been discussed by a number of Bugis scholars[1] as well as scholars from western countries.[2] *Siriq* is central to the Bugis world view, and is regarded as the soul and the spirit of each individual in the society. Errington defines *siriq* as 'dignity, honour or shame'. She draws parallels with *malu* (Indonesian), *isin* (Javanese),[3] *lek* (Balinese), and *hiya* (Tagalog). Similarly, Errington points out that 'a person who has *siriq* is sensitive to, hence vulnerable to, other people' (Errington 1989:145).[4] She notes that the term *siriq* is unique to South Sulawesi, but various senses of the term are found throughout Southeast Asia (Errington 1989:145). In a wider context, *siriq* is a compromising concept to the shame culture of in Mediterranean society where honour and shame have also played a dominant role in public life. Honour is fundamentally the public recognition of one's social standing (Baroja 1965).

For the Bugis, the notion of *siriq* is derived from *sumangeq* (B. energy of life), the life force of each individual in this society. Hamid Abdullah (1985:37) maintains that this notion is not only reflected in Bugis behaviour, but also in the Bugis social system and way of thinking. This means that *siriq* is viewed as a fundamental element in Bugis cosmology, as *jiwa* (I. soul), *kehormatan* (honour) and *martabat* (prestige). The Bugis scholar, La Side (1977:25–28) suggests a variety of meanings for *siriq*, namely *malu-malu* (I. shame), *segan/kerendahan-hati* (humility), *takut* (fear), *hina/aib* (disgrace), *iri-hati/dengki* (envy), *harga-diri* (self-respect), *kehormatan* (honour), and *kesusilaan* (morality).[5] These meanings are parallel to Matthes' definition in his Bugis-Dutch dictionary as *beschaamd*

1 For example, Mattulada (1974, 1995); Johan Nyompa et al. (1979); La Side (1977); A. Rahman Rahim (1982); Hamid Abdullah (1985); A. Zainal Abidin (1983); Laica Marzuki (1995) and many others.

2 For example, Errington (1977 and 1989); Millar (1983) and (1989); Brawn (1993); Robinson (1994, 1999 and 2001); Pelras (1996); Chabot (1996).

3 Keeler (1987:66) defines *isin* as 'vulnerability to interaction.'

4 Three other indigenous ethnic groups (Makassarese, Torajanese and Mandarnese) in South Sulawesi also employ *siriq* as a fundamental principle, but its application varies slightly in degree and practice. See, for example, Chabot (1996) and Natzir Said (1984) for Makassarese; Baharuddin Lopa (1984) for Mandarnese, and C. Salombe (1984) for Torajanese.

5 See also A. Rahman Rahim (1982:109–110).

(ashamed), *schroomvallig* (timid), *verlegen* (shy), *schaamte* (shame), *eergevoel* (pride, sense of honour), *schande* (disgrace) and *wangunst* (envy) (Matthes 1874).

Ultimately, *siriq* is related to *onro* [B. social status (Robinson 2001), social standing (Chabot 1996), social location (Millar 1983,1989), social place (Errington 1989; Acciaioli 1989)]; one has to know her/his place or who she/he is in relation to others (B. *naisseng onrona*). *Siriq* has special significance in Bugis society simply because one's place in relation to others is always a matter of concern. Even if status (that is *onro*) is theoretically determined by birth, achieved status is as important as ascribed status to ascertain one's social location (Robinson 2001:25), and it has to be continually demonstrated and acknowledged. Thus, a male family member will defend the *siriq* of a female relative because any attack on her *siriq* devalues or fails to acknowledge her social location or status, and by extension, that of her family and relations. This applies to husbands and affinal kin, as much as to cognatic kin, since a marriage implies at least equal status between the sets of relations (Millar 1989).

Mattulada (1974, 1995) argues *siriq* is an abstract term, though its concretely perceptible results may be experienced and observed. It has similarities with the notion of honour, described in Mediterranean culture, where honour is translated as 'the value of a person in his own eyes, but also in the eyes of his society' (Pitt-Rivers 1965:21). One's honour depends on the interpretation of one's action by herself/himself from others (Robinson 1999:243), and is learned in the course of daily activities or through wise advice from elders.

When speaking of one's own *siriq*, the concept indicates that one feels embarrassed about the situation. The consequence of *siriq* may result in a fatal action, such as killing the person who makes one face *siriq*. Indeed, killing people because of *siriq* is culturally acceptable for the Bugis. As Baroja states in relation to the Mediterranean concept of honour 'the loss of honour is equated with the loss of life' (1965:85). This is because to kill someone in consideration of her/his wrong doing is also acceptable since death is regarded as more appropriate for him/her than staying alive in a state of *siriq*. This echoes the Bugis notion.

Siriq in Bugis, like honour in the Mediterranean, can be used as a legitimation of violence. The cultural repercussions of defending *siriq* for Bugis can only be understood if we relate it to other beliefs. For example, there is a saying in Bugis, *cellaq topi na doang* (B. when it becomes red, it proves it is a shrimp)[6] which

6 Hamid Abdullah (1985:39) cites a similar Makassar saying: *éjatongpi na doang*, explaining that a shrimp is grey before it is cooked, and becomes red after frying. Andaya (1979:369) expresses the outcome of defending *siriq* among Makassarese: 'as a shrimp is red (when

means the outcome in defending *siriq* is destiny (B. *wéré*, M. *saré*). Life is nothing without dignity, and a person who does not have dignity is considered to be non-human (B. *tennia niq rupa tau*). As in Mediterranean society, honour is related to reputation and life, while dishonour is connected to infamy and death (Baroja, 1965:85).

In Bugis, this is summed up in the following saying:

Siriq-é mitu tariase tau	Only with *siriq* are we called human
Narékko déq ni siriqta,	
tanianik tau	If we have no *siriq*, we are not human
Rupa tau mani asengna	That's called: human in form only
Naia tau déq é siriqna	The person who is without *siriq*
Dé it ri lainna olokolo-é	is no different from an animal

ERRINGTON 1989:1467

This saying not only indicates the significance of *siriq* in one's life, but also emphasises the Bugis' notion of what it means to be human. Since a family shares one *siriq* (*masséddi siriq*), an individual has to behave appropriately in a *siriq* situation because they represent the family *siriq*,[8] *to masiriq* (people who are being shamed and who are responsible to defend family *siriq*) have to act in response to transgressions by family members or others. Consequently, for the Bugis it is better to die defending *siriq* (*maté ri siriqna*) than to remain alive without dignity (*maté siriq*). For the Bugis, only for *siriq* we are alive (*siriq émmi rionroang ri lino*). This proverb does not just carry a sense of social identity, but also self respect. One who has no *siriq* (*déggaga siriqna*) is similar to a living corpse or an animal (*olokoloq*). Therefore, one should maintain her/his *siriq* in order to continue to enjoy the respect of others.

But this is not to say that if one feels *siriq*, one automatically kills someone who causes *siriq*. *To masiriq* has to behave appropriately in a *siriq* situation, depending on the level of *siriq*, because he/she represents the family *siriq*. Muhammad Sikki et al. (1998:49), for example, indicate three levels of *siriq* on

cooked) and unbleached cotton is white, so must we accept what occurs, but we must first of all make an effort.'

7 See also Mattulada (1995:64–65) and Abdullah (1985:41–42) for a similar saying.

8 Here family refers to whoever feels part of the family who is being shamed. In Bugis, a family does not solely involve *sianang* (B. nuclear family), but may embrace extended family based on blood relation and *passilessurengeng* (siblinghood, even without family or village of origin relation), or *passaribbattangang* in Makassar terms. This relatedness is called *assiwolong-polongeng* and associates people to share one *siriq* and differentiates between family and *to laing*, literally meaning other people, but carrying the sense of outsider.

the basis of how people react. The first level of *siriq* is that *siriq* which can still be tolerated (I. *wajar jika didiamkan*). For example, people look down on an adult man who has no job. Instead of responding to the humiliation in a negative way, he uses his *siriq* as a challenge to find a job. The second level of *siriq* is that *siriq* which is supposed to be followed by anger (I. *reaksi marah*). For instance, if someone steals someone else's goods without feeling guilty, this sense of the thieves remorselessness should prompt an angry reaction in order to emphasise the perpetrator's behaviour. Finally, there is the level of *siriq* which has to be paid for with killing (*dibayar dengan nyawa*), as in an honour killing in response to, for example, incidents of elopement (B. *silariang*, see Sahariah's case below), or in cases of incest.[9]

There is a Bugis saying: 'If one's *siriq* is offended, one would act without a word' (*narékko siriqna naranreng tenrirenrengina nariéwa*) (A. Hasan Machmud 1976:60). This saying indicates the moral duty of someone whose *siriq* is violated. In other words, *siriq* has positive and negative applications (see Nurul Ilmi Idrus and Bennett 2003:47–49). *Siriq* as honour may appear to be a positive motivator. For instance, because of *siriq* someone attempts to motivate him/herself to achieve a standard of excellence, measured by material wealth, social status, level of education etc. In contrast, *siriq* as shame may force an individual to seek vengeance against the one who causes *siriq*. For example, in *silariang* (elopement), the men as well as the women are in danger of being killed by the women's male kin to maintain the *siriq* of the family. However, in marriage by abduction (*rilariang*), only the man is in danger of being killed, while the woman is in no danger of punishment because she is taken against her will (*silariang* and *rilariang* are further discussed in Chapter 3).

An individual who dies defending *siriq* (*maté ri siriqna*) is considered to die in sugar and coconut milk (*maté ri gollai, maté ri santangi*), meaning he dies in a sweet and delicious death. This notion implies that he has undergone an honourable and responsible death for the sake of the family.[10] For that reason, the resolution of questions of *siriq* may be accomplished through either taking the law into one's own hands (I. *main hakim sendiri*) or through a customary court (*pengadilan adat*). Since *siriq* is a part of adat, there is a Bugis saying related to this: adat does not recognize children and grandchildren (B. *adeq é*

9 In November 1999, *Fajar*—a local newspaper—reported the court hearings of an honour killing. A man killed his mother and his older brother because of their incestuous relationship, which he said both had admitted. Moreover, they allowed him to do whatever he pleased because they realized the shame (*Fajar* 1, 10 and 11 November 1999).

10 See, for example, Hamid Abdullah (1985:37–61), Errington (1989:144–52) and Mattulada (1995:61–65).

temmakkéanaq temmakké eppo) (Hamid Abdullah 1985:20). The gist of this saying is that anybody who collides with adat has to be treated the same. Thus whoever causes *siriq*, she/he would be treated equally. *Siriq* exists in every aspect of Bugis life, but the most common and concrete acts which can cause offence to *siriq* are associated with courtship and marriage (Mattulada 1995:62 and Hamid Abdullah 1985:37).

Siriq is significant for analysing gender relations in Bugis society (Robinson 2001:26 and 1999:242–243, Millar 1989 and 1983). Even though *to masiriq* refers to male and female kin, in general men are described by the term. It is regarded as more appropriate if women's feeling of *siriq* is defended by their male kinsmen (Millar 1983:484), who are obliged to respond if *siriq* is transgressed (Robinson 2001:27). While sons, particularly the eldest son, act as the first defenders of the family in the context of *siriq*, daughters are the ones who must be protected by their siblings and other kinsmen in order to guard family *siriq* (Hamid Abdullah 1985:130–131). On this point, men's control of female sexuality is sustained by the code of *siriq* (Robinson 1999:243). Brawn—who conducted research in Bone (South Sulawesi)—argues that Bone women do not have *siriq* because they cannot defend themselves from *siriq* situations (Brawn 1993:60). On this point, however, it is not that women have no *siriq*. Rather, since women are the primary symbols of *siriq*, it is considered more honourable if they stay calm rather than defending their *siriq* themselves. However, women can also take the active role of *to masiriq*, as shown in the following example.

Sahariah: A Female To Masiriq

I conducted an interview with a female prisoner (Sahariah) in Maros jail[11] who had killed her niece's sweetheart, Muhlis, because of *siriq*. He had dated her niece, Nia, for months in a clandestine courtship. This relationship was forbidden because Muhlis had never made a formal proposal to Nia's parents. On the day of the killing, someone told Sahariah that Nia and Muhlis were going to elope. She went looking for them on her way back from working in her rice fields in order to ask Nia to go home. Nia, however, refused to return home and

11 I visited women in prison to find out the reasons they were imprisoned and how they were related to marital violence. I chose two prisons, one in the metropolitan city of Makassar and another in Kotamadya Pare-Pare (Municipality). In fact, the prison in Makassar caught fire in 1999, consequently women prisoners were relocated to Maros. I was directed to conduct my interviews in Maros Prison (LP Maros) with fourteen women convicted of various crimes—six murderers, three drug offenders, two thieves, one case of abortion, one case of *siriq*, and one case of deception. However, only 13 were successfully interviewed, as one of them escaped from the court after the court hearing. Interviews were conducted on 5–6 December 2000. See discussion of other cases in Chapter 7.

Muhlis would not let Nia leave and even scolded Sahariah. Sahariah felt that her *siriq* was disregarded, not only because of Nia's refusal, but also because of Muhlis' scolding. In response, Sahariah stabbed Muhlis in the chest with a large knife (I. *parang*) which she used in wet-rice cultivation. He died in front of Nia and Sahariah. Then, Sahariah went home and her family called the police to pick her up at Nia's parents' house to protect her from the anger of Muhlis' family.[12] Sahariah proudly stated that:

> Although I never planned to kill him, I thought this was the way it should be. I did the right thing. If I did not kill him, he would kill me some day because he always threatened that he was going to kill me. He did not expect that I was going to kill him because he said: 'What can a woman do?' But I did it, I killed him. Most importantly, I defended my family *siriq*. I felt satisfied, though I have been sentenced for seven and a half years.
>
> SAHARIAH, 30 years, unmarried, farmer, never attended school, interviewed on 6 December 2000

When I asked who had demanded that she defend the family's *siriq*, she replied that it was not necessary to wait for a command from the members of her family. Then, she said:

> Nia didn't have a brother, her father was too old to defend himself, I didn't have a husband, so I felt that I was responsible as the *to masiriq* of the family towards Nia and her sweetheart's wrong-doing.
>
> SAHARIAH, 6 December 2000

This case involves a woman becoming a *to masiriq* for the family when the male members of the family are not available to fill this role. Sahariah's act occurred because of her feeling of sharing one *siriq* (*masséddi siriq*), and indicates how a woman can express her feeling of *siriq* in a *siriq* situation through killing. For her family and for people who understood what was going on, Sahariah was not acting as a male, but as the defender of her family *siriq*. For others, however, she could be considered a 'devil woman'. People in the jail commented that it could be difficult for Sahariah to find a prospective husband, not only because she was a killer, but also because she would be in

12 In such cases, it is assumed that one goes to the police station to protect oneself. Otherwise, one could be subject to an act of taking the law into one's own hands (I. *main hakim sendiri*), as reported by local newspapers in Makassar (see, for example, Zohra A. Baso and Nurul Ilmi Idrus 2002:205).

her late 30s when she is released from prison. From this point of view, it is obvious that the lessened possibility of finding a partner in the future is not only related to her crime which indicates her non-modest behaviour (*déqna malebbiq*), but is also connected with her age. Sahariah realized this, but during the interview, Sahariah never expressed regret.

In addition, women also participate in controlling *siriq*. For example, when men are around, instead of asking the men to get away from the women, older women usually ask young women to keep away from men in order to protect themselves from *siriq*. In the past, when a woman and a man were found stealing a glance at a man, it was already reckoned as a transgression of *siriq*.[13] Hence, there is always a dichotomisation of good/bad that sexualises male and female behaviour.

Masculine and Feminine: *Siriq* and Sexuality in Bugis Philosophy

I begin this section with a poem written by a young Bugis artist—Udhin Palisuri (2002:67)—because it encapsulates the subject I am going to discuss.

Tidak Boleh Karena Tradisi	**Prohibition Because of Tradition**
Sejak kecil	Since childhood
Orang Bugis-Makassar	The Bugis-Makassarese
Hidup dari tidak boleh	Live with prohibition
Tidak boleh ini	Not allowed this
Tidak boleh itu	Not allowed that
Tidak boleh begini	Not allowed like this
Tidak boleh begitu	Not allowed like that
Tidak boleh karena tradisi	Not allowed because of tradition
Tidak boleh karena pappaseng	Not allowed because of aphorism
Tidak boleh karena pamali	Not allowed because of taboo
Orang Bugis-Makassar	The Bugis-Makassarese
Hidupnya berkalang adat	Live based on custom
Tak ingin melanggar sumpah	Have no desire to collide with
ucapan leluhurnya.	words of the ancestors.

13 Chabot (1996) gives a similar account in regard to social intercourse between the sexes for the Makassarese.

This poem reflects how the lives of the Bugis (and Makassarese) are surrounded by multiple prohibitions based on custom, and fear of the consequences they may face if they do not practise what they have been told by their elders.

Hamid Abdullah, a Bugis scholar, argues that because women are the symbols of family *siriq*, they have to be closely monitored. Their behaviours are not only observed by their parents, but also by their close and distant family members (Hamid Abdullah 1985:131). For instance, if one's sister is being harassed by another man, the social location of the whole family is threatened as a result. Therefore, a woman is potentially the pride of her family and at the same time is potentially the destroyer of family honour.

The notion that *siriq* depends upon women's behaviour is reflected in Bugis *adat* that a woman should at all times be under someone's protection. If she is single, no matter how old she is, she is under the care and protection of her parents, her brothers (if any), and/or other male relatives; once she marries, she is under her husband's protection. Parental power is transformed into conjugal power and transferred to her husband. Thus, to maintain *siriq*, pressure is not just experienced by the women who are being protected, but also by their male relatives who act as *to masiriq* (B. *siriq* defender).

Abdullah notes that people who may not understand this situation would assume that this control is aimed at restricting women's freedom. In fact, he argues, this control takes place in order to prevent any 'improper behaviour' in which women may engage and to protect women from any forbidden contact, which would be seen as a violation of adat. A Bugis woman may become involved in public activities which are considered appropriate for women. In doing so, however, she is controlled by adat which is practised in the life of the Bugis family. Any violation of these norms has to be handled by adat in accordance with the values of Bugis society (Hamid Abdullah 1985:131).

A Bugis woman is placed in a 'position of honour,' as a jewel (*intang paramata*) of the family, but her freedom is restricted. From this perspective, *siriq* may legitimate any kind of violence against her and, at the same time, it may become a potential source of violence since *to masiriq*—who can be men or women—have the power to define what behaviour transgresses *siriq*. However, such restrictions are difficult to sustain these days since women attend school and work outside home.[14]

Although women in Kulo participated in this trend to become educated and move into the work force, in practice, they often found themselves caught in a

14 In South Sulawesi, participation rates of those who are economically active (TPAK) is 45 percent for female and 83 percent for male in 2009, to compare with TPAK for female and male in 2000, which are 28 percent and 70 percent respectively (BPS 2011).

contradiction between working in the modern economy and the expectation that women should not be in situations where the family honour could be under threat. Ati's case below illustrates this dilemma.

When Ati finished her study at the university in Makassar, she was asked by her elder sister, Rapiah, to come to Irian Jaya (now West Papua). Rapiah had found a job for Ati as an office worker through a friend, Lela. Ati was allowed by her parents to go to West Papua because it was hard to find work in Makassar. Ati did not know that the job offered by her sister was in a hotel, a place that people in Kulo still consider to be full of negative values (for example, bad girl, a place for whores). It was not that Ati did not like the job, it was only because the office was in a hotel. Ati worked half-heartedly, while she tried to find another job without her sister's knowledge. When she got another job, as she did not tell her sister that she had left the former job, her sister had no idea until Lela called and asked for Ati because she had been absent from the office for a week without any notice. Ati told them that she felt ashamed because she worked at a hotel. She thought that people in Kulo would gossip in a negative way about her job, regardless of what she was doing. After a long exchange of explanations and advice, Ati, Rapiah and Lela came to an agreement that Ati should go back to her former office. This is because Rapiah felt ashamed since she was the one who had asked the job for Ati. Besides, Lela already trusted Ati to be the money manager in the hotel based on Rapiah's recommendation. Rapiah called her parents in Kulo to explain about Ati's job because her parents were concerned about it. When I revisited the village at the end of 2002, Pak Bakri as well as his wife told me about Ati and their anxiety about her working in a hotel. After I explained to them, they seemed to understand that working in a hotel was not as bad as they thought. But the following day, I heard Ibu Bakri talking about what Ati was actually doing in West Papua, based on my explanation. Later, I asked her why she had to explain Ati's situation in West Papua to others. She said: 'So that people know' (I. *Supaya orang tahu*). Then, I came to understand that the anxiety experienced by Pak Bakri and his wife was not just about Ati and her job, but also about how to convince their neighbours about Ati's job. Thus, Ati's fear was well founded.

These restrictions are expressed through a number of symbols related to women's vulnerability in social interaction. Elders said: a woman is like a mirror (B. *makkunraié padai kacaé*). A *lontaraq* cited by Matthes states:

> A woman is like a glass. When she is gossiped about for an alleged wrongdoing, the glass is cracked. If the gossip is true, the glass is broken and worthless.

> *Apaq iatu riasengngé makkunrai riébaraq i kaca. Iana engka biritta temma decénna, riébaraq nitu mallesseq. Narékko mannessani pangkaukenna riébaraq ni pada tosa kacaé, reppaq ni degga buaq-buaqna.*[15]
>
> MATTHES 1972:102

However, regardless of whether or not the gossip is true, the glass (B. *kaca*) is cracked.[16] Once a glass is broken (*reppaq*), it becomes worthless (*déggaga buaq-buaqna*). The symbol of women as *kaca* reflects the women's vulnerability in everyday social interaction.

A similar image is used in a contemporary popular Bugis song entitled *Anaq Daraé* (Young Women)[17] which exemplifies women's vulnerability in their interactions with men:

Anaq Daraé	**Young Women**
Nappai ritangngaq-tangngaq	Only a quick stare
Nappai rikebbiq mata	Only a side glance
Naseng to mélo rialéna	She thinks I have fallen in love
Nasenni icanring aléna	She thinks I have become her boyfriend
Nappai ricanring-canring	Only a temptation
Nappai rikebbiq-kebbiq	Only stealing a glance at her
Nabbéréanni aléna	She has surrendered herself
Nasengngi méloq ipubéné	She thinks I will marry her
Idiq tu anaq daraé	We are young girls
Ajaq lalo mumalléré	Don't let yourselves be tempted
Idiq tu anaq daraé	We are young girls
Pada jagaiwi aléwé	Take care of yourselves
Padaki camming rasaé	We women are like a mirror
Reppaq na reppaq no	Once we are broken
Déggaga bettuanna	We mean nothing

15 Despite the fact that the *lontaraq* I quoted from Matthes is concerned with *pappangajaq* (B. advice) for *arung makkunrai* (noble woman), this *pappangajaq* is relevant to the everyday life of the Bugis, whether or not they are *arung* (noble descent). The text was transliterated by Mukhlis Hadrawi (1April 2000).

16 In a similar account, Mattulada (1995:441) also analyses the symbol of women as a glass in relation to women's social role.

17 This song was written by a male writer—Harun Husein—and sung by a male singer—Amal Mangile.

Irapakkiq penné pinceng	Like a porcelain plate
Nabuang nareppaq	Fallen and broken
Nadéggaga burayanna.	It becomes worthless.

This song embodies the metaphors for the sexual double standard which surrounds women's lives. Men interpret conduct based on their own points of view. The notion of a woman as a mirror (B. *camming*) or a porcelain plate (*penné pinceng*) demonstrates that woman should be carefully protected since both mirrors and porcelain are easily broken. Once broken, they become worthless (*nadéggaga burayanna*). Furthermore, it is common for a man to steal a glance (*kebbiq-kebbiq*) at a woman, but such behaviour is not acceptable in the reverse. Women's desire is not to be openly expressed, as reflected in the lyric of the song: 'Don't let yourself be tempted' (*Ajaq lalo mumalléré*). Women have to restrain themselves from expressing desire, while men's desire should be demonstrated, as stated in the following *lontaraq*:

> Men's desire is like a leaky roof, it is open. Women's desire is like a corset. That is why men are desirous. Women's desire is hidden, which means it can be held steady.
>
> *Naia cinnana oroané padai timpoq sebboq é, marisaliwengngi. Naia cinnana makkunraié padai wekkeng situtuq é. Namakkuanna naro namasero manessa cinnana oroané. Naia cinnana makkunraié mallinrungi, bettuanna maperrengngi*[18]
>
> *Lontaraq Daramatasia*, p. 45

The Bugis term *maperrengngi* (B. able to hold steadily) is derived from the verb *perreng* (to hold).[19] This term carries the connotation that a woman's desire must be strictly controlled, not just by herself but also by her family because a woman's sexual purity has a significant impact on her status in Bugis society. On account of this, a woman is expected to enfold herself in her honour in order to be in a steady state (*perrengngi aléna*), otherwise, she is 'wild'. But the saying indicates that men become desirous of women precisely because women's desire is not visible (*padai wekkeng situtuq é*). In other words, women control men's desire through their own unexpressed desire. In spite of the fact

18 *Lontaraq Daramatasia* Roll 17/No.7, Arsip National Wilayah Makassar, transliterated by Mukhlis Hadrawi (10 August 2000).

19 In her discussion on cockfighting in Luwu, Errington (1989:152–4) analyses the importance of *apperrengngeng* (steadiness) for men in relation to bravery and *siriq*.

that this proverb comes from a *lontaraq*, it can be found applied in everyday life of the Bugis, especially when elders give advice to young people.

Alternatively, men have to be conscious (*maringngerrang*) because men's desire is visible (*marisaliwengngi*), *marisaliweng* deriving from the noun root *saliweng* which means outside, literally open. If a man has a good consciousness (*madécéng paringngerranna*), he encircles himself with his self-control in order to protect himself from deviant behaviour (*malaweng pangkaukeng*).[20] One who is conscious (*maringngerrang*) will behave appropriately. When a person is doing something wrong, or looks as if she/he is about to, another person present will warn her/him: 'Be conscious!' (*Padécéngi paringngerrammu!*).[21] By contrast, if one has done something wrong, others will say: 'He/she was not conscious' (*Déqna maringngerrang*).

Thus, male openness (*marisaliweng*) and female hiddenness (*maperreng*) reflect the dichotomy of Bugis constructions of male and female sexuality.[22] This complementarily is not just about the attributes of the masculine-feminine, but can also be associated with male-female behaviour in terms of sexuality. In fact, a woman's sexuality is firmly controlled because it is considered more shameful than the sexuality of men. This is reflected in a Bugis saying that 'men have only one *siriq*, women have ninety-nine' (*urané séddimi siriqna, makkunraié aséra pulona aséra siriqna*). These numbers are not to be taken literally; they merely serve to illustrate the vulnerability of women with regard to *siriq*.

Since a woman's body is often thought to represent the moral integrity of the family (and the society), breaking the code for conduct is considered to dishonour the family and the society. Hence, it is not to say that a woman cannot be open (B. *marisaliweng*) in expressing her desire, but such an openness is considered inappropriate (*deqna malebbiq*).[23] On the other hand, a man who is not able to express his desire openly is regarded as being 'not a man',

20 Bugis advice (I. *petuah* Bugis) states that there are five kinds of deviation (*alawengengngé*): deviation of heart (B. *malaweng ati*), deviation of speaking (*malaweng ada*), deviation of clothing (*malaweng caré-caré*), deviation of place of sitting (*malaweng tudangeng*), and deviation of behaviour (*malaweng pangkaukeng*) (A. Hasan Machmud 1976:45).

21 Errington (1989:89–90) concludes that an individual's *paringngerrang* (memory) in Luwu is associated with his/her concentration and awareness.

22 See, for example, Brenner's (1998) analysis on the relationship between men's/women's control of desire and potency in Javanese society; and Bennet (2003) on her discussion of the invisibility of female desire and visibility of male desire in Lombok.

23 See Bennett (2005:Chapter 2) for a discussion of inscriptive femininity and maiden's sexual desire among the Sasak in Lombok, Mataram.

that it, as an individual whose behaviour is contrary to his biological sex; such a man thus viewed as *calabai* (cross-gender).[24]

The Construction of Singlehood: Female *Malebbiq*, Male *Warani*

In her study of maidenhood, sexuality and modernity in Lombok (Mataram), Bennet (2002:1) describes maidenhood as a journey from girlhood to womanhood. In Bugis society, as in other societies, this journey begins after menarche and continues through the period before marriage takes place.

The Bugis terms for young adults are classified into *anaq dara wélang-pélang* and *kallolo campéngngaq*. *Anaq dara wélang-pélang* refers to a young unmarried girl who has been circumcised (B. *rikatteq*) and passed her first menstruation (*maddara; I. haid* or *mens*). *Kallolo campéngngaq* refers to a young unmarried boy who has had his first wet dream (*mimpi basah*; B. *mannippi*) and who has been circumcised (*risunnaq*).

In theory, the terms *wélang-pélang* and *campéngngaq* are genderless and can be paired with either *anaq dara* or *kallolo*. In practice, however, they are not used interchangeably. While both terms indicate single status, the notion of *campéngngaq* is related to masculine identity, as *kallolo campéngngaq* signifies a 'handsome boy', the notion of *wélang-pélang* is associated with feminine identity, as *anaq dara wélang-pélang* is identified as a 'single girl'.

In relation to the topic of circumcision, this practice is very common in Southeast Asia, including Indonesia. It is not only related to sociocultural mores (C. Geertz 1960), but is also associated with Islamic law for health purposes (Ahmad Ramali 1951). For the Bugis, circumcision is usually performed at the age of between 8 and 10 years for girls and between 10 and 12 years for boys, followed by a ceremony to indicate that the girl and boy are considered 'grown-up' (B. *malopponi*). However, the practice of circumcision has become a subject of debate around the world, subject to criticism by women's NGOs and the World Health Organization (WHO), which claim that circumcision infringes on women's rights, is medically unsafe, and should be eliminated. Debate also exists among religious leaders regarding whether or not the practice is obligatory according to Islamic law.[25] However, female circumcision in Bugis is a symbolic ritual, it is

24 Graham-Davies (2007) discusses five genders among the Bugis in South Sulawesi (men, women, *calabai, calalai* and *bissu*). See also Pelras (1996:165–167) who discusses *calabai, calalai,* and *bissu* in Bugis society.

25 See Husein Muhammad (2001:39–50) for a discussion of female circumcision.

just a tiny cut to the hood of the clitoris and has no impact on women's ability to clitoral orgasm (see Bennett 2002:136–137). Thus, the dichotomy of male-openness and female-hiddenness does not necessarily means that women are not allowed to experience sexual pleasure (see Chapter 5).

In Kulo, whenever a girl passes these rites de passage, she enters freedom in her circumscribed world. Elders usually warn girls saying: 'If you have been circumcised, do not be in a close proximity with a boy' (B. *Nakko purano rikatteq, ajaqmu paddéppéri alému rioroané*). This indicates that the time for seclusion for a girl starts after circumcision. At this stage, in spite of the fact that boys and girls may play together, boys have more freedom to socialize with the opposite sex, while girls are expected to keep their distance from boys. 'Formal' seclusion, however, begins after menarche because this is when parents start thinking about prospective husbands for their young daughters.

Following adolescence, Millar (1983:487–488) points out that in Bugis culture, a male is expected to behave aggressively as well as formally. The aggressiveness and the formality of a man's behaviour are associated with his performance and social location. By contrast, a woman's passive behaviour is associated with her honour. To complement the behaviour expected of men, women are supposed to be obedient and timid, not only to show honour (*alebbireng*), but also to prevent transgression of *siriq*.

Errington notes that the opposition of active-male and passive-female is connected to the function of each sex. Men are responsible for protecting the family and extending kinship networks, while women function not just to protect the 'blood'[26] of the family, but also to preserve the *siriq* of the family (Errington 1977:53). In this view, women are the *siriq* holders, therefore, they are expected to be calm and patient, qualities encompassed by the term *malebbiq* because to be *malebbiq* is also attached to *siriq*. *Malebbiq* describes appropriate women's behaviour, such as not showing aggressiveness. In theory, the term refers to both men and women. In practice, however, women are often expected to embody the term. According to elders in the village, the set of behaviours subsumed under *malebbiq* has become looser recently as compared to 25 to 30 years ago. In the past, an unmarried *malebbiq* woman was never seen or was hidden. Such a situation cannot be sustained at present because of women's opportunity to attend school and be involved in employment.

26 'Blood' in this sense is associated with social location (B. *onro*). That is women marry hypergamously and hence can increase the proportion of 'white blood' in their descendants, white blood being a marker of divine descent and hence high status.

Given that men are the *siriq* defenders, a man has to be brave (B. *warani*), lest he be labelled as an inadequate man or 'not a man', referred to as an *oroané pélloreng*. Similar to the notion of *malebbiq*, *warani* is also attached to *siriq*. Similar to *siriq*, a popular saying related to manhood states:

Waranié mitu tariase oroané	Only with bravery are we called men
Narekko péllorengngi oroané	If a man is timorous
Oroané mi asenna	He is a man in form only
Naia tau péllorengngé	The timorous man
déqna lainna calabaié.	is no different from a *calabai* cross gender

This saying articulates the attributes incumbent on Bugis men. In spite of the fact that to be *warani* is associated with a man's social function mentioned earlier, the label is also connected to his sexual potency. Boys are socialized to be *warani* and girls to be *malebbiq* from early childhood. I observed that when two boys were fighting, for example, a boy who could not fight or fight back would be teased by his peers: *'anaq pélloreng'* (a timid boy) or *'péllorengngi'* (he is timid). Nevertheless, when two girls were fighting, elders would say: 'keep *siriq* in yourself, be modest' (*taroi siriq alému, pakalebbiq i ampé-ampému*). Thus, male-*warani* and female-*malebbiq* affirm the complementarity of male and female behaviour from early childhood.

Virginity, Premarital Sex and Social Stigma

Keperawanan is an Indonesian term for virginity. It is a spiritual element of life and is very significant in the life of a young woman because it is linked to her sexual reputation as well as her marriageability. Despite the fact that premarital sex is unacceptable for both girls and boys, among his peers, a young boy who has had premarital sex will be regarded as a virile man and who has proved his masculinity. On the contrary, a young girl who engages in premarital sex will be labelled a damaged woman (B. *makkunrai masolang*), dirty woman (*makkunrai marotaq*), cheap woman (*makkunrai masémpo*), flabby stuff (*agaga makebbong*), or shameless woman (*makkunrai déggaga siriqna*). In contrast, there is no pejorative label for the man. Therefore, she is an agent of shame for the family.[27]

27 See also Bennett (2005a) for various popular terms of insult directed at women related to premarital sex in Lombok, Mataram, Eastern Indonesia.

This differentiation is due to the fact that preserving virginity which only affects women indicates a woman's purity and her successful preservation of family honour. Failure to preserve virginity is equated with failure to preserve family honour, that is, *siriq* (see Bennett 2002).

To compare with Bali, for example, despite the fact that premarital sex is unacceptable, Parker suggests that the Balinese have no cult related to the virginity of girls (Parker 1993:20). Bellows, however, draws attention to contemporary debates concerning the meaning of virginity for unmarried Balinese women. In this debate, adherence to tradition entails preserving virginity. Modernity is associated with free-sexual practice, attributed to foreign influence through tourism, which is posited as a threat to Balinese moral order. According to this logic, preserving virginity is akin to preserving traditional culture (Bellows, 2003).

In Indonesia, sexual relations outside marriage are similar to the western pejorative term 'free sex' translated as *seks bebas* (see, for example, Iwu D. Utomo 1997, Beazley 1999, Bennett 2002, Hull 2002). This is probably why premarital pregnancy in Indonesia is regarded as the result of free sex (I. *akibat pergaulan bebas*). Furthermore, it is difficult to determine whether or not premarital sexual relations in Indonesia are regarded as a step towards marital union (Hull 2002:5). This is particularly evident in South Sulawesi. Young men who practise sexual relations outside marriage are not certain whether or not they will marry their sexual partner, but young women strongly expect to marry the men they have sexual relations with.

To comment on avoiding pregnancy, I often heard youth advised to express sexual desire by *pacaran pas foto* (I. passport photo courtship) to describe the style of sexual play limited to the area of the body between the head and waist, that is, the part of the body captured in a standard passport photograph. This sex *pas foto* includes kissing, love-bites (hickey) and breast-fondling, without having genital sexual contact, as a way to prevent premarital pregnancy.[28]

In Bugis culture, a girl who has lost her virginity prior to marriage is viewed as a woman whose value as a 'pure girl' is lost. She is considered as *makkunrai maruttung tenriammusikeng*, which literally means a woman who is withered before being celebrated with a musical instrument, but carries the sense that a woman is withered before getting married.[29] This phrase articulates the belief that virginity is a spiritual element of life associated with religious belief. Thus,

28 Bennett (2002:147) examines the limits on sexual physical relationships between young men and women during courtship in Mataram as a way to engage in sexual play prior to marriage, while ensuring the girl remains a virgin.

29 Significantly, this is expressed in Indonesian phrase: *layu sebelum berkembang* (withered before blooming).

a woman who engages in premarital sex is customarily and religiously seen as having violated the sacrament of sexual relations, as she has permitted her private body (I. *aurat*) to be seen and touched by someone who is not her guardian (*muhrim*).

When talking about sexuality, either with young people, adults or elders, they instantly refer to sex in marriage because it is understood that sexuality merely belongs to married couples. Such an understanding is in line with the Population Development and the Development of Happy and Prosperous Families laws established in 1992, which recognize only married couples as sexual beings having legitimate access to information on family planning and services (Iwu D. Utomo 1999:4).

There is a popular local belief in Sulawesi that an encounter between a man and a woman may easily end in sexual activity. However, the double standard of morality seems to be evident because the warning not to be in close proximity is directed at girls, presumably because a man does not have the possibility of becoming pregnant as a result of his premarital sexual relations. For example, Pak Bakri told me, as I wrote in my diary:

> A man who has slept with many women does not leave any sign in his posture, but a woman who has slept with a man has already shown a big sign.
>
> *Iaro oroané namu siaga makkunrai naéwa sitinroang déggaga tanrana rialéna, naia makkunraié séddimi naéwa sitinroang mannessani tanrana.*
>
> PAK BAKRI, School Principal, 22 October 2000

Sitinroang is derived from the verb *tinro*, meaning sleep which, in this sense, carries the connotation of sexual intercourse. When I clarified what he meant by *tanra* (sign), I was told that it might refer to either gestures indicating non-virginity evident in her posture, or her visible pregnancy. The wedding of a pregnant girl is referred to as *botting makemmé* (a flat wedding),[30] not just because it is not celebrated with full feast, but also because such a wedding is not expected (see Robinson 1986, Millar 1989).[31] Yet, despite the shame caused by such a marriage, young girls are not left alone to solve such problems. In the

30 Robinson (1986:223) identifies such a marriage for the Soroakan as *kawin pisang goreng* (I. 'fried banana wedding').

31 In Indonesia, a pregnant girl is discharged from school. Khofifah I. Parawansa, the Minister of Women's Empowerment under Abdurrahman Wahid's presidency suggested the Department of Education and Culture consider whether a girl should be allowed to attend school after delivery (*Republika* 11 December 2000). Her argument is based on the

city this is not always the case: young girls who are pregnant out of marriage may have several risky alternatives to solve their problems, including unsafe abortion (B. *malleggaq*, I. *menggugurkan kandungan*). Such abortions may be self-induced, or carried out by a traditional abortion specialist (*dukun abortus*), and are sometimes life threatening.[32] Alternatively, pregnant girls may run away from home. If they reveal their situations, there are two possibilities—they are 'thrown out' (I. *dibuang*) by their parents, or married off quickly before the pregnancy becomes visible.[33] In Sidrap, the latter solution is the most common solution to the problem of premarital pregnancy.[34]

When such a marriage is unstable, elders usually comment that a marriage which is easy to make, referring to premarital pregnancy, is also easy to break. This is due to the fact that the woman's virginity in her first marriage is a value cherished in Bugis society because the Bugis attach the idea of sexual intercourse to marriage; so one is eligible to have sex because one is married. When a girl is not a virgin and marries a man other than her original lover, it will lead to conflict, or in an extreme cases, she will be divorced right after her non-virginity is recognized. Although, the bride cannot prove the groom is not virgin, the elders told me that the groom can find out whether or not the bride is a virgin on the first night of sexual intercourse after the wedding ceremony.[35] A male informant told me that if a woman were not a virgin, her vagina would be loose (B. *maloga*; I. *longgar*) and she

view that the better the education of the mothers, the better they educate their children, as education is seen by her as a bridge to a better life (Khofifah I. Parawansa 2002:77).

32 Local newspapers in Makassar have reported a number of cases of self-abortion and abortion through *dukun abortus* which ended with the death of either the baby or the mother or both.

33 For a thorough discussion on how urban Indonesian youth deal with premarital pregnancy and critique of the government policy which regards only married couples as sexual beings, see Iwu D. Utomo (1999).

34 In Sidrap, abortion is not just practiced by unmarried pregnant girls, but also by married women through *sanro malleggaq* (B. traditional practitioner for abortion). The reason for the latter is because they do not want to have more children after having, for example, three or more children. *Malleggaq* consists of two methods: massaging the woman's abdomen or drinking a plant concoction. Bennett (2001) discusses different experiences of single women who have induced abortion, showing that it is more traumatic for single women as many have no alternative.

35 In the previous era, the newlyweds were only allowed to have sex after all the ceremonials were completed, usually days, weeks, or even months after the ceremony of *nikah*. The postponement of consummation is illustrated in the La Galigo manuscript in the marriage between Sawerigading and I Wé Cuqdai (see Chapter 5 for discussion on *malam pertama* and virginity).

would not bleed (see Chapter 5). This would indicate she had already had sexual intercourse with another man before her husband. This is also the reason young women are afraid of using tampons during their menstrual periods because they fear being identified as non-virgins resulting from damage to the hymen caused by the tampon.

However, the virginity of the groom is not compulsory and is not a matter of concern. Even though girls expect to have a 'pure' husband (*suami yang masih suci*), there is the sense that his 'purity' cannot be proved. This sexual double standard is socially legitimated.

In the case of premarital pregnancy, the woman is usually blamed for her pregnancy and the baby will be regarded as an *anak zinah* (I. offspring as a result of premarital sex). The usual comment is: 'Who demanded you to surrender yourself to a man who is not your husband' (B. *Igassuroko mabbéré-angngi alému to rioroané tennia lakkaimmu*), implying that the woman shoulders the blame in such a case.

There is a saying in Bugis that one's character reflects his/her descent (*sipaémmi paompoq i assalengngé*) (A. Hasan Machmud 1976:103). This saying is actually directed at both father and mother, since a good person will educate her/his child as she/he has been educated, and education starts at home. If a child behaves improperly, it is commented that her/his parents have failed to educate her/him. However, in the case of premarital pregnancy, a common criticism directed at the woman and her child is that an *anak zinah* will follow her/his mother's behaviour. Even though the parental role is attached to both mother and father, the mother is regarded as the prime child carer, and in such cases, any problem related to the child's behaviour is associated with his/her mother.

Accordingly, a Bugis aphorism states:

> Love and desire are lovely things in which there are words that cannot be uttered, but the beauty of love will be meaningless when it is disgraced.
>
> *Tempeddingngi sia laosiwali cinnaé, lao tungkeq uddanié ritosipurénréngngé.*
>
> A. HASAN MACHMUD 1994:31–32

Such advice is usually given to lovers to warn them to be vigilant because it is believed that the boundary between love and disgrace is very small. Once it is crossed, it turns disgraceful.

A *lontaraq* cited by Matthes states:

> [A] woman is symbolized as green wood. A man is signified as a burning ember. Even if the wood is green, it will still burn if it is close to the ember.

> This is the reason why a woman is prohibited to be in close proximity with men. Because she will become insensitive to accidental physical contact with men if it has become a habit to be around men.
>
> *[I]a makkunraié rirapangngi aju mamata. Naia oroané rirapangngi wara api masua. Namuni mamata ajué naddeppéri wara api nanrépi ritu na paggangkanna. Makkuniro ébara'na nariattéang makkunraié biasa maddeppé' rioroané. Apa' dé'na matu' natakkini' uli'na rioroané nakko nabbiasaini sirua oroané.*[36]
>
> MATTHES 1872:103–104

While the symbol of woman as green wood (*aju mamata*) indicates the sensitivity of female sexuality in relation to the opposite sex, the symbol of man as an ember (*wara api*) suggests that a man can easily be tempted, in this sense, by a woman. If being in close proximity with men becomes a habit for a woman, it indicates that she has become insensitive to accidental physical contact with men (*déqna takkiniq uliqna ri oroané*). Therefore, women have to, as much as possible, move away from men in order to prevent any dishonourable behaviour. Hence, male-ember (*wara api*) and female-green wood (*aju mamata*) are not just about attributes of masculine-feminine, but are also associated with Bugis construction of male-female sexuality.

An egg (*telloq*) is another symbol for a woman. If an egg falls and breaks, it becomes worthless. The destiny of a woman who has fallen into a 'hole' (for example, premarital pregnancy) is equated with an egg. If someone attempts to marry her—whether the man who has impregnated her or another man who intends to save her and her family from shame (*massampo siriq*)—it is usually commented that a woman is like a broken egg, if it is scooped up, it will never be a pure egg because dirt will be scooped up along with it (*makkunraié padai telloq reppaq é, komusinrui, maccoéq i rotaq é*). Such a woman will be labelled with various popular insults, as mentioned earlier, such as a damaged woman (*makkunrai masolang*), and will never be returned to her original state (i.e. virgin). This is because a woman's virginity is regarded as a symbol of purity, and failure to sustain this purity is synonymous with losing her honour (Adriana et. al. 1998:4–5, Bennett 2002:78–82).

Gender symbolization, for example, women as mirror (*camming*), porcelain plate (*penné pinceng*), glass (*kaca*), green wood (*aju mamata*) or egg (*telloq*) reflects sexual asymmetry in Bugis society. As Ortner (1974:72) argues, the problem of sexual asymmetry is located at the level of cultural ideology and

36 The text was transliterated by Mukhlis Hadrawi (1 April 2000).

symbols. The following case encountered during my fieldwork in Kulo illustrates the way in which a woman's reputation is irrevocably damaged by a premarital pregnancy.

Nadirah and Aco: Loose Girl, Lecherous Boy

In Kulo, unmarried pregnant girls are usually successfully married off to whoever impregnates them. Nadirah was an exception. I first met Nadirah, a wedding decorator, when she decorated the house of my host family for their son's wedding. She was a twenty three year old woman who became pregnant out of marriage, and married the father of the child's father who acted to cover someone else's *siriq* (B. *passampo siriq*). This marriage was conducted in order to save face from shame (*massampo siriq*) and to provide a legal father for her baby.

The term *passampo siriq* in Bugis is gender neutral, referring equally to men and women. For this reason, elders forbid youth to eat something in a bowl lid or any other kitchen utensil lid. The bowl lid, for example, symbolizes a protector (*passampo*), in this sense a protector of *siriq* (*passampo siriq*). Thus, eating from the lid of a bowl reflects a Bugis saying: someone acts, someone else protects his shame (*ia mappugau, to laing sappoi siriqna*). If someone disregards this prohibition, it is believed that one day she/he may become a *passampo siriq*. I found several cases of *passampo siriq* in Makassar. For example, a man proposed to a woman he intended to marry, but his proposal was refused. Then, to save him and his family from shame (*massampo siriq*), he immediately proposed to another woman. In this case, this woman is the *passampo siriq*, regardless of whether or not the woman he married realized that she had become the *passampo siriq* of his family. This may also apply in the reverse, that a man becomes the *passampo siriq* of a woman and her family, as in Nadirah's case.

Returning to Nadirah's story, soon after recognising her pregnancy, she notified her boyfriend, Aco. But, he was not financially ready to marry her. When people started to gossip about her pregnancy, she urged him to marry her. Aco finally agreed after working hard and collecting a certain amount of money. Unfortunately, as Nadirah's mother was not aware of her daughter's pregnancy, his proposal was rejected because the expected *duiq ménréq*[37] for the wedding

---

37 Bridewealth in Bugis consists of two elements, namely *sompa* (B. rankprice) and *duiq ménréq* (spending money). *Sompa* is measured according to the ascriptive rank of

ceremony was beyond his capacity. Taken literally, *duiq ménréq* means money taken up, but the phrase is used to describe spending money for the wedding. Aco felt ashamed because of the refusal of his proposal. He left the village to save his face from shame because of proposal refusal (B. *madduta tenri tangke*), while Nadirah was left alone with her hidden problem. She finally told her mother when it was too late because Aco, in fact, had already married another woman from a neighbouring village when Nadirah's mother finally requested that he marry her daughter. On this account, his wife has become the *passampo siriq* of Aco and his family as a result of the refusal of his proposal from Nadirah's mother.

Informants told me that in addition to Nadirah's pregnancy, people also gossiped about her mother's silliness because she could not recognize the pregnancy of her daughter, while others could. In Bugis, elders are usually able to distinguish between virgin girl (*anaq dara*) and non-virgin girl (*tennia ni anaq dara*) by an examination of her body, for example, the sparkling of her eyes, expressed as 'she loses the spark of her eyes' (*marunttunni caya matanna*), a speedy pulse in her throat, or a deep hollow in the back of her knee. A girl who has these signs, whether or not she is pregnant, is called a damaged woman (*makkunrai masolang*) which carries the connotation that a girl has been sexually involved with the opposite sex and should marry the man who has had sexual relations with her. Otherwise, she is 'unsaleable'.

In order to save face (*massampo siriq*), Nadirah had to marry Aco's father under an agreement of *kawin-cerai* (I. divorce right after marriage) which is an offence under Islamic law, as the objective of marriage is to achieve a happy marriage and not to get a divorce afterwards (KHI, Chapter 2:3). Given that Nadirah and her son live with both her mother and her grandmother in the house, people said: 'They were given no respect by the man because they had no man who could guard them' (*ritua-tuaimi nasabaq déggaga mpuranéiwi*). This illustrates the importance of a man in regard to the *siriq* of the family. It appeared that if a man were there, the circumstances would have been different.

---

the bride, that is the sum of money called in former currency, *rellaq*, while *duiq menréq* is determined based on the ascending status of the bride (Millar 1989; Pelras 1996). At present, the *sompa* is only symbolic, being announced during the wedding ceremony, while spending money may be brought on the day of bringing the spending money (*mappaénréq balanca*) or on the day of the wedding, particularly for wealthy people. These days, when people talk about bridewealth, it usually refers to 'spending money'.

Nadirah's story became everybody's business in the village. Each time I asked someone about Nadirah, people would mention her premarital pregnancy, and her story was always an interesting topic to talk about. Even though people also talked about the irresponsible behaviour of Nadirah's son's biological father (Aco), people even felt sorry for Nadirah's family because of the refusal of his proposal. During an interview with Nadirah, she tried to explain her situation to me without even mentioning her unexpected pregnancy. She said that her son was a piteous little boy who had become the victim of her problematic marriage. Surprisingly, she still looks forward to having her son's father, Aco, back in the future, expecting that he will divorce his wife (see Chapter 6 for Nadirah's further story).

Nadirah has become an instance of a 'loose girl' who has to struggle by herself because of her 'wrong-doing' in the past. I was told that parents in Kulo warn their young girls, using Nadirah as a negative example.

Jodoh: 'My Heart Pulsed Like a Thunder'

A Bugis saying states even if you fly far away, if it is your fate, you will definitely meet your partner (*mau luttuq massuajang, ukiq siputanrai, namusilolongemmua*),[38] which means one should not be 'too easy' on her/his partner because one's *jodoh* (I. predestined marriage partner) will not go away. Correspondingly, Acciaioli (1989:277) analyses the relationship between *jodoh* and *sumangeq* (B. soul), as follows:

> If two youths are fated as marriage partners (*jodoh*), then the *sumangeq* of the girl's clitoris (*celle'-celle'*) will climb the steps of the house of the boy, making the distinctive sound '*cikukaq*. The *sumangeq* of the male penis (*lasso*) responds with 'Thanks be to God!' (*syukur*). The spirit of the woman's clitoris then returns to her house, as the woman then can confidently wait for the actual marriage proposal.
>
> ACCIAIOLI 1989:277

This illustrates that the spirit (*sumangeq*) of two of a kind (*siparukkuseng*, I. *sejodoh*) is derived from the response of *celleq-celleq* and *lasso*. This spirit is regarded as the fated partner (*parukkuseng, jodoh*) and is followed by the man's

38 A. Hasan Mahmud (1994:55) records slightly different words: *mau luttuq massuajang teppa réwéq mua pura siputotoq é*, which means even if one flies far away, one's fate will be met.

proposal. This indicates that the spirit of *jodoh* comes from both male and female. Therefore, elders always advise girls by saying: 'If you haven't been celebrated with musical instruments, don't surrender yourself to a man who is not your husband' (*Nakko déqpa riammusikekko, ajaq muabbéréangngi alému tu rioroané tennia lakkaimmu*). 'Celebrated with musical instruments' literally means wedding party and 'surrender' refers to sex. This implies that a woman cannot have sex with a man except her fated partner (*jodoh*), that is, her husband. It is considered inevitable that one will meet one's *jodoh*. Therefore, she has to wait. This advice is designed to warn girls about their sexuality in order to prevent any behaviour which may transgress *siriq*.

There is a narrative explanation of how a girl realizes that she has met her *jodoh*. A young married woman said: 'If you meet someone and your heart beats rapidly, that means you have met your *jodoh* and you cannot get away from it'. Expressing a similar belief, Rapiah, the eldest daughter of Pak Bakri, told a story about her *jodoh*. She was destined to a particular partner (I. *dijodoh-jodohkan*) by her roommate, Ani. Ani's male classmate, Arief—a shy man and a civil servant in West Papua who undertook further study in Makassar—was searching for a wife. Ani told Arief that she had a roommate who was ready to get married, but she had not found the 'right man' yet. Every time Arief met Ani at the university, he questioned her about her roommate, and sent his regards (I. *kirim salam*) to Rapiah. Given that Rapiah was worried about her marriageability at her age (28), she also kept asking about Arief's background. They never met, but Ani secretly showed Rapiah's picture to Arief, and Arief gave his picture to show to Rapiah because women are usually first shown the men's picture.

One day, Rapiah accidentally met Arief, who was with Ani and other friends at the university. Rapiah felt something strange in her heart, a feeling that she had never felt before, so did Arief, he told Ani afterwards. Rapiah told me about her feeling.

'My heart pulsed like a thunder', she said.

'My friend told me that if I felt thundering when I met a man, that was the sign that I had already met my *jodoh*', she continued.

'But, was he really my *jodoh*?' she asked herself a bit falteringly.

She evaluated her incidental meeting with Arief and said:

'It was mutual, I know he also felt the same, I could see from his eyes and motion'.

'I know God had sent me "Mr. Right"'

But, as a woman, Rapiah had to hold herself steady (B. *perrengngi aléna*) until she heard from Arief. In view of his thundering heart when he met Rapiah, Arief believed that Rapiah was his *jodoh*. Arief became more serious about the relationship and asked Ani if he could meet Rapiah in their boarding house. Rapiah was reluctant to meet him since she thought that Arief just wanted to date her. However, Arief agreed that they both expected to get married soon. Arief talked to his family, so did Rapiah. Two months later, they married. The story of Rapiah and Arief is discussed further in Chapter 3.

The hasty marriage of Rapiah was reasonable, not only because she had turned 28 when she first met Arief and felt that it was time for her to get married, but also because she believed that she had already met her *jodoh* sent by God. Given that they just met and got married without courtship, they thus agreed their matching was like *jodoh* which had fallen from the sky (I. *jodoh yang jatuh dari langit*), which carries the sense that the jodoh was sent by God. Therefore, courtship was a waste of time. After they married, Rapiah followed her husband to West Papua after finishing his study in Makassar and after the birth of their first child. They live happily in West Papua. During my fieldwork, Rapiah came to visit her family in Kulo, and delivered her second child, and I accompanied her during her delivery in the hospital.

Canring, Courtship and Social Observance

The English terms for boyfriend and girlfriend indicate the difference between male and female sweethearts. Terms related to these may vary across the archipelago, based on geographical areas and ethnic groups, but the most general term used in Indonesia is *pacar* (I. sweetheart). This term, like the Bugis term *canring* is genderless.

The Bugis term for courtship is *maccanring* which refers to the relationship between a girl and a boy in a state of affection. The term *silori,* which means mutual affection, is derived from the word *lori* or love; *silori* means mutual love and carries the connotation of romantic love between a man and a woman. *Maccanring* is not an alien term for people in Kulo, as I observed children playing at dating. Take, for example, three year old Udin when asked by his parents or siblings: 'Who is your girl friend?', 'Do you want to date her?' He would answer all the questions straight away with no shame. But, when similar questions were asked of his 'girl friend,' Nira, she would cast down her eyes and run way, and her mother would respond: 'She is in a state of feeling *siriq* (*masiriq i*)'. Nira's reaction portrays the image of a modest (*malebbiq*) girl, as she is not expected to show her desire for the opposite sex. The teasing is used to instil modesty. Nevertheless, I never found a boy dating a girl in her natal home.

In Indonesia, studies indicate that the duration of courtship has become increasingly significant with the later age at marriage (see, for example, Iwu

D. Utomo 1997; Bennett 2002). The style of courtship varies based on the acceptance of the family towards premarital relationships between men and women.[39] In Kulo, 'home courtship,' a term for dating at home, is very uncommon, not to mention 'dating out' in which a girl is asked to go out by her boyfriend with the consent of her parents. I was told of a case of 'home courtship' of *Pak* Bakri's second cousin, Halida, when I visited her in Rappang.

Halida's Home Courtship: *Diapelin*

In spite of the fact that the Indonesian popular term for 'home courtship', *diapelin*, is uncommon for youth in the village, and only happens under certain circumstances, youth are familiar with the term. I named Halida's courtship as 'home courtship' considering that it was a courtship under the surveillance of her family and there was no specific Bugis term for this.

Halida had three sisters and three brothers. She was the youngest daughter in the family, and the first daughter to get married. She married a widower who I was told had divorced his first wife because of her infidelity. His widower status had become a subject of debate between Halida and her parents and elder brothers. I was told by Halida's elder sister that Halida was married when she was still very young (17 years) and had skipped over (I. *melangkahi*, B. *mallellung*) her other three elder sisters because she was regarded as a 'bad girl'. When clarified, I discovered that she liked to go out alone, had a secret boyfriend (I. *pacaran bekstrit*), and consumed the drug ecstasy. Soon after her *pacaran bekstrit* with Anwar was discovered, in order to avoid a premarital pregnancy, she was urged to marry her boyfriend. Despite the controversy, this was a way to maintain *siriq*. But, before the marriage took place, there was a time during which they had a 'home courtship'.

In Kulo, such a courtship is very rare, not just because engagement is uncommon, but also because the period between acceptance of a proposal and the marriage is usually very short. During this time, the bride and the groom are considered to be in a stage of semi-seclusion and in a state of vulnerability

39 For example, Bennett (2002:160–161) identifies three types of courtship in Mataram: traditional courtship (*midang*), modern courtship practices (*pacaran moderen*) and secret courtship (*pacaran bekstrit*). *Midang* is the favourite type, expressed as 'sweeter than sugar and honey'.

(B. *arapo-rapong*) (see Millar 1989:76).[40] Therefore, parents are reluctant to have a long-term engagement in order to prevent a vulnerable transition between these stages.

Any period of courtship of this type is very short. Halida could be diapelin at home only because Anwar had been accepted as a prospective son-in-law by her parents.[41] But, this courtship was very rigid. It was held in the living room and the couple were accompanied by Halida's sisters or brothers or parents. Sometimes everybody was in the living room, especially because the TV was located there. Halida could not sit in close proximity with Anwar, though sitting opposite him was acceptable. Anwar had to leave before ten, otherwise he would be warned by Halida's brother by saying: 'It's time for Dunia Dalam Berita' (B. Dunia Dalam Berita *ni*).[42] On other occasions the brother would turn the TV volume louder to indicate that it was time for Anwar to leave. Going out together was impossible, unless Halida was accompanied by her relatives.

When I talked to Halida's mother, she explained how proud she was because Halida had found her jodoh when she was still very young and married by family approval (I. *kawin baik-baik*). When asked about her courtship, Halida's mother clarified that they met only at home, in contrast to the 'modern courtship' (*pacaran moderen*) of Pak Bakri's daughter, Ati, discussed below. Hence, Halida's 'home courtship' and early marriage was a recompense for her previous bad reputation (*pacaran bekstrit* and drug user) in order to restore the *siriq* of the family. Now, Halida and Anwar have a daughter from this marriage.

Pacaran Bekstrit: 'Meeting under the Tomato Tree'

> Girls and boys are very excited if there is a wedding party in the village because this occasion gives them an opportunity to see each other without the scrutiny of their relatives. A secret rendezvous is like meeting under a tomato tree, very romantic. It's public, but unrecognized.
>
> FARHAN, 20, single, graduated from high school, 5 June 2000

40 See also Van Gennep (1960:116–115) who discusses the transition from betrothal to marriage as a rite of passage.

41 See, for example, Bennett (2002:162–3) for a discussion of courtship and social regulation of marriage in Mataram, Lombok, Eastern Indonesia.

42 Dunia Dalam Berita is a TV news broadcast from Jakarta at 10 p.m. local time. This news has been generally used as a sign for a boyfriend to go home.

The commonest and the most popular type of courtship in Kulo is *pacaran bekstrit* (I. secret courtship). Young men expressed this type of courtship in a local Bugis phrase: 'Woman goes down [from stilt-house] to meet her sweetheart' (*Makkunraié turung tusita canrinna*). This passage carries the sense that a girl is going out to meet her sweetheart without her relatives consent. In spite of the fact that the saying reflects the idea that only the girl goes out to see her sweetheart, the practice is mutual. The emphasis of the saying indicates the construction of a courtship biased in favour of boys, because, in fact, this saying suggests a negative image of girls.

In the village, there are certain events in which men and women may see each other, such as harvest time (B. *éngngalang*), wedding parties (*pesta botting*) or non-obligatory evening prayers during fasting month (A. *tarawé*). The last two events are the most popular occasions for men and women to flirt and rendezvous, yet they are also moments where people must be on their guard for transgression of *siriq*.

The enjoyment of a rendezvous during harvest (*éngngalang*) is only for those who work as paid labourers, for example as *padderos*, a local term for paddy harvester. Males and females may tease each other on the way to the rice field, during harvesting (*madderos*), and on the way back home. A rendezvous is even more exciting during a wedding party (*pesta botting*) because it is usually enlivened with *elekton*, a music group accompanied by local singers. The music is not only enjoyed by the invited guests, but also by the audience who surround the host's house. The occasion usually starts after the sunset prayer (*magrib*). The opportunity for a *tarawé* rendezvous starts after breaking the fast (I. *buka puasa*) and sunset prayer. Girls go out with their girlfriends for *tarawé* to prevent their parents' suspicion. Then, girls and boys meet at the mosque or other places outside the home.

The opportunity for rendezvous for young males and females is expressed in a slogan: 'Meeting under the tomato tree' (I. *Bertemu di bawah pohon tomat*). The tomato tree symbolizes the spontaneity of the meeting or opportune courtship. It happens by chance and the youth just take the opportunity when it arises since the place is irrelevant. It can be beneath one's house, a tree, or near the host's house at a wedding, usually standing with hidden faces or in a squatting position. No matter, flirting and the rendezvous are still enjoyable. This is a common occurrence among the youth in the village during *éngngalang*, *pesta botting* or *tarawé*, regardless of whether or not the parents consent to their sweethearts. In Makassar, dating was popularly known as 'Saturday night rendezvous' (*kencan malam Minggu*). It was usually conducted either at the girl's house or out with the partner with or without a woman's parents' consent. The argument here is not that girls in the city are free from their family's scrutiny, despite the control being more flexible. Though strict parents do not allow their daughters to be dated at home, this arrangement is becoming more popular than letting a daughter go out with her boyfriend, in order to avoid any behaviour that may transgress *siriq*.

Pacaran bekstrit usually takes place at a certain location, such as in a girl's friend's house, or other places that would not arouse the family's suspicion. However, if the couple were found out, the girl would be chastised as well as hit, either by her father, brother or other male relatives, and would not be allowed to go out for a certain period of time because she was considered to have caused shame (B. *mappakasiriq-siriq*) to the family. The boy, on the other hand, would only be warned and be in no danger of physical punishment by his parents.

The wedding party of my hosts' son in Kulo represents an example of how such an occasion can become an arena for rendezvous. I observed that around the venue of the party, partners were everywhere and in every corner, enjoying the party and their dates. People could no longer recognize them as the surroundings were shadowy.

It was interesting to observe the contradictory behaviour of the bride and the singers. The bride cast down her face as a sign of her honour (*alebbireng*), in marked contrast to the attitude shown by the singers—three females and a male—who sang and danced erotically with sensuous movement, sexy voices and clothes, except the male singer who wore long pants and shirt. The songs were mostly *dangdut*, a contemporary Indonesian music form.[43] The newlyweds left the stage by ten because the bride was not allowed by her family to spend the first night in her husband's family's house.[44] As time went on, the more excited the male and female audiences were, the more erotic the singers became and at the same time, the male audiences expressed sexual interest in an increasingly demonstrative manner by whistling and yelling harassment, or even trying to touch the singers when they approached the audience while performing.

For the audience, this was a way to give encouragement to the singers. On this account, the suggestions and responses of the audience were contradictory and ambivalent. The audience enjoyed the entertainment, on the one

43 See Browne (2000) for discussion of gender implication of *dangdut* as a low-class popular music form.

44 In Bugis, the newlyweds usually spend their first night in the bride's family's house. This has various meanings, but is generally to protect the bride from the control of her husband's family in her new life, and there are several rituals related to this discussed in Chapter 4.

hand, but they responded negatively, on the other. Nevertheless, the manager of this music group perceived such entertainment indicated a successful performance. When I asked male audience members about this performance in relation to *siriq*, they commented: 'It didn't matter as long as they were not my sisters' (*Déqna marigaga assalaq tennia padakkunraikku*). Thus, they enjoyed the erotic performance of the singers, but they would not accept such behaviour in their sisters.

As Bugis women, the singers' erotic performance customarily transgressed their family *siriq*. But, the manager clarified that the singers were women who were neglected by their husbands, came from poor families, and became singers to make a living, except one of them, Nina, who was married to the piano player of the music group. Nina stopped singing after the newlyweds left the stage to avoid being involved in the erotic performance, as she was not allowed to by her husband. Nina said: 'If I sing that way, it is similar to shaming my husband in public.' This illustrates that married women are more vulnerable to the *siriq* of their husbands, while 'independent women' have more freedom to choose what behaviour should and should not be allowed, depending on their status in the community. People said: 'High status people behave carefully, while lower status—offering the example of the singers—act like the singers, they have no husband, less control and less *siriq*' (B. *makurassiriq*).

It was also interesting to note that the existence of this erotic performance in the Bakris son's wedding party contrasted with Pak Bakri's social image. He was known as a religious community leader and a primary school principal in Kulo. Even though the wedding party was considered successful in view of the crowd of people, the food served, and the contribution from the guests they got, I heard the Bakris and their families in the stilt-house during the reception complained about the female singers' appearance (their erotic attires as well as attitudes). Nevertheless, no one came to admonish the manager to stop the erotic show.

To return to the issue of *pacaran bekstrit,* the trysting youth became more unrecognisable by the crowd. When confirming their existence with Farhan, my assistant, he said: 'They were missing' (*Lenynyeq manenni*). Their 'missingness' comprises two imaginable meanings, either they had gone home or they were still somewhere there, hiding in a less visible space.

Pacaran Moderen: Ati's Dilemma

As I mentioned earlier, whenever a premarital pregnancy occurs, girls are warned and asked to learn from such cases or to be careful when engaging with the opposite sex. Ati, *Pak* Bakri's daughter, is an example of this. Ati had been accompanied by her boyfriend, Ridwan, to her village for her brother's wedding a day before the wedding ritual. The presence of her boyfriend in Pak Bakri's house caused concern to her family as well as the guests, not just because he had spent the night in *Pak* Bakri's house, but also because his presence was without *Pak* Bakri's consent. He felt as if they were demonstrating their modern courtship (I. *pacaran modern*) in public.

Even though Ati and Ridwan did not sleep in the same room in her parents' house, it was said that they were not married, but were spending the night together (*déppa nasipuaseng, nasiabbenniang*). Spending the night in her parents' house shocked *Pak* Bakri. However, *Ibu* Bakri responded in the opposite way. She even offered him a rented *baju* adat (customary shirt) to wear at the wedding. She was very proud that someone loved her daughter and expected that the two would marry.

Despite the fact that her father and brother were upset, there was no single *siriq* act, except gossip. I heard one of Ati's brothers grumbling about her 'wrong doing.' In contrast, the reaction to Ati's brother, Umar, whose girlfriend also spent the night in *Pak* Bakri's house for the wedding was, if anything, positive. People were discussing Umar in terms of his virility, while his girlfriend got the same response as Ati. The presence of Ati's boyfriend and Umar's girlfriend illustrates not only sexual double standards in the relationship between men and women, but also indicates that the response to *siriq* has become weak and more flexible as compared to the old days.

A few days after the wedding ritual, I was watching TV with *Pak* Bakri in the living room as usual after dinner when he opened the discussion about his anxiety over his daughter. He expressed his disappointment and his feeling of *siriq*. What was more interesting to note in this discussion, however, was that, instead of directly talking to his daughter, I was asked to mediate. Furthermore, instead of asking me to warn Ridwan, as I also knew him, I was told to warn Ati in Makassar about her 'cheap' behaviour with her boyfriend. *Pak* Bakri compared her unfavourably with his eldest daughter who had grown up in a more conservative way even though she also studied at the university in Makassar. The anxiety of *Pak* Bakri was reasonable since one of his daughters from his second wife had become pregnant outside of marriage. He was afraid the same thing would happen to Ati. When Ati's brothers met Ridwan in Makassar in Ati's boarding house during their *kencan malam Minggu*, they confidently admonished not only Ati, but also her boyfriend, complaining that their way of courtship was too public.

Pak Bakri himself regarded his daughter as an extremely 'cheap girl' (B. *anaq dara naliweq sémpona*) because she did not act as a modest girl (*anaq dara malebbiq*) and her boyfriend was considered as a young man without adat (*kalloloq déggaga adeqna*) because he thought Ridwan did not know what and/or when to appear properly. Their way of dating was expressed in Indonesian as 'no days without dating' (I. *tiada hari tanpa pacaran*) which describes lovers who date day and night. I tried to initiate a discussion about his son, Umar, and his girlfriend in the same way, but *Pak* Bakri would not be drawn in, probably because Umar was not a girl and his girlfriend was not his daughter. Ati was pursuing higher education in Makassar, which meant entering a modern way of life that was not compatible with the standard of village life or the standard of woman's nature (I. *kodrat wanita*)[45] propagated by the New Order. Living in the city gave her an aura of independence and freedom, including sexual liberation. But when she went to her village she faced the moral dilemma that what was accepted in the city was not necessarily accepted in the village.

This illustration portrays to some extent the ambivalent understanding that courtship (B. *maccanring*) is a familiar term for the people in Kulo, yet the practice itself has not been completely accepted, and a girl who can be dated is regarded as a 'loose girl.' This, however, is not applied to a boy who dates a girl, but a boy is expected to find a modest (*malebbiq*) girl. Thus, men and women are treated differently, not just in public, but also in private places.

Gender and Social Encounter in the House

> Houses in South Sulawesi are, however, more than functional shelters for their inhabitants, or aesthetically pleasing material objects. They are sacred (*sakral*) spaces in which people are born, marry and die and where these occasions are socially and ritually acknowledged.
>
> ROBINSON 1998C:169

For the Bugis, the house has a great importance.[46] Bugis cosmology divides the world into the upper world (B. *Boting Langiq*, the middle world (*Lino*) and the

45 Wieringa (1992:110) defines *kodrat wanita* as women who are '*lemah lembut* (soft and weak), don't speak out loudly, and certainly not in their own interest, don't push their own interests against those of husbands and fathers, but are instead compliant wives and mothers and dutiful daughters.'

46 See, for example, Fox (1993:141–142), in his article on Rotenese house design, which notes that the house is a 'remembering' place which is derived from its physical structure and a place to differentiate between 'inside' (the house) and 'outside' (other places). See also Robinson (1993) in her discussion of the importance of the house to the identity of people

PLATE 2.1 *Bugis cosmic house*

lower world (*Toddang Toja*), based on the myth of La Galigo (see Chapter 1).[47] This cosmological viewpoint is reflected in the structure of Bugis house which consists of a space under the roof (*rakkéang*), the body of the house (*alé bola*) and area beneath the house (*awa sao*) (Mattulada, 1998:106) (see Plate 2.1). This vertical ordering of a 'miniature cosmos' is typical in Southeast Asia (Reid 1988:66).

The *alé bola* is divided into three parts based on gender: the front, the middle and the back. Each part of the house has its own post and the central post, the house's navel (B. *posiq bola*), is located in the middle part of the house.[48] Either end has its own entrance. The room for the married couple is located in the middle of the house. A house without a middle part is usually divided by a door through which outsiders (*to laing*) are strictly forbidden to pass.

---

in South Sulawesi. Errington (1989:92) identifies the house's walls in Luwu as like a 'second skin around them,' to protect the inhabitants from the danger of the outside.

47 For example, Errington (1989:73) classifies the house in Luwu into three levels (*rekéang*, *kalé banua*, and *sulluq*). She equates these with upper, middle and lower levels of the world.

48 See Pelras (1996:221) for the basic structural unit of Bugis house. Southon (1995:95–96) also describes a similar structure for Butonese house (*boba, tonga* and *tambe*) which is parallel to the structure of the house. He notes that Bugis division of house is 'vertical and cosmological', while the division of Butonese house is 'horizontal and corporeal'.

Mattulada indicates the difference between a guest (*to polé*, literally means the 'one who comes') and family by describing their relationship with the house. A *to polé* cannot even step onto the lowest rung of the steps of the stilt house (I. *rumah panggung*; B. *bola riaseq*) without the permission of the host, unless she/he is regarded as family (Mattulada, 1995:56). But for the Bugis, people who are not related by blood can also be regarded as if a sibling (B. *passilessurengeng*, from the word *silessureng*, meaning sibling). A guest (*to polé*) who steps on the steps of the main entrance without the host's consent is regarded as transgressing the *siriq* of the family. This is also true if the guest climbs the steps at the back entrance.[49] Thus, *to polé*-front and family-back reflect the dualism between the guests and the families associated with the layout of the house (see Errington 1979).

In Kulo, *to polé* usually ascend the steps at the front of the house. The family or people who are considered as family may climb the steps at the back of the house, even though they may also ascend via the front of the house. At first glance, this arrangement is merely about different entrances between the family and outsiders (*to laing*). But, I observed that male family tended to enter the house from the front, while female family entered the house from the back. Furthermore, when there are guests in the living room, the female family members (particularly young girls) would enter the house from the back, especially if the guests were men. In contrast, male family members are reluctant to enter the back part of the house when women gather together. But the division of the house based on gender is not rigid. Indeed, women spend their time at the front part of the house when non-related men are not around (Pelras 1996:161).

In her article on *The Platform House: Expression of a Regional Identity in the Modern Indonesian Nation*, Robinson identifies domestic arrangements in relation to the interior division of space among the Bugis (as well as Makassarese and Mandarese): front-back, public-private, strangers-family, outsiders-intimates and others-us (Robinson 1993:228–242). The door mediating between the public and the private spaces of the house is off-limits to all but family members, and strangers/outsiders/others are prohibited to pass (Errington, 1979:9), unless permitted by the host.

This arrangement aims to divide the front and the back parts of the house.[50] The front is regarded as the place for guests and men, usually a space with no wall, symbolising 'freedom.' While the back part of the house is considered as the place for women and family, limited by walls in accordance

49 See Reid (1988:65) for typical 'front-back' division of Southeast Asian houses.

50 See Errington (1989:66–75) for a detailed discussion of direction in houses.

with the principle of 'protection'. For instance, when an unmarried girl (B. *anaq dara*) serves male guests with drinks and snacks, she is only allowed to bring them up to the middle part of the house or to the door between front and middle parts of the house. Thus, the wife or mother will bring the refreshment to the living room. This arrangement prevents the girl for coming into direct contact with the opposite sex, which may transgress the family *siriq*.[51] However, this arrangement has changed significantly in recent years. A girl may now bring light refreshment into the living room, but leaves the room as soon as possible.

In the contemporary Bugis house, despite the fact that modernity has influenced its structure, the basic principle of the house in regard to gender remains the same. For example, the room for the married couple is usually located close to the living room, while the room for girls is situated behind or next to this primary bedroom or in the middle of the house where the family room is positioned, a place where *to laing* are prohibited. A room for boys is at the back of the house, usually close to the back door, or at the side of the house with its own door to the outside, so they can come and go without encumbrance. This implies that the layout of the house not only dichotomises between family and *to laing*, as Errington (1979:9) reported in Luwu, but also shows the division between male and female spaces of social interaction within and around the house. Most importantly, this arrangement aims to 'protect' the female members of the family from any offence which may result in *siriq*.

Social interaction in the house indicates cross-gender relations in terms of proximity. While father-son relationship seems to be reserved, the mother-daughter relationship is warm and supportive. The mother is the mediator of the family, not only between father and son, but especially between father and daughter. Open discussion between members of the family usually takes place during dinner for urban people, as the members of the family usually gather in the afternoon. In the village, I observed a number of times both in the Bakris and in other families, that such moment occurs either at noon, during/after lunch or dinner. Unlike western culture, the family discussion is limited and formal. Children are not supposed to become involved in converzation among elders unless they are asked for their comment. Otherwise, they will be regarded as non-respectful children. Sister-brother relationships are passionate and warm, as reflected in the relationship between Wé Tenri Abéng and her twin brother, Sawérigading, the main protagonist described in the La Galigo epic.

51 Personal communication with the late *Pak* Anwar Ibrahim, a lecturer at the Department of Bugis Language, Faculty of Arts, Hasanuddin University (6 May 2000).

Previous studies of the Bugis, such as Millar (1983, 1989) and Pelras (1996) have portrayed the relationship between men and women as egalitarian in many respects. However, both my male and female informants stated that females are 'lower' than males.[52] Mattulada discusses Bugis women's role based on customary law (*pangngadereng*) from the *Lontaraq Latoa* which states that men and women may both be involved in deliberation (I. *permusyawaratan*), but women's opinions can only be used as a complement and not to make a final decision because women are considered to have 'physical' as well as 'psychological' weaknesses (Mattulada 1995:440). That women are fragile creatures has become a general ideology. But, I presume that Mattulada's argument in this sense is related to public decision-making, which is considered to be men's arena.

At the community level, village meetings best illustrate this role difference. Whilst both men and women have the right to speak in the forum, men have more authority than women. At the household level, the wife has the same right as the husband to express an opinion. Nevertheless, the final decision is usually in the hands of the husband for matters related to the outside. Take, for example, when *Pak* Bakri, his wife, *Ibu* Darma, and his daughter, Ati, were discussing the possibility of Ati becoming a civil servant. *Pak* Ali, from a neighbouring village, had promised 'to take care of it' in exchange for Rp3,000,000 (about US$300 at current exchange rates). *Ibu* Darma and Ati refused, assuming that there was no guarantee that the position would come through. But *Pak* Bakri decided to pay, even though he had to borrow some money from his father-in-law. In fact, he was deceived, his daughter did not become a civil servant. The money was gone and *Pak* Ali kept promising to repay, or sometimes hid whenever *Pak* Bakri came to his house. I witnessed Ati crying when she found out that her application was unsuccessful. When I asked why *Ibu* Darma did not prevent *Pak* Bakri from taking part in the deal, she said: 'It's his decision, I can give my opinion, but he is the one who makes the decision'. She further stated that because he is the head of the family (*kepala keluarga*), he has the authority to decide. This illustrates that decisions about relations with the outside are in the hands of men, regardless of whether or not women agree with the decisions. Ati was reluctant to comment on her father's action, not only because of the distance between them, but also because she thought that her opinions were worthless in this instance.

52 Helliwell's (1995:364) study exemplifies similar features on the inequality of Gerai in the Dayak 'egalitarian' society.

Conclusion

When speaking about *siriq*, one must realize that *siriq* is a concept which is linked to gender as well as honour and *onro*, but the defence of *siriq* can be performed by both sexes. This is supported by my argument in Sahariah's case, although the majority of *to masiriq* are males, she—as a woman—became a *to masiriq*. Thus, she acted as the agent to maintain *siriq* of the family. The examination of *siriq*, however, differs according to social status; the higher the status the more likely *siriq* to occur.

People are ambivalent about courtship. The many faces of courtship indicate that there are some negotiations, as well as tension in courtship, depending on the consent of parents, and local youth practices. Thus, courtship is a life style between two worlds. While courtship is traditionally unacceptable, its contemporary existence cannot be avoided and is considered as a part of the modern life style. Young girls and boys therefore experience a clash between tradition and modern life styles as well as a clash between parents and children. They still recognize the non-acceptability of courtship, but also cannot avoid it, as seen in the practice of 'meeting under the tomato tree', and '*pacaran moderen*'.

A number of Bugis symbols for women, such as mirror (*camming*), glass (*kaca*), porcelain plate (*penné pinceng*), green wood (*aju mamata*), and egg (*telloq*), reflect the vulnerability of women in everyday social interaction, particularly with the opposite sex.

In addition, the layout of Bugis' house mirrors the division between male and female spaces of social intercourse which aims to 'protect' female members of the family from any offence which may transgress *siriq*.

The Bugis construction of male and female sexuality is an important complementarity informing the Bugis concepts of gender differences associated with the spiritual potency and the function of each sex.

In the next chapter, I will discuss the notion of marriage and the importance of kinship in marriage, and how status is related to it, as well as discuss the various kinds of marriage practiced in Bugis society.

CHAPTER 3

Asséajingeng: Marriage, Family and Social Status

Introduction

Marriage, family and social status are three issues associated with kinship (B. *asséajingeng*) which will be the focus of discussion in this chapter. Mattulada suggests that:

> [T]o the present time in Bugis-Makassar society, the system of familial relations (the kinship system) still continues to be the dominant factor determining the pattern of behaviour in society.
>
> MATTULADA 1977:114

From this point of view, it is obvious that kinship ties are central to Bugis social relations, including social relations in marriage. I will begin to unpack the Bugis notion of marriage in order to understand how marriage is defined according to Bugis custom (I. adat) and Islam. The importance of looking at adat and Islam together stems from the fact that Bugis adat is vigorously influenced by Islam. Further I explore how traditional expectation associated with adat and Islam are influenced by the New Order Ideology.

Second, I explore the importance of kinship in the selection of marriage partners, how the notion of marriage relates to *asséajingeng*, and how social status is measured in association with marital status, since acknowledgment of status is critical to Bugis. Status is determined by looking at the status of both parents, since kinship is reckoned bilaterally. Kinship plays a significant role in Bugis marriage regardless of whether or not one marries within one's kin group. At the end of the chapter, I present various types of marriage offering an example of each type.

Kinship plays a fundamental role in Bugis marriage, not just in the choice of a marriage partner and the time of marriage, but also in marital relations and how a couple get married.

Bugis Notions of Marriage: Between Adat and Islam

The Bugis term for marriage—*sikalaibiné*—combines the nouns *lai*, meaning man and *bainé*, meaning woman, and thus carries the connotation of the

 | DOI 10.1163/9789004311947_004

combination of the husband and wife to form a conjugal pair, indicating the social relationship between the couple. Furthermore, marriage is articulated in terms of kinship (B. *asséajingeng*), derived from the word *séajing* which means family or kin.[1] Kinship for the Bugis is, as Acciaioli explains, 'a totalistic set of relations' (Acciaioli 2000:237).

Drawing on alliance theory, Leach divided marriage into two types. One is marriage that originates from the notion of two persons acting as private individuals, and the other kind is a systematically organised affair which forms part of a series of contractual arrangements between two social groups (Leach 1961:56). In Javanese culture, the former type encompasses a marriage which is an 'establishment of a new autonomous household' (H. Geertz 1961:55).[2] By contrast, marriage in Bugis culture involves the joining of two families into one, whether or not the 'actors' belong to the same kin group. This point of view is implied in the Bugis term for marriage—*siala*—which can be translated as 'to take each other' (Pelras, 1996:154). This implies that there is an act of exchange in which the groom's side takes the bride's, and vice versa, in order to form a new social alliance which plays an important role in kinship (*asséajingeng*).[3]

Because the majority of the Bugis profess Islam, their everyday life is inseparable from religious beliefs and practice. For the Bugis, marriage is an act of following the act of the Prophet (A. *Sunnah Rasul*); one is not a Prophet follower (B. *tennia ummaqna nabitta*) if one does not get married. Marriage is also regarded as a benevolent and purified act that establishes the rights and duties for both husband and wife, and protect any children born from the marriage. But, under this system what does marriage actually mean for men and women?

When asking this question of my informants—young unmarried men and women, as well as older people in Kulo—the answer was related to the central

1 *Asséajingeng* in Bugis can be classified into *rappé* and *sompung-lolo*. *Rappé* refers to a relationship based upon biological descent (consanguineal relatives) and *sompung-lolo* signifies a kin relationship involving one's marriage link (affinity) (Mattulada 1995:38).

2 In her analysis of women and industrialisation in Java, Brenner (1998:81) discusses a similar account of marriage for contemporary Laweyan society as a formation of independent households and business.

3 Bugis *asséajingeng*, according to *lontaraq* (palm leave manuscripts) includes *sianrasa-rasangngé nasiamasé-maséi* (B. suffering and understanding each other), *sipakario-rio* (cheering up each other), *tessicirinnaiéngngé risitinajaé* (loving each other properly), *sipaingeq rigauq patujué* (warning each other for good manners), *siaddampengngeng pulanaé* (always apologizing to each other) (A. Hasan Machmud 1976:44).

motive for marriage, that is, procreation.[4] Such response is associated with the following *lontaraq* entitled *Fikhi/Nikah*[5] the title of which means 'Marriage Principles,' which quotes the utterance of Prophet Muhammad:

> [G]et married and have children, have many children because it will become an indication that I will have lots of followers in the judgment day.
>
> *[A]bbainéo mennang abbija tokko, péga toi mennang wijammu karana majeppuqna ia upasitanra tepposengngi riko mennang rimaégana ummaqkuq riesso kiameq* (p. 4).[6]

The passage implies the appeal of marriage and having children. However, in contemporary Bugis society, the common Indonesian philosophy that 'many children, much fortune' (I. *banyak anak, banyak rezeki*) is no longer in effect, at least for the people in Kulo. They tend to have fewer children than in the past. The slow process of the transformation from a traditional familial, peasant mode of production to wage-labour mode of production in Sidrap has been concurrent with a decline in fertility (see, for example, Robinson 1999:252; Parker 1993:5). This can be seen from the continuing decrease in the birth rate.[7]

---

4 Robinson (1986:217) describes a similar view that instead of personal attachment to the spouse, having children is the primary aim of marriage in Soroako, South Sulawesi.

5 *Fikhi* (A.) is the codification of principles of conduct drawn by religious scholars from the Qur'an, *Hadith* (Traditions), analogy of those two sources, and consensus by Legalists (Federspiel 1995:59–60). Thus, *Fikhi/Nikah* is the codification of principles conduct related to marriage, or in Indonesia is known as *Fikhi Pernikahan.*

6 *Lontaraq Fikhi/Nikah,* Roll 37/No.11, nineteenth century, Arsip Nasional Wilayah Makassar, transliterated by Muhlis Hadrawi (3-3-2002).

7 For example, the Indonesian Population Census indicates a decrease in the total fertility rate (TFR) in South Sulawesi from 5.71 in 1971, to 4.88 in 1980, to 3.54 in 1990 to 2.56 in 2000, and 2.55 in 2010. In fact, the national TFR tends to increase from 2.34 in 2000 to 2.55 in 2010 (Sensus Penduduk-2010 [2011b]). The gradual change in the local level has gone hand-in-hand with the willingness of people to accept family planning, and Kulo is no exception. For instance, in the year 2000 (when I conducted my fieldwork) out of 1,877 individuals in the fertile age group, 1,242 were active acceptors of family planning. Among all contraception methods, the pill was the most favoured method (689) as compared to implants (193), injections (178), the IUD (170) and female sterilization (12) (Sidenreng Rappang in Figures 2001). However, more than ten years later, injections have become more common and dominant as compared to other contraceptive methods (Sidenreng Rappang in Figures 2014). Family planning is typically introduced or suggested during the third visit of a local midwife after the delivery of a child and before the end of the parturition period. In theory, mothers are offered

Despite the fact that both men and women expressed the importance of what Van Gennep called the third cycle of rite of passage, the transition from social puberty to adulthood (Van Gennep: 1960),[8] and of having children. There are differences between what marriage means for men and women, as can be seen in the divergent views of the purpose of marriage according to sex.

For women, the significance of marriage is connected to the notion of marriageability and 'saleability'. For example, an unmarried woman is regarded as an unsaleable maiden (B. *makkunrai déqna tarala*), or maiden who is left by the market (*makkunrai nawélai pasaq*) and is called a old maid (*makkunrai ladoq*), at the age of 35. Another specific motivation for women to get married is economic. As women commonly said: 'There is someone who looks for money for me' (*Engka sapparekki duiq*), thus making explicit the husband's role as breadwinner, but also implying the significance of women as money managers in the household. My female informants never vocalised the importance of marriage in relation to sexual needs, potentially because they were reluctant to express their opinion about sex, afraid of being labelled a flirtatious woman (B. *makkunrai mangngureq*).[9] By contrast, men expressed the view that marriage fulfilled sexual needs, articulated as 'biological' (I. *untuk memenuhi kebutuhan biologis*) as sex outside marriage is forbidden.

While a woman who remains unmarried is labelled as unsaleable, a man who remains unwed is suspected of having something wrong with him, a suspicion that is related to his sexuality: his penis does not 'turn on' (*déqna tettong lasona*). This phrase suggests that he is sexually impotent like a man who is suspected of having a penis but *déqna tettong lasona* who may be considered a *calabai* (cross-gender). Thus, while the marital status of a man is related to his sexual potency, the marriageability of a woman is connected to her sexual purity and commodified value. Even though males and females are prohibited from engaging in premarital sex, the stigma for females who break this prohibition is greater than for males. This embodies a sexual double standard in regard to female sexuality.

---

a choice between a number of contraception methods. In practice, however, the pill has frequently been suggested to mothers, presumably because it is cheap, easy to get, readily available in community health centres (I. *Puskesmas*) or from local midwives (*bidan*), and does not have to be implanted in the woman's body, which explains why the IUD is less popular than pills among women in the villages.

8 Van Gennep (1960:3) classifies stages of individual rites as pregnancy to birth, initiation rites, bethrothal to marriage, and the funeral.

9 For a detailed discussion of single women's motivations for marriage in Lombok, Mataram, Eastern Indonesia, see Bennett (2002:88–89).

Unmarried female status is described by the metaphor of a fruit. While a ripe fruit (I. *buah ranum*) is tasty and has high value, an overly ripe fruit (*buah yang terlalu masak*) is tasteless and cheap, and is expressed in Bugis, as withered (*makelléqni*). The same image is applied to women. Fruit peddlers in the traditional markets usually place ripe fruits in a separate basket from overly ripe fruits to distinguish their quality and price. If one tries to bargain for the ripe fruit, the peddler will respond: 'It's ripe, that's why it's more expensive than the other,' pointing his/her finger to the overly ripe fruits. Similarly, when a woman is considered 'over ripe', public opinion holds that her family should not demand a high bridewealth. The most important issue is that she be married. An 'overly ripe' woman is considered to be less fertile than a 'ripe' woman, and therefore of less 'value'.

Marriage according to Islam is a physical-emotional contract (I. *ikatan lahir bathin*) between a man and a woman in order to form a happy and everlasting family (the Marriage Law 1974, Chapter I:1).[10] This indicates that marriage is not only to unite husband and wife, as 'two in one', but it also reflects a religious dimension (*ibadah*) (see, for example, Rahmat Sudirman 1999:66–67). Masdar F. Mas'udi—an Islamic scholar—supports the principle that marriage is *aqd al-ibadah*, which means it legalises sexual relationships which are prohibited prior to marriage, thus arguing against the view that marriage is *aqad tamlik* (A. property contract) (1997:107–108). Furthermore, marriage ideally creates a harmonious (*sakinah*), safe (*mawaddah*) and merciful (*rahmah*) family, as stated in KHI (Chapter II:3). In other religions, such as Christianity, the sacrament of marriage is considered to join the bride and groom and is ritually performed by a priest or minister. In Islam, marriage is considered a sacred 'legal contract' between the ritual guardian of the bride in the paternal line, called *wali*, and the groom through a legalisation process termed *nikah*.[11] The concept of marriage in Islam itself is associated with the dichotomous concepts of *halal* (permitted) and *haram* (forbidden). Because sex outside of marriage is forbidden, marriage is the only way to legalise sexual activities

10 The foundation of marriage stated in the Marriage Law is aimed to prevent a temporary marriage or a contractual marriage (I. *kawin mut'ah*). In Indonesia it has been a subject of debate as to whether or not this type of marriage is legal. Many argue that *kawin mut'ah* is intended to impede sexual relations outside marriage. But, others claim that this kind of marriage is against Islamic Law.

11 The literal meaning of *nikah* is 'to gather' or 'to come together.' Metaphorically, *nikah* carries the sense of 'sexual relationship' or 'copulation'. Related terms, such as '*ar-rafats*' (A. flirt), '*taqrabuhuna*' (approach), '*hartsun*' (plant), '*lamastumun nisa*' (touch the woman/wife), '*taghasyaha*' (mix into), '*zawwaja*' or '*zauwj*' (partner) can be found in the Qur'an (Rahmat Sudirman 1999:68).

between a man and a woman. Therefore, one should marry to legalise the sexual relationship. Otherwise, sexual intercourse will be considered as fornication (I. *perzinahan*).[12] As stated in the Qur'an (*Al-Isra*: 32):

> Nor come nigh to adultery: for it is a shameful (deed) and an evil opening the road (to other evils).

The connection between evil and sexual congress drawn in this verse is similar to the notion of deviant behaviour (B. *malaweng pangkaukeng*) evoked by my informants to refer to any sexual relationship between woman and a man who are not married to one another. Indeed, Hamka, one of Indonesia's most influential Muslim scholars in his book *Tafsir* Al-Azhar, Juz XV, relates the above verse to a Hadith which states that if a woman and a man sits side by side, it is considered as if there is a third party, an evil (Hamka 1982:56). In such an atmosphere, it is assumed that the evil may control one's behaviour. Similarly, a Bugis aphorism (B. *paseng*) states:

> The message of elders to their children and grandchildren: a man and a woman should avoid being alone together because being alone together they may easily be tempted by an evil.
>
> *Ia naé pappasenna tomatoa rioloé ri an[a]q [e]ppona, ajaq lalo musitudangeng oroané sipaqdua iko makkunraié, apaq iatu assipaqdua-duangngé malomo nauttamai s[é]tammajaq.*[13]
>
> AHMAD YUNUS ET AL. 1991/1992:25

Being alone together [*assipaqdua-duangngé*, derived from *dua* (two)] is always considered to be three-in-one (a man, a woman, and an evil), instead of exclusively two persons, a man and a woman; and sexual desire is assumed to be human nature. Given this belief, men and women should avoid being in close proximity without someone else accompanying them in order to prevent sexual contact outside of marriage. This is not to imply that the prohibition is due to a lack of trust of one person in another, but as Syekh M.Y. Qardhawi (1993) argues, it aims to prevent both sexes from engaging in prohibited behaviour. This prohibition is not only related to the thought that the boundary between

12 For a thorough explanation of sexuality in Islam, see Bouhdiba (1985).

13 *Lontaraq Latoa* regulates how men should behave towards women (I. adat *laki-laki terhadap perempuan*), one rule is that men are not allowed to be in close proximity with women, even their close female relatives (in Rahman Rahim 1982:21).

haram and *halal* is very thin, but also to the value of virginity for women. Hamka, in this sense, tries to suggest a way to prevent behaviour which may lead to sexual conduct between the sexes outside marriage and the resulting risks (for example, extramarital pregnancy). In order to avoid this, one needs to marry (see below, Timing of Marriage). But for the Bugis, marrying is not as simple as 'turning over the palm of the hand' (I. *membalikkan telapak tangan*), which indicates that marriage is not an easy affair. There are a number of aspects that have to be considered, one of which is selecting the marriage partner.

Marriage Partner: Between Ideal and Pragmatic

For the Bugis, there are standards applied in the selection of a marriage partner: religion, kinship, status and personal qualities, and for this reason, selection of a partner is a matter which cannot be left to the young Bugis alone.[14] Each of these standards is examined below.

Religion

The foremost standard in the selection of marriage is that the prospective partners have to be Muslim, whether or not they are is originally from another religion. In Indonesia, there are different opinions on whether or not marriage with a convert is allowed. Some consider that no matter what the prior religion of the convert, marriage is prohibited. Others consider that as long as the non-Muslim converts to Islam, marriage is permissible.[15]

The prohibition of marriage between two persons of different religions is based on a verse in the Qur'an, as follows:

> Do not marry unbelieving women until they believe: a slave woman who believes is better than an unbelieving woman even though she attracts you. Nor marry (young women) to unbelievers until they believe: a man slave who believes is better than an unbeliever even though he attracts you. Unbelievers do (but) beckon you to the fire. But Allah beckons by His

14 In his study of neighbouring Makassarese in Bontoramba, Chabot (1996:179) demonstrates three standards of selection (kinship, status and personal qualities). Presumably the reason Chabot omits religion as a criterion for marriage is that everyone in Bontoramba was Muslim.

15 See also Abdurrahman (1992:71–72) for his criticism towards Chapter VI (40 and 44) of the Compillation of Islamic Law concerning marriage between Muslim and non-Muslim.

> Grace to the garden (of bliss) and forgiveness, and makes His Signs clear to mankind: that they may receive admonition.
>
> AL-BAQARAH:221

In addition, the Qur'an (*Al-Maidah*:5) states that a Muslim man may marry a non-Muslim woman who is a follower of the Book (A. *Ahlul Kitab*, for example, the Bible). Another verse (*Al-Kafirun*:6) states that your religion is yours and my religion is mine. Based on these three verses, Abdullah Siddik—an Indonesian Muslim scholar—argues that the first verse means that men and women are prohibited from marrying non-Muslims, the second verse means that only men can marry non-Muslims who are *Ahlul Kitab*, that is, either Christians or Jews because Islam and these other two religions are descended from the Prophet Ibrahim's family. Further, the third verse means that each person has the right to stay in her/his own religion (Siddik 1983:38–45). Siddik's argument that women may not marry non-Muslims is based on the notion that women are 'weak' (I. *lemah*), and may be persuaded to convert to their husband's religions (*murtad*). Thus, Siddik makes an exception and allows a Muslim man to marry a non-Muslim woman. His argument is simply following a system of religious classification. As Mary Daouglas (1978) points out in her book Purity and Danger, such classifications are arbitrary in themselves, are not logical, and are culturally determined. In the case under discussion, there seems to be some confusion about the justifcatio for the flexibility for men, for example, because Jews and Christians are followers of the Book or descendants of the Prophet's family, while the prohibition for women is on the basis of her stereotyped character, as if a husband cannot be influenced by his wife to change his religion.

In Kulo, marriages between Muslims and non-Muslims were largely unknown as the area is predominantly Islamic.[16] Such marriages are common, however, amongst the heterogeneous population in Makassar. Despite the above stereotypical determination of women's character, it was argued that if a woman sustains her choice to marry a non-Muslim, her non-Muslim partner must become a Muslim before marriage to prevent the woman changing her religion.[17] Thus, there is a 'bargain' here that no matter what religion and sex

16 Despite the lack of statistics on religion at the Subdistrict Office at Kulo, it is assumed that 99% of the population is Muslim (interview with one of the officials, Subdistrict Office, Kulo, Sidrap, 21-11-2000).

17 In Sidrap, there is another local religious belief called Tolotang. Tolotang consists of two groups, Tolotang Benteng and Tolotang Towani. While the former's beliefs is 'close' to Islam (they fast and pray, but also practice animism), the latter is 'close' to Hindu. But

the non-Muslim, inter-religious marriage is acceptable provided the non-Muslim partner converts to Islam.

Kinship

In addition to religion mentioned above, kinship is another aspects to be considered when selecting marriage partner. Bugis decent is traced bilaterally. That is kinship can be determined by both sides, from the mother as well as from the father, and both spouses retain their natal group membership after marriage (Pelras 1996:152; Millar 1989:25).

Marriage within existing kinship networks is regarded as ideal; the most desirable arrangement is marriage between cousins, either parallel or cross cousins (Pelras 1996:154). Mattulada identifies three types of ideal kin-based marriages in Bugis: appropriate matrimony (B. *assialang marola*), that is, marriage between first cousins (*sapposiseng*); coherent matrimony (*assialanna mémeng*), that is, marriage between second cousins (*sappokkadua*); and marriage that brings close one who is far (*ripaddeppéq mabélaé*), that is, marriage between *sappokkatellu* (third cousins) (Mattulada 1995:44). Although marriage with outsiders (*to laing*) becoming more common in contemporary Bugis society, I found during my fieldwork that marriage within kin groups still persists.

In the past, marriage between second or third cousins was most favoured by lower-ranking Bugis, while the high-ranking nobility ideally practise marriage between first cousins. This practice was accepted by the nobility, following the La Galigo heroes (Pelras 1996:155). Such ideal wedlock is implied in the Bugis classic literature of La Galigo. In one episode of La Galigo, *Ritumpanna Wélenrénngé*, for example, it is suggested that an endogamous marriage between Bugis of similar status is regarded as a 'good match' as is marriage between cousins (B. *mallaibiné massappo siseng*). This can be seen in the marriage between Sawérigading and his first cousin I Wé Cudaiq; and between Remmangrilangiq and his first cousin We Tenriabéng. The marriage between

Tolotang Benteng accept themselves as Muslim-Tolotang Benteng, and Tolotang Towani refuse to be called Hindus, except for their identity card because this belief is not recognised by the state as an official religion. Thus, I presume that when they were asked what religion they belong to during a census, some might answer Hindu, while others say Tolotang. Therefore, they are included in either Hindu or Others (see Chapter 1 for statistics). There is usually a tension in inter-marriage between a Muslim and a Tolotang Towani if both of them sustain their religion. I was told by the leader of the Tolotang Towani that marriage does not aim to bifurcate two families, but to unite two families, and a marriage between a man and a woman of different religion (for example, between Tolotang and non-Tolotang) cannot be tolerated by their respected elders (interview with Uwaq Launga, 11-3-2000).

Batara Guru and Wé Nyelliq Timoq—who is the daughter of Batara Guru's mother's brother—demonstrates a perfect marriage, that is, a marriage between cross cousins of similar status (Fachruddin Ambo Enre 1999:127–128). This preference is connected to the Bugis notions of proper (*sekapuq*) as opposed to improper (*tessikapuq*) which can be seen in terms of genealogical relation (I. *hubungan darah*) and hypergamy (A.P. Hamzah et al. 1984:101), see below.

Tessikapuq marriage—which refers to, for example, the incentuous marriage of siblings—is prohibited, and it is believed that such a marriage will ruin the life of the whole community. This is also well-illustrated in the manuscript edition of *Ritumpanna Wélenrénngé*, for example, in the love affair between Wé Tenrirawé and her twin brother Pallawagauq (Fachruddin Ambo Enre 1999:127); and the conflict which resulted from the request of Sawérigading to marry his twin sister, Wé Tenriabéng (Fachruddin Ambo Enre 1999:127; Muhammad Salim and Fachruddin Ambo Enre 1995:26–27). In contemporary Bugis society, the consequence of an incentuous relationship is to be killed or thouwn out (I. *dibuang*) by the family because it is regarded as a shameful act.

There are different perspectives among the Bugis from different classes. For example, the tendency for nobles (B. *arung*) to marry within the family (between cousins) is not only understood to protect the property of the family, but also to preserve their nobility through status-matching. For commoners, especially those in the villages, marriage within a kinship network is mainly undertaken because the prospective in-laws are already known by all concerned (Pelras 1996:154). In addition, there are also contrasting opinions between elders and youth regarding marriage within kinship networks or with outsiders (*to laing*). On the one hand, Bugis elders usually gives advice to youth that 'it is better if you marry within your family, if you marry with an outsider, she/he will behave like an outsider' (*Makessimmutoitu ko padaidiqkiq siala, nakko to laing, to laing mutotu sipaqna*). Therefore, marriage with *to laing* should be more carefully investigated than marriage within the family because elders are afraid that an outsider will continue to behave like an outsider (*massipaq to laing*) even within the family. *Massipaq to laing* carries the sense that someone does not behave as a part of a family, which goes against the notion of *siala*. On the other hand, the younger generation consider that marriage outside the kindred will extend kinship networks. As they said: 'We would have a new branch of family'. Such marriages are also thought to prevent clashes between the two families when the couple is in conflict, given the fact that conflict between husband and wife may involve the family of both sides. In addition, marriage within the kinship network is viewed as marriage between siblings, as youth expressed in a focus group discussion. For example, I quote a young woman who said: 'I cannot imagine marrying a man who is, for example, my cousin or my close relative because I would feel as if I were marrying my brother'.

For the Bugis, marriage to someone from outside of the kinship circle can aim 'to make a non-kin into kin' (Pelras 1996:154). This portrays the ambivalence of Bugis preferences for marriage partner selection. While endogamous marriages aim to prevent the other infiltrating the family, exogamous marriages are expected to make others into family members.

However, to restrict the tendency to marry with *to laing*, elders allow that: 'One may marry an outsider, as long as she/he is Bugis' (*namu to laing napubainé assalaq ugiq mua*). This advice is directed to both men and women, and indicates the preference for marriage within the ethnic group in order to maintain the notion of *siala*. Thus, a young man/woman who intends to marry a non-Bugis has to make sure that his/her prospective wife/husband understands the philosophy of Bugis marriage (see below).

Errington argues that the tendency for endogamous marriages among noble Bugis aims to concentrate spiritual potency of and to consolidate, the family (Errington 1977:52–56). This may not be possible if one marries with *to laing*, as a new branch is formed; the family becomes scattered and the centre becomes unclear. Nevertheless, marriage with *to laing* can be politically advantageous.[18] For example, Acciaioli illustrates the 'third tip' based on the Bugis philosophy of *tellu cappaq* (B. three tips), as a strategy to integrate themselves with a new community. He writes that

> The three tips (*tellu cappa*[*q*]) encompass the tongue, the knife blade, and the penis. If a Bugis cannot integrate himself with the local leaders by diplomatic consultation (by the tip of his tongue), he may have to resort to armed battle (by the tip of his knife blade). But, best of all, he will be able truly to integrate himself in the new community by marrying one (or more) of the local women (by the tip of his penis).
>
> ACCIAIOLI 2000:216

18 Bulbeck (1996) shows that for Makassar, where the nobility of a rising polity, Gowa in his case, are 'wife takers', while the nobility of a polity coming under Gowa's dominion are 'wife givers'. Marriage cements the precedence of Gowa. This is precisely the same as the marriage strategy described in Pelras' (2000) discussion of patron-client relations for the Bugis and Makassarese, and the exogamous hypergamous marriages among *arung* (B. king) in the Chronicle of Bone to strengthen both their authority and territory (Macknight and Paeni, n.d.). The importance of this is to show that status (*onro*) is distinct from kinship (*asséajingeng*).

Thus, exogamous marriage is beneficial for a man's social security and status in the community. In line with this idea, Abidin argues that 'only when you are adopted by a leader do you have four sides' (B. *sulapaq eppaq*) (cited in Morrell 1998:155–156),[19] a phrase that articulates a Bugis concept of perfection (see below). The best way to achieve the *sulapaq eppaq* is to marry the daughter of the influential leader of the community, and this, at the same time, means that the groom becomes a member of the family of the influential community leader.

Since marriage in Bugis society links not only husband and wife, but also ties the families of both sides (Millar 1989:26–28), as it is reflected in the term of *siala*—the bride has to accept the family of her husband as her own family, and vice versa. The following expression is frequently uttered by elders to young people:

> If you are looking for a prospective wife, find someone who also likes your family, because for the Bugis when one gets married, the families of both sides also 'get married'.
>
> *Nakko sappaqko bainé, ia mélorié to ri séajimmu, nasabaq idiqtu to ugiq-é nakko bottikkiq, bottittoi tu séajingngé.*

In spite of the fact that this expression seems to be directed to men in its everyday usage, it refers to both men and women. The sentiment, however, applies to both men and women. It would be possible to utter the directive 'look for husband' (*sappaq lakkai*) to a woman, but it would have a negative connotation since women should wait for a man to 'look for her' (*sappaq bainé*). The implied meaning of *siala* is reflected in the phrase '*bottittoi tu séajingngé*' (the family of both sides also gets married), mentioned above.

Status

In Indonesian society, marital status is considered to be a fundamental aspect of a person's social status (Locher-Scholten and Niehof 1987:9). For the Bugis, marriage is an arena where one indicates social location (that is, *onro*); the status of the bride and groom can be the same, or unequal, but it is more usual for women to marry up (Millar 1989 and Errington 1989). An individual's social status is determined by affiliation which can be from birth, marriage or allignment.[20]

---

19 See Morrell's (1998:154–156) analysis of quadrate domains of Bugis-Makassarese.

20 For a detailed discussion on kinship in Bugis social organisation, see Millar (1989: Chapter 11).

The Bugis hierarchical marriage system is associated with the woman's function as the symbol of family *siriq* (honour) and as the preserver of the purity of 'blood'. A woman determines or stabilises the degree of nobility of her family.[21] Many noble women get married at an advanced age or even become old maids as a consequence of their nobility As a result, it goes without saying that many noble women get married at an advanced age or even become old maids as a consequence of their noble status.[22] In his study of the Makassarese in Bontoramba, Chabot describes a woman as a ladder in relation to hypergamous marriage. If a woman is allowed to marry down, the ladder becomes slippery (cited in Errington 1977:53–54). Thus, it is better for a woman to stay unmarried than to marry down.

In the Bugis kingdom of Luwu, where Errington conducted her study, rank is based on three divisions, from the highest to the lowest: better people (*To Malebbiq*), [regular] people (*To Samaq*), and slaves (*Ata*) (Errington (1989:96). Despite the fact that a woman of *to samaq* should also marry up, her status is determined according to her personal qualities or her parents' social status. In the past, the bridewealth of a daughter could not be lower than that of her mother, which indicates that her status may not be lower than her mother's status (Millar 1989:70; Errington 1977:55–56). Therefore, it is apparent that *to samaq* may enhance the status of the bride or the groom by 'receiving' or 'giving' high bridewealth (Errington 1977:55–56).

I will describe the marriage of my host's son as an instance of exogamous marriage and its relationship to social status, that is, *onro*, as well as personal qualities. The *onro* of the girl's family was slightly higher, indicated by her father's job as a *saudagar ikan* (I. large-scale fish merchant) in Pinrang (a neighbouring regency) and his hajj status, compared to Pak Bakri's job as a primary school teacher. The bride (Mina) had graduated from high school, while the groom (Aco) graduated from the state university in Kendari, Southeast Sulawesi. I was told that the 'spending money' (B. *duiq ménréq*) was quite high (Rp 1,000,000 equal to US$100 at current currency) for the status of *to samaq* in the village in 2000. Therefore, their *onro* was reckoned comparable on both sides by taking into account all these factors. However, considering that both families are *to samaq*, no one worried too much about the detail of this marriage.

---

21 See Millar (1989:Chapter II) and Pelras (1996:155) on the assessment of marriage and social location of the Bugis; Palmier (1960:53–57) analyses headwife (*J. padmi*) and secondary wives (*selir*) of Javanese nobleman; and Boon (1977:Chapter VI) discusses hypergamy and status equality in Balinese marriage.

22 M. Adlin Sila (2002:11–12) notes the dilemma faced by female Arab Makassarese as a result of their Arab inheritance and status.

But *Pak* Bakri thought that the high 'spending money' would be recompensed with 'something' else in the future, as he told me one afternoon. For example, I often heard *Ibu* Darma—*Pak* Bakri's wife—mention how proud she was because her son had married a daughter of a *saudagar ikan* and a hajj. She identified herself and her family as becoming part of the social status of her in-laws, *maccoéq-coéqki ri ajié* (be the follower of the hajj). In addition, the father of the bride promised to find a job for the groom's younger brother, Farhan. But, the promise has never been fulfilled until the groom's younger brother decided to go to West Papua to find a job, following his older sister.

Personal Qualities

Another standar for an ideal partner is the personal qualities of the individul concerned. This standard is usually mentioned by Bugis elders, and is stated in *Lontaraq Fikhi/Nikah*,[23] which is in fact based on a *Hadith* (Sahih Muslim), as follows:

> A woman is selected as a spouse because of four characteristics: being rich, beautiful, good descent, and being religious. But, the most important characteristic is piety.
>
> *Rinikkaiwi makkunraié ri eppaé sipaq*: *sugiq-i, makessi-kessingngi, mappasiabbatirengngi, pagamai. Naékia paléi mennang ia pagamaé* (p. 4).

Having all these four qualities (*sugiq, makessi-kessing, mappasiabbatireng* and *pagama*), a woman is regarded as a 'perfect woman' having the four qualities of *sulapaq eppaq*. Each element has to support the other elements as a system. However, no one is perfect. In theory, being pious is considered to be the most important characteristic because it is believed that a religious woman can control her behaviour. Elders commented that 'if one is pious, one also has a good attitude' (*ko pagamai tu taué, makessittoi tu ampé-ampéna*), though in reality this is not always the case. It is nevertheless considered that the quality of being pious may lead someone to behave properly, to have an inner beauty and to be rich. Therefore, being pious may cover the other qualities. 'Rich', in this sense, is not necessarily connected with material wealth, but may also mean that she is *sombéréq* (friendly, rich in smiles) not only to her husband, but also to others, particularly members of the family. I frequently heard the Bugis say: 'his wife is friendly' (*masombéréq bainéna*) which means that she can get on

23 *Lontaraq Fikhi/Nikah*, Roll 37/No.11, nineteenth century, Arsip Nasional Wilayah Makassar, transliterated by Muhlis Hadrawi (3-3-2002).

with everybody. This is associated with a woman's informal behaviour, which has a great importance in Bugis *asseajingeng*. Members of her husband's family are reluctant to visit if the wife is not friendly (*sombéréq*), behaves as an outsider (*massipaq to laing*) and treats them as if they are not part of her family.

The husband is not expected to show his friendliness (*sombéréq*) overtly—as his wife does. This is connected to the formality of a man's behaviour and to the maintenance of his social location (Millar 1983:487). Hence, husband-formal and wife-informal mirror the dichotomisation of male and female interaction with others after marriage. This complementarity is not just about their interaction within the family or with others, but is also associated with spiritual potency to protect their social location. Thus, men and women behave appropriately in different in different situation.[24]

In a similar way, the testament (B. *wasiat*) detailing the characteristics of an ideal wife in *Lontaraq Fikhi/Nikah* is not synonymous with the characteristics for an ideal husband. A *lontaraq* states that a good leader is one who has the qualities of four sides (*sulapaq eppaq*), consisting of bravery (*warani*), cleverness (*macca*), wealth (*sugiq*) and leadership (*panrita*) (Mattulada 1995:35).[25] Though these characteristics do not specifically refer to the values of an ideal husband, they may be used to indicate a 'good' man, and it is usually assumed that leaders are men.

In theory—as in Bugis manuscripts—a man is expected to be brave (*warani*), so he can be the protector of his family, or family *siriq*; he is clever (*macca*), so he can be the role model; he is wealthy (*sugiq*), so he can maintain his family; and he is religious leader (*panrita*), so he can guide his family. Possessing all these characteristics (*to warani, to macca, to sugiq* and *to panrita*) indicates that a man has *sulapaq eppaq*; he is a 'perfect man'. Pelras suggests that the possession of these four qualities can be 'equated with nobility', especially if one intends to marry a high ranking woman (Pelras 2000:35). The most important characteristic is *panrita*. While *pagama* refers to an individual's piety, *panrita* signifies one's proficiency as a religious leader (I. *ulama*).

In general, Mattulada indicates that the ideal Bugis personality should be clever (B. *acca*), honest (*lempuq*), firm (*getteng*), and brave (*warani*). In order to maintain the principle of mutual respect (*sipakatauq*) in which attitudes are

24 See also Keeler's (1990) discussion on how the dimension of prestige/potency distinguishes male and female in the social life of Javanese.

25 See also Pelras (1996:210–215) on the valued qualities of the mythical and fictional heroes in Bugis.

controlled by honour (*siriq*) and social solidarity (*pessé*) (Mattulada 1998:139). Mattulada expresses these characteristics as follows:

> Persons with mutual respect, share one *siriq* and maintain *pessé*, and behave in manners befitting a Bugis: they are clever and honest, firm and brave, with the willingness of Allah.
>
> *Tau si-pakatauq, masseddi siriq, mappatettong pessé, ri-ikkeng sempugi-sempullolotaq: To-acca na Malempuq, Warani na Magetteng! Mappasanréq ri Élo-Ulléna Alla[t]aala.*[26]
>
> MATTULADA 1998:vi

This saying illustrates that the ideal personality of Bugis sociality (B. *sempugi sempullolotaq*, I. *sesama orang* Bugis) is based on the concept of mutual respect (*sipakatauq*), honour (*siriq*) and social solidarity (*pessé*), through which an individual is united with others through customary etiquette (*pangngadereng*). Significantly, Mattulada mentions the rhombus square (*sulapaq eppaq wolasuji*) based on a mythical belief of Bugis-Makassarese associated with the shape of the written script (consonantsa) (Mattulada 1995:8–9).[27] This shape symbolises the square of the human body (*sulapaq eppaqna taué*), which carries the sense of the wholeness of the human body. Top and bottom are the head and the feet; right and left are hands, signifying the perfect shape of the human body. Each side is connected and balanced with another. The four characteristics of male and female mentioned above symbolise the four sides (*sulapaq eppaqna*) of ideal Bugis personalities.[28]

In practice, in addition to the attribute of being a Muslim as the main requirement for a prospective marriage partner, Bugis people stress that the ideal prospective husband should have the ability to 'surround the kitchen seven times' (*mattuliling dapureng wékka pétu*).[29] The kitchen symbolises household affairs, and seven times stands for the days in a week. A similar phrase is found in

---

26 Indonesian translation: '*Manusia yang saling menghargai, menyatu dalam Siriq menegakkan Pessé; dalam Pribadi Manusia Sulawesi Selatan; ialah, orang Pandai dan Jujur; Berani dan Teguh; Berserah kepada Redha Allah Taala* (Mattulada 1998:vi).

27 A. Zainal Abidin (1999:1–2) discusses the origin and the meaning of *lontaraq* as the opus of culture of people in South Sulawesi.

28 See the parallelism between the square of human body and the gender relations in Bugis marriage in relation to the structure of Bugis house in Chapter 11.

29 A. Hasan Machmud (1994:31–32) describes a similar, but slightly different saying: *iapa nakkullé taué mabbainé narékko naulléni maggulilingiwi dapurengngé wékka pitu* (someone is able to marry only if he is able to surround the kitchen seven times).

Indonesia: 'able to keep the hearth burning' (I. *mampu mengepulkan asap dapur*). Both sayings carry the sense that the prospective husband is able to feed the members of the family every day, imposing on him the financial responsibility for his own family, as a good provider (*nalaoanni aléna*).[30] A prospective wife, on the other hand, should be able to face her husband (B. *moloi lakkainna*). The meaning of *moloi* is related to the ability to fulfil the emotional and physical needs of the husband, which encompass the need for a sexual partner and a household manager.[31] Each of them is expected to cope with the family of both sides, socially and economically whenever it is needed and is possible.

A girl is expected to learn the skills of household management from her mother during her maidenhood. On account of this, uxorilocal residence has become the preference of the newlyweds. However, I have never heard of anyone getting divorced because of failure to satisfy the emotional needs of her husband, and this is not listed as a reason for divorce in the list of cases provided by the Religious Court (I. the Pengadilan Agama) in Sidrap.[32] Yet, divorce because of conflict with the in-laws is very common, and is classified as 'disharmony'.

I attended a number of weddings in Sidrap as well as in Makassar and noted that the typical advice that is conveyed is that the husband is 'the head of the family' and the wife as 'the mother of the household', stated in the 1974 Marriage Law.[33] In addition to the ability of the husband to 'surround the kitchen seven times' (B. *mattuliling dapureng wékka pétu*) for the husband and the ability of the wife to serve the husband (*moloi lakkainna*) were also usually pronounced during the speech of marital advice (I. *nasihat perkawinan*) that was offered after the marriage contract (A. *akad nikah*).[34]

---

30 A similar phrase is found in Indonesia: 'able to keep the hearth burning' (I. *mampu mengepulkan asap dapur*), which carries the sense that the prospective husband has the capacity to feed members of the family every day.

31 The term *moloi* is cognate with the term *atut* for Javanese, described by H. Geertz (1961:73). McDonald and Abdurahman (1974:4) report of the Sundanese that beauty and morality are the most important factors for a prospective wife.

32 This is presumably because there are standard reasons for divorce for the Religious Court in Indonesia (see, for example, Jones et al. 1994, Nakamura 1981). Thus, failure to fulfill the emotional needs of the husband would be classified under the standard reasons.

33 Following the tension between the state and Islam (and local traditions) in the early days of the New Order as to whether or not the state should intervene in family matters, a secular Marriage Law was introduced on 2 Januray 1974 (See, Robinson 2000:164). The implementation of the Marriage Law was regulated under the State Regulation (*Peraturan Pemerintah*) No. 9/1975.

34 *Akad nikah* is a marriage ceremony performed by the groom in the presence of the *imam nikah* (the person who officiates at an Islamic ceremony).

In a focus group discussion in Kulo, I explored the perceptions of youth relating to the ideal wife and ideal husband. Male youth were quick to reply that an ideal wife is the one who bows down to her husband (B. *tunruq é rilakkainna*), which means they expect to have an obedient wife. My male unmarried informants expected to have a full time housewife who could concentrate on her domestic responsibilities. Why? A working-wife, according to the group members in this focus group was assumed to be too demanding (*maéga éloqna*) because she has more friends and has been more influenced by the outside world. However, their answers seemed to be ambivalent, as they also said: 'It is also good to have a working wife because she will have her own income, and it is all right as long as she does not neglect her domestic duties'.

The perceptions of young women regarding an 'ideal husband' also varied. His characteristics included an employed man (*urané engkaé jama-jamanna*), a man who has a house (*urané engkaé bolana*) and/or a man with good manners (*urané makessingngé sipaqna*). It was interesting to note, however, that none of them expected to have an 'obedient husband'. This is not only because an 'obedient wife' is idealised, but also because a powerful wife, or in their own words a 'wife who has too much power' tends to be socially criticised. A husband who participates in domestic affairs, for example, cooking and washing, is considered to be a 'less powerful husband' who is controlled by his wife. In contrast, a wife who spends more time outside the home is regarded as a 'bad wife'. From this point of view, it is assumed that while for the Bugis there has been no clear division concerning domestic and public roles between the husband and the wife, the influence of the development ideology of the New Order intensified the tendency for sexual stratification and specific gender roles in domestic life, discussed in Chapter 4.[35]

Timing of Marriage and Marriage of Minors

In addition to the above attributes—religion, kinship, status, personal qualities—age of marriage is another important factor for selecting a prospective bride/groom. For the Bugis, the desire for marriage is in accordance with the *sunnah*—which refers to acts that are optional, but meritorious if performed—of the Prophet Muhammad in which it is suggested that men and women get married

35 The official Indonesian state development ideology of a 'good wife' and 'good mother' is based on *Panca Dharma Wanita* (I. women's five principal duties): as appendages and companions to their husbands, procreators of the nation, mothers and educators of children, housekeepers, and members of Indonesian society. See Robinson (1998), Saraswati Sunindyo (1993, 1996), Julia I. Suryakusuma (1987, 1996), Istiadah (1995), and Sullivan (1983, 1994), Gerke (1993).

because marriage may preserve gaze (explain below) and honour. Thus, if a man is capable and intends to get married, and he is afraid that he cannot manage his passion, marriage becomes obligatory for him (Djuher 1983:54). This is in accord with the metaphorical definition of *akad nikah*: *akad* (A. contract) and *nikah* (sexual relationship). Thus, *akad nikah* is a contract of sexual relationship between a man and a woman which transforms from *haram* (forbidden) prior to marriage, to *halal* (permitted) after marriage (Ramulyo 1996:1–2).[36]

Corresponding to this prohibition on premarital sex, unmarried men and women are considered 'dangerous' in regard to sexuality (see Bennett 2002). It is believed that sex may start from one's eyes, since being unable to control one's gaze may lead to a more 'dangerous act' (for example, touching, kissing). Such sexual conduct may, then, contravene one's honour (B. *siriq*) because such behaviour is regarded as shameful.

Those who are incapable (usually referring to men) of self restraint are advised to fast in order to lessen their lust. In this regard, marriage or fasting is considered to be the way to manage sexual tension. In this connection, Imam Al-Gazali (1995:32), a great Islamic scholar, argues that sexual desire cannot be negated; it can only be controlled through marriage.[37] Furthermore, there is a testament (B. *wasiat*) in Bugis *lontaraq* which indicates that the utterance of the Prophet Muhammad states there are four actions which have to be taken immediately. These four actions are burying a corpse, marrying off daughters, feeding guests, and paying debts. The one relating to marriage is as follows:

> If you have a daughter, a young woman, and she can be married off, and there is a prospective husband, marry her off immediately.
>
> *Nakko engka anaqmu wélangpélang, bettuanna tau lolo, naweddinna mallakkai, naengkana maka mupasialangngi, pallakkainisisaq.*[38]
>
> S. BUDHISANTOSO ET AL. 1990:38

36 A *Hadith* (Nasa'i, Ibnu Majah, Tirmidzi) states that the boundary between *haram* (fornication) and *halal* (marriage) is the sound of tambourine and songs (Syaikh Kamil M. 'Uwaidah 1998:406) which indicates the importance of celebrating to inform the marriage.

37 A related *Hadith* (Bukhari-Muslim) states that if any of you is able to get married, the marriage will preserve your sight and reproduction (Husein Muhammad 2001:96).

38 A significant *Hadith* (at-Tarmudzi) states that if a pious man comes to propose to your daughter, marry them off. Otherwise, it may lead to a slander and damage the earth (Husein Muhammad 2001:96).

This *wasiat* carries the overtone that parents are expected to marry their daughters (*anaq dara wélangpélang*) off immediately after menarche.[39] In spite of the fact that this *lontaraq* has never been read directly by the majority of the Bugis in contemporary society, the *wasiat* circulates as an oral tradition, and is evoked in discussions of marriage of young women, especially among the Bugis in rural areas.

The emphasis of the *wasiat* on girls is relevant to the belief that raising a girl is ten times more difficult than rearing a boy. There is a saying frequently uttered by young men and women that 'looking for a lost spoon is more important than looking for a lost young boy'. This is not to argue that a boy is not as valuable as a girl, but the 'protection' of boys is loose compared to girls, and such 'protection' is closely associated with family honour.

I was told by *Pak* Bakri—my host—that early marriage occurs between families or the children of colleagues. But such marriages are usually very unstable because the bride and the groom are still so young. During my fieldwork, in Kulo, there was a case of an arranged marriage during my fieldwork between a 14 year old girl, Tati, and a 20 year old young man, Amal. Neither of them knew the other until they married. Their livelihood was supported by the family of both sides. In spite of the initial instability of this marriage, they stayed married because of the effort of both families to maintain the marriage. In addition to this case, I often heard people gossiping in mini-buses (*pété-pété*) when I was travelling around. Junior high school girls discussed a schoolmate who was going to get married, the marriage arranged by her parents.[40]

39 Several studies indicate this, for example, H. Geertz (1961), McDonald and Edeng Abdurahman (1974), Tim Peneliti (1988), Jones (1994), Bennett (2002), Platt (2010).

40 Based on the 1990 census report, Hull (2002:2) states the singulate age at first marriage (SMAM) in all provinces in Indonesia was over 20. Furthermore, in North Sumatra, Jakarta, South Sulawesi, East Nusa Tenggara, and Yogyakarta, SMAM was over 23. At the regency level, the 1998 National Socioeconomic Survey indicated that SMAM in all regencies in South Sulawesi was between 22 and 26 years; in Sidrap, Pangkep, Maros, Bantaeng and Bulukumba, it was over 24, while in Makassar—the capital city—it was over 26 (BPS Sulsel Online 2002). Despite the fact that the national and the regional statistics show high average age at first marriage, early marriage still occurs. The SMAM reflects the experience of all residents—those who marry young and those who delay marriage until their late 20s and early 30s. Even though the age at first marriage increases every year, it is not a revolutionary change, and therefore early marriage may still happen at the local level (Personal interview with Terry Hull, Canberra, 12-11-2002). In the national level (uban and rural), Population Census shows the slightly change of SMAM, from 23.5 (1990), 22.5 (2000), and 22.3 (2010) (Sensus Penduduk-2010 [2011b]).

There is a folk story related to early marriage and the well known veteran of Sidrap, Captain Usman Balo, the leader of Tentara Kemanan Rakyat (TKR, People Security Army).[41] He was described as a powerful man who was not only a heroic figure for the people of Sidrap, but also a person who could cause trauma to the villagers because of his womanising, especially towards young beautiful women. As a result, young women in his area were reluctant to go out or were even kept in the house by their parents in order to avoid Usman Balo's request to marry their daughters (*Fajar*, 9 January 2002). Even though early marriage was common in the past, parents were reluctant to marry their daughter with a much older man, not just because people would comment that 'he is supposed to be her father,' but also because he was bound to be polygynous.

Do girls get married younger if they are poor? Poverty is not always related to early marriage. Young girls and boys from poor families discontinue their educations if their parents cannot afford to pay. The highest level of education for poor young girls and boys is usually senior high school (SMU), but many did not even graduate from junior high school (SMP), as they are compelled to find jobs to support their families. An example of this was Ria, a 19 year old girl who graduated from senior high school in Rappang. Despite the fact that she intended to continue her education, her parents could not afford to continue to pay for her schooling. When I talked to her mother about the possibility of marrying Ria off, her mother said that no one had proposed to her yet. When I asked Ria what she wanted to do—get a job or get married, she chose both. She emphasised, however, that if she could not find a job, and someone proposed marriage to her, she wanted someone who had a job (B. *urané engkaé jama-jamanna*).

While waiting for the 'right man', Ria's father was attempting to find her a job in Makassar through a friend. A few months later, Ria was accepted as a factory worker in Makassar. The whole family was very excited and a small party was held to celebrate her new job as well as to release her ritually from her natal house and village. In Kulo, people usually hold a small festivity whenever anyone intends to leave the village, whether or not the departure is permanent. In spite of the fact that Ria was just a factory worker, she was still able to contribute some of her salary to her parents every time she returned home. Ria felt that living in the village with limited job opportunities gave her no

41 TKR is a local guerilla force in the Indonesian revolutionary era, who revolted due disappointment over the newly formed national army's refusal to recruit veterans of local guerilla forces in the struggle for national independence. TKR was led by Captain Usman Balo, a controversial figure because of his cruelty, bravery and womanising.

future, while working at the factory enabled her to meet various people in a different atmosphere. When I revisited the field in 2001, I heard that she had married a man who also worked in the same factory. In fact, Ria had to resign from her job. The company does not allow couples to work for them. But Ria's primary target had already been achieved. She had an employed husband, was pregnant with her first child, and they lived happily in Makassar.

In contemporary Bugis society, there is a wide range of views as to whether a young woman should be married off soon after menarche, or later. For example, elders suggest that young women should marry as soon as they begin menstruating in order to preserve the reputation of the family. In the past, the younger the girl, the better the match she could make, the higher the status of the groom, and the more prestige for the family. Therefore, in the past it was not surprising to find a girl who had not even experienced first menstruation when she married. However, no such cases of pre-pubescent marriage occurred during the period of my fieldwork.

Even though the Marriage Law of 1974 (Chapter II, 7:1) establishes that the minimum age of marriage as 16 for a female and 19 for a male, members of the younger generations suggested in a focus group that a female and a male should wait until they are mentally and physically ready to get married, indicated as age 20 for a female and 25 for the male. By this age, my interlocutors observed, the wife is considered able to face her husband (B. *moloi lakkainna*) and the husband is able to surround the kitchen seven times (*mattuliling dapureng wékka pétu*). Marriage at a younger age than this is considered potentially more unstable because the partners are not competent to perform marital obligations. This view was in line with cases of divorce in the Pengadilan Agama Sidrap in which parents had married off their daughters to men who did not even have jobs to maintain their families, which meant that the new couples depended financially on their parents. The impetus to early marriage in many of these cases arose from concern the girl would be 'unsaleable' if she waited. In other cases, the girl and the boy were sexually involved, and because the girl got pregnant, their parents married them off immediately. In such circumstances, these marriages were frequently unstable and ended in divorce, as I observed in a number of court hearings in the Sidrap Religious Court.

In Kulo, I recorded a number of reasons why parents attempt to marry off their daughters at a young age. First, parents wanted to preserve their reputations and to protect the family from shame. It is considered shameful if parents do not find a match for a fully grown daughter,[42] who will be labelled an

42 See also H. Geertz (1961:56), Masri Singarimbun and Manning (1974:5) for Javanese and McDonald and Edeng Abdurahman (1974:3–4) for Sundanese.

'unfortunate woman' if no one proposes to her; she then becomes a burden to her family. If a younger daughter is proposed to, and the elder daughter remains unmarried, the parents should pay the cost of 'skipping over' (B. *ilellung*) to the older daughter, usually paid from the part of the bridewealth that is 'spending money' (*duiq ménréq*), given by the groom of the younger daughter. The *duiq ménréq* is spread out on a table or on the floor. The eyes of the elder unmarried daughter are covered by a handkerchief and she is asked to use both hands to pick up as much as money she can. Alternatively, she may be given a piece or a set of jewellery by her parents in order to console her for the marriage of her younger sister. The amount of money or the kinds of gift given to the 'skipped over girl' varies, depending on the social status of the family and the number of 'skipped over sisters'. For example, the Akbars—*Pak* Bakri's lower class neighbours—gave a gold ring to their elder daughter as recompense for Ria's marriage. Ria 'skipped over' an elder sister (and a brother). In another instance, in a middle class family, I discovered that the parents gave a gold ring to each of their three daughters as a recompense for the marriage of their youngest daughter, Halida, who also had two elder brothers. A middle class woman in Makassar told me that she was given a gold and diamond bracelet as consolation for the marriage of her younger brother. While an elder sister should be paid for the cost of being 'skipped over' (*ilellung*), this is not the case between younger sister and elder brother, and between elder and younger brothers. In this sense, it indicates that while an unmarried young woman faces a social stigma as a result of *ilellung*, an unmarried young man does not. Consolation from *ilellung* is not significant for young men.

People usually comment: 'It is a pity she has been "skipped over" by her younger sister' (*Ilellungngi kasiq rianrinna*), or use a commodified metaphor: 'The elder hasn't been sold, so she is "skipped over by" the younger one' (*Deqpa natarala daénna jaji ilellungngi rianrinna*) which means that the elder hasn't been married (or is less saleable), but someone has proposed to her younger sister. However, it is more shameful if an older daughter is *ilellung* by her younger brother because of the notion that the younger son is more 'saleable' than the elder daughter. There is a joke usually expressed by unmarried daughters in regard to this compensation: 'I am waiting until all my younger sisters and brothers get married, so I can accumulate more money and/or jewellery before I myself get married'.

The fear of the early death of parents is another reason to marry off children quickly as parents are afraid of not witnessing their children's marriages. This applies to both daughters and sons. Another extreme reason is that parents want to get rid of the responsibility of taking care of an unmarried young woman (*anaq dara*). This sentiment illustrates how an *anaq dara* can become a burden for the family in the perception of the community. In Bugis, marrying an *anaq dara* entails transferring the major responsibility to her husband. Parents who have pubescent unmarried daughters experience a state of anxiety, especially after she has experienced several years of menarche.

In spite of the fact that the minimum legal age of marriage in Indonesia has been established in the 1974 Marriage Law, a dispensation can be requested through the Religious Court if the female's age is less than that stipulated in the law. I suspected at first that this dispensation might be used to perpetuate marriage below the minimum legal age. I was informed by the judges that I interviewed that before the young woman is given a dispensation to marry, she has to be examined. This examination is on an ad hoc basis to assess her physical and psychological conditions. For example, if the young woman is well developed physically, it is assumed that she is ready to marry. Her psychological condition is assessed based on her behaviour—whether she behaves in a childish or mature manner—and is also based on the evidence of her parents. Another factor considered is whether the young woman has already had a boyfriend. In fact, there were not many cases of dispensation of marriage (I. *dispensasi kawin*) of the minor provided by the Religious Court in Sidrap.[43] This is not to say, however, that underage females are not married, as people may lie in the first step of the procedure in the village office (*kelurahan*)[44] (the procedure of marriage registration is discussed in Chapter 6). For instance, if the female is 14, she can easily be registered with an age of 16 if officials 'turn a blind eye' based on the principle that one should not be hampered if the *jodoh* (pre-destined marriage partner) is before one's eyes. This circumstance has always been the concern of judges at the Sidrap Religious Court.

Marriage of minors, however, is not only a common phenomenon in Bugis culture, but also in other parts of Indonesia.[45] Underage marriage is more associated with arranged, not free-choice marriage.[46] Despite the fact that arranged

---

43 For example, there was only one case of dispensation of marriage filed in the Sidrap Religious Court in 2000, 2 and 4 cases in 2007 and 2009 respectively, and increases significantly to 25 (cases) in 2010 and triples (76 cases) in 2010 .

44 Personal interview with judges in Sidrap Religious Court (10-5-2000).

45 See, for example, H. Geertz (1961); Masri Singarimbun and Manning (1974); MacDonald and Edeng Abdurahman (1974); Niehof (1985); Jones (2001), and in Southeast Asia (Jones 1994), Bennett (2002), Platt (2010).

46 In August 2008, there was a controversial underage and arranged marriage between a 43 year old politician-cleric (Pujiono Cahyo Widayanto), popularly known as Syech Puji, the head of an Islamic boarding school (Ponpes Miftahul Jannah) in Semarang, Central Java and an 11 years and 10 months old (Lutfiana Ulfa), who had just begun studies at a local junior high school by unregistered marriage (*nikah siri*). As a result of this marriage,

marriages as well as free choice marriages involve the couple and parents from both sides, the couple is usually blamed for 'incorrect' choice of spouse in free-choice marriage, especially those who get married to outsiders (B. *to laing*).

In contemporary Bugis society, even though some parents in Kulo still consider the ideal age at first marriage for a young female to be between 15 and 17 years, extended possibilities for education and the opportunity to work in the paid workforce nevertheless raised the age of marriage. Bugis people in Kulo say that the current average age at first marriage is now 20 for a female and 25 for a male. Given that there is no high school in Kulo, females and males have to go to the subdistrict centre which is about 15 kilometres away to attend school, and this distance gives them the 'freedom' to socialise with others away from their place of origin.

There are various terms related to age of marriage. Given that 20 years of age at first marriage is currently the norm, a female who passes the age of 25 and is still unmarried will be labelled as *mangngaribini* (B. time for sunset prayer).[47] Her parents will start to ask her whether or not someone has already approached her, and the woman herself is often in a state of anxiety. When a woman turns 30, she will be called *isyani* (B. time for evening prayer), a time when a woman is considered to be *makelléqni*, the term used to describe an 'overly ripe and wrinkled fruit'. *Isyani* is considered a risky time and such a woman will often feel grief and become pessimistic, afraid of being an unsaleable woman (*makkunrai ladoq*).[48] A thirty-five year old unmarried woman is called *subuni*, a term that refers to the time for the early morning prayer. At this stage, in many cases, a woman is usually viewed as left behind by the market (*nawélaini pasaq*).

If a woman gets married after 35, she is commonly proposed to either by a widower or a married man. This illustrates that the term *subuni* refers both to a woman's age and the decreased possibility that she will find a marriage partner. In urban areas, however, the age of marriage is higher compared with rural areas. In Makassar, people state that the average age for first marriage is 25 for females and 30 for males. Even though similar Islamic terms are applied, the age at which each term evoked is quite different. Thus, 30, 35 and 40 are associated

---

on 24th November 2010, Syech Puji was sentenced to four years jail and a 60 million rupiah (approximately US$6,666) fine.

47 In Islam, there are five obligatory prayers: *dhuhur* (A. prayer before noon), *ashar* (afternoon prayer), *magrib* (sunset prayer), *isya* (evening prayer), and *subuh* (the early morning prayer).

48 Bennett (2002) also notes thirty as the age that single women in Mataram begin to fear that they are too old to attract a marriage partner.

with the terms *mangngaribi* (sunsent prayer), *isya* (evening prayer) and *subu* (early morning prayer).[49] While these terms are not used to label men, a man who reaches the age of 35 in a rural area and 40 in an urban area and is still not married is suspected of being sexually disfunctional, *déqna tettong lasona*, a Bugis local parlance for 'his penis does not turn on', and he may be deemed *calabai* (cross-gender). Nevertheless, it is the norm for a man to search for a prospective wife who is younger than him. This is not just linked to the belief that women age more quickly than men, but also to the structural hierarchy between husband and wife, as between older brother and little sister. There is a Bugis aphorism related to the criticism of men who marry older women: 'driving an old car' (*mattonang oto toa*), the woman being the old car (*oto toa*), 'driven' by her husband. This phrase refers not just to spousal age difference, but is also a crude reference to the sexual act. The option of marrying an older woman is strongly prohibited, and such marriage, in many cases, is rejected by the family of the groom, or at least they admit her half-heartedly.

The Status of Janda/Duda

The importance of marriage for individual status is reflected in the negative valuation of divorce and loss of a spouse through death, both referred to by the term *janda*. For women, this negative valuation stems from the notion that a woman's sexuality has already been activated, and also from the fact that she has greater structural autonomy. *Hadith* (Ibn Abbas) states that 'a *janda* has more rights for herself than her guardian' (Masdar F. Mas'udi 1997:98), which means that a *janda*[50] is more independent than an old maid or a young unmarried woman in terms of what she should and should not do, and it is not obligatory to provide a representative (A. *wali*) if she remarries. To return to the problematic quality of a divorced or widowed woman's sexuality, *janda* are typically assumed to seek out sex because it has become a 'habit'.[51] There is a joke frequently uttered by males: 'it's good to marry a *janda* because she "knows how to act" (B. *makessingi ko mabbainé jandakiq nasabaq missenni kédo*), meaning that a *janda* is a good match because of her sexual experience, which reflects the negative value of *janda*, who it is assumed are not modest (*deqna malebbiq*).

In addition to widow (I. *janda ditinggal mati*), divorcee (*janda bercerai*), and young divorcee/widow (*janda kembang*), in Kulo there is a fourth type of

49 *Mangngaribi, isya* and *subu* are parallel to Indonesian terms *magrib, isya* and *subuh*.

50 The Bugis term for divorcee/widow is *balu* or *walu*, but I never heard people use this term, and they use the term *janda* instead.

51 Brenner (1998:161–166) discusses the perceived danger of autonomous Solonese female traders in relation to sexuality and money.

janda—*janda tenri telleq*—which refers to a divorcee who was not divorced.[52] This is a *janda* who is neither divorced nor widowed, but a 'married woman' who was left by her husband in a state of uncertainty (discussed further in Chapter 6). Similarly, the term *duda*, applied to men, can be differentiated into widower (*duda ditinggal mati*) and divorcee (*duda bercerai*). Since a widow (*janda ditinggal mati*) receives her designation because of the death of her husband, she gets more respect socially than a divorced woman (*janda bercerai*). A young divorcee (*janda kembang*) is usually the result of an unsuccessful arranged marriage.

Given that the transition from single to married status is so important, both my interviews and observations indicated that it is better from the individual's point of view to be a widow/divorcee (*janda*) than an old maid (B. *makkunrai ladoq*). This is because being a *janda* means that one has already experienced marriage. Despite this popular view, a woman with the status of *janda* is given less respect than an old maid, and whatever she does is often regarded as 'all wrong' (I. *serba salah*). People will talk about her as they please, and it is very easy for her to be accused of, for example, being a flirtatious woman, a woman who yearns for sex, a woman who may take someone else's husband and other negative values. To marry a *janda* is also *serba salah*, especially for an unmarried man. It is very hard for parents to accept a son's marriage to a *janda*, particularly a divorced woman (*janda bercerai*). Even if she does not have any children from her previous marriage, parents are reluctant for their son to marry such a woman. But when *janda* and *duda* are married, people will say: 'It's a perfect match' because both are reactivated sexually.

The circumstances in West Java are quite the reverse because the status of *janda* is not disgraceful; women can easily remarry a *duda* or become second wives. A woman with multiple marriages (I. *suka kawin cerai*) indicates that she is attractive to men (McDonald and Edeng Abdurahman 1974; Yasmin Al-Hadar 1977; Jones 1994). Among the Bugis, being a divorcee is already considered shameful, not to mention being a serial divorcee. This difference is because of different ideals of marriage. For Bugis, marriage is ideally a monogamous lifelong union.

Even though the statuses of *janda* and *duda* are considered shameful for both men and women, the stigma placed on *janda* is greater than that accorded to *duda*. I observed that when people were talking about a *duda*, discussion was frequently oriented towards 'who he is going to marry' or 'how he is going

52 In regard to remarriage after divorce, McDonald and Edeng Abdurrahman (1974) divided divorces in West Java into two types: divorces as the result of arranged and unconsummated marriages and 'chronic divorcers.'

to approach a prospective wife' rather than 'why did he get divorced,' or whether he is 'dangerous' as a *duda.*

A Bugis popular song entitled *Janda Callédaq é*[53] (B. A Flirtatious Divorcee) illustrates the stigmatised position of *janda.*

Janda Callédaq é	**Flirtatious Divorcee**
Nigaro asenna anrittaq?	What's your younger sister's name?
Janda callédaq é	A flirtatious divorcee
Magello tappana rita mata	Looking at her, she is beautiful
Janda callédaq é	A flirtatious divorcee
Nigaro janda callédaq é	Who is that flirtatious *janda*
Méga ro kédo-kédona	Moves so much [seductively]
Purani maggincung	She has put on her lipstick
Purani mabbeddaq	She has put on face powder
Igaro janda callédaq é	Who is that flirtatious *janda*
Micawa-cawa cabbéruq	Laughing and smiling
Napaita ro posiqna	Showing her navel
Napakédo-kédo poncinna	Shaking her hips
Kallolo pancanringengngé	A young handsome playboy
Naccoéri janda callédaq é	Following the flirtatious *janda*
Nakkutana kégakiq monro anri?	Asking where do you live younger sister?
Tomatoa cakkindiq-kindiq é	A flirtatious elder
Naddeppéri janda callédaq é	Approaching the flirtatious *janda*
Makkutana niga asetta anri	What is your name, younger sister
Janda callédaq é	A flirtatious divorcee
Asenna Sitti Bondéng	Her name is Sitti Bondéng
Anaqna Amboq Sakkaq	The daughter of Ambo Sakka
Monro ri Balang Caddi	Lives in Balang Caddi
Nigaro janda callédaq é	Who is that flirtatious divorcee
Mégaro kédo-kédona	Moves so much [seductively]
Purani ro maggincung	She has put on her lipstick
Purani ro mabbeddaq	She has put on her face powder

53 The song is written and sung by Zaenal Abidin Haz, and produced by Abadi Records. The words are taken from the transcript supplied with the cassette.

The whole song illustrates how the status of *janda* is disrespected. For example, the phrase 'flirtatious divorcee' (B. *janda callédaq é*), 'move so much [seductively]' (*maéga kédo-kédona*), 'she has put on her lipstick' (*purani maggincung*) and 'she has put on her face powder' (*purani mabbeddaq*) are typical labels for a *janda* to indicate that she is trying to attract men's attention. More than that, the lyrics 'young handsome playboy' (*kallolo paccanringengngé*) and flirtatious elder (*tomatoa cakkindiq- kindiq é*) are mentioned to counter the flirtatious behavior of *janda*, but explain to some extent that it is men's nature to seek women (for example, to approach or to flirt with *janda*).[54] The case of *Ibu* Warnidah discussed below further illustrates the extent to which a *janda* is considered to have been disgraced.

Ibu Warnidah's Story: A Janda Bercerai

Ibu Warnidah, a forty year old woman, had been a *janda* for over ten years. In the initial part of the interview, *Ibu* Warnidah first explained what kind of *janda* she was. She differentiated herself from other *janda* calling herself an unflirtatious divorcee (B. *janda déqna mangngureq*) in this way emphasising that she did not fit the stereotype.

Ibu Warnidah worked as a paddy harvester (*padderos*), and her ex-husband (Basir) was an official in the *kantor desa* (I. village office) situated not far from their house. Even though they did not have children, she described her marriage as a happy one until students from Makassar came for KKN in 1988.[55] One of the students, named Sukma, had an affair with her husband during the KKN period.

Ibu Warnidah's very public case involved not only *Ibu* Warnidah and her husband, but also her family and some community leaders in the village. She attempted to do whatever she could in order to get her husband back, including publicly slapping the young student, Sukma, but was unsuccessful. Ironically, Basir left *Ibu* Warnidah and stayed with his sister and continued his affair with the female student, even though Sukma had already left the village after completing her KKN, because he considered himself to have been shamed by *Ibu* Warnidah as a result of the slapping. In fact, this affair finally ended after *Ibu* Warnidah wrote a letter to Sukma's parents and explained what was going

54 In a seminar on 'Pornography from the Perspective of Gender Equality,' implemented by Women's Forum in collaboration with Bureau of Religious Prosperity and Women's Empowerment of South Sulawesi, on 16 January 2002, at Sedona Hotel, Makassar, a *janda* (one of the participants) begged the police (who was one of the presenters) to destroy casettes on the market which contained stigmatisations of *janda*.

55 KKN, which stands for *Kuliah Kerja Nyata*, is an obligatory rural social action internship for advanced university students over a period of three months.

on between her husband and their daughter. *Ibu* Warnidah and Basir eventually reunited. But, instead of staying in their house, they left Kulo and lived in the neighbouring village in her husband's sister's house, to save face after the shame of the incident. During that time, however, Basir had an affair with another woman who lived in the neighbouring village. *Ibu* Warnidah could no longer tolerate Basir's infidelity. She also felt that she could not compete with the new woman, who was a beautiful, rich *janda*. This illustrates to some extent that *janda* lacks respect, that *janda* can easily take someone else's husband just because she is beautiful and/or rich. There was a joke associated with this. People said: 'It is okay to marry a *janda*, as long as she is beautiful and rich.' The joke indicates that a *janda* becomes valuable solely because of her attractiveness and wealth, through which a man may enjoy and take advantage of her.

During their separation, *Ibu* Warnidah acted as if she did not want a divorce, not only because she was waiting for her husband to initiate the divorce to avoid the cost, but also because she wanted to slow down the process of Basir's second marriage. They separated for one year until Ibu Warnidah decided to get a divorce on the advice of her family. During this time *Ibu* Warnidah was travelling to and from Malaysia to make a living. As soon as she got a divorce in 1990, she went to Malaysia and decided to live there permanently; while her ex-husband married the *janda*.

But every time *Ibu* Warnidah visited the village, her ex-husband always came to see her without his second wife's knowledge. In 2000, Basir begged her to remarry him, promised to change his behaviour and never to leave her. People suspected that this was probably because he did not have any children from his second marriage either. But when I asked *Ibu* Warnidah about Basir's desire to remarry her, she said it was because his second wife did not 'serve' him (*déqna issengngi moloi lakkainna*) as well as *Ibu* Warnidah had. If the former were true, this man was infertile. But in the village, infertility is blamed on the woman, as I observed that it was a woman who was expected to seek treatment, as *Ibu* Warnidah had done during her marriage. If the latter were the case, *Ibu* Warnidah's family suspected he would find another woman in the future.

Ibu Warnidah agreed to remarry as long as Basir divorced his second wife. This resulted in tension between *Ibu* Warnidah and her family. She was considered 'too easy' on Basir given that she could easily forgive what he had done to her. Despite endless tension with her family as well as community concerns, I was told when I revisited the village in January 2002 that they finally remarried in Malaysia in 2001, eleven years after the divorce, though without Basir first divorcing his second wife. People commented that it was because they were fated to be a couple (*jodoh*) that made them reunite, noting the effort *Ibu*

Warnidah's family had made to prevent *Ibu* Warnidah from remarrying Basir. I could see the happiness of this fated couple when I spent the night in their house on my way to Tawau (Sabah, Malaysia) for fieldwork in 2007. I shall return to discuss remarrying according to the Marriage Law in Chapter 6.

When I asked her primary motive for remarrying Basir. She replied quickly that she still loved him deep in her heart, and realised that her husband did not have any children from his second wife, assuring her that the absence of offspring was not solely because of her infertility. This reflects the burden of lack of children on women (see Parker 1989:356). She said that she had to balance his good and bad attitudes, and the only mistake he had made during their marriage was his infidelity. But, most of all, she was sick of being a *janda*. As she said: 'Even though I was not a flirtatious *janda*, it was still better to have a husband'. Her point of view exemplifies women's fear of the position of *janda*, and underscores the importance of marriage for women in particular.

Types of Marriage

In South Sulawesi, marriages vary according to how they are brought about. Marriage for the Bugis includes marriage by proposal, either arranged marriage or free-choice marriage; and marriage by elopement (B. *silariang*), abduction (*rilariang*) and giving herself (*najjuluang aléna*).[56]

Marriage by Proposal

Marriage by proposal consists of arranged marriage and free-choice marriage.

Arranged Marriage

There are various forms of arranged marriage. The first type is a marriage arranged by the two sets of parents without the girl's consent, essentially a forced marriage. This type of marriage is particularly common if the parents are from a wealthy family. In a forced marriage, the girl is usually reluctant to prepare herself for the nuptials.

An arranged marriage, however, is not always forced. While there are arranged marriages in which the girl is forced to marry a man against her will, others take their feelings and preferences into account. Arranged marriages may occur either within the kinship group or outside the circle of kinship. In the latter case, marriages are commonly arranged between children of

56 Sila (2002:8) discusses three types of shameful marriages (M. *annyala*) among the Makassar *sayyid* community in Cikoang: *silariang, nilariang* and *erangkalé*.

colleagues or business partners. Such arrangements are attempted to form both a successful couple and to establish economic ties (see Robinson 1986:216 and 1999:258), as well as to preserve status-matching between the two families.

Arranged marriage among Madurese has been well described by Niehof (1985:Chapter IV) based on her fieldwork between 1977 and 1979. She found that most marriages were arranged by parents with variation in different areas as to whether the marriage is organised between kin or non-kin.[57] Other studies, located in Central and West Java, indicate that 67 to 70 percent of the marriages of female respondents were arranged by their parents in the early 1970s and 1980s (Chapon 1976: Table 10; Tim Peneliti 1988: Table 13). While Niehof's ethnographic as well as demographic study found that kinship ties, the reputation of the family and social class are the bases of arranged marriages, Chapon and Tim Peneliti looked at the differential effects of demographic dimensions (for example, age, economic status, education) of parentally arranged marriages in Central and West Java.

Based on a focus group discussion with young people in Kulo, it appears that arranged marriages, though they still exist, may not be as prevalent as they used to be due to the desire to attend school and to participate in the work force. Young men and women refuse this kind of arrangement (usually among their kin) for various reasons. First, marriage within extended family may not expand the kinship networks (B. *asséajingeng*). Romantic love is another reason to refuse an arranged marriage. One young woman stated: 'I cannot imagine how to live (read: sleep) with a stranger if I get married with someone I don't love (*silori*) or someone I don't know'. Others explained that getting married with kin (*séajing*) is similar to marrying one's brother/sister, particularly between first cousins because they considered it is too close or in Pelras's term 'too hot' (Pelras 1996:154). While arranged marriage still exists, marriages between first cousins, though in favour for nobles, appear to be very rare in contemporary Bugis society. The following story illustrates the case of a forced arranged marriage.

Hartati's Unsuccessful Arranged Marriage

Hartati was a seventeen-year old, thin and depressed girl who called herself the victim of an arranged and early marriage where I met her in the Pengadilan Agama Sidrap. She stated:

57 For example, in Potandu 72.5 percent of marriage was arranged between non-kins, and 48.9 percent of arranged marriage in Tamben was between kins (Niehof 1985:112).

> I was married to my second cousin, Rasyid, when I was 15 years old, when I had not even finished my Junior High School. He worked as a gold retailer in Kupang (West Timor). I still wanted to play with friends of my age, but I could not refuse my mother's decision because I was afraid to commit a sin. When we were married, he never persuaded me to accept him. When we lived together in my mother's house for eight months, my marriage had still not been consummated. For me it was important because we did not know each other until we got married. My mother was trying to sustain our relationship, but she did not know what I wanted, and she never asked me, while I was too ashamed to talk about it. That was why the problem was never solved.
>
> HARTATI, 17 Years, Junior High School, housewife, divorced, no children, interviewed on 2 March 2000

After eight months of unsuccessful marriage, her husband finally left since it was shameful to stay with his wife while he felt that he was not 'accepted' as a husband. They had been separated for over two years at the time of interview. Instead of examining what happened, Hartati's mother and family even accused her of being the one who caused their shame (B. *mappakasiriq-siriq*) because she was abandoned by her husband, regardless of the reason. The action of her husband was even justified by her family. Accordingly, Hartati felt that no one stood up for her, she had no one to share her feelings with, not even a friend because she was not allowed to go out in view of her uncertain status after her separation. Her family was trying to arrange a divorce, expecting her to get married soon in order to save the honour of the family (her further story is discussed in Chapter 6).

Since consideration of women's views is not regarded as important in an arranged marriage, women tend to become the 'victims' of this arrangement. In spite of the fact that young people dislike arranged marriages, it is still difficult to refuse parents' wishes, especially when the youths still live in the village, have discontinued their education and/or are jobless. Refusing their parents is believed to be sinful act (I. *berdosa*) that may affect one's future life. A girl is usually warned that she may find it difficult to find a partner or may experience an unhappy marriage later if she refuses the marriage her parents seek to arrange. Hence, following the parents' behest is a way of avoiding sin (*dosa*), but with the expectation that later the girl may get divorced. When I was returning from the Pengadilan Agama Sidrap one afternoon in a minibus (*pété-pété*), I overheard a girl talking to her friend about her parents who had arranged her marriage with someone she didn't know. She said: 'I do not want to get married yet, but I am afraid to refuse my parents' behest, afraid to be sinful and damned (*kualat*).

A young man who comes from a family accustomed to arranged marriages, however, may still have a chance to choose his partner based on his parents' consent. For example, a young man said: 'I can choose a girl from all the prospective girls shown to me.'

The second type of arranged marriage by proposal is when a young man asks his parents to arrange his marriage with someone he likes and/or intends to marry with the consent of the girl. When the girl is still very young, she is 'reserved' (B. *ritaro*) for him until she is considered mature enough to be a wife or they accept marriage beforehand (*kawissoroq*), which is like suspended marriage (I. *kawin gantung*) for Sundanese, Javanese and Maduresе (McDonald and Edeng Abdurahman 1974; Hull and Hull 1987; Jones 1994 and 2001; Niehof 1985). For the Bugis, when a girl has been 'reserved' (B. *ritaro*) since childhood, she has to be secluded to protect her from any behaviour that may adversely affect her following her first menstruation. In marriage beforehand (*kawissoroq*), legalization of marriage (A. *akad nikah*) is performed, accompanied by the Bugis ritual of presenting 'rice and palm sugar sauce' (B. *palopo*),[58] and bridewealth (see Millar 1989:75–76).

These marriages are not consummated until the two families decide that the couple is able to live together as a married couple. During the seclusion and waiting periods, the girl is trained by her mother to be a wife, including how to manage domestic activities. While in rural areas, the girl who has been 'reserved' usually discontinues her education, in urban areas, the girl generally continues her education.[59]

In Kulo, in particular, *kawissoroq* may take place nowadays because the day of the *akad nikah* and wedding party is not on the same day, usually because of the consideration of 'good day and time' (B. *mattanra esso*) for the ritual. I asked Ibu Masriah (a local *pattanra esso*, day decider, see Plate 3.1) to explain the basis for deciding the day and time according to her *lontaraq* calendar. She said that

58 Rice (made from sticky rice) symbolises the spirit of life and palm sugar sauce (made from brown sugar and coconut milk which is sweet and delicious) symbolises good fortune and happiness. This type of 'main refreshment' is usually served in Bugis rituals, such as marriage, birthing, circumcision or Idul Fitri, the celebration of Fasting Month.

59 Hull and Hull's (1987:108) finding in Java illustrates that *kawin gantung* is to give time for the parents to accumulate money for a more elaborated wedding party, in addition to separation because of study commitment or work, as well as the inavailability of housing. Niehof's (1985:111) study in Madura indicates that *kawin gantung* aims to protect the girl against premarital sexual relations. Similarly Jones (2001:72) analyses the relationship between *kawin gantung* and non-consummation in Java, he found that there was a short delay in initiation of sexual relation, that is no longer than one year in most cases, and, in fact, first sexual relations at very young age still occured.

PLATE 3.1 *The day decider, Ibu Masriah*

Monday (*Asénéng*) between 11 and 12 o'clock (*tangngasso*) is an instance of a good day and time for legalization of marriage (I. *nikah*), with a sign of a 'square,' on the calendar indicating the 'spirit of life.' It is believed that the couple will have a virtuous life if this day and time are chosen. But the sign on the calendar between 6 p.m. and 8 p.m. on that day (usually the time for a wedding reception to begin) was a 'circle' or 'hole' (B. *lobbang*) which means 'empty', any activity at this time resulting in 'bad' fortune.[60] Thus, instead of using the same day for the *nikah* and the wedding reception, they choose another auspicious day and time.

Aside from this calendar, Tuesday (B. *Salasa*) is believed to be a 'bad day', based on the name of the day—*Salasa*—due to fear that the ritual may be in disarray (*massala-salang*). During the period between the day of *nikah* and the day of the wedding party, the marriage remains unconsummated.[61]

Regardless of whether it is a 'good day' (*esso makessing*) or 'bad day' (*esso majaq*), both *ritaro* and *kawissoroq* are, to some extent, very risky, especially if

60 Interview with Ibu Masriah (1-8-2002).

61 Hull and Hull (1987) analyse the relationship between an arranged marriage or free-choice marriage and consummation of marriage. In the former case, consummation delay frequently took place, while in the latter case the marriage couple usually consummate the marriage without delay unless there are some pragmatic reasons to suspend (for example, work or study commitment).

either bride or groom becomes interested in someone else during the seclusion and waiting periods. Such an interest threatens to transgress the *siriq* of both sides, especially if the girl is unwilling to carry on with the arrangement. In the *ritaro* state, the two families may resolve the problem peacefully or it may end with conflict between them. However, in *kawissoroq*, the circumstance is more complicated because they also have to deal with the Pengadilan Agama in order to divorce the young pair.

But there are cases in which an arranged marriage is successful. The couple stay married and live happily. The following story exemplifies a successful arranged marriage.

Mustari's Successful 'Modern' Arranged Marriage

In contemporary Bugis society, arranged marriage can be modified into a 'modern' arrangement, that is, a marriage arranged with the consent of both parties. The marriage of Mustari and Eni is an instance of this type of arrangement, initiated by the girl's relatives without resulting in shame to the female side.

Mustari (35 years) is a young retailer who traded between Kulo and Malaysia selling various kinds of clothes and bedding from Makassar. He used to study at a university in Makassar, but discontinued his education as he was more interested in making his own living and felt that continuing his study did not guarantee he would find a job related to his education.

Mustari did not have a girlfriend at the time of my fieldwork, but his father (his mother had passed away a few years before) as well as his elder sister kept asking him to get married. His father thought that he was already able to 'surround the kitchen seven times' (B. *mattuliling dapureng wékka pétu*) and was afraid that he would not be able to witness his son's wedding if Mustari waited much longer. Most of all, Mustari had reached the age of thirty-five, and he was afraid that people would start suspecting about his single status.

His elder sister, *Ibu* Darma (*Pak* Bakri's wife), helped Mustari's father to find a prospective wife for him. Her son's mother-in-law (*baiseng*), *Haji* Ramlah, 'offered' her niece, Eni (18 years) whom she considered able to 'face' her husband (*moloi lakkainna*) since she had been at home for over a year after quitting school. Mustari was shown Eni's picture, and vice versa. *Haji* Ramlah said that Eni agreed to marry him, but Mustari was unsure as to whether to proceed because he had only the word of *Haji* Ramlah that the girl was willing. Mustari finally decided to marry her only after he met her and made sure that the girl wanted to get married. When I asked Mustari why he had to wait for a year to decide to marry her, he said that he did not want to take the risk of an unsuccessful marriage because it was not just shameful, but also a waste of money and time. Eni, on the other

PLATE 3.2 *A happy arranged marriage couple, Mustari and Eni*

hand, agreed to marry Mustari because he already had a job as a successful young retailer and she considered she was ready to get married (see Plate 3.2). The 'modern' arrangement of this marriage could be observed from their relationship before marriage; Eni along with Mustari went to buy all their marriage gifts in Makassar without being accompanied by her siblings.

Mustari finally married Eni with a full feast in Kulo and had their honeymoon (I. *bulan madu*) in Malaysia for a few weeks. This indicates the 'modern life style' of Mustari since *bulan madu* is not common among village people. They now live happily, even though Mustari has to leave her sometimes because of his job as a retailer. Mustari's case illustrates that despite the fact that his wife was willing to marry him, he himself was afraid of the risk of an unsuccessful arranged marriage. Otherwise, he would have had a free-choice marriage.

Free-Choice Marriage

> In a community where marriage was once a family affair, the arrangement of a marriage by two families taking account of the need to establish a harmonious and economically viable household, the young are now in the grip of a desire for free choice marriage based on romantic love.
>
> ROBINSON 2000b:158

Marriage with one's own sweetheart (B. *canring*) is now common among the Bugis, both in urban and rural areas. Free-choice marriage may occur with or without parental agreement, which can be seen as an 'advance in personal autonomy,' but in such circumstances the bride and the groom take more risks in the marriage (Robinson 1999:258). Although this type of marriage is not favoured by parents in Kulo, it is acceptable in some circumstances because, for instance, of the children's opportunity for education. Another reason is that parents avoid the future risk of an arranged marriage being unsuccessful, since the bride and the groom bear the risk (Robinson 1999:258).

In Kulo, despite the fact that parents allow their children to marry their sweethearts, they are usually reluctant to see their daughters dating openly in order to avoid gossip. Pubescent girls are usually advised to carefully guard themselves (B. *matutui aléna*). They are told not to be too hasty and aggressive when they are in love, because such a relationship will become flat (*makemmé*) when they get married, the love having 'run out' during the dating period. Such a marriage is said to be a 'short-lasting marriage', and is related to the Bugis saying: 'If it is easy to get you, it is also easy to throw you away' (*nakko magampakko ritangkeq, magampang tokko riabbéang*) which indicates the importance of being careful (*makkalitutu*) in regard to dating.

The marriage of my host's elder daughter, Rapiah (to Arief), and elder son, Aco (to Mina), were instances of free-choice marriages in Kulo. Neither lived with their parents because they sought further education in Makassar (the capital city of South Sulawesi) and in Kendari (Southeast Sulawesi) respectively. They both found their own match outside their kinship group. While Rapiah arranged all the requirements for marriage, including the amount of 'spending money' (*duiq ménréq*) the man's side should bring, Aco first had to consult his parents, given that they would have to prepare the spending money as a result of his inability to provide it himself.

Before sending delegates to Rapiah's family for the marriage proposal, Rapiah's prospective mother-in-law (Arief's mother) asked her to meet and discuss the spending money without first asking her parents' consent (her prospective father-in-law lived in West Papua and had married another woman). The prospective mother-in-law suggested a certain amount of spending money, while Rapiah told her the amount of money she expected to be brought. There was a tension between them at the time of discussion. According to Arief's mother, the amount of mothey she offered was standard spending money in her village (Maros) which was Rp3,000,000 (US$300 at current exchange rates), while Rapiah claimed that the amount offered was lower than the standard spending money in her village (Kulo) in 1997. The solution was that they came to a compromise and agreed that the amount should be half way between the two, mediated by Arief. They also agreed what kind of wedding gifts should be brought. Then, Rapiah informed her parents to accept whatever had been decided between her and Arief's mother without any objection. This kind of procedure indicates Rapiah's personal autonomy concerning her marriage and that any matter related to it was accepted by her parents.

Both arranged and free-choice marriages are always preceded by the presentation of a proposal (B. *madduta*). In both types of marriage, there is a ritual at the end of the ceremony in Bugis marriage called *mappasiéwa ada* (appeasing), a term derived from the two words *siéwa* (mutually) and *ada* (utterance) which carries the sense in English of talking to each other.[62]

In a 'traditional' arranged marriage, the role of the ritual is to introduce the bride to the groom and to encourage them to talk to each other. In practice, however, they are not expected to talk to each other to show their honour (*alebbireng*).

While in a 'traditional' arranged marriage, such ritual is vital, especially if the girl does not know her husband prior to marriage, in a free-choice marriage, such ritual is held to conclude formally the whole ritual in marriage ceremony. This ritual cannot be implemented in marriages other than arranged and free-choice marriages, such as marriage by elopement (*silariang*), abduction (*rilariang*) or bringing herself (*najjuluang aléna*).

Marriage by Silariang, Rilariang *and* Najjuluang Aléna

For the Bugis (and Makassarese), there are three types of elopement (*kawin lari*): (1) elopement with the mutual agreement of the individuals concerned (*silariang*); (2) a woman is carried off by a man without her consent (*rilariang*); and (3) a woman brings herself to a man in order to be married (*najjuluang aléna*). Although these categories of marriage exist in Bugis society, the most common type of marriage today is free-choice.

The three forms of elopements—*silariang, rilariang* and *najjuluang aléna*—initially involve, in Leach's words, 'persons acting as private individuals' (Leach 1961), whether or not they will have a reconciliation (*maddeceng*), derived from the word goodness (*décéng*), in the near future.

Informants explained that elopements (I. *kawin lari*)—*silariang, rilariang* or *najjuluang aléna*—are based on love (*cinta*), or in more radical terms 'excessive love' (*terlalu cinta, cinta mati*), either romantic love or unrequited love (*cinta bertepuk sebelah tangan*).

62 In a similar account, Chabot (1996:226) discusses *pabbajikang* as a ritual to appease the bride and the groom for their refusal to consummate an arranged marriage.

Silariang

Silariang is an offence against Bugis custom (adat), Islam and state laws. *Silariang* is against adat law because a marriage, according to Bugis adat, has to be preceded by a proposal (*madduta*) and other customary requirements. It is against Islam, because in Islam, marriage should not only be preceded by making a proposal (I. *peminangan*), but also should meet essential principles (A. *rukun*) and prerequisites (*syarat*), discussed in greater detail in Chapter 6. It is against state law as it is regarded as a kidnapping, if the family of the bride reports the case to the police.

Given that *silariang* takes place between a man and a woman with mutual consent, they are both at risk of being killed by their families. In the capital city of Makassar, the eloping couple, called *to massala* (B. the ones who are *silariang*, M. *tomanynyaqlaq*) usually go to the closest *imam* (I. the person who officiates at an Islamic wedding ritual), whether or not the *imam* is legal, or find a safe place to protect themselves from family anger. The *imam* tries to look for some consensus to solve the problem since the consent of the woman's representative (A. *wali*) is required under Islamic law. The *wali* of a *silariang* woman usually allows the *imam* to do whatever he pleases in order to avoid being connected to any shame related to the bride. When there is a hint of negotiation from the woman's side, the *imam*—who at this stage becomes the go-between—will get in touch with the family in order to marry the couple in the ordinary way. Another way to try to maintain *siriq* is through reconciliation (B. *maddéceng*). *Maddéceng* usually takes place a few years after elopement or when the couple already has offspring. In such a case, the children are the 'instruments' to persuade their parents, through a go-between, to accept the marriage. The go-between may be a respected member of the family or a person (for example, friend) who is known by both families, so she/he can negotiate between the two families using customary procedures. For the middle class, this is usually followed by a reconciliation feast (*pesta maddéceng*) to celebrate the fact that the couple have been accepted back into the family.

Silariang may occur for three reasons. The first is to avoid a forced marriage by parents due to the fact that the girl has her own sweetheart (*canring*). This may happen before or after her sweetheart proposes. The former takes place when the man thinks that it is not possible to propose since the women's parents are in negotiation with another man and may refuse to agree with the man their daughter wishes to marry. The latter option is chosen after a proposal has been refused. When the first alternative is chosen, that is, before the presentation of a proposal (*madduta massuro*), the man's side is blamed. The woman's side will say: 'He has never proposed to the girl'. On the other hand, the second choice may seem to be a 'good' reason for them to commit *silariang*. It is difficult to say whether it is better to propose than do nothing before *silariang* becomes an option, since *silariang* will be followed by tension and dangerous acts (for example, killing) on both sides as the result of *siriq*. Indeed, refusing a proposal also results in *siriq* on the groom's side.

The second reason for *silariang* is a difference in status between a man and a woman.[63] A woman's high status may lead to rejection of the proposal of a man of lower status.[64] The usual comment was that the status of the man and the woman did not match (*déqna siratang*). 'Buying blood' (*mangngelli dara*) may become a solution if the family on the woman's side agrees to negotiate. A problem may arise when the man's side cannot afford to pay for 'buying blood' to recompense his lower status.

The other reason for *silariang* is because the man's family cannot afford the part of the bridewealth, that is, the spending money (*duiq ménréq*), as a Bugis marriage is accompanied by the presentation of a bridewealth by the man's side to the woman's side (Pelras 1996:155–156). High bridewealth is best illustrated in La Galigo epic. The bridewealth of I Wé Cuqdai given by Sawérigading took three months to carry from the ship to the land, reflecting the quantity of the bridewealth (Kern 1989:223). To the outsider, Bugis bridewealth may seem to be the 'purchase' of a woman. The Bugis themselves, however, perceive this bridewealth as an honour for the woman and her family based on the assumption that a woman cannot be obtained as easily as a wild woman on the street. High bridewealth is also used as an admonition that marriage is not as easy to turn as the palm of one's hand. It is expected that when the spouses are in conflict, the couple will think thoroughly before breaking their marriage up. In other words, high bridewealth is one of the bases of marital stability.

A high bridewealth may also be used as a strategy to refuse a lower status man's proposal[65] in order to sustain social status and prestige. The sum of

---

63 Chabot (1996:242) in his study of the neighbouring Makassarese in the 1940s wrote that women's parents may refuse to give the *imam* the right to act as a *wali* (A. ritual guardian of the bride in a paternal line) for a *silariang* (B. elopement) if she is found in a forbidden contact situation with a man of a lower status. Taking the woman back is preferred, since allowing her to marry a man of a lower status results in even more *siriq*.

64 See Pelras (1996) and Millar (1983 and 1989) concerning social status in relation to Bugis marriage.

65 A man of a lower rank may be asked to bring high bridewealth, which is thought cannot be afforded, as a way to reject the proposal. However, there is a possibility that a man, because of his lower rank and the high possibility of denial, provides a high bridewealth in order to surprise the woman's family and to counterbalance his lower status, which is expressed in Indonesian: *terima tidak terima* (accept or not really accepting [the proposal]), indicating that he can afford the high bridewealth.

money for the bridewealth varies from one family to another, depending on the descent rank, wealth, and/or level of education (Millar 1989). In addition, when a woman performs the pilgrimage to Mecca (I. *hajjah*) at her father's expense, this may count in the bridewealth because the parents consider as an addition to her status, particularly for a new *hajjah*. When a man is going to propose to a *hajjah*, a forewarning takes place so he can take into consideration the intended bridewealth. Such a case usually becomes the topic of interesting gossip among the community, expressed as: 'He will be asked for a high bridewealth because the woman is a *hajjah* (B. *ritangngi maega, nasabaq hajjiwi makkunraié*). There is a joke related to this that a man who marries a *hajjah* does not have to perform pilgrimage to Mecca because he will *naik haji* (means performing pilgrimage to Mecca) by being her husband. But, in this sense *naik haji* refers to the husband who climbs on top of his wife's body to engage in sexual intercourse in top-husband/down-wife position.

Millar (1989:101) argues that the process of determinating the amount of bridewealth is like a game. The bridewealth is sometimes not disclosed by the woman's party in an attempt to sustain their prestige. The man's side, on the other hand, refrains from asking in order to avoid any suspicion about their ability to satisfy the other party's expectation and to find the most appropriate status for their children. In this regard, the question may arise: how do they determine the bridewealth? Usually, the man's side examines the woman's side in terms of the woman's descent rank and achieved status and/or finds out the amount of bridewealth previously given to her sister, which must be more than the bridewealth given to her. In the past, the bridewealth of one's daughter was based on her mother's bridewealth. Both sides try to demonstrate their best, but avoid offending the other side because it involves the social position of both sides. In spite of Bugis high bridewealth, the cost of marriage by elopement (*silariang*) in South Sulawesi is usually lower than that of customary marriage or even nil.[66]

66 A local newspaper reported a case of *silariang* in Desa Libureng (Bone) and its consequence. The couple got married by elopement in Luwu at the end of 1999. Six months later they revealed to the woman's family their intention to *maddéceng* (B. reconcile). Fortunately, the idea of *maddéceng* was approved. The couple went back peacefully to the woman's family in Bone, and it was suggested they report to *kepala desa* (I. village head) in regard to their return and to arrange a letter related to *surat nikah* (marriage certificate) which indicates that the couple got married by *kawin liar*. But, the *kepala desa* demanded Rp. 2,500,000 (approximately US$280 at current exchange rates) as a penalty of their *silariang* that had resulted in shame not only to their family, but also to the community of the village. If they did not pay, the couple and the family of both sides would have to leave the village and they would not be allowed to enter the village unless the *kepala desa*

Unlike marriage by elopement (I. *kawin lari*) in Mataram and marriage by capture (*ngerorod*) in Bali, *silariang* in Bugis does not unquestionably result in a family's ultimate acquiescence. While the implementation of *kawin lari* and *ngerorod* are 'tolerated' by the Sasak of Mataram and Balinese local adat respectively, and is sometimes encouraged, *silariang* in Bugis is the reverse.[67] *Silariang* is a shame as well as a solution. It is regarded as shame because it does not follow the customary procedure of marriage, and 'solution' because it is an alternative way to get married whether or not the couple subsequently marry legally.

In Sidrap, I heard of several cases of *silariang*, but the *to massala* chose to go to an *imam liar*, a term that literally means 'wild' *imam* but indicates an illegal *imam* instead, and asked him to marry them by *kawin liar* (illegal marriage).[68] However, the number of cases of *silariang* by *kawin liar* cannot be counted since such a marriage is not registered by the *imam liar*. He is reluctant to register the marriage because, as an *imam liar* said: 'It's illegal according to the state, so it is pointless to have a marriage registration.' But he told me that many of his clients are a result of elopement (B. *silariang*) and abduction (*rilariang*).[69]

Rilariang

Similar to *silariang*, abduction, termed *rilariang*, is a kind of shameful marriage. However, abduction occurs against a woman's will. A woman is usually forced to accept *rilariang* because a man is in love with her, but he receives no love in return. An example of this is Ramlah's case, a young woman I interviewed in the Detention Centre (Lembaga Pemasyarakatan, LP) in Pare-Pare who had been *rilariang* by Burhan, a close friend of her husband. Her story is as follows.

Ramlah's Story: A Case of Rilariang

Ramlah was a 19 year old married woman whose husband Sapri was in Malaysia to make a living. Burhan, who lived in the same house with her, that is, her mother-in-law's house, asked her to accompany him to a wedding party of his family in a village far from Pare-Pare. Ramlah refused at first because her

---

stepped down. Afraid of the threat, they paid the penalty, but the *kepala desa* refused to sign a proof of payment (*Fajar*, 9-6-2000).

67 For a detailed discussion on *kawin lari* in Mataram, see, for example, Bennett (2002: 205–216); and for *ngerorod* in Bali, see Boon (1977:121–124).

68 *Imam liar* and *kawin liar* are discussed in Chapter 6.

69 Interview with *imam liar* Desa Mario, Kecamatan Kulo, Kabupaten Sidrap on 1-8-2002.

mother-in-law could not accompany them, but her mother-in-law asked her to go with Burhan to be the family representative of Sapri at the wedding. Finally, she agreed to go as she felt that Burhan was her husband's close friend and had thus become part of her husband's family. She never realised that Burhan had been in love with her since her husband left for Malaysia. She did not realise that Burhan was taking this trip as an opportunity to try to seduce her.

After two days, they went back to Pare-Pare and Burhan fell more in love with her. As he knew that Ramlah had refused him, he arranged a scenario under the supervision of his traditional healer (B. *sanro*) in order to attract Ramlah's attention. Love magic, symbolised by *simaq*[70] was given to Ramlah by force. According to his *dukun*, the only way to take her was by *rilariang*. Later, Ramlah realised that she had been bewitched (*risanroi*) when a neighbour saw smoke accidentally coming out from the house like a light one night, and perceived it was a sign of magic, as a result of *cinta ritollaq, sanro maqgauq* (traditional healer acts as love is refused).

The following day, Ramlah was forced to follow Burhan to Makassar, a big city she had never visited before. She was forcefully abducted and left with nothing but the clothes she was wearing. In Makassar, Ramlah stayed in Burhan's sister's house, watched over by Burhan's sister and brother-in-law. She was 'married off' the following day, without her consent by an *imam liar* in Makassar. There were only three of them: the *imam*, Burhan and Ramlah. She was shown a piece of paper, a 'marriage certificate' (*sureq nikka*), that was different from what she got with her first husband, and was told that they were officially 'husband and wife'. Though she realised that this marriage was strange, she could not get away. She was trapped and under intimidation during the *rilariang* period. Following a threat to report him to the police by Ramlah's mother, Burhan brought Ramlah to Kolaka (Southeast Sulawesi) in order to get her away from her family.

Once she was left at the house in Kolaka, she used the opportunity to call her mother-in-law in Pare-Pare to clear up the situation, but did not find her at home. Further, she was informed by her husband's family that her husband, Sapri, had come back from Malaysia after being informed that his wife had been abducted by Burhan. She was not expected back since her husband was going to get a 'second wife' with his family at his mother's behest to save face from *siriq* (*massampo siriq*). She called her mother and told her where she was. Her mother then sent someone to pick her up in Kolaka, but she was afraid to

70 *Simaq*, a symbol of love magic from a traditional healer, is a small square shape, covered with black material. It is believed that when a person touches this object, s/he will fall in love with the one who applied this magic.

leave for two reasons. First, she had been away with Burhan, who she considered as an illegal husband for over a month and forcefully consummated the 'marriage.' Second, she was afraid to face the reality if her first husband married another woman.

Following the failure of her first delegate, Ramlah's mother came accompanied by a policeman to pick her up, Burhan was arrested for a crime against morals (I. *kejahatan kesusilaan*, GOI Chapter XIV:297), and Ramlah and her mother returned to Pare-Pare. However, the following day, Ramlah was also arrested for the same crime, having been reported by her husband for elopement (*silariang*) instead of abduction (*rilariang*).

When the interview was conducted, she had been held for two months in house detention at the subdistrict level (I. *Sektor*), one month in an office of the counsel for the prosecution (*kejaksaan*)—detainees are kept here when the *Sektor* is full,[71] and one month under house arrest (*tahanan rumah*), all in Pare-Pare. She was then released after her first-husband withdrew the accusation. Sapri refused to take a second wife after Ramlah explained the real situation. Though her husband often visited her in jail as well as in her mother's house, Sapri had not taken her to his mother's house, waiting until his mother became cool, and accepted that she had been the victim of these series of events.

Later she was asked to be a witness in court for the case against Burhan, but she was again sentenced to jail in Pare-Pare, accused of a similar crime as Burhan. Ramlah was accused on this occasion because she was regarded as 'having two husbands' at the same time. According to Bugis culture, based on Islamic teaching, a woman must not be involved in a polyandrous marriage since in such a marriage, the father of any baby born cannot be identified. The accusation was similar to the first, though it was not clear who had made the complaint, she said. Instead of explaining why she had to be arrested for the second time, the attorney equivocated saying: 'You just have to undergo this situation, it is only for a week, then you will be released' (4 December 2000). This situation reflects the fragility of the law, particularly for ordinary people like Ramlah, who are ignorant in regard to law. Ramlah is not just a victim of an illegal marriage (*kawin liar*), but also of the law. Burhan, on the other hand, was convicted and imprisoned. Even though I happened to see him from a distance in jail in Pare-Pare while he was on a break with other prisoners, I was not allowed to talk to him for security reasons.

---

71 *Kejaksaan* is an office of the counsel for the prosecution. Detainees are kept here when the *Sektor* is full, under entrusted status.

Sapri had promised to have an adat ceremony when Ramlah was released from jail in order to clear up the previous disgrace. In this case, he felt obliged to protect his wife and his in-laws' *siriq* as well as his family *siriq* because his emotional attachment to his in-laws would directly influence his own face in the community.

In *rilariang* cases, the union may or may not work out. In Ramlah's case, she finally separated from Burhan, since she had never consented to the union, and unfortunately she was forced to have sex with Burhan during the period of the abduction because Burhan told her that they were 'legally' married.

In Kulo, I was told that there was also a case of *rilariang* when I revisited the village at the end of 2002. A girl, Emma, was *rilariang* by her boyfriend, Karim. Afraid of her family's anger, she was reluctant to go home unless he married her. The families of both Emma and Karim looked for them for days. Karim's family were afraid that he was at risk of being killed. If the couple were caught, they would probably be killed because of *siriq*. But the problem was mediated by a community figure (I. *tokoh masyarakat*). When they were found, the families of both sides, along with the *tokoh masyarakat*, deliberated over the problem and came to the conclusion that the couple had to be married. Regardless of whether or not they had premarital sex, the boy had to marry her, otherwise it would be difficult for the girl to find a prospective husband in the future. They finally got married, though not with a full feast.

According to *imam liar* Desa Mario, there were also many cases in which the girl was forced by her boyfriend to 'run' and be married by the *imam liar*. In such cases, the girl had to accept the marriage and remain in a state of fear since she was afraid of her family's anger.

Najjuluang Aléna

Najjuluang aléna is a gendered term for another kind of shameful marriage, which is directed at a woman who brings herself to a man in order to be married, and not the reverse. *Najjuluang aléna* is closely related to the Bugis phrase *botting tenri sompa*, which means a marriage which occurs without bridewealth. In the context of Bugis marriage, *najjuluang aléna* is regarded as the most disgraceful type of marriage because the woman takes herself to the man whom she expects to marry her.

There are many possible factors contributing to a woman's interest in this type of marriage. A woman may wish to acquire good descent from a man because of his nobility, piety, or other qualities. But the most common reason is that a woman expects to attain protection from a man with whom she may feel secure. *Najjuluang aléna* may become an option when a woman is forced by her parents to marry another man who is not her sweetheart. Still another reason is the unwillingness of a man to marry her if they have already had premarital relations. For the woman, *najjuluang aléna* is a way to protect herself from her family's anger. In such a case, a man will face a difficult situation because, like it or not, he has to marry her. A very common reason for this type of marriage is because a woman gets pregnant (B. *mattampuq*). In the phrase *anré riolo, baca rimunri* which means 'eat' first, 'read' later, and refers to sex prior to marriage, *anré* refers to premarital sexual relations and *baca* signifies legalisation and celebration of the marriage. This saying carries the connotation that a woman has premarital sex with a man who has not yet become her husband.

The situation is even worse and more complicated if the man refuses to marry the woman, and she has nowhere to go. In such a case, she not only faces *siriq* towards her own family and surrounding community, but also towards the man himself. Her family may even blame her as she is considered to be 'too cheap'. In public, she may show admirable behaviour, but there is a bad course of action behind the scenes, only discovered as her pregnancy, for instance, becomes visible. This is usually expressed by an Indonesian saying: *diam-diam makan di dalam* (quietly eat inside) which means that she seems to surprise others with her wrong doing because she is known as a good girl (I. *gadis baik-baik*; B. *anaq dara malebbiq*). While this physical evidence later becomes an object of gossip in society, the man does not experience a similar social stigma.

In spite of the fact that I never heard a case of *najjuluang aléna* (with the exception of Nadirah's specific case discussed in Chapter 2), I was told by *imam liar* Desa Mario that some of his clients came to him because of this kind of elopement.

A local daily newspaper reported that the most common crime in Pare-Pare (see Map 1.2) was *silariang*. Although this newspaper did not publish the total number of cases reported, it was predicted that there were more cases than had actually been reported. The head of the city police of Pare-Pare, JR Sitinjak, pointed out that *silariang* had recently been reported more frequently in Pare-Pare (*Fajar*, 15 January 2002). In the past, such cases were rarely reported to the police, especially because *silariang* was regarded as transgressing family *siriq*.

Cases reported to the police consisted of two main types. In the first type, parents reported that their daughter has been carried off (*rilariang*) by her partner or eloped (*silariang*). Despite the fact that *najjuluang aléna* is not included in the report. It might be possible that this type of marriage was classified by the police as either *rilariang* or *silariang*.

The *silariang* report usually came from the family of a broken marriage. For instance, a wife *silariang* with her lover because her husband left her and neglected his marital responsibilities. *Silariang* is an alternative for a woman with uncertain status (married, but separated). There are also cases in which the husband reported the desertion of his wife as *silariang* with another man. It was highlighted that cases of desertion in marriage were usually due to the existence of prior marital conflict.

Elopement used not to be reported as it was not considered a criminal action and therefore not the business of the police. Even though *silariang* is regarded as a crime (kidnapping) under Indonesian Criminal Code (KUHP), such cases are only processed after being reported to the police. Unreported cases are invisible and remain a family affair. However, this attitude is changing significantly, as people have started reporting such cases instead of handling them as family affairs,[72] and expect some follow-up soon after.

However, the police consider that dealing with such cases is a dilemma. While the case might be based on mutual agreement between a man and a woman (*silariang*), her family may report that the woman has been abducted by another man (*rilariang*). For that reason, the police have to handle these problems cautiously, particularly given the issue of *siriq*. The police often act as a 'mediating bridge' between the man and the woman's family to prevent both sides from committing further crime, such as killing.

Conclusion

Marriage is universal among the Bugis, as in other ethnic groups across the archipelago, and is ideally a monogamous lifelong union. Men and women are expected to get married, otherwise certain stigmatising labels will be attached to them. While the labels for women are connected with their commodified value, the labels for men are related to their sexual potency. But the negative labels associated with age—*mangngaribini* (B. sunset prayer), *isyani* (evening prayer), and *subuni* early (morning prayer)—are only attached to unmarried women. Regardless of the negative values attached to *janda*, being an old maid is even worse given that the status of *janda* means that she has been previously 'saleable', while an old maid is wholly 'unsaleable'.

Bugis men and women have similar as well as different aspirations for marriage. Both realise the importance of changing from single to married status. While for men this aspiration is attributed to biological needs, the women's aspiration to marry is discussed in term of social status.

72 In the last five years, local newspapers, such as *Fajar, Pedoman Rakyat and Berita Kota*, have continuously reported cases of *silariang*.

However, this is not to argue that women neglect a desire for sex and for life companionship. Rather, expressing such desires may affect the value of their maidenhood. Although both men and women acknowledged the importance of having children, which indicates the importance of reproduction for both sexes, personal attachment was rarely articulated because it is not a matter that is supposed to be openly expressed.

In theory, the notion of ideal husbands and wives are both connected to personal qualities. In practice, however, economic capability (able to *mattuliling dapureng wékka pétu*) is emphasised for men and domestic abilities (able to be *to bola*) are stressed for women, reinforcing the position of the husband as the head of the family (as breadwinner) and the wife as the housekeeper, established in the 1974 Marriage Law under the New Order ideology which promulgated the ideal state of womanhood.

In the bilateral Bugis society, kinship plays an important role in marriage. That is why when discussing marriage in Bugis, one should realise that this union must be viewed in relation to kinship, as marriage is perceived as forming two families into one (B. *siala*), as a social alliance, in addition to a rite of passage in the life cycle of the individual. This is not to argue, however, that marriage with an outsider (*to laing*) is prohibited, given that an exogamous marriage may politically benefit the family, and as Pelras argues, make an 'outsider' (*to laing*) into 'insider' (*tennia to laing*). In addition, the importance of marriage for the Bugis is related to social status (*onro*). The degree of one's *onro* may be raised, stay the same or even fall as a result of the union, whether or not one is married within one's kin group, since *onro* and kinship are two different concerns.

The presentation of various types of marriage indicates the gradual transition from arranged marriage to free-choice marriage. This also leads to a transfer of responsibility from family to the couple, though this does not necessarily indicate that parents take no responsibility in regard to types of marriage, particularly free-choice marriage. As Pak Bakri said:

> We are parents, our feeling is always attached to the children, wherever they go, we always worry about them, their health, marital stability or their economic circumstance, if they cannot handle any of them, they can always come home and stay with us (22 October 2000).

While there is a recent trend towards free-choice marriages, arranged marriages with the consent of the bride and the groom reflect another recent transition from forced marriage to marriage by consent. The risks of such marriages therefore are borne by the couples' families as well as the couple themselves.

Although no one ever imagines that he/she may engage in any kind of shameful marriage (*silariang, rilariang* or *najjuluang aléna*) for various reasons such marriages happen, and may result in legal action or the possibility of marriages not recognised by the state. My data suggests that cultural (for example, bridewealth, nobility, ideal partner, virginity) and religious (for example, belief, parent's consent) elements are the major motivations to opt for such marriages, as such factors often lead to illegal actions to facilitate marriages, desired by one or both parties.

The discussion on types of marriage in this chapter suggests that there are certain situations in which women become powerful agents. For example, in the free-choice marriage of Rapiah where she acted as an agent in deciding matters related to her own wedding, including when the man's family could come to propose to her, how much the bridewealth (*duiq ménréq*) should be given and what kinds of wedding presents the man's family should bring. In another instance, a woman excercises agency when she approaches the man she expects to marry and asks him to marry her, as in the case of *najjuluang aléna*.

In the next chapter, I will discuss the dynamics of marital life, which include the expected behaviour of husbands and wives, a gendered division of labour in Bugis marriage, and how women exercise social power.

CHAPTER 4

Assikalaibinéngeng: The Couple, the House and the Household

> Households are important in feminist analysis because they organize a large part of women's domestic/reproductive labour. As a result, both the composition and the organization of households have a direct impact on women's lives, and in particular on their ability to gain access to resources, to labour and to income.
>
> MOORE, 1988:55

Introduction

Jones (2002:219) argues that the household is the basis to an understanding of gender relations in Indonesia. Considering that marriage for the Bugis involves 'taking to each other', household dynamics rely on kinship relations as well as marital ideology.

This chapter deals with the nature and dynamics of Bugis households. I begin by unpacking the concepts of *makkunrai,* which may be glossed as 'woman' and *oroané,* a term that means 'man' to understand how these terms are related to the expected behaviours of husbands and wives in conjugal relationships, and how space in the Bugis house is connected to gender relations in marriage. Further, I discuss the ideology of *assikalaibinéngeng,* that is 'marital life', by examining norms and traditions surrounding the conjugal relationship. Then, I examine living arrangements and household composition as well as the most common types of residence after marriage, considering the positive aspects as well as the shortcomings of each type.

The discussion is continued by examining contradictory ideology in the separate spheres by examining women's mobility, women's work and how they identify themselves. In addition, I discuss consumerism as a part of modern life, a way for gaining status and strengthening women's domestic dominance and how consumerism is associated with gender relations in marriage.

In the subsequent section, I present *Lontaraq Daramatasia,*[1] a 20th century Bugis manuscript, which addresses aspects of marital life (*assikalabinéngeng*) and discuss how this relates to everyday practice. This is followed by using the

1 *Lontaraq Daramatasia,* Roll 17/No. 17, 20th century, Arsip Nasional Wilayah Makassar.

 | DOI 10.1163/9789004311947_005

case of Bakris to examine the nature of marriage and its change. I conclude this chapter by presenting three case studies to examine the relationship between money, power and violence in the household.

The House and the Notions of *Makkunrai* and *Oroané*

Apart from the ideal partner discussed in Chapter 3, when a man and a woman are married, there are behavioural expectations related to their marital status as well as their household and social responsibilities.

For the Bugis, as for other Indonesians, marriage is the entry point to adulthood for both men and women. In theory, to become an adult, a woman should pass through at least four steps: become a woman (*mancaji makkunrai*), become aware of her domestic responsibilities (*mancaji misseng dapureng*), become a household manager (*mancaji I Mattaro*) and become one in all circumstances (*mancaji baliperriq*) (see below).[2] To start with, a woman is expected to become a woman, articulated through the term *mancaji makkunrai*. The Bugis word *mancaji* means 'become'. The term *makkunrai*, translated as 'woman', is derived from the prefix *makké*, indicating possession, and the noun *unrai*, which refers to a covering for the body. Thus, to become a woman, one should cover the body. The notion of a body-covering indicates that she should not only protect her *aurat* (an Indonesian term that refers to those parts of the body which cannot be visible and is frequently a reference to genitals) but must also preserve the family from *siriq*. Her obligation to protect her family from *siriq* reflects the notion that a woman is the symbol of the *siriq* of the family. Hence, to *mancaji makkunrai* is not just about covering her body, but also associated with protecting her honour.

The second step is to 'become aware of her domestic responsibilities', referred to with the phrase *mancaji misseng dapureng*. The term *misseng* means 'be cognisant of' and *dapureng* means 'kitchen'. This phrase, therefore, conveys the sense that she should have the ability to do domestic chores, including cooking, cleaning, washing and taking care of children. Given that the house is a woman's arena, she should be the one who dominates domestic chores.

The next step is to 'become a household manager', articulated through the statement *mancaji I Mattaro*.[3] *Mattaro* is a Bugis term meaning 'able to store' derived from the verb *taro*, to store. The term *taro* in this sense implies an

2 Said discusses the development of female behavioural expectations in Bugis- Makassarese (cited by Ahkam Jayadi 2002).

3 *I* is an article indicating a woman (such as I Suri), *La* is for a man (such as *La* Muhtar).

image of a rice container (*pabbaresseng*), which is usually placed in the house; rice signifies the spirit of life and rice-metaphors are frequently used to refer to women. For example, the 'contents of the rice container', termed *liseq pabbaresseng* is a metaphor used to refer to women. Further, the term for rice seed, *biné*, is cognate for the word *biné/bainé*, which means woman or wife. It is taboo to have an empty rice container (*pabbaresseng*) in the house because it indicates that the household's livelihood is not sustainable. Thus, *I Mattaro* carries the connotation that a woman must have the ability to manage household earnings. This signifies the position of the wife as the money manager in the household as well as the money spender. In this sense, women have to balance the income and the expenses of the household. A wife who is not able to be a household manager, that is *I Mattaro*, in the household (*assikalaibinéngeng*) is referred to as a leaky washbasin (*bokoroq sebboq*). If one puts water in a *bokoroq sebboq*, the water drains away. Thus, the wife who is considered *bokoroq sebboq* will spend all the money she has, no matter how much.

Finally, she is expected to become one in all circumstances, a sentiment expressed in the Bugis phrase *mancaji baliperri*. *Bali* in Bugis means mutual and *perriq* means smarting. This phrase, then, implies that husband and wife will help each other in any circumstance, in happiness as well as difficulty (*sibaliperriq*). Thus a household problem is off-limits to the outsider, unless it cannot be handled internally. The concept of *sibaliperriq* is related to a verse in the *Qur'an* (Al-Baqarah:187) which states that the wife is a dress/protector for the husband and vice versa. Hence, husband and wife protect each other.

In practice, all these four elements have become important measures of women's abilities, in an ideal sense. But *misseng dapureng* is the most significant indication of an ideal wife. For example, despite the fact that attending school has continued to become more common, people usually question an educated bride's ability in the kitchen, by asking if she is 'able to run the kitchen' (*macca muiga maddapureng*?), implying that those who attend school have no time to learn about household chores. Therefore, in the early period of marriage, a new bride usually focuses her attention on the kitchen to show her interest in household activities and to gain respect from her in-laws, by for example, helping other women in the kitchen. The daughter-in-law of *Pak* Bakri is an example of this. Whenever Mina and her husband, Aco, came to Kulo, she spent most of her time in the kitchen, especially during the preparation of meals. Rapiah, *Pak* Bakri's eldest daughter, who came to visit from West Papua once, commented on Mina's busy hours: '*Ibu* Ilmi, look at Mina, she tries to show her good behaviour to the family'. Mina's mother, who once came to visit her in-laws in Kulo, also encouraged Mina to help women in the kitchen to show that she had taught her daughter appropriate feminine tasks.

In addition to being the income provider and the protector of the family, to be a man, that is an *oroané*, a Bugis man is expected to be patient, so he can control himself from any evil temptation, that is, any behaviour that may affect his status. Being patient is seen as a remedy for passion. There is a Bugis aphorism (*paseng*) which is directed at men and women, as follows:

> Women, take care of yourselves to preserve your honour.
> Men, take care of yourselves to maintain your patience.
>
> *É makkunrai, sappo i alému nasabaq siriqmu.*
> *É oroané, sappo i alému nasabaq asabbarakeng*
>
> A. HASAN MACHMUD 1976:44–5.

This *paseng* reflects the idea that a woman's behaviour is related to her honour, as women are the symbol of family *siriq* while a man's honour is associated with his patience, as it mirrors his spiritual potency. In order to maintain *siriq*, women have to behave properly, that is modestly (*malebbiq*) because to be *malebbiq* also contributes to Bugis *siriq*. To preserve his patience, a man, or *oroané*, has to be in a state of conscious (*maringngerrang*). Thus, the honour of women (*siriq*) and the patience of men (*asabbarakeng*) reflect the complementarity of men and women in social interaction.

Referring to a verse in the Qur'an, *Lontaraq Budi Istiharah* states that 'God is the friend of a patient man, an impatient man is the friend of evil'. Therefore, a man should control himself from the temptation of evil. In the relationship between husband and wife, a man should be patient with his wife because a woman uses her mouth as an instrument for her protection (Ahmad Yunus et al. 1990:118).[4] Hence, there is a joke usually directed at women that a woman has two mouths, an upward mouth and a downward mouth (*makkunraié dua i timunna, timung riaseq na timung riawa*). While the term *timung riaseq* refers to her mouth, *timung riawa* refers to her vagina. This joke stereotypes women as chatterboxes. Therefore, people usually commented that one should not be surprised if a woman was a chatterbox because they have two mouths, expressed in Indonesian: *'tidak heran kalau perempuan cerewet karena punya dua mulut'*.

While in relation to his sexuality, man's desire (B. *cinnana oroané*) is open (*marisaliweng*); in social performance, a man is expected to be able to control (*maperreng*) his social behaviour to indicate his moral rectitude. To hold

4 In a Malay novel entitled *Bilik 69*, a cognate expression is described: that women use their mouth as their weapon (*senjatanya ialah mulutnya*) (Hooker 1997:76).

himself in a steady state (*perrengngi aléna*), a man should also be in a state of awareness (*maringngerrang*).[5] For example, if a man is severely angry in public, he is seen as a person who cannot control himself; this is particularly the case for high status people. Angry outbursts lower a man's status and spiritual potency, aspects which are central to everyday life.[6] If commoners act in a similar manner, people will say: 'That is the way lower status people behave.' Apart from being *tomasiriq* of the family, being angry in public is equated with allowing dirt to enter one's soul.

Furthermore, a man is considered to have achieved adulthood (B. *makkalépuqni*) after being married (*purani botting*), and his ability independently to support his family (*mattuliling dapureng wékka pétu*) is the most significant indicator of a capable husband. A man is regarded as standing on his own feet (*nalaoanni aléna*), which implies that he has become an independent husband. In a broader sense, this designation usually refers to a family that moves from uxorilocal residence in the wife's family compound to neolocal residence. In this type of residence, the husband becomes the 'head of the house' (*pangngulu bola*); the word *pangngulu* is derived from the noun *ulu*, which means 'head,' and the word *bola*, which means 'house'. The wife is the *to ri bola*, that is the 'person who is the house', meaning the housekeeper. This term is derived from the word *to*, which means 'person', and *ri bola*, which means 'in the house'. These two terms indicate that both husband and wife are connected to the *bola*, the house. But, husband—*pangngulu*—and wife—*to ri bola*—do not necessarily indicate the opposition of superior versus inferior. It rather signifies that the 'head' without the 'body' will fall, and the 'body' without the 'head' will be blind which implies that the existence of both is complementary. For example, I often heard people comment about an unmarried man who already had a house, evoking a Bugis maxim meaning he has a house without step (*engka bolana, tapiq déggaga addénénna*), referring to a Bugis stilt-house. The step is a metaphor for the wife. Given that the wife carries the spirit, or *sumangeq*, of the house, and the house is the women's arena, a house without a wife is similar to a house with no *sumangeq* because it has no housekeeper (*déggaga to ri bolana*). Therefore, such a man should marry soon in order to energise the life spirit of his house. If a man says to a single woman that he is looking for a step for his house, this may have two meanings: either he is interested in proposing to her or he is asking her to find him another woman to be his wife, the former being the most common.

5 For further discussions of *maringngerrang*, see Errington (1983, 1989) and Acciaioli (1989).

6 See Keeler (1990) and Brenner (1998) for discussion of status and spiritual potency among Javanese.

During my study in Australia, whenever I went home, people usually commented: 'Your house becomes "alive" when you are around', which reflects the woman's attachment to the house.

Thus, while the Bugis man is recognised by the outside world as the provider, a Bugis woman is identified with the house (Robinson 2001:27). A woman's ability in the household is based on the notion of a woman as housekeeper (*to ri bola*, also *pajaga biliq* or *pangngonro bola*). If a husband is asked 'who is with you?' (*iga ta sibawa*?) and the answer is '*to ri bolaé*', it means that he is with his wife. This notion is in line with a Bugis saying that the most precious place for a woman is in the house (*tampaq kaminang malebbiq é ri séséna makkunraié, ianaritu ri bolaé*).

Errington has noted parallelism between the Bugis house and the human body (Errington 1979:13); the relationship between husband and wife can be analysed based on the structure of the house. The house consists of rafters (*rakkéang*), the body of the house (*alé bola*) and beneath the house (*awa bola*), which correspond to the head, torso and feet of the body, respectively.[7] For Bugis, just as the head and the feet are the most vulnerable parts of human body and touching these parts may result in violent chastisement, the openings in the roof and beneath the house can also be dangerous (Errington, 1979:13), and have to be under the guard of the protector of the family, that is, the *pangngulu bola*, or husband. The torso is where most human functions take place, just as domestic activities are located in the *alé bola*, the body of the house, dominated by the wife.

While the husband protects the two extremities of the house which have a direct connection with the outside world, the wife is the keeper of the middle part of the house. Thus the correspondence of *rakkéang* and head, *alé bola* and torso, and *awa bola* and feet with the head/foot associated with the husband and torso associated with the wife not only symbolises the cosmology of the house and human body, but is also associated with the function of husband and wife in the household (*assikalaibinéngeng*).

The Ideology of *Assikalaibinéngeng*

In Bugis, husband and wife are considered to be 'two-in-one'. This is reflected in the Bugis terms that combine the words for man and woman into a single term (*mallaibiné*, *sikalaibiné*, and *sipubainé*). In *Lontaraq Budi Istiharah Indar*

7 See Errington for her examination of the parallelism between the Bugis house and the human body based on its space and function (Errington 1979).

Bustanil Arifin, mallaibiné is symbolised as an orange. If an orange is bitter, the whole orange becomes bitter and visa versa, it will never be a half bitter and half sweet (P3B, 1999:61), reflecting the complementarity between husband and wife. Therefore, husband and wife have to work hand-in-hand in managing their household life (*sibaliperriq*). This indicates that they equally belong to each other. This mutual belongingness is also reflected in how husband and wife are addressed; the wife is *bainéna* X (the wife of X); the husband is *lakkainna* Y (husband of Y).[8] The teknonymous term of address will be further discussed in Chapter 5.

While the Javanese local terms for house, getting married, household and spouse are related words: *omah, omah-omahan, somahan* and *semah* (H. Geertz 1961:55), the Bugis term for the house (*bola*) is not related to the other terms, getting married (*mabbainé/mallakkai*), household (*onro sikalabinéng*), and spouse (*baine/lakkai*). The terms for getting married and spouse are gendered, but the Bugis term for household (*onro sikalabinéng*) reflects the tie between husband and wife. This term is derived from the noun *onro* meaning place and *sikalabinéng* referring to household affairs. *Onro sikalabinéng* carries the sense of a family unit where husband, wife and other members of the family are considered a whole.

The newlyweds are usually advised by elders to run their household based on a philosophy of fire (B. *api*) and water (*uaé*). If fire meets with fire, it will burn (*api masua*), but if fire meets water, the fire will be extinguished. To put this another way, if one is angry, the other party should be quiet. This piece of advice is usually given during the formal speech of marital advice (*nasihat perkawinan*) after the ritual marriage contract (*akad nikah*).

The Bugis term for marriage is derived from the Bugis term *siala*, as I mentioned earlier in Chapter 3. There is, therefore, an 'intersecting duty' between husband and wife and the members of both families. For example, if a person from the family of the husband comes to ask for money or goods, these are given by the wife, while the husband deals with requests from the wife's family. This 'intersecting duty' develops an image of sharing and integration between the two families, no matter whether they are single or double-income families. But because the wife is usually the money manager in the household, she commonly manages such family requests with the consent of her husband.

Furthermore, the relationship between husband and wife is expressed in a Bugis saying: 'a wife follows her husband's forefinger' (*bainé maccuéi ripajjelloqna lakkainna*). The literal meaning of this saying reflects the idea that a wife

8 See also Millar (1983:485).

should follow her husband's will.[9] In this context, however, the saying is applied when the husband plays the role of *tomasiriq* of the family, particularly of the women.

In analysing gender relations in a Bugis household, we should look back to the rituals associated this. For example, prior to marriage, a mother encourages her son to expect that his wife will be obedient to him after marriage. This is implied in one of the ceremonial processions in a Bugis wedding after the ritual of marriage contract (*akad nikah*), called the touching each other, or *mappasikarawa,* from the verb *karawa*, which means to touch. Since *akad nikah* is performed between the groom and the bride's guardian (A. *wali*), the bride usually waits in a separate (locked) room accompanied by her family, for the arrival of her husband. Soon after the *akad nikah* is completed, the groom comes to the bride's room to touch her legally for the first time. The groom, escorted by his family, knocks at the door of the bride's room and offers a number of coins for the door keepers, without which the door will not be opened. So, there is always a 'tension' between the door keepers of the bride and the grooms' escorts, which is sometimes followed by competition between the two to accelerate or slow down the groom's effort to enter the bride's room. This is intended to show that the bride is not easy to meet (B. *déqna magampang riduppai*).

During this touching ceremony (*mappasikarawa*), the bride usually sits on the bed, with her back to the door, or at least not daring to look at her husband's face in order to show her honour (*alebbireng*), bride and groom accompanied by their respective families. Despite the fact that the term *mappasikarawa* carries the sense of touching each other, the ritual is only for the husband to touch his wife without any counter-touching from his wife.

In Bugis, it is believed that the 'first touch' in this ceremony reflects the future relationship between husband and wife. So touching the crown of the wife's head, the part that the groom's escorts (usually women) try to get the groom to touch, symbolises her future obedience (*ripatunruq rilakkainna*),[10] while touching her chest or shaking her hand symbolises equality between the couple. Consequently, the family of the bride endeavours to protect her from being touched on any part of her head because the women's family does not expect her to be treated arbitrarily by her husband. There is therefore usually a struggle

9 This is similar to the situation described by Chabot (1996) for the neighbouring Makassarese that the wife stands on the index finger of the husband (*bainéa amménténgi ripanjojjoqna buraqnéa*).

10 See also A.P. Hamzah et al. (1984:111) on their discussion on various 'first touch' in the *mappasikarawa* ceremony.

between the family of the bride and the family of the groom during this ritual. Nevertheless, the expectation that a wife should be obedient is very strong, reflecting the ambiguity of this symbolic touch in the wedding rites (Nurul Ilmi Idrus 2001:51), since the commonest first touch in this *mappasikarawa* ritual is shaking the bride's hand or touching her chest.

The *mappasikarawa* ceremony is not just about gender relations in Bugis marriage. It is also about whether or not the couple are well matched. *Ibu* Masriah, my *lontaraq* reader, explained that the parts of the women's body which are subject to touching during the *mappasikarawa* ceremony are associated with the couples' compatibility. For example, if the groom touches the bride's chest it indicates good prospects for livelihood (*maliseq-liseq*), her shoulder suggests the spouses will be equal (*mallémpaq*), and her arm indicates good health (*masumangeq*); thus, all of these touches mean the couple will have good fortune in the future. But touching the bride's forehead is associated with a lack of spirit (*maponcoq sungeq* or *déqna silampéreng*) and indicates bad fortune; the marriage will either be in conflict or end in a divorce. Such rituals are still practised by the Bugis in both rural and urban areas, and if something happens in the relationship between the couple in the future, elders usually refer back to this ritual and analyse what eventuated then as precursor of future events.

Another Bugis practice I observed during my fieldwork was that a wife can avoid being subordinate to her husband by 'putting a key in her mouth and biting it' during the *akad nikah* ritual. The key symbolises that the husband's power is 'locked out', and the action of biting indicates the wife will become the 'power holder' in the family. Still another symbol is when both the bride and the groom are asked to stand up from the bed after the *mappasikarawa* ceremony. Whoever stands up first is believed to become 'superior' to her/his partner. In such a ritual, each of them competes, and there is always a 'winner' and a 'loser'. Although all these rituals are merely symbolic of the quality of the future relationship between husband and wife, people tend to believe they will influence the couple's relationship in the future and as a result appear to cause anxiety in the 'loser'.

Bugis women are more than equal to their husbands in the household. As noted above, when a woman gets married, she is the money manager as well as money spender, while her husband is the income provider. This is reflected in a Bugis saying: 'the woman's domain is around the house, the man's domain reaches "the border of the sky" (horizon)' (Pelras 1996:161) which indicates a clear-cut division of roles between men and women. This is not to argue that women cannot participate in public life, or vice versa, it is rather to indicate what Pelras portrays as 'the basis of their partnership in caring for each other's concerns' (Pelras 1996:160), or in Millar's words, roles that are 'distinctly different, but complementary' (Millar 1983:486).

Nevertheless, the idea that the wife is the 'boss' at home is the basis for women's prestige with the outside world. For example, a wife who is successful in public life, but fails to perform her domestic responsibilities is considered unsuccessful as a wife. Husbands who have working wives frequently say: 'Do not forget your family' (I. *Jangan lupa keluarga*); 'Put family ahead of your work' (*Utamakan keluarga dari pada kerja*); 'Do not ignore your kids and your husband' (*Jangan lupa anak dan suami*) or express other similar sentiments, asserting women's primary responsibilities in the domestic sphere.

Alwy Rahman discusses the public-domestic division in the orientation of 'space and interaction' in the wedding ritual in South Sulawesi. He argues that in such a ritual, the association of men and the front of the house and women with the middle and back of the house is the basis of women's domestication because, in fact, the middle and the back parts of the house are the places where most domestic work is performed (Alwy Rahman 1998:7).

I observed in Kulo, however, that in the preparations for a wedding reception, men at the front were as busy as women in the middle and at the back parts of the house. Take for example the wedding preparations for Pak Bakri's son. In a village, a commoner wedding reception usually takes place under the stilt-house, where men build a temporary stage (B. *lamming*) where the bridal couple, the children-in-waiting, and their parents sit. The men also construct a reception space, including a fence and entrance (I. *pintu baruga*). While the basic materials used in the construction of the *lamming* is wood, the fence and the entrance are made from bamboo, both obtained and carried from distant gardens by men. Men also carried the rented chairs and tables from the truck to the location of the wedding reception. On another occasion, I saw men construct an extended stilt-house for the wedding (B. *bola sambung*) in the space around the kitchen and the living room (see also Robinson 1986, Millar 1989). This addition gave women more space to prepare the food, not only for the wedding reception, but also for the people who contributed to the preparations for the reception; and the extended living room provided more space for the guests to sit in. In addition, men carried water from the pool formed by water flowing from the mountain through connected bamboo or from the well, to be used for cooking, boiling and cooking rice in huge quantities outside the house. Thus, the association of men with the house-front and women with the house-middle and back in the wedding ritual, described by Alwy Rahman as symbolising the domestication of women, is irrelevant for people in Kulo and its surrounds, because both the front and the back/middle parts of the house are full of work before, during and after the ritual. This dualism is simply about the division of labour,[11] which distinguishes the kinds of works as women-cooking and men-construction rather than the space where they happen. The division is flexible, given that men and women may help each other in both spheres.

In her study of gender in Bugis, Millar suggests that the Western construction of public and private division for men and women does not apply to the Bugis (Millar 1983:477). Thus, Rosaldo's (1976) claim, which identifies men with public life and women with domestic life as the basis for women's subordination,[12] is irrelevant for the Bugis; rather, this spatial division is associated with a gendered division of labour conceptually, albeit not rigid in practice.

Living Arrangements and Household Structure

In this section I am going to discuss the structure of the household to see whether extended or nuclear family is dominant household structure, and which type is preferred for the married couple.

In Indonesia, however, no data from any census provides statistics on family structure (such as nuclear family or extended family). The census records data on families consisting of husband, wife and children, while other members of the family who live in thc same house are not counted. Only the state family card (I. *kartu keluarga*) includes the members of extended families beyond the nuclear family.[13] But, the Indonesian census provides data on extended families, based on non-nuclear relatives of household head[14] (excluding servants and others) and results over time show the co-resident extended family in decline: 10 percent in 1980, 9.2 in 1990, and 8.3 in intercensal survey of 1995 (Jones 2002:225, Table 18.4).

My observations indicate that although the nuclear family is more common in the capital city of Makassar, the extended family groups—which consist of husband, wife, children and other members of family, such as grandparents,

11 See also Pelras (1996:162) for the domestic-public division of labour between men and women.

12 In her later publication Rosaldo (1980) questions the universality of women's subordination based on the division of male-public and female-domestic. See also Strathern (1980) and Ortner and Whitehead (1981) for critical discussion of cross-cultural evaluation of sex and gender.

13 Personal interview with Terry Hull (12 November 2002).

14 Non-nuclear relatives of household head consist of grandchildren, parents, parents-in-law and other non-nuclear relatives.

aunts, sister/brothers, or cousins—are still common in the district capital as well as in the village.

For a double-income family in the city, waged domestic labour service (such as a maid or a childcarer) is becoming more common. Thus, a couple should be financially independent in paying their own bills and expenses, including the maintenance of a domestic helper. This independence is presumably one reason why age at first marriage in the city is higher than that in the village.[15]

For the Bugis, considering that kinship is bilateral, newlyweds may live with either the parents of the wife or the parents of the husband (Millar 1989:25; 1983:488). Nevertheless, uxorilocal residence is a common preference for a newly married couple (Pelras 1996:161); a husband comes to live with his wife, but retains his own natal group membership.

In the patrilocal family structure of the Balinese, a new bride becomes a complete stranger in her husband's family and lose her natal group membership (Robinson 2000b:143–4). For the Bugis, the shift from single to married is said to enhance women's social status, and since uxorilocal residence is common for the newlyweds, it is the husband who becomes the stranger in his wife's family compound.

The preference for living with the family of the wife is said to be due to the fact that a wife may still learn from her mother about how to manage a household, and also because of emotional attachment and cooperative relations between daughter and mother (Millar 1983:488). In any case, uxorilocal residence provides women the support of their kinfolk, both in daily activities and when conflict arise with the new husband, especially in arranged marriages or marriages of minors.

Another common reason for living with parents is economic: if the couple is regarded as incapable of running their own household, the parents of the bride take responsibility for the extended family. Even if the couple is financially capable, they are not prohibited from staying with their parents. The daughter is usually the one who takes care of her parents, and indeed inherits the house. This differs from the Javanese situation, where a couple living with parents maintain their own kitchen, reflecting the autonomy of Javanese marriage (H. Geertz 1961:75). In Bugis, newlyweds usually share their parents' kitchen, reinforcing the view that Bugis marriage is about kin ties; but the son-in-law may contribute or even take over the expenses related to this common kitchen.

---

15 For example, Chang and Jones in their study of marriage patterns and household formation in peninsula Malaysia demonstrate the relationship between later age at marriage and the convention of neolocal residence after marriage (Chang and Jones 1990).

In Kulo, because of economic uncertainty, many men migrate in search of fortune (*massompeq*), for example to Malaysia or other parts of Indonesia, leaving the family in the village. Many successful migrants (*passompeq*) take their families to Malaysia or send money home and visit once in a while. In exceptional cases, the husband leaves the wife and children with nothing. In this event, the wife commonly become *janda tenri telleq*, that is, separated but not divorced, abandoned without financial support. In such cases, the women often move back to their parents along with their children (see the case of Rahmatiah in Chapter 6).

Moving back to one's parents house, however, is not always acceptable for lower status families because they may already live in poverty and cannot maintain the returning daughter and her children. Take for instance *Ibu* Aminah, a forty-year-old mother with three children, who had been separated from her husband since 1997 without financial support for the children. Her eldest son, Safar, (who was 16 years old) did not continue his studies beyond primary school because he had to help his mother to make a living, as a paddy harvester (*padderos*). Despite her poverty, *Ibu* Aminah had to pay someone else to take care of her other two children, aged 5 and 3, when she and Safar went out to the rice fields. *Ibu* Aminah's case reflects a consequence of the transformation of the local economy from a family and village-based mode of production to a waged labour mode of production.

Unlike *Ibu* Aminah, *Ibu* Kasmawati, a middle-class, divorced woman who lived with two children, did not have to pay someone to care for her children because her children attended the school where she worked as a primary school teacher; indeed, her house was just behind the school. In *Ibu* Kasmawati's case, it was not that she could not move back to her own parents' home after her divorce. Rather, she had become accustomed to living in a nuclear family. Further, childcare was not an issue since her work place was close to her house.

Despite the specificity of the two cases presented above, most working women in the village prefer to stay in an extended family compound because it ensures that their children and domestic chores are taken care of by other members of the family while they are away for work.

For the Bugis, even though virilocal residence is not prohibited, this arrangement is not common. After all of the weddings I attended in Kulo, the newlyweds stayed with the family of the bride or in a neolocal residence, including *Pak* Bakri's son and *Ibu* Bakri's younger brother. This is because virilocal residence in many cases resulted in conflict, particularly with the female-in-laws, consisting of the bride's mother-in-law (*matuang makkunrai*) and/or sister-in-law (*ipaq makkunrai*). However, based on my observation of court hearings and interviews with a judge in the Pengadilan Agama Sidrap, such conflict, although common in Sidrap, is not legal grounds for divorce, but is subsumed under incompatibility (see Chapter 6 for the grounds for divorce). Whether this is an incompatibility between the couple or the families can be observed during the court hearing. In contrast, Millar's findings in Soppeng—where she conducted her fieldwork—indicate that 'the relationship between female-in-laws is often warm and supportive' (Millar, 1983:488).

'Good luck staying with your mother-in-law' is a comment frequently uttered to a wife who lives with her in-laws. This comment implies that the bride will be under the control of her mother-in-law. Living with the in-laws is popularly known as living in the 'beautiful housing complex of the in-laws' (I. *perumahan mertua indah*). This terminology ironically reflects the naming practices of the highly desirable new urban housing estates. The phrase has negative connotation, such as lack of independence and being controlled by the in-laws.[16] For example, the mother controls her daughter-in-law in serving her husband, spending money, determining when to have children or managing the household. It is very difficult to argue with one's mother-in-law because the couple have been taught since childhood to listen to parents or elders (B. *mangkalinga ada to matoa*). Thus, the wife as well as the husband are afraid of being sinful.

Living away from the in-laws is said to improve the relationship between the wife and her in-laws because they do not often meet. I was curious to know why conflicts between a daughter-in-law and her mother-in-law are more common than between a son-in-law and his mother and father-in-law. When I asked the women who usually rested under the stilt-house of the Bakris, one spoke for all of them, saying:

> *Ibu* Ilmi, how can two money managers be in the same house? Who is going to manage what? It is better for them to live separately. Otherwise, they won't get along (16 August 2000).

The two money managers refer to the mother and the daughter-in-law. Hence, one can see why virilocal residence is avoided as much as possible by newlyweds, not only to avoid conflict with the bride's in-laws, but also to avoid being sinful towards her mother-in-law. Even though money is not always a cause of conflict, this sentiment reflects to some extent the significance of the wife as

16 In contrast Mitchell (1994) in her study of women age hierarchy among egalitarian Andean peasant society indicates that the control of older women over younger ones in reproducing and provisioning the household by organising labour in extended post marital residence carries a sense of prestige rather than negative.

money holder in the household, and the dilemma she faces when living virilocally. Since the wife is the *to ri bola* with the house as her main arena, it is reasonable to suggest that having two *to ri bola* in the same house is a source of potential conflict, that is, conflict between a senior mother and a young wife.

Contradictory Ideology in the Separate Spheres

Alwy Rahman discussed women's domestication on the basis of 'time and space' by classifying women in association with the domestic and night and men in association with the public and day (Alwy Rahman 1998:7–13). He articulates that women's mobility during the daytime is within a very limited radius, while men may move freely over an extensive radius. Time spent working during the night is longer for women compared to men. Accordingly, women are the last people to go to bed at night, but the first to get up in the morning.[17]

This reminds one of the popular English saying: 'a man works from rise to set of sun, a woman's work is never done'. In Indonesia, this saying has been adjusted into: 'a woman's work is never done, days and nights, from rise of sun to the close of her husband's eyes'.

In Kulo, women could easily mobilise themselves during the day, for example, to shop at the market (the closest market was in Rappang—Pasar Rappang is 10 Km from Kulo), visit family, or attend parties. Small merchant women moved from one house to another to sell their goods (clothes are the most common goods sold by women) or in the market on market days (B. *wettu pasaq*) which occur only three days out of the week—Tuesday, Friday and Sunday.

Wedding parties around the village were always big entertainments for village residents and also a time for young girls and boys to rendezvous (discussed in Chapter 2). But if the party were outside of the village (e.g. in Rappang or Pangkajene), wedding guests had to make arrangements with a mini-bus driver (I. *sopir pété-pété*), to make sure that they had a ride to the party and would be driven by a familiar driver, as I overheard people discussing in the mini-bus (*pété-pété*).

The judgment given by Rahman on this account was based on the New Order gender ideology which constructed this male-public/female-domestic dichotomy. Indeed, it was common to hear the following expression from

17 Bennett (2002:177–8) discusses female vulnerability in terms of the differential regulations concerning gendered time and space in courtship in Mataram, Lombok, Eastern Indonesia.

women when they are not at home: 'I want to go home soon because I have to cook' (*Èlo'ka lisu magatti' nasaba' élo'ka' mannasu*), or something similar. Female officials in village or subdistrict offices (Kantor Desa or Kantor Kecamatan) or local clinics (Puskesmas) spent some of their working hours at the market buying daily needs. If there were a party that day, women office workers frequently went home earlier than they should in order to prepare food for the family before attending the party. When they went home after the party, they had to cook dinner, wash the dishes, then go to sleep earlier than non-working women because they had to finish their domestic chores before going to the office the following morning. Thus, it was also very common for female staff to come to the office late, and return home earlier from work, a practice that was understood amongst their colleagues. Non-working women spent most of their time at home. Their unemployment and domestic responsibilities restricted their mobility, but their lives were more relaxed because they had no set working hours or external work place.

The related dichotomies of female-domestic-day and male-public-night are more appropriately evaluated in terms of their vulnerability. Errington identifies the private-public division in terms of vulnerability and space through the dualism of house-safe space and outside-dangerous space (1979:10). Given that women are identified with the house, and 'the house is the haven for female honour' (Robinson 1993:238), women are considered to be more vulnerable in the outside world, especially at night and even if they are accompanied by male relatives.[18] Despite the danger of public spaces, girls are allowed to go out, usually with friends, to watch the entertainment at wedding parties after the evening prayer because the crowd of the wedding makes the outside less vulnerable. People are surrounded by other people, which provides protection especially as the time of a wedding reception is often a period of transition (twilight, right before dawn, and high noon) which can be especially dangerous to human beings (Errington 1979:10).

In the 1970s, there was a tendency amongst feminist scholars to dichotomise society into male and female spheres, contrasting production-reproduction, public-private and culture-nature as economic, political, and cultural models respectively. In the 1980s, this dichotomization was integrated to a more social and cultural construction concept that stresses male–female roles, symbolic meanings attached to the sexes, and their social, economic and political implications (Ortner and Whitehead 1984).

18 See, for example, Bennett's discussion on vulnerability of women in Lombok with the outside world, especially during the night (Bennett 2002:170–3).

Many Bugis women are involved as wage labourers and income earners in the formal (such as civil servant, teacher) and informal economies (agriculture). Women's contributions to the household income cannot be denied, or at least cannot be considered merely as 'pin money'.[19]

In Kulo, however, there is a problem in defining women's work. Housewives who make significant contributions to the family income as a result of their participation in agricultural and small-scale market production are still identified as housewives rather than working women.[20] The state policy under the New Order identified men as providers while women's labour and productivity in public is not part of the development strategy, and this has intensified the identification of women with the home.[21] For example, when I asked women in Kulo about their employment status, they inevitably identified themselves as housewives (I. *ibu rumah tangga*). If I asked further concerning their participation in agriculture, they said that they only helped their husbands (*bantu-bantu suami*). But when the former question is asked to working women in the formal sector (such as teacher, administrative staff), they do not consider themselves as *bantu-bantu suami*. This clearly indicates that when a wife is involved in informal work, such as selling things on credit (B. *mappaccicil*), wet-rice agriculture, and the production of brown sugar, her involvement was regarded as no more than *bantu-bantu suami*. Similarly, when a husband shared responsibility for the household activities, it was no more than helping the wife (*bantu-bantu istri*). This is not just because the image of income-provider has attached to the husband, but also because female informal works are classified as non-works. However, the income received from wives' employment—whether it is formal or informal work—is united with their husbands' earnings as family income which is controlled by women.

For instance, I talked to a woman rice vendor named *Ibu* Nanna in Pasar Rappang whose husband was a farmer. She told me that her income was used to pay for daily expenses and her husband's income was saved in the bank under their name; *Ibu* Nanna and her husband planned to use their savings to perform hajj in Mecca, an indicator of additional personal and social status. In spite of the fact that her income as a rice vendor was an important contribution to her

19 See, for example, Hardyastuti Suhatmini and Bambang Hudayana (1991); Grijn et al. (1992).

20 See Moore (1988: Chapter III) for a detailed discussion on understanding of women's work.

21 Apart from the negative effects of the New Order ideology for women, as many social scientists argue, Gerke (1993) and Robinson (1994) look at the positive side of Family Planning Programme on women. While Gerke's impression relies on the increasing autonomy of women, Robinson views it as a way to discipline women.

family, she described herself to be a helper to her husband. In local statistics, such a household is considered to have a single, rather than a double income. But in a household where the wife works in a formal sector (such as teacher of official staff), it is considered as double income household. Single and single-parent working women are regarded as income providers only if they are the only ones who support their families. Therefore, the social recognition of women's participation outside their primary responsibilities is clearer when they are unmarried or are single parents or working in the formal sector.

A lack of statistics on female-headed households from both village and sub-district offices (Kantor Desa and Kantor Kecamatan) in Kulo indicates that their existence is not officially acknowledged. The head of the household is often identified as a man, usually the eldest man in the house which evokes the state label of the dualism of the husband as *kepala keluarga* (I. the head of the household) and the wife as *ibu rumah tangga* (the mother of the household) under the Marriage Law of 1974 (see Sullivan 1994), which does not fit the cultural category of the relationship between husband and wife on the basis of complementarity. Thus, *de facto*, women are the heads of the household, but *de jure*, their existence is not recognised under this category in local statistics. This intensifies the gender distinction between the head of the household and the wife. On a national level, the population census indicates a decline in *de jure* female household headship: 16.3% in 1971, 14.2% in 1980, 13.3% in 1990 and 12.7% in 1995. Jones argues that this gradual reduction largely results from a decline in widowhood, divorce, death rates and divorce rates, and the narrowing age gap between couples (Jones 2002:220). The number increases to 14% in 2000 (BPS 2000) and 14,4% in 2012 (BPS 2013). In Kulo, *de facto*, women head the household because of, for example, the death of the husband, divorce, or separation (B. *janda tenri telleq*), particularly separation because of migration for work.

It is also evident that the wife plays an important role in enhancing social status of middle class families through her informal participation in the economy, such as a trader, termed a *pajjakarta*, that is a man or a woman who trades in goods purchased originally in Jakarta or Surabaya.

Pajjakarta: Consumerism, Status and Women's Domestic Dominance

There are many factors that indicate social status in Kulo, as in other neighbouring regencies and in the capital city of Makassar. One of these is through social performance using clothes and accessories. Sidrap, Pare-Pare and Pinrang are three neighbouring regencies in South Sulawesi (see map 1.2) that are well known for their successful female traders (*pajjakarta*) and their highly competitive pattern of consumerism. Trends in appearance which lead to consumerism are indicators of 'modern life' and a way to show social status. This pattern of 'modern life' comes from Jakarta, Surabaya or neighbouring countries like Malaysia, where many people migrate to make a living. The flow of modern ideas and goods is brought by traders (*pajjakarta*) who travel back and forth between either Sidrap, Pare-Pare, or Pinrang and Jakarta through the nearby harbour in Pare-Pare. These traders buy things (mostly clothes and accessories) for cash in Jakarta and re-sell them on credit or for cash (either at the market or at home). I initially wondered whether selling for cash would be more profitable since the circulation on the trader's investment would be quicker than selling on credit. But a successful middle-class female *pajjakarta*, *Haji* Farida,[22] at the central market in Pangkajene, told me that even though selling on credit takes ten months to finalise, the price is tripled. So she can recoup her capital after the third payment. Despite the fact that her customers realise that paying on credit is more expensive, it is much easier for them to pay this way. So, there is mutual benefit for *pajjakarta* and their customers.

One morning, when I was in the Pasar Pangkajene at *Haji* Farida's shop, I observed a female civil servant, *Ibu* Tati, who bought a set of clothes, a bag, and high-heeled slippers, all for Rp1.000.000,- (US$100 at current exchange rates) on credit. I heard from *Haji* Farida that she would pay all her debt from her salary (I. *potong gaji*) through the official treasurer (*bendahara*) in her office. But, I did not see any document signed by *Ibu* Tati agreeing to the terms for payment. When *Ibu* Tati left, I asked *Haji* Farida about the payment. Responding to my curiosity, she smiled and said: 'We trust each other (*saling percaya*)'. The treasurer in *Ibu* Tati's office had known *Haji* Farida for a long time, not only because her husband worked at the same office as *Ibu* Tati, but also such payment was common without any letter of consent.

Haji Farida enjoyed collecting money through the *bendahara* rather than collecting it from one person directly, not just because it was easier for her, but also because her middle class status made it inappropriate for her to collect money directly. People who were not working in her husband's office usually came to her to pay, or if they did not, her assistant, Hasnah, who was her status inferior, would collect the debt. *Haji* Farida would collect money only on a special case. For example, when the debt was unpaid for a few months, but such case was very rare. Thus, there is a mutual relationship between *Haji* Farida

---

22 In Indonesia, the initial *ibu* is replaced by *Haji* after performing pilgrimage to Mecca. Despite the terms being *Haji* for male and *Hajjah* for female, *Haji* is usually used for both sexes, and is commonly pronounced *aji* (for instance, Aji Nur).

and Hasnah. On the one hand, *Haji* Farida provided for the basic needs of Hasnah, while Hasnah provided her assistance to *Haji* Farida. Hasnah looked after the shop, for example, and did domestic chores, especially when *Haji* Farida went to Jakarta to shop, while Hasnah also sold her own goods (such as soft drink, cigarettes, lollies and chips). Every time *Haji* Farida returned from Jakarta, Hasnah received presents, such as clothes, slippers, a bag or other accessories. Thus Hasnah, like *Haji* Farida's customers, would never miss out on the latest style of attire and accessories.[23]

Every month, *Haji* Farida attended her husband's office for *arisan Dharma Wanita*, a regular social gathering of Dharma Wanita members, all of whom contribute to, and take turns at winning, an aggregate sum of money. At the same time, *Haji* Farida brought her goods to sell and collected money from the official treasurer. She would wear her latest style of attire and accessories to attract other women (I. *ibu-ibu*) to buy or to place orders if they were interested in high status goods like clothes, gold bracelets, bags or slippers.[24] Hence, *Haji* Farida acted as a model for promotion of her wares and what is popularly called *toko berjalan* (I. walking shop). She told me that instead of ordering similar clothing, sometimes her customers asked to buy the outfit she was wearing because it was the latest trendy style. I wondered how she dealt with her husband's salary. She said: 'It has been taken care of'. She clarified that she had obtained a loan from the bank, which she then used as capital for her business. She repaid this loan directly through her husband's salary. Her husband received none of his monthly salary. I suspected that this was a way to prevent her husband from using his salary for 'something else', given that she had a much greater income of her own than her husband. She added that 'a husband's money belongs to his wife, but not vice versa', and I have heard such an expression several times. Indeed, in the city of Makassar, women often said: 'When the husband's salary is in the wife's pocket, don't he dare to ask how to spend' or 'your money is mine, my money is mine too', underscoring the view that women are the money managers of the household.

Every time *Ibu* Farida's husband, *Haji* Gaffar, needed money, for example, to buy fuel for their car or cigarettes, he would ask *Haji* Faridah (see H. Geertz 1961:123). He always made a joke about his domineering wife, that things 'depended on the boss'. But *Haji* Gaffar apparently did not feel that he had been subordinated by his wife just because she earned more money than he did as a successful *pajjakarta*.

---

23 See, for example, Pelras (2000) for detailed discussion of patron-client relationship among the Bugis-Makassarese.

24 See, for example, Djadiningrat-Nieuwenhuis (1987:41–2) for her analysis of trading among Javanese *priyayi* women.

At the market, I observed how male and female traders invited people to stop by at their shops. Female traders were more skilled at this than male traders, without letting themselves be 'cheap'. They said: 'Please stop by' (B. *Léppakkiq mai*) or 'Please browse' (*Itamukkiq*). If a customer finally decided to stop by, they continued to attract the customer by saying: 'Please look' (*Kitangngaq mui*); or 'That's the latest model' (*Modéléq paling mabarué*); 'This dress suits you' (*Sikanakkanakkiq bajué*), or other expressions that might persuade the customer to buy at a good price. This is similar to the situation observed by Brenner (1998) among the Javanese batik traders where female and male traders act to persuade their customers in different ways. While women are more active in persuading their customers to buy batik at a good price, male traders feel reluctant to do so because it may lower their status. But for Bugis male traders, it is not because this may lower their status, it is just that they were not as good as female traders, female success being indicated not just because 'the customers buy', but also because the goods were sold at a 'good price'. Money was obtained from the outside, and brought home for the social status of the family. But for the Bugis, having money is not enough to gain high status; it is supposed to be displayed, by for example, appearance.

In Sidrap, particularly in Rappang and its surrounds, appearance has become one of the primary concerns; consumerism affects daily life. People—particularly women—constantly compete with each other. For example, if a woman first wore the most recent style of attire, like *Haji* Farida, she would be 'admired by others', and would gain satisfaction by 'satisfying others'. Others try to perform their best in order to gain status in the eyes of their associates. The culture of 'satisfying others' is a philosophy which has been developed by people in Sidrap, as in Pare-Pare and Pinrang. An example was given by *Pak* Akhmad; he already had a watch, but his wife asked him to buy a new one on credit. When I asked the reason, he said that his wife was afraid that people might criticise him for wearing an old watch since a judge has high social prestige. There is a saying related to this pattern of consumerism: 'let the water run out, as long as it has been boiled' (*taro metti, kopura mua nrédé*), which means that one prefers to be in debt in order to display status and to be judged favourably for glorious appearance.

A middle class woman and a civil servant, *Ibu* Hamidah, told me a related Indonesian saying: 'let one be poor as long as one kept up appearances' (*biar miskin asal penampilan*). To clarify what she meant, one night a lower class woman and her daughter walked to a wedding party of a neighbour. Pointing to them, *Ibu* Hamidah told me: 'Look at them, their appearance is like rich women, wearing trendy attire and accessories which are still on credit, but they walk because they have no car'. The social pressure to gain status has led to consumerism, often at great cost. In fact, one's status is not always gained in this way, especially for lower class people since one's status is not based only on appearance.

This pattern of consumerism affects gender relations in marriage. There is an ambiguity in this pattern. While husbands expected their wives to perform their best, they also discouraged their wives from going along with whatever happens to be the prevailing fashion (*ikut-ikutan mode*) because Islam does not teach you to be extravagant with money (*foya-foya*). For example, I often heard husbands complain about their wives glorious appearance, but at the same time they were also proud of them because, to some extent, it indicated their social status. Thus, the social pressure and the great cost of consumerism may be in a different degree in different status levels because of the ability to meet the costs.

In a party, apart from what they wear and how they are treated according to their status, we can also observe how people from different classes behave. Millar's finding in Soppeng, where she conducted her study, identifies how guests are placed according to their status in a Bugis wedding (Millar 1989). One night, when *Ibu* Hamidah got back from a wedding party, she directly had her dinner at home. I wondered why she did not have her dinner at the party. She said: 'We usually do not eat much in a party, we just take a very small portion of food, and do not finish it, otherwise it shows that we are poor and do not have anything to eat at home'. Hence, not only one's appearance and order of seating are of concern for status, but also how one eats at a party.

Lontaraq Daramatasia:[25] *Assikalaibinéngeng* in Bugis Manuscript

Lontaraq Daramatasia is a Bugis manuscript showing heavy Arabic influence, written in the 20th century.[26] The manuscript deals with the dynamics of the relationship between husband and wife and offers marital guidance. The text

25 There are a number of version of Daramatasia manuscripts. For example, Djamaris (1983:79–96) transliterated another version of Daramatasia manuscript based on van Ronkel catalogue (Notulen, 28 April 1868). M.D. Nor (1989) collected six Malaysian stories (*hikayat*), including Hikayat Daramatasia in a book entitled *Antologi Enam Hikayat*. While the basic story of these versions is similar with *Lontaraq Daramatasia*, the ending of each version is different from each other. *Lontaraq Daramatasia* continues the story after the death of Daramatasia's husband, and that she was proposed to by a number of men and decided to marry Ahmad (see Chapter V).

26 In her article on women and Islam in the 1920s Malay fiction, Hooker (1994) discusses the tone of Islam, in the love story of Hikayat Faridah Hanom and Hikayat *Percintaan Kasih Kemudaan*.

begins with an illustration of the happy family of Daramatasia and Saéheq Bilmaqrupi, who had a daughter, Indara Dewi.[27] Then the text narrative states that God plans to test Daramatasia's husband (B. *riuji ri Allataala*). For that purpose, according to the text, God caused sin enters Saéheq Bilmaqrupi's body, who subsequently was under the spell of evil whenever his wife cut her hair without his consent. One evening when he was eating, the oil lamp was just to go out. When Daramatasia attempted to look for a lamp wick, she recalled the an utterance of our Prophet (Muhammad) (*adanna Nabitta*):

> Any woman who leaves her husband when he is eating, is considered a rebellious wife—both towards Allah's command and her husband.
>
> *Nigi-nigi makkunrai moloiwi manré lakkainna nakkeddéq mpélaiwi dorakai ri Allataala nénniya risurona, na madorakatoi ri lakkainna* (*Lontaraq Daramatasia*, p. 7).

The message of the Prophet Muhammad, according to this *lontaraq*, illustrates that the rebelliousness of the wife is not just related to her husband, but also to Allah. Therefore, if Daramatasia becomes a disobedient wife, she is not only being rebellious to her husband, but also to Allah. If Daramatasia becomes a disobedient wife, she is thus not just being rebellious towards her husband, but also towards Allah. In practice, when the husband is eating, the wife should be in his side. Leaving her husband while he is eating is tabooed by elders (*nappémmaliangngi tomatoaé*), among the Bugis, not just because it shows her indifference and impoliteness, as she usually 'serves' her husband during meals, putting the food onto his plate, pouring his beverage into his glass, and so on. In addition, this is the time for the members of the family to have open discussions.

To keep the lamp from going out, to avoid both walking out on her husband (*mpélai lakkainna*) while he was eating and leaving her daughter (who was sleeping in her lap) lest the girl cried, she cut seven strands of her hair to use as a lamp wick (*kuretteq pitu lampaq kuala sunggu ri pajjennangengngé*). Knowing that Daramatasia had cut her hair without his consent, her husband was severely angry (*temmaka caiqna*) because she usually first asked his permission before doing anything. Hence, she cast her out and told her to return to her parents. He ignored her apology and even hit her with a rattan cane until

27 The name of their daughter is mentioned in two slightly different spellings. At the beginning it was Cindara Dewi, another time it was Indara Dewi. Hence, I use Indara Dewi to standardise the name.

she fainted when she asked to stay to take care of their daughter (*taronaq monro ri bolataq taranakakkiq anaqtaq*), promising to cook and do her husband's laundry (*kiala aréggaq pannasu-nasu mutarekkiq dapurettaq, kiala aréqga passessaq-sessaq sessakengngiq pakéattaq*) if she was only allowed to stay with them (see Hooker 1997:77–8). When she regained consciousness, her husband beat her again and she was once more told to return to her mother (*lao mémenno riyaq ri indoqmu*). She finally left for her parents' home, but only after having asked permission from her husband (*nalao sujuq riolona lakkainna*). By doing this, she showed her respect for him despite his violent behaviour, as in Islam a wife is not allowed to leave the house without her husband's permission; moreover, he still might change his mind. But he did not, and Daramatasia left.

However, when she got to her parents' house, they turned her away, as they realized that her arrival in the middle of the night unaccompanied by her husband meant there was something wrong between the couple (*déq kumaéloq timparekko tangeq nasabaq déq muengka nawattu ri tangnga bennié, majeppuq magellikotu lakkaimmu namuengka lettuq ri tangnga bennié*). Her parents were reluctant to accept Daramatasia lest they accept a 'rebellious wife' (*téa sisengnga mitai makkunrai doraka ri lakkainna*). Further, Daramatasia's mother was afraid of being sinful to God (*mitauqkaq ri Allataala nennia ri surona*) if she let Daramatasia to the house.

Finally, Daramatasia left without having a place to go, but whenever she needed something, she prayed to God (*Allataala*), and her request was immediately granted. When she wanted to pray, she could not find any water for her ritual ablution before prayers (A. *wudhu*), and she also needed clean clothes to wear for praying. God commanded Jibril (the archangel Gabriel) to prepare blouse (B. *waju*) and a sarong (*lipaq*), and to provide her with a golden pool full of water from heaven (*kollang pulaweng polé ri Surugaé*). After her afternoon prayer (*sempajang Assaraq*), Jibril told Daramatasia that God wanted her to pray two *rakaat* (A. an essential unit of prayer ritual), wash her face with water brought by Jibril from heaven, and return to her husband (*réweq rilakkaimmu*). Daramatasia's face became luminous (*maccéia*) and younger (*malolo tangngarenna*). Before she departed, Jibril told her that both her husband and her daughter had suffered since she had left (*maseroto anrasa-rasana ri munrimmu*). When she came home, Saéheq Bil-maqrupi apologised (*pakarajaiangngaq addampeng andiq*) for what he had done to her. Three days later, he died (*naréweq ripammaséna Allataala*).

There are a number of messages in this *lontaraq*, but the main message is that the wife should be obedient to her husband. For example, Daramatasia was given a number of things from heaven by God during her journey, as rewards for being an obedient wife. Before she is asked to return to her husband, she is beautified, which reflects the importance of the of the wife's beauty to her husband. But what about the latter's violent behaviour? One may say that according to this text, the husband is entitled to be violent to his wife, as becomes apparent, for example, from the fact that Daramatasia's mother approves of her son-in-law's behaviour. Analogously, Daramatasia accepted her husband's anger as being 'her fault', even though she had acted for the sake of her husband and her daughter. In Bugis, it is acceptable for the husband to 'warn' his wife when she neglects her domestic tasks. It is also common for the wife to ask her husband for permission to cut her hair. But I never encountered any case where a wife was cast out by her husband because she cut her hair without his permission. The text demonstrates the importance of the husband's consent for the wife before she engages in any activity.

When Daramatasia had returned and after Saéheq Bil-maqrupi listened to the story of her journey, he became aware of (B. *talingeq*) and asked for forgiveness because of his 'wrong doing' to Daramatasia. But Daramatasia replied:

> My excellency Saéheq Bil-maqrupi, God forgives you, and it is His command [for a wife to be obedient] and Muhammad is Allah's messenger to lead you to well-being.
>
> *O Puwakku Saéheq Bil-maqrupi, Allataala maddampengekkiq sibawa risurona naia ritu Muhammadeq tau masserié nennia assalamakeng* (*Lontaraq Daramatasia*, p. 36).

Daramatasia accepts her husband's violent behaviour because it is Allah's command that she must be obedient. Otherwise, she would be being sinful towards her husband, and this is understood as akin to a sin against God (*dorakai ri Allataala nennia ri surona*). On this account, the husband is identified with God. The importance of the wife's obedience is reflected in the following statement made by Daramatasia at the end of the text:

> My fellow females, dedicate yourselves to your husbands. According to the Prophet s.a.w.,[28] a wife is under her husband's command. The Prophet s.a.w. also states that there are no deeds better than a wife obeying her husband's command.

28 s.a.w. stands for *sallallahu alaihi wasallam*, meaning 'the blessing of God be upon him and peace,' a phrase pronounced or written after mention of the name of the Prophet Muhammad (Federspiel 1995).

> *[O] pada-padakkuq makkunrai, patuju laloi kasuwiammu rilakkaimmu. Rimakkedanna Nabi s.a.w. naia makkunraié ilaleng paréntanai lakkainna. Makkedda toi Nabitta s.a.w., déq amalaq masero lebbiq nennia masero décéng napogauq makkunraié engkaé lakkainna sangngadinna tumaningiéngngi passurona lakkainna napoéloq é* (*Lontaraq Daramatasia,* p. 48).

This statement emphasises that not only is the husband entitled to the obedience of his wife, but the wife herself supports this idea as well. Despite Saéheq Bil-maqrupi's apology, this *lontaraq* reflects the male-dominated orientation of the text, and suggests that violence against one's wife is a legitimate measure. This message is related to a textual interpretation of a verse in the Qur'an (*An-Nisa*:34) that emphasizes the obedience of the wife to the husband. That verse is, in turn, supported by a textual interpretation of some Hadith, according to which a wife has to obey her husband and must not reject his demand for sexual intercourse, which stresses women's subordination in marital life.[29] In fact, the Qur'anic verse explains that 'the good wife is obedient and harmonious in her husband's presence, in his absence guards his reputation and property and her own virtue, as ordained by Allah'. In case of marital conflict, there are four steps to be followed by both husband and wife, measures which are often recommended by religious leaders (I. *ulama*) in their sermons, and have to be taken in the following order: first, verbal advice or admonition may be sufficient; if not, sexual relations may be suspended; if this is not effective either, some slight 'physical correction' may be applied. While the latter is permissible, it is not advisable, and all authorities unanimously disapprove of any sort of cruelty, including even persistent nagging. If all these measures fail, it is recommended to summon a family council.[30]

In Bugis marital life (B. *assikalaibinéngngeng*), violence against wives is acceptable, but only for certain reasons, for instance, if a wife behaves in a manner that brings *siriq* (shame) upon her family, or by committing adultery with another man. In the past, not only the unfaithful wife was killed, but also the man she had an affair with. In such cases, the killing was culturally acceptable and not considered a crime. Indeed, in instances like these, the husbands are acting as *to masiriq.* Even though killing because of *siriq* is still culturally acceptable today, it now has to be brought to court. For the Bugis point of view, an adulterous wife is more shameful than an adulterous husband who goes

29 See Istiadah (1995:6–7) for a discussion of neo-modernist interpretations of the Qur'an and Hadith.

30 For a discussion of marital violence in Bugis society, see Nurul Ilmi Idrus (2001) and Nurul Ilmi Idrus and Bennett (2003).

astray, and it is very easy to divorce a woman who is deemed unfaithful. In such cases, the divorce is hastened, and soon after the divorce is granted, the husband is married to another woman.

In addition, the manuscript also provides marital guidance for the wife based on the words of the Prophet Muhammad, among others:

> [I]f a wife cooks her husband's meal, she will be kept away from hell…for washing her husband's, she will be recompensed with cleansing herself of sin as clean as the clothes…for praying for her husband's goodness, the door of heaven will be opened for her (*Lontaraq Daramatasia,* pp. 50–3).[31]

All a wife's deeds for the sake of her husband will be rewarded in heaven with something which is beneficial because, according to this text, Allah requires the wife to work for her husband (*naékia naélorekko Allataala makkarésoangngi lakkaimmu*).

Within the context of the ideas outlined above, the 'cooking duties' of the wife (*mannasuangngi lakkainna*) not only pertain to providing meals for her husband, but also providing meals for the children and other member of the family who live in the same house. But when the husband is not present at lunch or dinner, his meal portion will be put aside before others enjoy the food cooked by the *to ri bola* (B. the wife). In addition, I frequently heard a joking remark amongst young married women in the village when they were washing clothes near the well: 'The more you wash, the more good works you have' (*Mangking maéga musessaq, mangking maéga amalaqmu*). The women would joke that way to entertain themselves when men were not around; they viewed doing the laundry as a good deed rather than a burden. Women also pray for their husband (*tuling méllauangngi décéng lakkainna*). More precisely, they usually will pray for their husband's health, safety, and fortune, implying that without these qualities the husbands would not be able to 'surround the kitchen seven times' (*mattuliling dapureng wékka pétu*) (see Chapter 3).

In contrast, this *lontaraq* also states the recompense for the wife's bad behaviour towards her husband based on the words of the Prophet Muhammad, among others:

> [I]f a wife always has bad thoughts about her husband , she will forever cry in hell…if she is always angry with her husband, she will be thrown to hell by an angel…if she lies to her husband, or does something without

31 For complete and original texts of *Lontaraq Daramatasia* pertaining to 'good behaviours' of the wife towards her husband (quoted texts are bold), see Appendix 4.1.

> her husband's consent, she will be beaten in hell similar to the way 40 thieves are beaten (*Lontaraq Daramatasia,* p. 53–5).[32]

Thus, while a wife's good behaviour toward her husband is associated with heaven (B. *suruga*), in this *lontaraq* bad behaviour is linked to hell (*ranaka*). In practice, elders advise married women to be always pleasant towards their husbands (*tuli macenning atinna ri lakkainna*), and to be faithful to them (*malempuq rilakkainna*). Yet rather than relating such such behaviour directly to a wife's fate in afterlife, the elders hold that it is conducive to the fortune and happiness of marital life (*assikalaibinéngeng*) in this life on earth.

While the largest portion of the text of the *Lontaraq Daramatasia* provides guidance for the wife, a small portion is directed to the husband, based on the words of the Prophet Muhammad. For example, the best deeds enacted of a husband are to take care of his wife (*piaraéngngi bainéna*), or to provide her with food (*anréna*), money (*balancana*), and clothing (*pakéanna*). He is also obliged to prevent her from engaging in bad behaviour (*gauq majaq*) and to guide her to behave in a good manner (*gauq madécéng*). However, the *lontaraq* does not mention any bad behaviour of the husband towards his wife that might affect his life after death. All good behaviour toward his wife arises out of his above mentioned duties and does not imply that he will go to heaven. Likewise, his bad acts are not associated with going to hell. This reveals that the text mainly addresses wives. In practice, man's economic and moral obligations in Bugis society are reflected in the image of ideal prospective husband who has the ability to 'surround the kitchen seven times' (*mattuliling dapureng wékka pétu*) and to be the role model in his family, as I discussed in Chapter III.

Although the influence of Islam is significant in the *lontaraq* under discussion here, much of its content is not consistent with the teaching of Islam, and it is thus possible that the reference to Allah (B. *Allataala*) and the Prophet (*Nabitta*) in the manuscript merely serves the purpose of legitimazing the message of this *lontaraq*.

The application of the values in this *lontaraq* bolsters the idea of the 'natural authority' of the father which was constructed by the New Order through its development policy that defined Indonesian women as subordinate to men within the family and the state (see Robinson 2000b). It is not clear whether or not the *Lontaraq Daramatasia* influenced the secular Marriage Law of 1974, but this ideology existed long before that law was introduced under Islamic influence, identifying the husband as the head of the household (*kepala rumah*

32 For complete and original texts of *Lontaraq Daramatasia* with reference to 'bad behaviours' of the wife (quoted texts are bold), see Appendix 4.2.

tangga) and the wife as the mother of the household (*ibu rumah tangga*), it reflects the structural relationship between husband and wife (see Chapter 1).

In the following section, I discuss the nature of the Bakris and the struggle between the forces of tradition and those of change.

The Bakris: The Narrative of the Nature of Marriage and its Change

Pak Bakri's household consists of *Pak* Bakri—the head of a primary school in Kulo—and *Ibu* Darma or *Ibu* Bakri, a housewife, their two youngest children and *Ibu* Darma's father, whose wife died a few years ago. They have seven children (three daughters and four sons); two of their daughters are married, one resides in West Papua and the other is in Kalimantan, and a son is also married and lives in another regency (Pangkep). They are all married to Bugis. The other two children, Ati and Umar, are continuing their studies at public and private universities in Makassar. Hence, there were only five people living in the house when I did my fieldwork in 2000. The Bakris used to live elsewhere but moved to *Ibu* Darma's parents' house after the death of her mother. As *Ibu* Darma is the eldest daughter in the family, it was her responsibility to take care of her father. The house was left to *Ibu* Darma but I heard that there was tension between *Ibu* Darma and her younger sister, *Ibu* Marwah, who lived in Malaysia. *Ibu* Marwah contested whether the house was left to herself or to *Ibu* Darma, given that she used to take care of her parents before migrating to Malaysia.[33]

Daily activities in the house started early in the morning, at five. *Ibu* Darma was the first person to get up, while other members of the family still embraced their pillows tightly. After her morning prayer, *Ibu* Darma's daily routine started by boiling a pan of water, carrying several buckets of water, preparing breakfast for all members of the family, drying the chocolate seeds, laundering, cleaning, cooking, folding the dry clothing in the afternoon or in the evening or whenever possible, preparing dinner and washing dishes. She had no time to relax

33 There is no rigid regulation in terms of inheritance. Even though there is the notion of '*mallempaq oroané, majjujung makkunrai*' which implies that man gets two portion, woman gets one. In practice, they are equally distributed and the distribution is not rigid and is situational. I encountered during my fieldwork that parents usually divide their property to their children equally, then bequeath their house to the eldest or youngest daughter or to eldest son, depending on considerations, such as who they live with in their old age, or who among their children does not have a house. Others make an arrangement that the house can be sold by their children after their death and the money divided equally.

until she went to bed at ten after completing her domestic chores. I could see how tired she was whenever I saw her lying in front of the TV in the evening. One evening she told me: 'I need an energiser battery'.

During harvest time, after returning from school, *Pak* Bakri and *Ibu* Darma went to the chocolate garden and returned before six. The youngest child (three years old) was tended by their second youngest son, Farhan, who was 20 years old. During the day, Farhan and *Pak* Bakri helped *Ibu* Darma to carry water to the kitchen from the water pool (I. *kolam air*) or well downstairs.

Pak Bakri got up early in the morning as well. However, he returned to bed after his early morning prayer. He got up just before seven, took a shower and went to school, which was located right in front of the house. His nights were spent with his friends playing cards, either in the house or at his friend's after evening prayer.

Ibu Darma's father usually spent his day under the stilt-house, reading, lying down, or playing with his youngest grandchild, while greeting anybody who passed the house. He would watch TV in the afternoon after finishing his afternoon prayer. To protect themselves from bad spirits, everybody usually bathed and was home before twilight because this period of transition is regarded as dangerous.[34]

Pak Bakri spent most of his time outside; it was very difficult to find him during the day. But he was usually at home during the evening prayer. *Ibu* Darma was often around the house, but not necessarily inside. Women usually gathered together under the stilt-house after lunch. There were two bamboo couches under the stilt-house of *Pak* Bakri, one was used by *ibu-ibu* to sit on or lie down and talk to each other, while *Ibu* Darma's father lied down on another bamboo couch.

Even though *Pak* Bakri accepted the idea that the relationship between husband and wife among people in Kulo is equal and complementary, he himself showed a 'different picture'. He usually denigrated *Ibu* Darma for her lack of education. For example, every time I went home, *Ibu* Darma usually welcomed me with a number of questions regarding what I had done during the day. Even though I was not disturbed by her questions, *Pak* Bakri usually scolded *Ibu* Darma by saying: 'Why do you always ask *Ibu* Ilmi, she is not a kid' (*Kenapa selalu tanya-tanya* Ibu Ilmi, *dia bukan anak kecil*). Then, Pak Bakri would criticise her, by telling me: 'That's the way she speaks because of her lack of education' (*Begitulah kalau orang tidak berpendidikan bu, urusan orang mau diurusi*). To me, her curiosity showed her interest in my work.

---

34 See Errington (1979 and 1989) for a discussion on danger and the transition of time in Luwu, South Sulawesi.

In Bugis, any activity related to internal family affairs is customarily regarded as the wife's business, including money management. This is why when a husband controls the money, he will be called a parsimonious husband (B. *lakkai matunreng*). This is the case in *Pak* Bakri's family. *Pak* Bakri used to give his salary to his wife, but he changed the arrangement after he had relationships with a number of different woman between 1979 and 1995. Responding to my curiosity about the switching of money management, *Pak* Bakri defended himself by saying it was not because he was a parsimonious husband (*lakkai matunreng*), but because *Ibu* Darma was incapable of managing the household income, while *Pak* Bakri always had to save money for the children's education. This seemed to be reasonable since two of their children were continuing their education in Makassar. He explained that such a plan was beyond *Ibu* Darma's ability because of her low education, which *Pak* Bakri always emphasised whenever he talked about his wife or whenever she did something he considered 'wrong'.

However, his eldest daughter, Rapiah, suggested that this transfer of responsibility was due to the fact that *Pak* Bakri had to finance his children from his second wife, now 'divorced' (see below). Thus, he was afraid that it would be difficult for him to control the money if it was managed by his first wife. He tried to assure me that the recent arrangement was the right decision, and that his wife could get money anytime from his pocket. However, when I inquired with *Ibu* Darma, she told me of her disappointment because every single Rupiah (Indonesian currency) had to be accounted for to her husband. In spite of the fact that she was psychologically denigrated by her husband on the daily basis, I never witnessed *Ibu* Darma physically abused by her husband.

Another interesting comment on this arrangement was made by *Pak* Akhmad, a judge in the Pengadilan Agama in Sidrap, who was also the money manager in his family. He, too, refused to be called a parsimonious husband, or *lakkai matunreng*, and argued that as long as all the family needs could be fulfilled, particularly if the husband was the only income-provider in the family, there was nothing to complain about.

Since it is common for wives to be the money managers no matter whether they have a single or double income in the family, wives will feel denigrated by any change to this general pattern, and a husband who handles the family income is viewed in a negative light by others. It is also a question of power. Unlike Javanese, who consider that handling money is coarse (I. *kasar*) and devalues women (see, for example, Hatley 1990, Keeler 1990 and Sullivan 1994), in Bugis, money is seen as one of the sources of women's social power which may be used to establish prestige and social status of the family. I heard from *ibu-ibu* that 'if we don't hold money, we have no power', giving *Ibu* Kasmawati and *Ibu* Darma as examples who are not money managers in the family. Then, the *ibu-ibu* said: 'If men hold the money they may spend it on something else, such as an affair with another woman' (see Brenner 1995:80).[35] Men also acknowledge the attachment of women with money management. The typical comment is that the wife is the boss when it deals with money. While men as money managers has a negative value for the Bugis (such as *lakkai matunreng, lakkai macukkéréng*),[36] this is the reverse for women (see below). A number of studies in Java indicate similar account of the conception of gender and money management that women are competent in money management, while men are incompetent to do so (see, for example, H. Geertz 1961:123; Hull 1975:113). Errington notes that such economic power is in marked contrast to the greatest prestige of spiritual potency and perceives women's assumed high prestige based on their control of money as 'an optical illusion based on the importation of Eurocentric ideas about the relations of power and prestige' (1990:7). In other words, women should control the source of spiritual potency in order to achieve the highest social prestige (Robinson 2001:26).

Money, Power and Violence

Money, power and violence are three aspects that are interrelated. To explain the connection, I present three case studies of family dynamics in this section—the cases of *Ibu* Kasmawati, *Ibu* Halimah and *Ibu* Darma.

Ibu *Kasmawati's Story: Money and Male Control*

Since Bugis women are usually the money managers in the household, women whose husbands control the money view this as a form of economic violence. For example, one informant, *Ibu* Kasmawati, stated:

> Even though my husband gave me all his salary every month, every single Rupiah (Indonesian currency) spent had to be reported to him and any expense had to be according to his decision (B. *éloqnapi najaji*), not only with his money, but also with my money. I did not even have the right to

35 See Robinson who discusses the contradictory point between Sullivan, Hatley, and Keeler, on the one hand and Brenner, on the other, in terms of gender ideology and self-control for the Javanese (Robinson 2001:22).

36 *Lakkai macukkéréng* is a term used to describe a husband's behaviour who wants to know every single cent/penny spent by his wife. This term is even more negative than the term *lakkai matunréng.*

> use my own money as I pleased. He usually counted the money according to 'how many grams of gold' we could buy with the money I spent. He did not take into account that every day we had to buy food and other daily basic needs. He is really an inquisitive husband (B. *lakkai macukkereng*). I was so sorry because it is usually the wife who controls the money (Kasmawati, 39 years, primary school teacher, divorced with two children, interviewed 22 January 2001).

Ten years after this marriage, which began in 1994, money management was not the only problem in *Ibu* Kasmawati's marriage. Her husband, *Pak* Alam, became violent when he became sexually impotent (B. *déqna tettong lasona*). After that, he was quick to anger not only with his wife, but also with their children. *Pak* Alam also used to scold her using terms such as unlucky woman (*makkunrai macilaka*) and devil woman (*makkunrai sétang*). He kicked and slapped her, dated another woman before the divorce, and threw stones at his wife either in the house or elsewhere in view of others, including in the school where both of them worked as teachers. There is a rumour in the village that *Pak* Alam was bewitched (*risanroi*) with very strong magic (*saraddasi mallino*) by someone who was jealous of his family's social well-being. The rumour was spread by *Ibu* Kasmawati based on advice she received from a traditional healer. This seemed quite reasonable to her since they alone represented middle class social status among the villagers in Kulo. She accepted *Pak* Alam's violence for this reason. But, she told me that she tried to camouflage *Pak* Alam's sexual impotence to prevent him from feeling shame, as she stated that it was more honourable for him to be known as a sick man because of bewitching rather than as an impotent man. *Pak* Alam, on the contrary, married another woman in the same year of their divorce (1998), but still controlled his ex-wife's daily life. For instance, when he came to visit their children, who were under the custody of *Ibu* Kasmawati, he asked them suspicious questions concerning people who came to the house, to find out whether or not his ex-wife had a relationship with another man. *Pak* Alam's second marriage appeared to be a strategy to conceal his sexual inability and to return his self-confidence. In fact, he did not have any children from this marriage.

Ibu Kasmawati's case suggests that her husband's control of money was a way of controlling her. In addition, *Pak* Alam's sexual impotence resulted in a lack of masculine power as a penis is termed 'a man's gun' in Bugis (*pattémbaqna urané*). Upon losing this 'gun' (sexual impotence means losing his power), violence became an alternative means of demonstrating his masculine power.

Ibu *Halimah's Story: Negotiating Economic Difficulties*

In other situations, such as in the economic division of labour, men who do not work or have no earning power in the family may use this as an excuse for domestic violence. Take for instance the case of *Ibu* Halimah in the following story.

In Rappang (see Map 1.2), *Ibu* Halimah's violent marriage was a very public case. I first met *Ibu* Halimah, a mother of seven children when I visited her house one day with my assistant, Farhan. *Ibu* Halimah is the first cousin of my host, *Pak* Bakri. I had been introduced to her daughters, her son and her son-in-law at the wedding party of *Pak* Bakri's son, Aco. *Ibu* Halimah and one of her daughters, Rahmi, were not present because they were in Jakarta to visit her eldest son when Aco was married. But, according to one source, they did not attend because Aco had previously been *dijodohkan*, that is destined to a particular partner, with Rahmi, a match Aco had refused because he thought they were second cousins (*sappokkadua*) and that this was too close for marriage. Farhan told me that *Ibu* Halimah's husband, *Pak* Tamrin, also refused to attend this wedding. Before they left, I was invited by one of her daughters to visit their house.

After the wedding, *Pak* Bakri's wife, *Ibu* Darma, explained to me what had happened in *Ibu* Halimah's marriage. Her husband was unemployed for years. He used to be a successful trader in West Papua. *Ibu* Halimah and her seven children returned to Rappang from West Papua because her mother was sick, followed by the return of her husband a few years afterwards. They started a new business in Rappang, opening a shop at the market, but it was not successful, unlike when they were in West Papua. Rapiah, *Pak* Bakri's eldest daughter, told me that *Pak* Tamrin was involved in incidents of sexual harassment, including with female customers and *Ibu* Halimah's first cousin. I was told that the cause of his bankruptcy was his unacceptable behaviour which was said to be the carrier of his misfortune (B. *pacilakai*) because people were reluctant to visit his store for fear of sexual harassment, which had become public knowledge in Rappang. As a result, *Pak* Tamrin started to sell their property until they were bankrupt.

To survive, *Ibu* Halimah and her children sold cakes in the market and catered for parties. Her youngest married daughter, Halida, who helped her husband in the market, contributed to the daily expense for food, and her eldest son, who worked as a contractor in the capital city of Jakarta, routinely sent money for their bills.

Pak Tamrin, however, became quick to anger and jealous of his wife. For example, he would get angry if his wife went out and returned late. He would ask a number of questions: where had she gone, what had she done, and to whom had she talked? *Ibu* Halimah was indifferent initially, but *Pak* Tamrin became more jealous and violent. Tension arose, not only between *Ibu* Halimah and *Pak* Tamrin, but also between *Pak* Tamrin and his children, who took the side of their mother. If there were male guests in the house, *Pak* Tamrin would get mad even if a guest were a member of *Ibu* Halimah's family. Despite their ongoing quarrels, *Pak* Tamrin never let her sleep in a separate room and became angry if *Ibu* Halimah refused to sleep with him. Once, *Ibu* Halimah could no longer take her husband's attitude, she left the house and stayed in her youngest daughter's house for about three months. During this time, her husband did not have any idea where she was. When he realised that she was staying with his youngest daughter, he came to see her, asked for forgiveness and promised to behave. But he never changed.

This attitude caused problems in the business run by *Ibu* Halimah and her daughters because people were reluctant to come to their house to order catering. But when she went to the market or came to her customers' houses to negotiate orders, *Pak* Tamrin would get jealous. Thus people commented to his behaviour in a Bugis saying: 'He wants a cat, but he does not want a mouse, he wants to eat, but he does not want to work' (B. *Élo'mi méong téa balao, élo'mi andé téa éco*). Ibu Halimah told me that to run such a business she had to be progressive, promoting her business and being friendly without letting herself be cheap. But this was unacceptable to her husband, who lacked confidence because of his unemployment, while *Ibu* Halimah had to feed herself and her children. In addition to this, according to one source, *Pak* Tamrin's anger and jealousy was one of the reasons why their other three daughters found it difficult to find a match.

Considering that *Pak* Tamrin was not able to 'surround the kitchen seven times' (*mattuliling dapureng wékka pétu*) or as the provider of the family, his violent behaviour aims to show his power over his wife to compensate his lack of confidence because of his unemployment status. Thus, in this case, violent in marriage was a situational event because,[37] according to *Ibu* Halimah, he was not that kind of person when he was the breadwinner.

But, everybody in the house was sick of *Pak* Tamrin's attitude. Thus, *Ibu* Halimah and her children decided to ask her eldest son in Jakarta to take his father and to prevent him from returning to Rappang. Hence, he lived in Jakarta, supported financially by his eldest son. *Ibu* Halimah and her children

37 Dobash and Dobash (1979) have analysed domestic violence based on situational contexts. On this account, violent behaviours can be best understood in terms of a range of interactions and consequences.

in Rappang enjoyed life without her husband. Her business was also smooth without him around.

Ibu *Darma's Story:* Pak *Bakri's Infidelity*

One late afternoon in the middle of July 2000, when I was helping *Ibu* Darma, *Pak* Bakri's wife, to fold clean clothes, we were talking about her past life, the period of time when her husband left her and her children for another woman. She was reluctant to tell me at first, but the story came out, as she knew that her eldest daughter, a friend of mine, had told me part of it already.

Pak Bakri left *Ibu* Darma in 1979 when they had five children and she was one month pregnant with her sixth child, Farhan, who later became my assistant. *Pak* Bakri then married a *janda* with four children, a teacher at the school where he worked. According to *Ibu* Darma, her husband married a flirtatious woman (B. *makkunrai callédaq*) who was left by her first husband because she had a relationship with another man. *Ibu* Darma was the one who took care of the children, while *Pak* Bakri came once in a while. Despite his infidelity, she always expected him back one day. She not only prayed, but also used witchcraft (*massanro*) to encourage *Pak* Bakri's return, as she believed that he had been bewitched by love magic by his second wife.[38]

During the day, she and her children lived in the same house as when her husband was still with her, and slept at her parents' house at night, a few houses from her own house in Kulo. *Pak* Bakri lived in Rappang (15 km from Kulo) with his second wife (*Ibu* Ros) and four children from her previous marriage, plus four children from this second marriage. During this time, the relationship between *Ibu* Darma and her in-laws was amicable and her parents also did not interfere in her marriage since they also expected the two to be reunited one day because they had children from this marriage. So, in this case, both his and her in-laws supported her. The divorce was prevented in consideration of the children.

I asked why she did not report her husband to his boss for polygamy, based on the PP No.10/1983 (see Chapter 1). As a village woman, *Ibu* Darma did not understand PP10. But apart from that she preferred to be sharing with another wife (B. *ripammarué*) than to be a divorcee. This was not only because she was afraid of the status of *janda,* but also because she was afraid of losing financial support for the children. Even though she had a wet-rice field, it was only enough to meet her daily expenses; she needed *Pak* Bakri's support for the education of the children. In fact, *Pak* Bakri's second marriage was an illegal marriage (*kawin liar*)

38 See, for example, Bennett (2000) in her detailed discussion of love magic in Lombok, Mataram, Eastern Indonesia.

which means that the marriage was unregistered and illegal. Therefore, this marriage would have no effect on his status as a civil servant even if *Ibu* Darma had reported his second marriage. In fact, she knew that her husband's second marriage to *Ibu* Ros was *kawin liar* only after a few years of their separation (*kawin liar* will be discussed in Chapter 6).

But *Ibu* Darma made contrary statements about her relationship with her husband. On the one hand, she said she kept out of the way whenever her husband visited the children in her house in order to avoid any conversation about divorce. On the other hand, she still engaged in sexual intercourse with *Pak* Bakri. *Ibu* Darma was afraid to refuse to have sex with *Pak* Bakri because she was still his wife. Hence, sexual intercourse was an act of 'duty' rather than an act of sexual satisfaction for both. She said that because he was her husband, so it was her duty to serve him (I. *namanya suami bu, kita harus ladeni*). However, *Pak* Bakri finally 'divorced' his second wife after fifteen years of marriage. Then, he had a relationship with another woman before he returned to his first wife in 1995. 'Play boy' was the label given to him by his sons for his infidelities with other women. The reason why *Pak* Bakri 'divorced' his second wife was not clear, but he justified it by saying it was time for him to return to his first wife and children after four years—the time between leaving his second wife and returning to his first wife—living in uncertainty away from his own family. During this period he lived with his mother. He stated that he needed a 'home'.

When I asked why he had married *Ibu* Ros, he defended himself saying that marriage was a mistake (*kekhilafan*) because he had never planned to have another wife other than *Ibu* Darma. He suggested that others should be careful when 'speaking about other people' because he believed that it might rebound on them. For instance, he had disapproved of his cousin, *Pak* Amir's plural marriage. But, a few years after his criticism, he himself had married for a second time, and a year after his first wife died he married for a third time, though it was suggested by his children who pitied him of being a lonely man in his olden age.

Conclusion

When men and women enter married life, they have certain expectations about the behaviours and duties connected to the household. Despite their differences, they both expect to help each other (B. *sibaliperriq*). This term implies the understanding that both husband and wife should contribute to, and take responsibility for, the household.

While the wife is identified with the house and the husband is identified with the outside world in search of family fortune, this is by no means a strict and permanent gender division. Rather, each party can play a part in the other's domain. Regardless of the different roles between husband and wife, they are complementary.

The idea that the wife is the boss at home is associated with her role not only as the money manager and money spender, but also as the decision maker for most of the matters related to household life. Any contrasting arrangement is regarded as a violation of local practice in marital life (*assikalaibinéngeng*).

While women become more dynamic because of the opportunity to work outside home, their house-based identity is intensified by the New Order since their labour productivity is not part of the development ideology. Thus, sentiment arises to working women which affirm their primary responsibilities in the domestic sphere, as reflected in the ideology of Bugis, *assikalibinéngeng*.

The Bugis bilateral kinship system allows newlyweds to live either with the family of the bride or the family of the groom. In the village, however, uxorilocal residence after marriage is the most common pattern, not only for newlyweds, but also for couples who have been married for longer periods. Emotional support, economic dependency and prevention of conflict between female in-laws are the predominant reasons newlyweds prefer uxorilocal residence. Although neolocal residence is preferred by more independent couples, this is not favoured by double-income families because of the difficulty of childcare. While in the city, waged domestic helpers can assist a working wife, people in the village rely mostly on familial relationships and domestic helpers are very rare. Thus, the extended family is very significant and is more likely to involve uxorilocal residence.

The local philosophy that one should 'let the water run out as long as it has been boiled' (B. *taro metti, kopura mui nrédé*) has been an important element in stimulating a new pattern of consumerism. Given that having money is not enough to provide social status, people compete with each other to establish rank, and trading as a *pajjakarta* is one of the most popular local ways for middle class to earn money, particularly for women acting as *pajjakarta* who advocate this consumerism to improve their own economic and enhance social status. Being female *pajjakarta* and advocating pattern of consumerism give an avenue for women to act as an agent to strengthen their domestic dominance and to be more dynamic in everyday life, as in the case of *Ibu* Farida. In contrast, this pattern also creates social pressure and affects gender relations within marriage because people compete each other to 'satisfy others' and to demonstrate status in a great cost.

Three cases presented in this chapter indicate the link between money, power, and violence in Bugis marriage. These instances reflect the view that violence against women in the household is not just caused by male unemployment, but also extramarital relations as well as sexual impotence, as the virile functioning of a man's penis is seen as one of the indicators of masculinity.

Lontaraq Daramatasia is a Bugis manuscript related to marital life (*assikalaibinéngeng*). This 20th century manuscript contains Islamic influences, indicated by referring to God (*Allataala*) and the Prophet (*Nabitta*). The dynamics of *assikalaibinéngeng* illustrated in this manuscript indicate a wife's domestic and moral duties and husband's economic and moral obligations to maintain and to guide the wife, the text provides less guidance for the husband. In this text a wife's dedication to her husband is connected to life after death, either in heaven or hell, but the man's fate is not resultant his performance as a husband. Despite the Islamic influence of the text, they are not necessarily similar to official Islam, compelling me to suggest that Islamic terms are used to merely legitimate the content of the manuscript. Many of the content in this manuscript are significant in the everyday practice of Bugis marital life, even though they are not perfectly the same.

In the next chapter, I will discuss beliefs and sexual manners from the ideology of Islam, adat, and how they are significant with everyday sexual practices among the Bugis.

CHAPTER 5

Beliefs and Sexual Manners: Islam, *Lontaraq* and Everyday Practices

Introduction

Bugis notions of sexuality are related to tradition as well as Islamic values. These act both to legitimate and to reproduce the accepted order of the sexual universe. It examines the belief systems that surround sexuality within marriage among the Bugis.

It draws upon written traditions derived from Bugis manuscripts that deal with the relationship between husband and wife and are subsumed under the genre of *Lontaraq Assikalaibinéngeng* (B. *lontaraq* marital life).[1] The manuscripts considered here were written between the 17th and 20th centuries (though some of them are undated) and come from a number of sources, including the Arsip National Wilayah Makassar and the Menzies Library at the Australian National University. Additionally, some of the ideas in this chapter are in circulation as oral tradition and are part of local sexual beliefs.

The chapter begins with a discussion on sexuality by examining how sexuality is regulated through Islam and manuscripts, which I refer to as *lontaraq*, and how these *lontaraq* are interpreted and interrelated to each other. In the second part of the chapter, I discuss the first night (I. *malam pertama*) of newlyweds, the virginity of the new bride, how newlyweds should behave, and rituals related to the control of the young couple's sexuality. Further I discuss sexual positions in relation to Bugis cosmology and reproduction, followed by a discussion of sex and symbols by examining the images and symbols of the vagina and penis found in *lontaraq* sources. The chapter ends with manners for sexual intercourse, the importance of self purification after intercourse, and the significance of these in the sexual life of the marital couple.

I argue that Islamic beliefs about sexuality, coming out of written as well as oral traditions, affect the daily sexual lives of Bugis, not just because Islam is the dominant ideology which cannot be separated from local practice, but also because *lontaraq* have a sacred value for the Bugis.

---

1 I am indebted to Mukhlis Hadrawi and Anwar Ibrahim (1999) for many of the texts that comprise *Lontaraq Assikalaibinéngeng* as well as their transliterations of *lontaraq* (written between the seventeenth and twentieth centuries) presented in this chapter.

 | DOI 10.1163/9789004311947_006

Islam and *Lontaraq* on Sexuality

Bugis and Islamic thought on sexuality invariably illustrates the relationships between men and women. Sexual life includes the complexity of emotion, feeling, personality, attitude and social character related to sex acts and sexual behaviours.

Sexual life—psychologically, socially and culturally—is regulated in the teachings of Islam. According to Islam, sexual intercourse is an act that can only be legitimated through marriage ties. Islam differentiates between sex in marriage and sex outside of marriage in order to make clear the difference between what is permitted (A. *halal*) and forbidden (*haram*). The sacrament of marriage (*nikah*) relates to the regulation of sexual practices. The disapproval of sex outside marriage is not merely about prohibition, it aims to regulate sexual practices (Bouhdiba, 1985:14). Islam dichotomises sexual life into sex as religious duty (*ibadah*) and sex as fornication (*zinah*). The former can be accomplished through marriage and brings reward (*pahala*), while the latter is conducted outside of legalized marriage and brings punishment from the society during one's lifetime as well as from God after death (Rahmat Sudirman 1999:42–43). Within Islam, marriage has at least three objectives: to legalize sexual practices between a man and a woman, to have children, and to achieve a peaceful life.

Bouhdiba (1985) stresses that sexual intercourse in Islam is one of the pillars of legal marriage (A. *nikah*), significantly the Qur'an (*Al-Imran*:14) states that sexual intercourse is one of the joys and pleasures from God. Citing Muhammad's words, Brook suggests that sex within marriage is supposed to be enjoyed by both the husband and wife, that foreplay and flirting are encouraged, and that sexual intercourse without foreplay is considered an act of cruelty to women (Brook 1995:39).

In Islam, the relationship between husband and wife (including sexual intercourse) is based on the principle of 'knowing good manners' (A. *mu'asyarah bil-ma'ruf*); *mu'asyarah* derived from the word for family, relative, close friend, termed *usyrah*, and the term *al-ma'ruf* from the root *urf*, meaning custom, habit, or culture. Thus, the phrase *mu'asyarah bil-ma'ruf* can be translated as social intercourse based on religious values and human culture (Husein Muhammad 2001:106–15).[2] This principle is reflected in a number of verses in the Qur'an and Hadith. For example, the Qur'an states 'a husband should behave in a good manner towards his wife' (*An-Nisa*:19); 'the wife is a dress/protector for the

2 This principle can be found in a number of verses of the *Qur'an*. For example, *Al-Baqarah* (233), *At-Taubah* (24), *Al-Hajj* (13), *Asy-Syu'ara'* (14), and *Al-Mujadalah* (22).

husband and vice versa' (*Al-Baqarah*:187); 'men and women have equal rights and duties' (*Al-Baqarah*:228); and 'husband and wife should love each other' (*Ar-Rum*: 21). Considering that the husband is responsible for providing for his wife's maintenance (I. *nafkah lahir*) and conjugal rights (*nafkah batin*) at least once in four months, failure to perform these duties gives a wife the right to ask for a divorce.

However, there are some verses in the Qur'an which are interpreted by some as a form of women's subordination. The most popular one is *Al-Baqarah* (223) which states:

> Your wives are your tillage, go in therefore unto your tillage in what manner soever ye will.

This verse is often interpreted to mean that a man may have intercourse with his wife whenever he wants, ignoring the woman's consent. It can be argued that it was a response to the behaviour of some men who liked to have anal sex, which Islamic law prohibits.[3] The verse warns that the wife's womb is the tillage for the man to plant his sperm, and the parable is intended to reveal that a husband should 'visit' his wife in the 'appropriate place' to prevent anal intercourse. This interpretation is supported by two Hadith (Abu Daud and at-Turmudzi) prohibiting anal intercourse. In addition, a Hadith (Ahmad bin Hanbal) states that a couple who have anal sex with the consent of both partners must be divorced, not to mention if a husband forces his wife to do it (Husein Muhammad 2001:113–4), reinforcing the prohibition of non-vaginal intercourse, considered a sinful act.

Furthermore, several Hadith articulate equality between husband and wife. For example, 'the best husband is the one who does the best for his wife' (Hadith at-Turmudzi); 'I like to dress up for my wife as I like my wife to dress up for me' (Hadith Ibnu Abas in Muhammad, ibid); 'the Prophet prohibits a husband to perform *azl* (coitus interuptus) without his wife's consent' (Hadith Ibn Majah) (in Masdar F. Mas'udi 1997:118).

However, as with the verse from the Qur'an cited above, several Hadith are also interpreted to mean that women must be obedient to their husbands. The most popular one states that 'an angel will denounce a wife until morning if she refuses to have sex with her husband' (Hadith Abu Hurairah in Masdar F. Mas'udi 1997:112). This Hadith has been taken to mean that the wife must not refuse her husband's desire to have sex in whatever fashion. In fact, the notion of 'refusing' in this Hadith is actually directed at a wife who refuses to have sex with her

3 For details see Masdar F. Mas'udi (1997:110–1).

husband 'without any reason,' and refusing in itself is not meant to be sinful (see Istiadah 1995:8, Masdar F. Mas'udi 1997:107–8, Husein Muhammad 2001:98–9). This affirms that there is still room for husbands and wives to negotiate sex. To strengthen this argument, a verse in the Qur'an (*Al-Baqarah*:228) states that wives are entitled to receive rewards for the duties they perform for their husbands.

Such interpretations are challenged by those promoting more equitable marital relations. For example, Shinta Nuriyah, the wife of Abdurrahman Wahid, the fourth president of Indonesia, commented that women's sexual and reproductive rights are violated in the name of 'harmony' by misinterpretations of the Qur'an and Hadith in which the sacred meaning of sexual intercourse is lost (*Kompas*, 29 July 2000). Johan Effendy, the previous State Secretary of Indonesia, notes that the texts in the Qur'an have to be re-examined contextually through historical and social methods because the present situation is different from the past (Kompas, 22 August 2000), when the verse was revealed. Both Shinta Nuriah and Johan Effendy recognize that the strictly literal interpretation of the Qur'an have resulted in the misinterpretation of the texts.[4]

Bugis manuscripts, called *lontaraq*, record the relationship between husbands and wives. For example, a manuscript called *Ajaran Tentang Etika*,[5] the title of which means 'Teachings about Ethics', describes marital obligations between a husband and wife. In this text, one of the duties of the husband is not only to provide his wife's material needs (food, clothing, shelter), but also to fulfil her sexual needs (B. *arusuq toi turusi éloqna naponyamengngé makkunrainna*). One of the wife's duties is to provide her husband's food and clothing and to welcome her husband to have sex (*malebbiq égang ritu makkunraié tarimaéngngi eloqna oroanéna*). The wife may refuse her husband's sexual advances if she is sick (*engka peddiqna*) or menstruating (*maddaragi*). In addition, a wife may ask for a divorce if her husband is impotent or infertile (*maténi napesunna*) or if the husband is overly sexually demanding and unable to control himself (*lebbi nawessui tennaullé perrengngi*). The wife therefore has both duties as well as rights in conjugal relations.

4 Masdar F. Mas'udi classifies verses of the Qur'an into 'fundamental' and 'instrumental' principles of religious teaching. While he refers the former to 'fixed principles' which are egalitarian and emphasise equal justice, the latter are concerned with the 'technical principles' of the teachings of Islam. For example, how women should dress or how women can inherit (Masdar F. Mas'udi 1994:15–9).

5 *Lontaraq Ajaran Tentang Etika,* Roll 62/No.26, seventeenth century, Arsip National Wilayah Makassar, transliterated by Mukhlis Hadrawi in June 2000; and *Lontaraq Budi Istikharah* (in A. Rahman Rahim 1982:37–9).

Even though the teachings of Islam and the content of *lontaraq* are interrelated, they are not the same. For example, it is stated in the *lontaraq* mentioned above that the husband is the substitute of God—*Allataala*—in the world (*apa iatu oroané passullénai Allataala rialéna ri lino*), that the wife should honour her husband after intercourse (*riélorengngi makkunraié mappakaraja ri oroanéna kopurai massita lakkainna*) by making obeisance (*sujuq*), and that all these actions will be rewarded in the afterlife (*sujuq-i koritu koamengngi nalolongang enrengngé nyamekkininnawa mattiq riakheraq*). Expressing a similar sentiment, a Hadith recounts Muhammad's words: 'If I ask someone to make obeisance, I will ask the wife to bow to her husband'. The implied meaning of this Hadith (Abu Hurairah) is that a person cannot perform obeisance other than to God. Thus, if someone performs his/her obeisance to someone else, it is the wife to her husband, which indicates the honour of the husband over his wife after God (Abdul Jalil Mohd. Hasan 1993:118).

Thus, an examination of what Islam (through the Qur'an and Hadith) says about sexuality reveals that these *lontaraq* contain an Islamic influence. The *lontaraq* that I quote may not be read by the majority of the Bugis, especially young people, but the message has been passed on by elders through oral tradition. The authority of *lontaraq* is not only because they are loaded with Islamic influence, but also because the content of *lontaraq* is framed as tradition passed down from elders through use of opening phrases like 'the elders say' (B. *makkeddai to matoaé*), these are 'the elders words' (*adanna to matoaé*), or this is 'the message of the elders' (*pappasenna to matoaé*). Thus, *lontaraq* are legitimated by evoking the authority of elders.

Bugis are brought up to listen to their elders (*mangkalinga ada to matoa*). Whether or not one agrees with elders' utterances, at least she/he is listening, and anyone who confronts elders' word is regarded as sinful. Thus, the content of *lontaraq* is imbued with Islamic values and elders' authority.

In addition to this authority, *lontaraq* are often preceded with the phrase 'the *lontaraq* states' (*makkeddai lontaraq é*); in this way, the *lontaraq* itself is regarded as having a spiritual, sacred. As Sweeney states:

> Social participation in the consumption of literature not only limits the content to what is accepted by the group as a whole; it also increases the normative influence of whatever fiction is tolerated, legitimizing and reinforcing its didactic effect.
>
> SWEENEY 1980:28

Sweeney's point is that the writer (of Malay literature) is not just concerned about the content of the text itself, but what the audience can get from the text and how the text is legitimated through consumption of the text.

Beliefs on Sexuality: Body Care

Sexuality is expressed in historically and culturally specific ways (Manderson 1995:2), and so varies from one culture to another. In their study of *Myth and Sexual Behaviour* of the Bugis in *lontaraq*, Muhlis Hadrawi and Anwar Ibrahim (1999:27) argue that myth [belief from cultural tradition] is one of the aspects which forms the discourse of sexuality of the [Bugis] marriage. Such belief is expressed through *Lontaraq Assikalaibinéngeng* in the forms of behaviour, magic formulae (*jappi-jappi*), and through the circulation of oral tradition.

For the Bugis, sexuality is understood in terms of a variety of folk beliefs. During fieldwork, I found that such beliefs are passed from one generation to another as oral traditions. Examples of these folk beliefs include the notion that frequent male masturbation will deplete sperm, a virgin girl will bleed as a result of first intercourse on the first night of her marriage, and pregnancy can be prevented by jumping about or sitting against a warm pan immediately after having sexual intercourse.

A unique belief from a *lontaraq* entitled *Bunga Rampai Lontaraq*,[6] the title of which means 'Anthology of *Lontaraq* relates to the use of semen as a youth-preserving salve that can be smeared on the body, particularly the face. During my fieldwork, I found that smearing semen around the face is a common practice. The following two statements detail this practice. Both of these statements indicate the importance of using procreative fluids to maintain beauty. The second statement testifies to the significance of returning what has been spent—that is *manni*, which is conceived as the mixture of the man's and woman's procreative fluids. To specify what they meant by the term *manni*, each of the women revealed that this substance is the fluid that flows out of her vagina after intercourse.

> I usually smear my husband's *manni* around my face because I was told by elders that this may make me stay young. Look at me: people usually comment that I still look young in my late thirties.
>
> MARDIAH, 39, two children, interviewed on 10 October 2000

> If a woman wants to stay young, she should take care of herself (B. *parakai aléna*). One of the ways of doing this is by, for example, smearing *manni* on her face. It is a remedy for my body. I believe that by practising this, *manni* is spent, but then returned to my body.
>
> ASNI, 40, three children, interviewed on 25 September 2000

6 *Bunga Rampai Lontaraq*, Roll 45/No. 23, undated, Arsip National Wilayah Makassar.

Women sometimes characterize the fluid that flows from their vaginas after intercourse as their husbands' seminal fluid, expressed as 'what men have' (I. *laki-laki punya*) or 'what comes from men' (*dari laki-laki*).[7] But when women talked about the importance of beauty and health, they referred to 'spent fluid', that is the *manni* (semen), but what they meant was a mix between women's vaginal fluid and men's semen. Further, Asni articulates in the second statement that fluid which comes from the body has to be returned to the body.

However, I have never heard that the liquid from the vagina is wiped on the face of the husband for cosmetic reasons. I discovered two related *lontaraq*—*Bunga Rampai Agama*-A[8] and *Bunga Rampai Lontaraq*—associated with the use of procreative fluids. The treatment described in the texts of *Bunga Rampai Agama*-A is how the husband treats his wife after intercourse. After wiping the *manni* consisting of his semen and his wife's vaginal fluid on his wife with the palm of his right hand, the husband pronounces the following magical formula (B. *jappi-jappi*):

Uakketta mmalai uaé matasaqna	I intend to get the boiled fluid
I Ali na Patima	of Ali and Fatima
Satijjang	which spurt at the same time
Pégollao junnuq	wherever the fluid goes
Pégo polé	wherever the fluid comes
Réweqko rionrommu	return to your place.

'Boiled fluid' in this sense refers to the mixture of vaginal fluid and semen. Ali and Fatima symbolize the penis and the vagina.[9] Thus, sexual intercourse signifies the meeting between Ali and Fatimah.

In *Bunga Rampai Lontaraq*, the following *jappi-jappi* is pronounced by the husband after mixing his semen (*uaé kollanna kalkausareq*, from the blade of his penis) and his wife's vaginal fluid (from the opening of her vagina) after intercourse:

7 Women use the Indonesian phrases 'what men have' (*laki-laki punya*) or 'what comes from men' (*dari laki-laki*) or in Bugis 'what belongs to the man' (*anunna oroané*) or 'comes from the man' (*polé ri oroané*) to refer to semen without specifically mentioning it. Such avoidance is related to taboos on talking about matters related to sex, sexuality or sexual organs.

8 *Lontara Bunga Rampai Agama*-A, Roll 48/No. 18, eighteenth century, Arsip National Wilayah Makassar.

9 Fatima is the Prophet Muhammad's daughter and Ali is her husband, the Prophet's cousin and disciple.

Waduq, wadiq, maniq, manikeng	The mixed fluid
mani riparéweq	the fluid is returned
tajang mapparéweq	brightness returns
t[a]jang ri apparéweqki	brightness is returned
ritongkoq uleng tépu	to complete the moon
nasalipuri caiana nurung Muhammaq	covered by the light of Muhammad
énréqko maccaia ri rupanna Fatima	bright Fatima's face
muasseri tubunna	strengthen her body
muallebbang ri atinna	spread in her heart
muraddeq rinyawana	be in her soul
napakéo temmaté-temmatoa	she will not die or become old
mumalolo pulana	always stay young.
Kumpayakung.	Let this be so.

These two manuscripts implicitly state the importance of returning 'spent fluid' and energy to the body, while the second one also alludes to health (B. *muasseri tubunna*) and beauty (*temmaté-temmatoa*). After pronouncing the above magical formula (*jappi-jappi*), the text states that the husband should lightly smear the fluid on his wife's body, from her forehead to her navel.

Another Bugis folk belief is that a husband should gently push on his wife's vagina with the heel of his foot immediately after sexual intercourse. This practice is believed not only to return the vagina to its original position, but also to tighten the vagina and make her stay young. Some elders told me that this practice protects the women's body from becoming 'withered'. In line with this, these elders can tell which women are taken care of by their husbands and which women are not. To clarify the difference between these two cases, I asked an elder, *Haji* Rukiah (62), to differentiate a woman who had been taken care of by her husband/herself (*riparakai rilakkainna/naparakai aléna*) and a woman who had not been (*déq riparakai rilakkainna/déq naparakai aléna*). The point she made is that the posture of woman of the former category is 'fresh' (I. *segar*), while the latter is 'withered' (I. *layu*). Therefore the practice of pushing the wife's vagina is a belief in traditional healing for the health of women's bodies associated with sexual pleasure. To convince me what she said, she showed me two married women as examples of both 'fresh' and 'withered' women.

In addition, elders also advise a couple to drink lots of water after intercourse in order to return their energy. The energy spent during intercourse was described by an elder as follows:

> During intercourse, hundreds of our tendons (I. *urat-urat*) are broken off. Hence, it is important to care for our bodies in order to preserve them from becoming withered. If a woman does not take care of her body, she will get old very quick because taking care of the body reconnects broken tendons to one another.
>
> HAJI DAWIAH, 65 years, interviewed on 10 October 2000

While this statement reflects the significance of caring for the woman's body—to strengthen tendons—it clarifies the local belief on the principle logic of body care. In addition, tightening the vagina constitutes care for the husband. There are two interchangeable terms used in this sense: 'loose vagina' and 'wet vagina'. While the former results from regular sexual intercourse, the latter is associated with lack of vaginal care. Consequently, women are advised by elders to take care of their vagina by, for example, drinking traditional juice. Turmeric juice is the most common juice suggested since it is believed it lessens the moisture of women's vagina. A traditional concoction made of betel leaves (B. *dauppacci*) is also recommended for washing the vagina. These beliefs reflect the significance of a wife's body care in association with a husband's pleasure. But both 'loose vagina' and 'wet vagina' are quite difficult to separate and define. When women talk about these terms, they are grouped together and related to the care of vagina and prospective brides, who are assumed to be virgins, are also advised in this way.

Newlyweds, *Malam Pertama*, and Virginity

The wedding night or first night (I. *malam pertama*) refers to the first night of sexual intercourse of newlyweds, which is considered to be an eagerly awaited moment, not only for the newlyweds, but also for the families of both sides. Nevertheless, the bride usually has ambivalent feelings about this moment. In spite of the fact that the bride is excited because this will become her first experience of sexual intercourse with her husband, it is also a threatening night for her because she has been informed that the first night of intercourse is a nightmare. My female informants described the experience of their first night (*malam pertama*) as painful. In reality the experience may vary from one person to another. As LeMoncheck, a feminist philosopher, states:

> Sex can be scary, passionate, funny, unsuccessful, unsafe, painful, boring, publicly humiliating, privatly beautiful, extremely personal, consciously

> political, cheerfully avoided, or regrettably absent, each in a different women's life, or all in a single life.
>
> LEMONCHECK 1997:23

From this point of view, sex can be either pleasurable or offensive, or it can be both. Some female informants told me the enjoyed of the 'first night' (*malam pertama*) in the way they were treated by their husband, but sexual intercourse itself was described as painful. A new bride who cries and gets hurt in the first night of her sexual intercourse is considered to be a 'successful bride' because it indicates that she is a pure virgin and is automatically regarded as having had no previous experience of intercourse.

Malam pertama, or the first night of sexual intercourse, does not necessarily take place on the first night of the wedding since a traditional Bugis wedding usually extends over several days. But, after the first intercourse, the family of the bride and the groom are concerned about the bride's virginity. The mother of the bride asks for proof, such as a piece of white fabric—a symbol of purity—with a spot of blood as evidence of her virginity. The bride usually keeps it as a memento of the proof of her purity. The mother of the groom asks her son about whether or not the bride was a virgin, inquiring 'did she bleed?' (B. *maddaramuiga*?). The result then becomes public knowledge.

In the old days, newlyweds were not allowed to sleep together if guests were still present or until the whole ritual was completed. I observed in a number of cases that a new bride who spent her time in her wedding bedroom, regardless of whether or not she had sexual intercourse with her husband, often became the subject of gossip or faced negative responses. I heard comments such as: 'she is eager to have sex with her husband'; 'she is being too aggressive with her husband'; or 'she does not want the guests to be around as it is time for her to have sex with her husband.' In one instance, I observed that a woman who was a close relative of the groom left the house because she considered herself disrespected (I. *tidak dihargai*) by the fact that the bride spent most of her time in her room while the relatives, both close and distant, were still there. In another case, I heard female elders murmur angrily for similar reason. If the negative response comes from the family of the groom, it may shame the family of the bride. Hence, it is up to the family of the bride to control the bride's behaviour.

There is a game played by the bride's relatives and the new groom and his escorts on the first night of the marriage. Her relatives try to hide the new bride from her husband to delay the first night of sexual intercourse. The higher the status of the couple, and this is especially the case for nobles, the more rituals are performed and the longer the delay before the first night of intercourse. Although the practice of such games has now been modified, the expectation that women should not show interest in sex remains significant. To show respect to the guests, the groom usually accompanies male members of the family by, for example, playing cards or talking to them. Since male sexual interest is considered to be part of his nature, the groom is usually teased by other men about his desire to have sex with his wife (as soon as possible).

Sexual Position, Bugis Cosmology and Reproduction

In her book *The Tao of Islam*, Murata (1998), a Japanese scholar, elucidates the meanings of 'unity' and 'dualism' in the relationship between men and women. In a chapter entitled 'Macrocosmic Marriage'. Murata discusses the relationship between the sky and the earth[10] which is an analogy for the relationship between *yang* and *yin*, a man and a woman, a husband and a wife. In analysing the relationship between men and women, however, Murata reveals her liberal thought by not indicating that the sky/man and the earth/woman analogy is based on the top/down position of the sky and the earth. She bases her argument on Chinese cosmology which describes the universe in the frame of *yang* and *yin*, emphasising 'harmony and equilibrium'. Murata applies her argument to an analysis of the Qur'an and Hadith, through which she denotes an understanding of Islam concerning men and women as giving them 'complementary functions.' A verse in the Qur'an (*Adz-dza-ri-yat*: 49) states that 'everything is created in pairs'. This suggests that the existence of one has no meaning without the presence of the other. In other words, husband and wife are two-in-one. Significantly, the Islamic scholar, Ibn Al-'Arabi (as cited by Murata, 1998:197) suggests that God created the sky and the earth as a set of supra-formal provisions and as a sign of God's creations. God created 'the earth as the wife' and 'the sky as the husband'. The sky reveals the vision from God to the earth just as a man transmits his sperm in the body of a woman through sexual. In addition, Murata states:

> Because of her beauty and kindness, the sky is deeply in love with the earth. The sky is married to the earth not because it is his duty, but because the sky intended to achieve enjoyment and happiness.[11]
>
> MURATA 1992:197

10 A verse in the Qur'an (*Al-Baqarah*:19) states that Allah (God) created sky and earth and the shift between night and day are evidence of His power.

11 Translated from an Indonesian version: '*Dikarenakan keindahan and kebaikannya, bumi menjadi sangat dicintai. Langit mengawininya bukan karena kewajiban, melainkan juga untuk mendapatkan kenikmatan dan kesenangan*' (Murata 1992:197).

In this account, Murata tries to make sense, in terms of the Islamic cosmology, of the complementary relationship between men and women and sky and earth, and the consequences of this relationship.

In the La Galigo Bugis epic, cosmological marriage can be analysed on the three levels: the upper world or sky (B. *Boting Langiq*) as the husband, the middle world or earth (*Alé Lino/Kawa*) as the child/ren and the lower world, or earth (*Pérétiwi/Toddang Toja/Uriq Liu*) as the wife. While the sky (*Boting Langiq*) is occupied by a ruler of the sky (*déwata*) named Patotoq é and his wife, named Datu Palingeq, and the lower world (*Toddang Toja*) is occupied by Guru ri Selleq and his wife, Sinauq Toja, the middle world (*Alé Lino*) is still uninhabited (*masua tau ri awa langiq*). One of Patoto'é's advisers, Rukkelleng Mpoba, who had visited the lower world (*Pérétiwi*), suggests Patotoé fill up the middle world (*Alé Lino*) with his descendents (*rijajiammu*), so that the *Alé Lino* is not uninhabited (*ajaq naoro lobbang linoé*). If this were not done, there could be no god because there were no human beings. The following dialogue expresses the advice of Patoto'é's advisor to fill up the earth (Muhammad Salim and Fachruddin Ambo Enre 1995):

> Rukkelleng Mpoba [a heavenly servant] added submissively,
> 'There is absolutely no one
> to acknowledge Batara [= Patotoq é, the creator] as lord,
> to show reverence to *Pérétiwi* [the lower world].
> Why, lord, do you not send down one of your family
> to appear on earth
> so that the world may not remain empty
> and so that earth may be filled with brightness?
> You are not god, lord, if people are lacking
> below sky and above *Pérétiwi*
> to acknowledge Batara as lord'.
> Yet Patotoq é [the creator] stayed silent; he answered not a word.
> Then three times Ruma Makompong [another heavenly servant] addressed him
> before La Patigana [= Patotoq é] turned and spoke,
> 'I agree to go up to the palace *kuta pareppaq é* [? the four-square fort]
> to inform the mother of La Rumpang Mégga [his consort] of this.
> She will then consent
> to place a child below the sky'.[12]

12 Loosely translated by Campbell Macknight (7 April 2003).

> *Maddaung wali Rukkelleng Mpoba,*
> *'Lé namasuaq mua na sia*
> *mattampa puang lé ri Batara,*
> *mappaleq wali lé ri Pérétiwi.*
> *Tammaga Puang muloq séua rijajiammu,*
> *tabbareq bareq ri atawareng,*
> *ajaq naonro lobbang linoé*
> *makkatajangeng ri atawareng.*
> *Teddéwata iq, Puang, rékkua masuaq tau*
> *ri awa langiq, lé ri manéqna Pérétiwié*
> *mattampa puang lé ri Batara'.*
> *Ala mettéq ga Patotoq é, ala mabbali ada sélappaq*
> *Nawékkatellu paddéweq ada Ruma Makompong*
> *nainappa na ngkiling makkeda La Patigana,*
> *'Taro aq ménréq ri sao kuta pareppaq é*
> *paissengi wi allingérenna La Rumpang Mégga*
> *Napoéloq pi Datu Palingéq*
> *taroé tuneq ri awa langiq'* (p. 58).

Despite the fact that Patotoq é is the ruler of the sky, he considers that only with his wife's consent, can the middle world of *Alé Lino* be filled up. The dialogue between Patotoq é and Datu Palingéq is as follows:

> [Patotoq é gets ready and goes out with his retinue.]
> Patotoq é [the creator] declared to his cherished wife,
> 'Why, dear Datu Palingéq [royal mother],
> do we not send down our offspring and create a child in *Kawaq* [on earth],
> letting him abandon our divine nature
> so that the world may not remain empty
> and so that brightness may shine below sky?
> We are not gods, dear, if people are lacking
> below sky to acknowledge Batara as lord'.
> Datu Palingéq replied,
> 'How indeed, Aji Patotoq [lord creator],
> if you wish
> to send down a child to the world itself,
> could there be brave people to confront you?'
> Patotoq é rejoiced greatly
> that his cherished wife agreed to send down a child.
> Palingéq é [the mother, = Datu Palingéq] declared,

'It would be good, Aji Patotoq [lord creator],
to send an order down to *Toddang Toja* [the Lower World]
to bring up our brothers and sisters,
to bring up here
all our first cousins, our nieces and nephews,
and all
from Toddang Toja [the Lower World] and from *Boting Langiq* [the Upper World]
come together here in the palace *kuta pareppaq é* [? the four-square fort],
all we divine leaders sitting together.
Let it be our common desire to act in common to place a child in Kawaq [on earth]'.[13]

Kua adanna Patotoq é ri makkunrai ripawekkeqna,
'Temmaga waé Datu Palingéq anri
tauloq rijajiatta, tabbareq bareq tuneq ri Kawaq,
massaliang ngi aju sengkonang siasettaé,
ajaq naonro lobbang linoé
makkatajangeng ri awa langiq.
Teddéwataiq anri rékkua masuaq tau
ri awa langiq mattampa puang lé ri Batara'.
Mabbali ada Datu Palingéq,
'Magi ro waé Aji Patotoq
na é rékkua lé maélo' ko
panonnoq tuneq ri Alé Lino,
maka inai to warani pang éwai o?'
Natalloq rio Patotoq é lé rituruqna panonnoq tuneq
Ri makkunrai ripawekkeqna.
Kua adanna Palingéq é,
'Madécéng sia Aji Patotoq,
massuroé kko ri Toddang Toja
patarakkaq i sélingéretta
napatarakkaq maneng ngi mai
sappo sisetta, anauréta,
narini maneng mai timummung,
ri Toddang Toja, ri Botting Langiq,
ri sao kuta pareppaq é,

13 Loosely translated by Campbell Macknight (7 April 2003).

> *tasicokkongeng maneng ponratu.*
> *Pada éloqpiq, tapada taro tuneq ri Kawaq'* (p. 60).

This dialogue illustrates that the woman's point of view is taken into account in making a decision. Hence, *Datuq Palingéq* invites their siblings, first cousins and nephews/nieces (B. *massélingéreng sappo sisetta, anauréta*) from the lower world, *Toddang Toja*, and the upper world, *Boting Langiq*, to discuss the plan, considering that only by all their agreement can the middle world of *Alé Lino* be occupied (*pada éloqpiq, tapada taro tuneq ri Kawaq*). The result of the meeting determines that Batara Guru from the upper world of *Boting Langiq*—the eldest son of Patotoq é and Datuq Palingéq—should be the first inhabitant in the middle world of *Alé Lino*. Wé Nyelliq Timoq—Batara Guru's first cousin and the eldest daughter of Guru ri Selleq and Sinauq Toja—comes up from the lower world of *Toddang Toja* to be the wife of Batara Guru. The marriage between the son of the ruler of the upper world and the daughter of the ruler of the lower world results in the birth of Batara Lattuq in the middle world. Three elements are explicitly illustrated in this cosmic marriage: first, the ideal marriage occurs between first cousins (*sapposiseng*) of noble descent (*assialang marola*); second, marriage takes place between a man and woman of different worlds, but the same social location in order to consolidate their 'white blood', a phrase that articulates Bugis concept of nobility; finally, the birth of Batara Lattuq (the son) indicates the significance of procreation, as a consequence of love and affection, in this instance between Wé Nyelliq Timoq and Batara Guru.

The initiative to reside in the middle world and the first dweller there (the husband, Batara Guru) came from the upper world, while the partner (Wé Nyelliq Timoq) of the first dweller came from the lower world. These three levels of the world based on Bugis cosmology reflect the sexual position during intercourse. For example, when people talk about this, both men and women state that during sexual intercourse the husband should be on top of the wife; the would-be baby is in the middle because when the wife conceives, the resulting child's position is in the middle between the prospective mother and father.

This top-husband and bottom-wife position, some feminists claim, leads one to make the opposition of the active versus passive partner in sexual intercourse. But this is not necessarily the case in Bugis culture, given that the wife can also be in the top position, though it is not encouraged. The former position has become the ideal and the most common style of intercourse within marriage. Nevertheless, instead of analysing this position in terms of active and passive roles in sexual intercourse, one could argue that such a position is associated with local understandings of reproduction. Indeed, Bugis express the belief that to conceive more easily, in addition to being on the bottom, the wife should also put a pillow under her buttocks in order better to retain the mixed procreative fluids, so that this fluid will not flow out of her vagina. This practise is particularly advisable for those who have been married for some time and do not yet have children. Therefore, the idealism of husband-top-active and wife-bottom-passive is not just about an ideologically constructed sexual position in sexual intercourse within marriage, but it is also associated with fertility. As Connell argues that '[g]ender is social practice that constantly refers to bodies and what bodies do, it is not social practice reduced to the body' (Connell 2000:27).

The importance of reproduction for the couple is expressed in teknonymous term of address. When the couple have children, the wife and the husband are called by the name of the first child. For example, Pak Bakri is known as father of Rapiah's (B. *amboqna Rapiah*) and Ibu Bakri as mother of Rapiah (*emmaqna Rapiah*) (see Robinson 1985:51 and Millar 1983:485). This indicates that the couple have gained full acceptance for their union.

Given that women are supposed to be modest (*malebbiq*), it is considered bad for a woman to initiate sexual intercourse. Thus it is common to hear that a wife who initiates sexual intercourse is considered to be a flirtatious wife (*mangngureq*) and is disapproved of; an ideal wife is one who awaits her husband's sexual initiative (Nurul Ilmi Idrus 2001, Nurul Ilmi Idrus and Bennett 2003). Such idealism is reflected in a *lontaraq* that states:

> There are four kinds of behaviour that a wife should have in order to be loved by her husband: First, if she hides her desire when facing her husband. Second, if she is always happy when facing her husband. Third, if she arouses her husband's desire. Fourth, if she has a mutually balanced relationship with her husband. If she has already performed these four elements and she is still abandoned by her husband, it is considered her fate.
>
> *Eppa buangenna ampéna makkunraié nariélori rioroanéna: Maséuanna, dékko napateddéngngi napasunna makkunraié mangngolo rioroanéna. Maqduanna, marajarioé rékko mangngoloi makkunraié rioroanéna. Matellunna, rékko paola éloq i makkunraié rioroanéna. Maeppaqna, rékko mappasilasai makkunraié rioroanéna. Narékko napogauqniro eppaq é uangenna naritéaimopa rioroanéna inaritu toto oki pura onro.*[14]

---

14 *Lontaraq Pesanan-Pesanan Berlaki-Bini*, MAK No. 74, p. 93–94 (Macknight microfilm 1972: reel 5).

At first glance, there seems to be a contradiction between the first and the third requirements. On the one hand, a wife should hide her desire when facing her husband (B. *dékko*[15] *napateddengngi napasunna makkunraié mangngolo ri oroanéna*); on the other, she should arouse her husband's desire (*rékko paola eloqi makkunraié rioroanéna*). It is therefore implied in this sex-related *lontaraq* that even though a woman is not expected to initiate sexual intercourse, she is responsible for attracting her husband's attention.

These expectations are impressed upon a prospective bride or new wife on a daily basis. For example, prior to marriage, the mother of a prospective bride advises her daughter to be modest (*malebbiq*) or even to 'sell herself dear' (I. *jual mahal*) in bed in the sense that she should await her husband's initiative and not show her own desire. *Jual mahal* literally means 'to sell dear', but carries the sense that she should show reluctance to grant a favour to her huband. Paradoxically, a mother also encourages her daugther to be attractive, so her husband will always be passionate towards her (B. *nasanging macinna oroanéna mitai*). This is best illustrated in the epic La Galigo which describes how Batara Lattu', the son of the ruler of the middle world, persuades his wife, Wé Datu Sengngeng, to enjoy their first night together (Muhammad Salim and Fachruddin Ambo Enre 2000):

> Batara Lattu' moved up,
> sat on the golden [wedding] throne
> and embraced his wife.
> Yet Wé Datu Sengngeng shrank
> from the touch of the man whose renown she shared.
> Batara Lattu' said
> 'Turn here, dear Highness,
> and show me the full oval of your face [read *mabbojoq*]
> if I may see your gaze turn on me,
> sacred maid-servants by the thousand are yours to take'.[16]
>
> *Natarakkaqna* Batara Lattuq *ménré*
> *macokkong ri ménéq lamming mpulawengngé*
> *méssang ngi luséq makkunrainna.*
> *Ala wedding ga* Wé Datuq Sengngeng
> *ritampa' jari oroané sébirittana.*
> *Kua adanna* Batara Lattuq,

15 The word *rékko* and *dékko*, meaning 'if' or 'that', are used interchangeably in this *lontaraq*.

16 Loosely translated by Campbell Macknight (9 May 2003).

'Giling ko mai, Anri Ponratu,
paleppangi aq rupa mabboja
kupémmagga i turung rupanna,
muala mua bissu pattudang tebbanna sebbu' (p. 178).

[Other supporters too offer gifts until Wé Datuq Sengngeng eventually relents and Batara Lattuq wins his suit. He declares his wish to retire inside the bedroom.]

Wé Datuq Sengngeng's reluctance to welcome her husband is reflected in the statement 'Yet Wé Datuq Sengngeng shrank', indicating that she is 'selling herself dear' (I. *jual mahal*) to her husband. 'Sacred maid-servants by the thousand are yours to take' reflects Batara Lattuq's effort to persuade his wife by offering her gifts.[17] Only after a long seduction did Wé Datuq Sengngeng allow Batara Lattuq to hold her hand and lead her to their wedding bedroom.

In parallel to the above, the expectations of the wife towards her husband are also described in the same manuscript:

> Behaviour that a wife expects from a husband: first, that he is obedient; second, that he is deeply affectionate to his wife; third, that he is kind-hearted; fourth, that he has a mutually balanced relationship with his wife.
>
> *Gauq nalorié makkunraié: Maséuanna, mapatoé. Madduanna, rékko matellengngi oroané ri makkunraié. Matellunna, rékko malaboi oroané rimakkunraié. Maeppaqna, dékko mappasilasai oroané rimakkunrainna.*

Regardless of the similarity of the fourth element of mutuality for the wife (B. *rékko mappasilasai makkunraié ri oroanéna*) and for the husband (*dékko mappasilasai oroané rimakkunrainna*), the expectations of the husband and the wife in this manuscript are different from each other. While a husband's expectations towards his wife are associated with her sexual attractiveness and availability, the wife's expectations are related to her husband's ability to fulfil appropriate roles in marriage. A wife's expectations, as represented in this text, reflect the view that a wife is not expected to express intentions and interests associated with sex.

It is interesting to note, however, that the first behaviour expected by the wife of her husband is 'one who is obedient' (*mapatoé*). One may ask, what is

17 Batara Lattuq offered a number of presents to persuade his wife, and they were mentioned repeatedly in this prose, until Wé Datuq Sengngeng was willing to sleep with him.

the relationship between obedience (*mapato*) and sexual life? Is not the wife expected to be obedient? The usual comment related to male sexuality is that 'a man is unable control his desire' (*oroané déqna ullé tahangngi cinnana*). This notion that men's desire is uncontrollable is reflected in La Galigo (Muhammad Salim and Fachruddin Ambo Enre 2000):

> Yet Wé Datuq Sengngeng stayed silent;
> she answered not a word
> to the husband whose renown she shared.
> Batara Lattuq could not find a way to restrain desire;
> he could not put away his keen anticipation as one might fold up a good cloth;
> he could not store up his desire to be with her as one might roll up a piece of silk;
> he was infatuated with his wife.
> He could not hold in check
> his saliva running like a stream
> to which he chose to pay no attention.
> Then La Rumpang Langiq [Batara Lattuq] stood up
> and embraced his wife,
> he took her within the sarong,
> then they went and entered the chamber,
> they crept beneath the net,
> they sprang on to the bed,
> they lay together on the sleeping mat,
> they lay sharing his wife's golden cushion.[18]
>
> *Ala mettéq ga* Wé Datuq Sengngeng,
> *ala mabbali ada sélappaq*
> *lé oroané sébirittana.*
> *Tenna bajéqni perreng cinnana* Batara Lattuq
> *leppiq dusiq i mecciq kéloqna*
> *lulung géssa i cinna béasa*
> *pabongngoq é ngngi ri makkunrai.*
> *Tennaullé ni paleppengi wi*
> *diméng mallari soloq éloqna,*
> *téa na sia ripamaureq.*
> *Natijjang ronnang* La Rumpang Langiq

18 Loosely translated by Campbell Macknight (9 May 2003).

nasalikking ngi makkunrainna,
pangalai wi luangeng sampuq,
nalaoang ngi ronnang muttama ri goarié,
nasellukang ngi riulampué
naléccéngang ngi ri palakkaé,
nawellengang ngi ri baritué,
leuq mangnguruq talaja kati makkunrainna (p. 182 and 184).

Male desire is reflected in the statement that Batara Lattu could not control or manage his desire. Such uncontrollable desire is reflected in a common Bugis saying that states men's desire is nine, women's desire is only one (B. *naia cinnana oroané asérai, naia cinnana makkunraié seddimi*). Thus, in this sense, obedience (*mapato*) to the wife controls the husband's desire. For example, when a husband wants to have sex with his wife and she hides her desire (*napateddéngngi napasunna*) or 'sells herself dear' (*jual mahal*), she controls her husband's desire.

The examination of desire (*cinna*) is best illustrated in two conversations, between Daramatasia and two groups of men who intends to propose to her after the death of her husband, Saéheq Bil-maqrupi, in the manuscript entitled *Daramatasia*.[19] The first conversation is between Daramatasia and the seven brothers (*oroané pitué mappadaoroané*), and second between her and the three brothers (*oroané tellué mappadaoroané*). Three days after the death of Daramatasia's husband, the seven brothers come to visit her with the intention of proposing marriage to her. The first conversation is as follows:

Daramatasia:
If anyone can answer my question, he can take the place of [my husband] Saéheq Bil-maqrupi.
Narékko engka pakatajangekkaq pakkutanakuq iana kuala passéllé polé ri Saéheq Bil-maqrupi.

The seven brothers (*oroané pitué mappadaoroané*):
Please state your question so we can hear, one of us will have the answer to your question.
Poadai maé pakkutanamu nariéngkalinga kaleséddikku ia pitue pakatajangakko pakkutanamu.

19 See *Lontaraq Daramatasia,* Roll 17/No. 17, twentieth century, Arsip Nasional Wilayah Makassar. This part of story is not found in other versions of *Daramatasia* manuscript.

> Daramatasia:
> How great is a man's desire for a woman? And how great is a woman's desire for a man?
> *Siaga égana cinnana oroané ri makkunraié, siagato cinnana makkunraié rioroanéna?*

The seven brothers (*oroané pitué mappadaoroané,* who answer the question in unison):

A man's desire for a woman is one. A woman's desire for a man is nine. *Naia cinnana oroané ri makkunraié seddimi. Naia cinnana makkunraié ri oroané asérai.*

> Daramatasia:
> How loose you are and how inadequate your honour, why do you come to me if you only have one desire? It is I who should come to you because I have nine.
> *Arugimmutu nennia akurassirisemmutu paléq, magi naiko laoikaq mai na séddimi cinnamu, sitinajannatu iaq laoiko nasabaq aséra cinnakuq.*

Hearing how Daramatasia responds negatively to their answer, the seven brothers (*oroané pitué*) leave Daramatasia's house immediately, ashamed because none of them could properly answer her question.

On the seventh day after her husband's death, the three borthers (*oroané tellué mappadaoroané*, the eldest Hasang; the middle one, Huseng; and the youngest, Ahemadeq)[20]—come, also intending to propose to Daramatasia. The second conversation takes place as follows:

> The three brothers (*oroané tellué mappadaoroané*):
> We three brothers come to you, so you can choose one of us to take the place of [your late husband] Saéheq Bil-maqrupi.
> *Aga nangkau' mai lao riko tellu mappadaoroané maéloqkaq mupiléi kalaséddikku muala passéllé polé ri* Saéheq Bil-maqrupi.

> Daramatasia:
> Even though it is only a week has elapsed since the death of Saéheq Bilmaqrupi if one of you can answer my question, he can take the place of [my late husband] Saéheq Bil-maqrupi.

20 The original names from *lontaraq* for theses there brothers are Hasang, Huseng and Ahemade. A Malaysian text, 'The Hikayat Muhammad Hanafiyah' states that Hasan and Husen are the sons of Ali with Fatimah; while Muhammad Hanafiyyah (Ahmad), is Hasan's third son with another woman (Brakel 1975:203).

Mauniro pitumpenni maténa réweqna ripammaséna Allataala Saéheq Bil-maqrupi *narékko engka patajangekkaq pakkutanakuq iana kuala passéllé polé ri* Saéheq Bil-maqrupi.

The three brothers (*oroané tellué mappadaoroané*):
Daramatasia, please state your question, so we can hear, one of us will answer the question, if the Almighty wills.
Daramatasia poadani mai pakkutanamu nariengkalinga kalaséddikku naélorang Allataala pakatajangekko.

Daramatasia:
How great is a man's desire for a woman? And how great is a woman's desire for a man?
Siagaro cinnana oroané rimakkunraié, siagato cinnana makkunraié rioroanéna?

Hasang and Huseng:
A man's desire for a woman is one. A woman's desire for a man is nine.
Naia cinnana oroané ri makkunraié seddimi. Naia cinnana makkunraié rioroané asérai.

Daramatasia:
How inadequate your honour and how loose you are, why do you come to me if you only have one desire? It is I who should come to you because I have nine.
Akurassirisemmutu paléq nennia arugimmu, magi naiko laoi mai na séddimi cinnamu. Iaqga sitinaja laoiko nasabaq aséra cinnakuq.

Shamed by Daramatasia's response, Hasang and Huseng leave. But Ahemadeq (the youngest brother) stays and has his own answer. He says: 'It is true that a man has one desire for a woman, while a woman has nine desires for a man (*tongenggi adaé makkedaé séddi cinnana oroané ri makkunraié, aséra cinnana makkunraié ri oroané. Makkunraié saba'na enrengé atajanénna*). But there is an explanation for that.'

Ahemadeq goes on to describe why Adam and Eve (Hawa) were expelled from heaven because they were found eating the forbidden fruit (B. *aju tubi*) in heaven by an angel (*malaékaq*). When they were caught, the *aju tubi* was still in Adam's throat, so he squeezed his neck, and the fruit became the Adam's apple (*caridoq*). Eve, however, devoured many *aju tubi* and her neck and chest became conspicuously bulky. Ahemadeq concludes that men's desire is weaker because the *aju tubi* is only in Adam's throat while women's desire is 'ample' because Eve has eaten many of the *aju tubi* that are deep down in her chest. Had Eve not been more desirous than her mate to eat the *aju tubi*, the couple would not have been expelled from heaven, as Eve would have been able to hide her transgression from the angle because she could still have hidden her transgression from the angel, just as did Adam. Based on this story, Ahemadeq' makes the point that women should not have more desire than men, or at least should not show their desire openly as such desire is dangerous. After listening to Ahemadeq's parable of men's and women's desire, Daramatasia tells him: 'You are the one who is allowed by God to take the place of Saéheq Bil-maqrupi' (*Ikonatu naéloreng Allataala kuala passéllé pole Saéheq Bil-maqrupi*).

Therefore, instead of nine desire-woman and one desire man, there is a reversal: man has nine desires, while woman has only one (*cinnana oroané asséra, cinnana makkunraié seddimi*) in order to protect the honour of the family. This 'nine/one' parable not only aims at demonstrating the contrast between the desires of men and women, but also at reflecting the notion that man's desire desire is supposed to be 'open' (*marisaliweng*), while women's desire should be placed 'behind the scenes' (*maperreng*) which reflect the dichotomy of Bugis constructions of male and female sexuality, as discussed in Chapter II.

But, Daramatasia's statement above also implies that because the man is the one who comes forward to propose marriage, he should have more desire than the woman to whom he proposes. This is not to say that women cannot expres their desire as men do, it just means that the sexes have different ways of expressing desire (see below).

In her account of women's status in Islam, Brook cites Ali's statement[21] that in Islam 'Almighty God created sexual desire in ten parts then He gave nine parts to women and one to men' (Brook 1995:39). Based on this statement, Islam holds that a wife can initiate a divorce if her husband does not fulfill her her sexual desire at least once in every four months. Yet among the Bugis, people are taught the opposite; since men are believed to be sexually desirous and are unable to control their lust (B. *déqna ullé tahangngi cinnana*), women are taught to control their behaviour towards men, which is similar to the argument given by Brook (1995:40) regarding Christian teachings on sexuality.

For the Bugis, the idea that women are sexually desirous is in contrast with the notion of modesty (*malebbiq*). Thus, in order to control women's nine parts of sexual desire that are postulated not only by Islam, but also by seven brothers and Hasang and Huseng in the two conversations quoted above, the Bugis

21 Ali is the husband of the Prophet Muhammad's beloved daughter, Fatimah.

apply the contrary parable (nine parts to men and one to women), as is explained by Ahemadeq and accepted as the correct answer by Daramatasia in the second conversation. This is not to say that the Bugis hold an idea that contradict Islam. Rather, desirous women will threaten the *siriq*, that is, the honour of the family. Women are moreover regarded as being 'naturally weak' and thus can easily be sexually tempted. It is the task of their *siriq* defender (*to masiriq*) to protect them from men who 'by nature' have a strong desire.

It is interesting to note, however, that while Islam is the dominant ideology of the Bugis, the parable of sexual desire between men and women is incompatible with Bugis practice. With regard to Islamic belief, Brook (1995:38–40) establishes a link between women's desire and the justification of clitoridectomy, seclusion and veiling for Muslim women. Among the Bugis, however, the practice of female circumcision and the accompanying ritual are a public statement signalling that the girls are grown up (B. *malopponi*) and that they must begin to guard themselves from male peers because being around men will threaten their *siriq*. Thus, circumcision is not related to lessening women's desire in Bugis society, as it is in many Muslim countries around the world.[22]

In sexual intercourse, since man's desire (*cinnana oroané*) is nine, he should be the one who approaches his wife; because woman's desire (*cinnana makkunraié*) is only one, she should wait. Despite the fact that women can also initiate sex with their husband, it is considered modest (*malebbiq*) to wait for the husband's initiative. Thus, man/nine (*aséra*) and woman/one (*séddi*) reflect the construction of male and female desires. In line with this, there is the misconception that men are sexual experts, which implies that they are the ones who know best what women actually need (Segal 1994). Thus, in sexual relations, there is a close connection between masculine and feminine attitudes and the perceived biological nature of the sexes. This connection echoes the persistent stereotypes described by Oakley (1996:36), namely, that a female 'open vagina' as well as her stereotypical 'feminine personality' (dependent, passive, nonaggressive as well as submissive) reflect her 'receptiveness.' From this point of view, a man's penis and masculine personality (independent, active, aggressive) may be regarded as mirroring his hegemony. In other words, a penis entering a vagina signifies an active/passive relationship in sexual intercourse. In daily practice, women have to restrain themselves from expressing desire, while men's desire should be demonstrated, as discussed in Chapter 2.

---

22 Muhammad Husein (2001:40–1) discusses how male circumcision is medically positive,enabling men to avoid premature ejaculation and increasing pleasure in sexual intercourse, while female circumcision aims to lessen female sexual pleasure.

Sex and Symbols

The image of a vagina I offer below is originally from a manuscript entitled *Lontara Sebboq* which means *Hole Lontaraq*, which I adopted from Alwy Rachman (1998:4).

The image consists of a circle, a triangle and a crown, each of which has a symbolic meaning (see Diagram 5.1). This image tells us that the circle symbolizes the hole of the vagina; the triangle, the shape of the vagina; and the crown, the pubic hair.[23] The vagina is symbolized as a rose (B. *bunga sibollo*),[24] and the 'door' of vagina is named the 'door' of the rose (*timung bunga sibollo*). Entering the hole of the vagina is similar to 'entering the door to a rose', and is epitomised as Yusuf—a prophet in Islam famed for his handsomeness—bringing a fortune.

In *lontaraq*, sexual intercourse is understood through symbols. The actors (husband and wife) and the sex organs (vagina and penis) are symbolized using the names of honourable people in the history of Islam, Ali (the cousin and disciple of Muhammad, the husband) and Fatimah (his wife) represent penis and vagina respectively (Muhlis Hadrawi and Anwar Ibrahim, 1999:32).

In Bugis, there are a number of symbols used to describe the penis (*laso, laseq*) as well as the vagina (*sombiq*). For example, the penis is symbolized as the index finger on the right hand and the vagina as the joining between thumb and index finger of the left hand, forming a circle. Sexual intercourse is symbolized by inserting the index finger in to the hole of the circle. Another symbol for penis is as a 'man's gun' (*pattémbaqna oroané*) and a woman's vagina is symbolized as the target for the gun to shoot.

Sexual activity is always followed or accompanied with prayers or magic formulae (*jappi-jappi*). The pronouncing of prayer during sexual intercourse signals the interaction between human-beings and God. It also differentiates between the sexual relations of human beings and animals. It is believed that

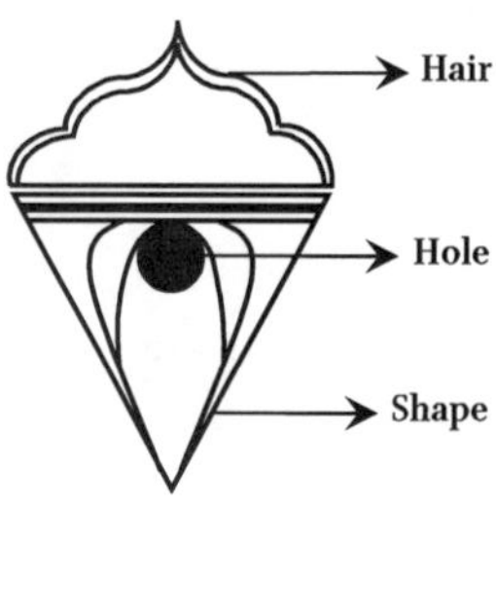

DIAGRAM 5.1
The Image of the Vagina

23 In Indonesia, hair is commonly expressed as the crown of women (I. *mahkota wanita*).

24 In Bugis, a girl is usually symbolized as a rose, a pubescent girl is regarded as a 'rose-bud'.

sexual intercourse without prayer is like the copulation of animals, and the desire is viewed as a sinful desire. This reflects the belief that sexual intercourse is not just a biological concern, but also has a religious significance.

Lontaraq Bunga Rampai Agama-B,[25] a manuscript the title of which means 'Anthology of Religion,' illustrates that one of the functions of prayer is to chase sin away because it always tries to tempt human beings to transgress (I. *khilaf*) and lose control during intercourse (Muhlis Hadrawi and Anwar Ibrahim 1999:33). In addition, prayer has an impact on the future behaviour of the unborn baby. A message of the elders (B. *pappasenna tomatoaé*) states that sinful sexual intercourse will result in the birth of a sin-child. As stated in *lontaraq*: 'Bad behaviour [of parents] will be bequeathed in the behaviour of their children' (*gauq majaq namanaq i torimunrimmu*) (S. Budhisantoso et al. 1990:39). Although this does not specifically refer to behaviour in sexual intercourse, this is the implied meaning of this wise aphorism (*paseng*). Correspondingly, the manuscript *Tata Cara Hubungan Suami Istri*,[26] the title of which means 'The Etiquette of Marital Relationships,' explains that a wise man is one who always keeps the name of God in his mind in order to control his behaviour during intercourse. If he does so, sin cannot interfere with his sexual activities. I often heard men teas each other to the groom when they talk about sex that no matter how desirous he is to have sex his wife in the first night of marriage, he has to always keep the name of God in his mind before having sex.

In manuscript *Ilmu Tarekat*,[27] which deals with 'Mysticism,' the use of the symbol of Ali and Fatimah is stated in the following magical formula (*jappi-jappi*):

Iko Patima, iaq I Ali	You are Fatimah, I am Ali
usarakengngi (Alépuq) riwatakkalékuq	I require (*Alif*)[28] in my body
lapaleng (Allah) riwatakkalému	the text (Allah) in your body
ukkarengngaq tangeqna Patima	please open the door of Fatimah
nauttamaq Ali	Ali can enter [the door]
Barakkaq Laa Ilaaha Illallahu.	In the blessing of Allah (God).

Since the magical formula (*jappi-jappi*) begins with 'you are Fatima, I am Ali', it indicates that this formula should be said by the husband in foreplay.

25 *Lontara Bunga Rampai Agama*-B, Roll 32/No.8, undated, Arsip Nasional Wilayah Makassar.

26 *Lontaraq Tata Cara Hubungan Suami Istri*, Roll 26/No.18, twentieth century, Arsip Nasional Wilayah Makassar.

27 *Lontaraq Ilmu Tarekat*, Roll 26/No.13, undated, Arsip Nasional Wilayah Makassar.

28 *Alif* is the first letter in the Al-Qur'an. In this account, the letter *alif* symbolizes the first person (for example, Ali).

The requirement of *Alif* in Ali's body and the text Allah in Fatimah's body reflects the religious significance of the initiation of Ali to Fatimah in sexual intercourse. The request of Ali to open the 'door' of Fatimah—the door signifies Fatimah's vagina—indicates that Ali, the initiator, is ready to enter the vagina.

The following formula is uttered by the wife when her husband is about to insert his penis into her vagina in the penetration phase of sexual intercourse:

Iko Ali puttamaq	You, Ali, insert
I Usupeq asenna katauwammu	Yusuf[29] is the name of your penis
Laqu' asenna mannimmu	Laqu' is the name of your sperm
Koca'i lakoci' Patima	penetrates Fatimah
koci' wadu wadi mani manikeng	penetrates until [I am] stimulated
soddi laserakku	I am wet
Barakka Lailaaha Illallahu	In the blessing of Allah
Muhammadarrasulullah	and the Prophet Muhammad

This formula states the request of Fatimah to be penetrated by Ali, 'I am wet' (*soddi laserakku*) indicates that Fatimah is ready to be entered. Although Fatimah states her request, the activities are implemented by Ali. Thus, both formulae reflect the active part of the husband and the receptiveness of the wife in sexual intercourse. From foreplay to penetration, the name of Allah is always mentioned in order to avoid the interference of evil. Each activity during sex is symbolically based on Islamic ethics as a guide to control human behaviour during intercourse.

There are various magical formulae circulated by elders to couples. Those formulae contain what the husband as well as the wife should utter in the initial phase of intercourse in order to chase sin away. In practice, however, such formulae are replaced by silently uttering the prayer *Bismillahirrahmaanirrahim*, which in Arabic means 'in the name of Allah the All Merciful, the Beneficient.' However, it does not mean that no one use such formula in every day life, the uttering of *Bismillahirrahmanirrahim* is uttered for the practical reason to keep one in a state of counscious, so no one other than him/herself is in control of him/her.

Bugis believe that sexual intercourse without religious significance is similar to sinful intercourse (B. *padai setangngé*) and is considered to be in a state of unconsciousness (*déqna maringngerrang*). This is presumably why elders usually remind newlyweds to be conscious (*maringngerrang*), by saying: 'Be

29 In Bugis language, Yusuf is pronounced as *Usupe*.

conscious, do not be like sin riding a horse', so you will have good children' (*Padécengi paringngérrammu, ajaq mupada sétang makkinnyarangngé namakessitto matu anaq mujajiang*). Sin is the husband and horse is the wife. Being conscious in this sense is associated with the cultural and religious significance of intercourse; one should always be in control.

Manners in Sexual Intercourse: From *Lontaraq* to Practice

Sexuality in marriage is a sequential activity which begins with a 'game' of desire (foreplay), proceeds into the art of romantic love (intercourse) and ends with an affection built upon sexual gratification (orgasm).

Lontaraq Assikalaibinéngeng provides a guide to sexual manners from the beginning to the end of sexual intercourse. By combining a number of manuscripts, Muhlis Hadrawi and Anwar Ibrahim have chronologically divided sexual intercourse into three steps, namely: pre-, during- and post-sexual intercourse (Muhlis Hadrawi and Anwar Ibrahim 1999:36). These three steps are preceded with some activities as well as the reciting of magical formulae (*jappi-jappi*) to be uttered by the husband in order to stimulate his wife's desire and described in *Lontara Tata Cara Hubungan Suami Istri, Bunga Rampai Budaya*[30] and *Bunga Rampai Lontaraq*.

The activity that should precede foreplay, as illustrated in the *Lontaraq Tata Cara Hubungan Suami Istri,* is begun by performing ablutions to cleanse the body from dirt (A. *najis*)[31] and a minor purification (*wudhu*) before entering the mosquito net (I. *kelambu*).[32] A wise husband will ask his wife whether or not she welcomes (B. *halalakiangngi*) his body for sexual activity. Then, the husband greets his wife by saying the Arabic phrase *Assalaamu Alaikum' ya baburrahmati,* which means 'Peace be upon you, merciful door.'[33] A welcomed husband will be greeted with her response in Arabic *Wa Alaikumussalam ya*

30 *Lontaraq Bunga Rampai Budaya,* Roll 35/No.15, twentieth century, Arsip Nasional Wilayah Makassar.

31 Islam regulates that one has to cleanse her/himself 'before' (by *wudhu*) and 'after' (by *istinja* which covers the whole of the ritual intended to keep the anus pure) sexual intercourse.

32 Mosquito nets, termed *kelambu,* are used over beds to protect from mosquito bites when sleeping. People in the city tend to use insecticides rather than mosquito nets, for convenience. In the past, however, mosquito nets were more common in both villages and urban areas.

33 Similar greeting is also found in the text *Ilmu Tarikat* (no roll number and date), Arsip Nasional Wilayah Makassar.

sadikul aminin, which means 'peace be upon you, faithful friend', and indicates the wife's readiness to make love.

In theory, based on this *lontaraq*, the wife's welcoming attitude is signalled by her saying 'I allow my body in the name of Allah', to which the husband will reply 'I accept your consent'. In practice, I found during my fieldwork that such utterances are replaced with the husband of squeezing (B. *makkobbiq*) his wife's thigh to signal his desire to make love. The acceptance of the wife will be indicated either by smiling (*macawa cabbéru*) or by remining quiet; otherwise she refuses her husband. For example, a male informant told me:

> When I squeeze my wife's thigh, she automatically knows that I want to have sex with her. Her unwillingness will show right after the squeezing. Her smile indicates her acceptance, and refusal can be seen from the knitting of her brow.
>
> MALIK, 45, interviewed on 11 September 2000

A female informant used similar, but slightly different words:

> My husband usually squeezes my thigh when he requests to have sex. If I am in the mood, I will respond with a smile. Otherwise, either I will say 'maybe later' or I just keep away from him.
>
> RUKIAH, 38, interviewed on 11 September 2000

These utterances/actions reflect the mutual respect between husband and wife in sexual relations and the importance of the wife's sexual consent. Corresponding to the squeezing analogy, a piece advice usually given by elders to the wife is 'when your husband wants you to have sex, you should serve him as soon as you can, to ensure your good fortune' (B. *nakko nakobbiqko lakkaimmu, pitujui magatti, namakkoto gattiqna pole dalléqmu*). In this sense, sexual intercourse is not just about biological needs, but also related to the prosperity of the couple. Conversely, I have never heard the expression in the reverse, that when a husband serves his wife, good fortune will ensue (Nurul Ilmi Idrus, 2001:46). Similarly, I did not find any comparable advice directed at the husband. Hence, this strengthens the view that it is the husband who initiates sex and not vice versa. This is not to say that a wife cannot initiate to have sex, but it is not idealized.

The texts assert that foreplay[34] starts by touching the wife's sensitive areas in order to stimulate her. In line with this, a *Hadith* states that when a husband

34 In Islam, the term *mula'anah* refers to foreplay. The Prophet Muhammad condemns a husband who has intercourse with his wife without foreplay (Rahmat Sudirman 1999:129).

is going to have sex with his wife, he should not treat his wife like a camel, he should start with caresses, persuasion, and kissing (Masdar F. Mas'udi 1997:118).

Lontaraq Tata Cara Hubungan Suami Istri and *Bunga Rampai Lontaraq* provide a description of the acts of foreplay. Even though these descriptions have some differences in terms of the parts of the body to be touched as well as the magical formulae (*jappi-jappi*) to be pronounced, the objectives are similar. In the *lontaraq Tata Cara Hubungan Suami Istri*, foreplay consists of 'touching' and 'kissing'.

In 'touching', a husband is expected to touch his wife in various parts of her body (right hand,[35] the tendon of her heel, the crown of her head, her chest to her breast, under her stomach, her navel, and her clitoris). Kissing his wife from the crown of her head to her nipples represents to the second part of foreplay. The kissing consist of twelve parts—the crown of her head, ears, eyebrows, eyes, nose, lips, chest, neck, nape of neck, hand, between her breast, and nipple—which are regarded as women's sensitive areas, and are kissed during foreplay as indication of love and affection. No movement in these touching and kissing phases without mentioning the name of Allah.

I talked to a number of men both in Sidrap and Makassar, they indicate that touching and kissing parts of the body before having sex are very common activities during forplay. All of them also stated the importance of mentioning the name of Allah, though it is commonly mentioned in the beginning of the conduct. For example, *Pak* Saleh stated:

> When having sex without 'warming up' like touching and kissing, I feel that we just 'do it', not really enjoy it, right? I like to play it first before actually go to the main part of making love because we make it through playing, then love it. That's why, it is called 'making love'...it always starts with the name of Allah...ya ya, just in the beginning.
>
> SALEH, 40, interviewed on 3 July 2009

Pak Saleh's statement indicates the importance of warming up (*pemanasan*), as expressed in the term 'to play' (*main-main*), through touching (*sentuh*) and kissing (*cium*). While, every part of touching and kissing movement head with mentioning the name of Allah is idealised, my interlocutors explained that they did it only in the beginning of the first movement by silently uttering the prayer *Bismillahirrahmanirrahim*.

---

35 In Islam, every time someone starts to do something, one always starts with the right (such as right hand), except when going the toilet, when one goes in with the left leg and comes out with the right leg.

An elder man I met in Sidrap explained that touching and kissing not just related to warming up, but also to manner in sexual intercourse. He emphasized that 'when one have sex without forplay, he actually has no respect to his partner.' Thus, this significantly shows that touching and kissing are not solely about how to enjoy sex, but it is also about how to respect to each other.

Bunga Rampai Lontaraq calls these kisses the 'twelve kissings' (B. *pabbau seppuloduaq*), which indicates that there are twelve parts of a woman's body that regarded as women's sensitive areas and which, therefore, are kissed during foreplay as an indication of love and affection. Therefore, kissing these parts will give pleasantness (*anyamengngeng*) to the woman. Kissing is followed by caressing from her stomach to her vagina three times, then lifting her right and left legs one at a time by saying '*Alhamdulillah*' (A. Praise the God) to finalize the foreplay and to lead to sexual intercourse at which point the husband asks his wife's acceptance.

However, none of the sexual activities during foreplay mentioned in *Lontaraq Assikalaibinéngeng* indicate any actions that should be implemented by the wife, except pronouncing magical fomulae (B. *jappi-jappi*) (Muhlis Hadrawi and Anwar Ibrahim 1999:40). For example, *Lontaraq Cenninrara*[36] provides the following magical formulae (*jappi-jappi*) for the wife to utter during foreplay:

> The enjoyment is located under my navel,
> so stimulate around my vagina
> like what has been experienced by Ali and Fatimah.
>
> *Kuriawana posiqku palué nyameng,*
> *pappénéqdingangngaq bulu-bulu lénalanu*
> *padai assijakkasidara'na Ali Patima.*[37]

The content of this formula implies the expectation of the wife to be stimulated in a certain sensitive part of her body where she can feel the pleasure of touching during foreplay. However, when a wife pronounces such a formula,

---

36 *Lontaraq Cenninrara,* Roll 47/No.18, undated, Arsip Nasional Wilayah Makassar. Different formula, but for similar purpose is also found in the *lontaraq Bunga Rampai Agama*-A, see footnote 8.

37 This is closely related to a Malay love magic manuscript called *Perhimpunan Gunawan Bagi Laki-Laki and Perempuan* from the early twentieth century (inscription of *Compendium*), written by Khatijah Terong of Pulau Penyengat and transliterated by Ding Choo Ming. This manual is almost exclusively for women's use (see Mukherjee 1997).

she usually does so silently. Therefore, a husband never hears what is actually being requested by his wife. The elders say that any formula related to sex is usually repeated in her heart.

Another formula which is uttered by the wife at the end of foreplay is as follows:

> Open the vagina when [the penis] arrives
> like a horseman rides.
>
> *Tattimpa'ko lébana Utuma*
> *makkeddaé pajarangi tonang ri anynyarang.*

This formula is an invitation to the husband using the analogy of the horse as the vagina and the rider as the penis. This again implies the top/husband and bottom/wife position in sexual intercourse, a position in which the receptiveness of the wife is idealized. As noted previously, this position is related to the expected behaviour of the wife as modest (*malebbiq*), and who acts properly in front of her husband. A female informant stated:

> I cannot imagine asking my husband to have sex, I am very ashamed to express my feelings. My mother taught me to wait until he asks for it. During intercourse, I cannot even look at my husband's face.
>
> ERNA, 35, three children, interviewed on 1 April 2000

Even those who are sexually desiring expressed their reluctance to ask for sex. For instance, another female informant said:

> Ibu Ilmi, you know I am a sexually desiring woman [she looked around to make sure no one heard her]. But, it is still difficult for me to express my desire to have sex with my husband. Even if I have the courage, when I am about to tell him, I cannot. I do not know how to say it, so I just wait.
>
> NANNA, 38, two children, interviewed on 1 April 2000

For women who do have the courage to express desire, the articulation of that desire is not something they can say every time they want to have sex. For example, a third female informant told me:

> I do not think that my husband will say that I am flirtatious if I ask him for sex, maybe he even appreciates that I have the courage to say so. But whenever I do, I always think he may think that I am flirtatious

> and at the same time I think he is supposed to ask me rather than the reverse.
>
> MULIATI 29, one child, interviewed on 1 April 2000

These three statements indicate that it is not impossible for a wife to initiate sex. Though exploring their sexuality can be desirable, women are reluctant to do so. While the first statement from Erna indicates that she had no intention to initiate sex, the other two passages reflect some women's ambivalent feelings about initiating sex. Thus, sexual initiation is not just about whether or not someone has the courage to speak or to initiate, but is also linked to how women think about initiating sex and how women think their husbands will react to their expressions of desire. During my fieldwork, I frequently found that the way women were taught by their mothers or elders affected the way women thought about sex and dealt with their sexual lives.

Following foreplay is the penetration phase which is considered a core phase of intercourse, and results in orgasm, indicated by the flow of fluid from the husband and the wife repectively (Muhlis Hadrawi and Anwar Ibrahim 1999:42). I would argue, however, that having been sexually penetrated does not automatically mean that every woman will experience orgasm, as many women experienced non-orgasmic intercourse, and lack of orgasm is not uncommon. While there is no specific Bugis term for orgasm, people usually link orgasm with pleasure (B. *nyameng*), pleasantness (*anyamengeng*) or pleasant feelings (*manyameng*).

Although women do not commonly discuss orgasm with their husbands, women were willing to talk about orgasm explicitly during informal social gatherings (for example, *arisan*) when no men were present. Take, for instance, the following interview with *Ibu* Risma (37) in Makassar.

> Ilmi: Do you usually have foreplay before having sex?
> Risma: Sometimes, yes. But sometimes, he just 'comes'.
> Ilmi: How do you feel if you have sex without foreplay?
> Risma: It is disgusting (*jijay*). I like foreplay, it makes me feel affectionate. 'Quick sex' is like this, he is coming, finishing, and snoring. Sex without foreplay is like soup with no salt, tasteless.
> Ilmi: Do you usually have an orgasm?
> Risma: Not in 'quick sex' like that. But in 'normal sex' [sex with foreplay and orgasm], I can have my orgasm.
> [My informants referred to orgasm with various terms, such as 'orgasm' (I. *orgasme*), 'climax' (*klimaks*), 'peak' (*puncak*), 'losing the pupil of the eyes' (*hilang bola mata hitam*).]

Ilmi: How do you describe orgasm?
Risma: It is hard to explain how pleasant it is. But how can I have an orgasm during 'quick sex'? It gives me a headache.
Ilmi: Do you ever discuss sex with your husband?
Risma: No, I am ashamed (*malu*). I just grumble (*ngomel*) whenever we have 'quick sex'. But I am a hypocrit (*munafik*) too because I grumbled, but I did not tell him. So, it is worthless (interviewed on 21 April 2000).

The contrast Risma draws between 'normal sex' and 'quick sex' implies her awareness of the importance of foreplay and orgasm in sexual life, reflected in her comment that sex without foreplay is 'tasteless soup', and sex without orgasm causes headaches. This is a very typical comment for women in urban areas.

The following interview with *Pak* Nasir (39) is parallel to *Ibu* Risma's interview:

Ilmi: Do you usually have foreplay before having sex?
Nasir: Yes and no. It depends on my mood. Sometimes, I do not want to 'play', I just want to have sex.
Ilmi: How do you describe sex without foreplay?
Nasir: It is like sex without love. I am coming, having sex, and sleeping.
Ilmi: Didn't you think about your wife's feelings?
Nasir: My wife didn't complain. So, what's the big deal?
Ilmi: Do you usually have an orgasm?
Nasir: Of course I do. Men always do.
Ilmi: How do you feel?
Nasir: Delicious! (*enak*).
Ilmi: What about your wife's orgasm?
Nasir: I think if I had an orgasm, she did, too.
Ilmi: Do you ever discuss sex with your wife?
Nasir: No, we just do it. If I want to have sex, I just squeeze my wife's thigh. She never says no.
Ilmi: Do you think she always wants it?
Nasir: Why not? Sex is so good (*enak*) (interviewed on 2 May 2000).

This interview indicates that *Pak* Nasir realizes the significance of foreplay, reflected by his statement 'sex without love'. However, he thinks the fact that he had an orgasm indicates that his wife did too, particularly given the fact that she did not complain. This is a typical comment for urban men in regard to orgasm. Both interviewees admit they do not discuss sex. While *Ibu* Risma's view indicates her reluctance to talk about sex with her husband because of shame, *Pak* Nasir seems to be careless in regard to discussion of sex, or the pleasure of his wife.

Two manuscripts—*Tata Cara Hubungan Sexual* and *Bunga Rampai Lontaraq*—prescribe the ideal conduct of the couple during the penetration phase. Both manuscripts clarify how the husband prepares himself for this stage. For instance, he is advised to concentrate his heart, to calm down his feelings, and to regulate his breath. In addition, the texts also describe the techniques he should use in touching the 'door' of the vagina. Every single movement in this phase is followed by saying *'La Ilaha Illallah'* (A. there is no God except Allah). This is to remind the husband of God's spirit, who gives an unequaled pleasure. In the *Lontaraq Ilmu Tarekat*[38] sexual intercourse is described as the entry of the Prophet Yusuf through the door of Fatimah. Entering this door signifies Yusuf's entry to heaven. Fatimah's 'door' consists of four sides, each side with a 'doorkeeper'. The four doors are equivalent to four walls and the sensitive areas of the women's vagina, reflecting the perfection of the form of the door of the vagina (B. *sulapaq eppaq*). Each of the doors is like each of the wives of the Prophet Muhammad, all of whom were in 'harmony'.

Before coming to the penetration phase, the husband utters a mantra 'please open Fatimah's white cummerbund' (*timpakengngaq bekkeng puténa Patima*), a phrase in which the opening of the woman's clothes and the opening of her body are treated as analogous. When the wife shows her acceptance, this incantation will be followed by another magical formula from *Lontaraq Bunga Rampai Agama-A*,[39] uttered by the husband:

> My body faces *Ka'bah*[40]
> my heart faces *Baitul Amur*[41]
> my soul faces *God in Arasy*[42]
>
> *Tubukku mangngolo rikabbaé*
> *atikku' mangngolo ri Baitulla Amuré'*
> *nyawaku' mangngolo ri Puang ri Araseng.*

---

38 These images of the door of the vagina are from *Lontaraq Ilmu Tarekat*, see footnote 28.

39 *Lontara Bunga Rampai Agama*-A, Roll 48/No. 18, eighteenth century, Arsip National Wilayah Makassar.

40 *Ka'bah* is the small cubicle shrine in the Great Mosque of Mekkah which contains the famous black Stone of Mekkah. It represents the direction (A. *kiblah*) to which Muslims turn in praying.

41 *Baitul Amur* is peaceful house.

42 *Arasy* is a mysterious 'place' of God (Allah) which cannot be understood by a logical thinking (A. *ghaib*).

This magical formula implies that the position of the husband is akin to the position of a Muslim when praying. This is because sexual intercourse is also regarded as an act of religious duty (A. *ibadah*), and is therefore considered a sacred action. A text in *Lontara Assikalabinéngeng* which states: *'Narékko muputtamai kalammu, isoqi nappaseqmu. Narékko muredduqi kalammu, muasseppungengngi nappaseqmu'* (When you push your penis, hold your breath. When you pull your penis, release your breath). This saying implies that aims to control one's sex feeling and emotions, to be calm and relax during sexual intervourse, as this has an implication towards one's sex stamina Muhlis Hadrawi (2009:153–4).

The four 'doors' of the vagina are guarded by Hatijah (right-side), Salamah (left-side), Aisyah (top-side) and Maemuna (bottom-side), the names of the wives of the Prophet Muhammad (see Diagram 5.2 below). These four women are symbolized as ideal wives. *Lontaraq Budi Istikharah,*[43] for example, states that four people who are loved by Prophet Muhammad are: Sitti Hatijah, Sitti Aisyah, Sitti Ummu Salamah and Sitti Maemuna.

Lontaraq Ilmu Tarekat also describes how to touch each of these doors, as follows:

- If you intend to touch the top-side of a woman's vagina (Aisyah), your thighs should touch hers and you should support her hip as high as four fingers.
- If you intend to touch the down-side of a woman's vagina (Maemunah), your navel should touch her navel.

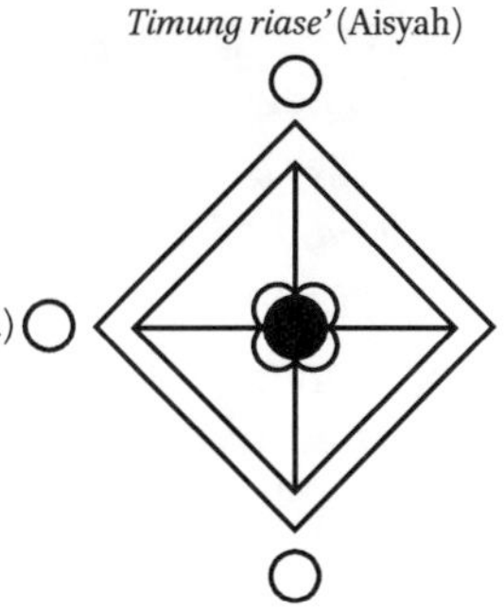

DIAGRAM 5.2 *The Image of the Vagina's Doors*[44]

43 *Lontaraq Budi Istikharah* (P3B 1999).

44 This image of the vagina's doors is originally from *Lontaraq Ilmu Tarekat,* which I adopted from Muhlis Hadrawi and Anwar Ibrahim (1999:34).

- If you intend to touch the right-side of a woman's vagina (Hatijah), ben your right leg and straighten out her left leg.
- If you intend to touch the left-side of a woman's vagina (Salamah), bend your left leg and straighten out her right leg.

Each touch is then followed by a greeting along with the name of each door-keeper, such as the Arabic phrase '*Assalamu Alaikum ya* Aisyah,' which means 'peace be upon you, Aisyah.' Such phrases are the instructions for the correct way to touch each side of the vagina.

The saying of the phrase *Basmalah*, which means 'with the name of Allah' accompanies the man's penetration of the woman's vagina with his penis. When the penis enters the vagina, the husband says *Alif* marking the initiation of the intercourse phase. When the whole penis is inside the vagina, he says 'light of light, light of illumination' (*nurung caia, nurung maccaia*), which demonstrates his feeling of pleasure. The husband's breath follows the 'in and out' of his penis.

Corresponding to this, a Hadith states that the Prophet Muhammad prohibits a husband to *azl*—an Arabic term that refers to the man's withdrawal of his penis—without his wife's consent (Masdar F. Mas'udi 1997:118). Another Hadith states that when a husband has reached orgasm but his wife has not, he should not pull out his penis until his wife has reached orgasm. These two Hadith underscore the significance of not only the husband's sexual pleasure, but also the wife's. In practice, however, orgasm is not discussed. Many don't even understand what orgasm is, particularly those in the village. One informant explained that sometimes she 'feels good', another time she has headache after having sex. Another informant even questioned me about the liquid came out from her vagina every time after having sex, not to mention orgasm.

Lontaraq Ilmu Tarikat describes the wife's feelings before and after sexual intercourse. The wife will feel 'beloved' if her husband asks to make love before sleeping. On the contrary, she will feel as if she is treated like a 'servant' if she is awakened from sleep for sexual intercourse (Muslis Hadrawi and Anwar Ibrahim 1999:51). The final phase Muhlis Hadrawi and Anwar Ibrahim describe is 'post-sexual intercourse, the phase after climax is reached'. They conclude that there are three aspects involved in this phase: 'magical, health, and psychological' (Muhlis Hadrawi and Anwar Ibrahim 1999:47–48). These three aspects are reflected in the couple's interaction after intercourse, reference to which are found in four related *lontaraq*: *Bunga Rampai Budaya, Bunga Rampai Lontaraq, Bunga Rampai Agama*, and *Ilmu Tarikat.*

Magical aspects are reflected in the magical incantations (*jappi-jappi*) uttered after intercourse, described in the post-coitus instructions in several *lontaraq* that reflect the spiritual element of sexual practice.[45] *Bunga Rampai Lontaraq* and *Bunga Rampai Agama*-A describe the health significance related to body care discussed previously. The psychological element is portrayed in the *Lontaraq Ilmu Tarikat* which describes the attitude of the husband toward his wife after intercourse; and the *Lontaraq Bunga Rampai Budaya* addresses the purification of the body. These will be discussed in the following section.

Mandi Junub: Cultural and Religious Purifications

Mandi junub is an Indonesian term for a bath after sexual intercourse; it is like cleansing the body of dirt, not because sexual intercourse is viwed as dirty, but because the activity makes both husband and wife sweat and fill with fluid. *Mandi junub* is required not only before a religious duty, but also before one leaves the house after sexual intercourse. But whether or not one will pray or go out afterwards, *mandi junub* is an obligatory ritual for both men and women.

Elders usually warn 'do not leave the house if you are not clean' (B. *aja' muwélai bolaé nakko dé'mu mapaccing*). The implied meaning of this admonition is to keep one's body free of dirt. So if there is an accident when one is out, one will be ready to face death in a state of cleanliness.

The text *Bunga Rampai Budaya* prescribes the magical formula to be used when performing *mandi junub*, by saying:

Uniakangngi tubukku	I intend my body
ujunnuki nyawakuq	to ritually purify my soul
ujunnuki rahasiakuq	to ritually purify my secret parts
uniakangngi upaccingi tubukkuq	I intend to clean my body
ri laleng ri saliweng	inside and outside
marana' mallaibini.	with children, husband and my wife

One then drinks water, saying:

> I intend to clean my hair
> a thread of hair which is passed on by words [texts]
> There is no God except Allah and Muhammad is His Prophet

45 In *Bunga Rampai Lontaraq, Bunga Rampai Agama, Ilmu Tarekat, Tata Cara Hubungan Suami Istri,* and *Cenninrara.*

Uniakangngi upaccingi gemme'kuq'
cilampaé naola-olaé lapaleng
La ilaha Illallah Muhammadang Rasulullah.

The practitioner then drinks three swallows of water to finish the process of purifying the body after having sex. Drinking water itself functions to return energy to the body. The above incantation (*jappi-jappi*) covers the complete purification of the body, from the ends of the hair (*gemmeq*) to the end of the toes, from the inside to the outside (*ri laleng ri saliweng*). This indicates that all parts of the body need to be cleaned after having sex. The practice and the importance of *mandi junub* is expressed in the following statements:

> I usually take a shower right after having sex with my husband because I feel disgusting without *mandi junub,* and I cannot do anything else before doing it, particularly if I want to pray or go out.
>
> AISYAH, 36, interviewed on 1 June 2000

> My husband and I usually have a shower right after intercourse. This is fun because we shower, hug and kiss each other. I enjoy this *mandi junub*.
>
> NARTI, 38, interviewed on 1 June 2000

> We will not sleep before taking a shower. It is just like missing something if we do not do it. Even though we are very tired, we can not sleep without *mandi junub*.
>
> SIDA, 40, interviewed on 1 June 2000

In addition to this, the attention the husband gives his wife by, for instance, massaging her body and/or hugging her, portrays the emotional meaning of the final phase, so that his wife will not feel ignored after making love. In line with, I often heard from women complaining their husband's manner after sexual intercourse because they just sleep after making love, as if there is no one besides him, and snorking.

The religious meaning can be seen from the incantations (*jappi-jappi*) uttered at the end of intercourse, which symbolize that interaction between God and humans always takes place. The integration of these meanings reflects the comprehensiveness of the activity, which encompasses all three steps of sexual intercourse.

In the village and in the city, incantations (*jappi-jappi*) related to sexual intercourse are still significant in the sexual lives of Bugis. Elders usually have incantations (*jappi-jappi*) of their own and pass them to the younger generation.

Young people, especially girls, ask elders to teach them, for example, how to be attractive to the opposite sex, how to find a soul-mate or pre-destined partner (I. *jodoh*) as soon as possible, and how 'to bind' (B. *sioq*, I. *mengikat*) a husband with magical formulae (*jappi-jappi*).

Conclusion

Bugis sexuality is shaped by an integration of 'Islamic' and local values. Islamic teaching (based on the Qur'an and Hadith) is found in *lontaraq*, many of which I found during my fieldwork to be interpretated in oral tradition similar to how the Qur'an and the Hadith are interpreted.

The manuscripts associated with the conjugal, sexual relationship indicates the ideal activities between the couple before, during, and after intercourse which reflects the notion that the husband is active/aggressive and the wife is passive/obedient. This is related to the sexual values in Bugis marriage, described in the written traditions of *Lontaraq Assikalaibinéngeng*. This tendency is not just related to position in sexual intercourse based on a cosmological view, but also to the enactment of male bravery (*warani*) and female modesty (*malebbiq*) in social intercourse.

The names of God, Kuranic Prophets and other personage Islamic names related to Islam, such as Allataala (God), Nabitta (the Prophet), and the reference to other personage well known in Islam, such as Saéhe' Bil-Ma'rupi, Hasang, Huseng, Ahemade (as discussed in *Lontaraq Daramatasia*) are intertwined with local Islamic beliefs, and at the same time lend the *lontaraq* authority. This serves the sole purpose of legitimating the message of the text. The influence of Islam in this text, however, is not necessarily similar to the teaching of Islam which identifies women as subordinates to men. The application of values in this lontaraq bolsters the idea of 'natural authority' of the father, which was constructed by the New Order regime through its development policy defining Indonesian women as subordinate to men within the family and the state (see Robinson 2000). It is not clear whether or not the Lontara' Daramatasi has infuenced the secular Marriage Law of 1974, but this ideology has existed long before that law was introduced under Islamic influence, which identifies the husband as the head of the husehold (I. *kepala rumah tangga*) and the wife as the mother of the household (ibu rumah tangga), reflecting the structural relationship between husband and wife.

Yet, there is an important element absent in this *lontaraq*, namely, the period of *iddah*, an Arabic term that refers to the period for a widow or divorcee has to wait before she is allowed to remarry. *Iddah* needs to be observed for the duration of three menstrual periods by a divorcee and four months and ten days for a widow (as discussed in Chapter 6). In the *lontaraq Daramatasia*, Daramatasia accepts the proposal of Ahmade's proposal a week after her husband's death, which indicates that she does not observe the proper period of *iddah* required by Islamic law. In everyday practice, however, *iddah* is practiced by Muslims. While a widow or female divorcee has to wait at least for the end of *iddah* before remarrying, in many cases this period of waiting is even longer. This is one of the ways the wife shows loyalty towards her late husband, and a woman who gets married not longer after the end of her *iddah* is usually regarded as sexually desirous, and as publicly demonstrating these desires through marriage.

The authority of a widow to make her own decision with regard to remarriage is reflected in the text because there is no description relating to any consent and direct involvement of Daramatasia's parents when it comes to her second marriage. In Islam, this personal authority is related to a Hadith (Ibn Abbas) which states that 'a widow/divorcee has more right for herself than her guardian' (Masdar Mas'udi 1997:98). Among the Bugis, however, widow rarely remarry without parental consent because marriage involves the merging of two families into one, as is reflected in the Bugis term for marriage—*siala*—which means 'to take each other'.

Despite the fact that Bugis values do not prohibit women from being sexually aggressive with their husbands, it is not encouraged, and it is not 'appropriate' for a wife to take an active role. I have never heard a mother encourage her daughter to initiate sex with her husband, but being attractive to her husband is always encouraged. On this matter, female elders play as an important part in teaching young women about how they should behave with their husbands.

The message within *lontaraq* provides the details of ideal manners in sexual intercourse. However, these are not always comprehensively followed in the daily conduct of sexual interaction. In spite of the comprehensiveness of the acts (for example, touching and kissing) and incantations (*jappi-jappi*) in the *lontaraq*, contemporary practice is simplified. Nonetheless, they commonly imbue sexual intercourse with religious meaning.

Even though written traditions related to sexual intercourse are not read by the majority of the Bugis, the message in the manuscripts of *Lontaraq Assikalaibinéngeng*, passed on by elders, regulates sexual behaviour. None of the *lontaraq* I have discussed in this chapter contains the name of the author of the text. They do, however, often contain the names of the owners which show clearly that the *lontaraq* are oriented toward men.

In the following chapter, I will focus my discussion on the Islamic court and customary practices in relation to marriage, divorce and reconciliation.

CHAPTER 6

Marriage, Divorce and Reconciliation: State Law, Islam and Local Practice

Introduction

Examining marriage, divorce and reconciliation in Bugis society sets one thinking about how daily life can be regulated by various cultural, religious and legal forces. In this chapter I examine the dynamics of marriage, divorce and reconciliation within Bugis society, by relating them to state regulations, Islam and local practice. I focus on how the use of Indonesian civil law on marriage in the form of Marriage Law No.1/1974 and local practices and norms of marriage, its dissolution, reconciliations in their purpose, yet open to contraventions and circumventions. In bringing out these issues, my observations will be based on how religious judges handle marital cases in the Religious Court (Pengadilan Agama) in Sidrap, a regency in South Sulawesi.[1] This chapter consolidates the 'local discourse' aspects that were raised in the previous chapter. The emphasis here is on the role of religious judges in the courts in relation to marriage disputes, which have become part of the daily activities in the Pengadilan Agama. Furthermore, I examine how 'wild/unregulated officiants' (*imam liar*), have arisen in South Sulawesi to fulfil a need around the implementation of forms of marriages and divorces which are not legally recognized by the state, but are socially acceptable, if not necessary, for the community's various responses.

In this chapter, I begin with a discussion of marriage requirements and procedures. I continue by discussing the practice of polygyny, forced marriage and 'wild' marriage, divorce, and reconciliation. Cases of patterns of socially offensive and unofficial marriages are examined to depict both the coherence and contradictions in local practice in relation to Islamic rules and state laws. In the subsequent section, I discuss divorce, reconciliation and how people consult others about their marital issues in order to explore how people manage their problems and how the judges deal with them in court. This chapter is based on interviews, observations of court hearings and of everyday social practice, as well as from a focus group discussion.

1 In his book *Meninjau Hukum Adat di Indonesia*, Soejono Soekanto (1981:17) argues that there are more adat laws in Indonesia than the laws regulated by the state.

 | DOI 10.1163/9789004311947_007

Marriage Requirements and Procedures: Between Adat and Islamic Law

Requirements for Marriage

In contemporary Bugis society, the majority of Bugis consider that a man and a woman who intend to get married should follow the marriage requirements specified in the state 1974 Marriage Law, or in their own words, based on religion (I. *sesuai dengan agama*), as the majority of people understand this as a state regulation related to Islam. In spite of the fact that the majority of the community where I conducted my research accepted this secular law, some use illegal marriage (*kawin liar,* literally 'wild' marriage) as an alternative to legitimate cohabitation, which I will discuss later in this chapter.

In Indonesia, when one is talking about Muslim marriage, one should consider at least four state regulations: *Undang-Undang Perkawinan* No.1/1974 (the Marriage Law) and *Peraturan Pemerintah* No.9/1975 (the State Regulation No.9/1975), *Instruksi Presiden* No.1/1991 (the Presidential Instruction No.1/1991) in relation to *Kompilasi Hukum Islam* (Compilation of Islamic Law), together with *Peraturan Pemerintah* No.10/1983 (PP10) which is appended to regulate the marriage, divorce and sexual behaviour of civil servants (see Chapter 1).

A verse in the Qur'an (*An-Nisa*:21) states that marriage is a firm contract (A. *mitsaq al-ghaliz*). Therefore, marriage cannot be broken off without a legitimate reason. In Islam, any act of law has to include two aspects: an essential principle (I. *rukun*) and a prerequisite (*syarat*). In regard to marriage, the essential principles, or *rukun,*[2] are the presence of the bride, the groom, the *wali,*[3] a term that refers to the nearest male relatives in the bride's or groom's paternal line, two male witnesses (*saksi*), and the granting of consent by the bride's family during the wedding ceremony (*ijab-kabul*).

In addition to the essential principles (*rukun*) of marriage, there are eight prerequisites (*syarat*) for the bride and groom. The *syarat,* or prerequisites, for the bride are that she must be a Muslim woman, heterosexual, unmarried, and not in a period of *iddah,* or waiting period;[4] she has given her consent to her

---

2 *Lontaraq Fikhi/Nikah,* Roll 37/No.11 (p. 5), nineteenth century, Arsip Nasional Wilayah Makassar, transliterated by Muhlis Hadrawi (3-3-2002). This *lontaraq* provides a similar *rukun nikah,* consisting of *ijab-kabul* (B. *duaé lapaleng assikadong*), the bride (*makkunrai ripubainé*), the groom (*oroané mabbainé*), guardian (*owalli*), and two witnesses (*duaé sabbinna*).

3 *Wali* (A.) consists of *wali nasab,* as explained above, and *wali hakim* who acts as a *wali* on behalf of the father or male relatives of the bride if the *wali nasab* cannot be present.

4 *Iddah* (A.) refers to the period of abstention from sexual relation imposed on a widow or a divorced woman, or a woman whose marriage has been annulled, before she may remarry.

wali; the groom is not her *muhrim*, a term that indicates a degree of consanguinity between a man and a woman that renders marriage impossible, but gives them the right of association; she has never been cursed (A. *li'an*) by the prospective groom; and she is not undertaking a pilgrimage.

The *syarat*, or prerequisites, for the groom are: he has to be a Muslim and a heterosexual; he cannot already have four wives at the same time nor have a wife who is forbidden to be the co-wife[5] of the prospective bride; he is not the *muhrim* of the bride (see above) and is not being forced to marry the bride; he knows that his wife is not forbidden to marry him; and he is not undertaking pilgrimage. In regard to the *syarat* for the representative (*wali*) of the bride and for the witnesses (*saksi*): they should be a mature, just, and Muslim; physically and psychologically healthy; and understand the aim of the consent granted by the bride's family (*ijab-kabul*). For the *wali,* he should not be the representative of anyone else at the same time.[6]

Although there are some similarities between the *syarat* for the bride and the groom, it is particularly interesting to note that one of the *syarat* for the groom is that 'he is not forced to marry the bride.' This is not a *syarat* for the bride, although it is stated in the Marriage Law that marriage cannot be implemented without the consent of both parties (KHI, Chapter IV, 17:2). This indicates that the legal prohibition of forced marriage does not only relate to the groom, but also to the bride. The question is why this *syarat* is not stated explicitly for the bride? Does this indicate that a woman's consent is not an important issue in marriage? A woman's agreement may be a clear oral or written statement, hints, or a silent act, as long as an obvious refusal does not exist (KHI, Chapter IV, 16:2). In fact, this *syarat* regarding free consent is not stated in the manuscript *Fikhi/Nikah,* (Marriage Principles) either for the bride or for the groom,[7] which reflects that the manuscript *Fikhi/Nikah* is a Bugis 'domesticated' version of Islam. Consent for marriage in relation to customary notions

---

There are two types of *iddah,* one is *iddah* because of the death of the husband (a period of four months and ten days), and the other is *iddah* because of divorce (a hundred-day waiting period or three menstrual periods) (See Chapter V and VII for a discussion of *iddah*).

5 Marriage is prohibited between a man and a woman because they are related by close family ties (I. *pertalian nasab*, such as mother, aunt); by marriage (*pertalian semenda*, such as mother-in-law, stepmother); and by those who have suckled at the same breast (*pertalian sesusuan*) (KHI, Chapter VI:39).

6 *Buku Pegawai Pencatat Nikah dan Pembantu Pegawai Pencatat Nikah* (P3N&P3N, 1997/1998).

7 In *Lontaraq Fikhi/Nikah* (p. 9), there are only four *syarat nikah* for the groom: he must be a heterosexual male, legally able to marry the bride, who must be legally able to be a co-wife of any existing wife, and he cannot have four wives at the same time.

of marriage is discussed below. The following section will discuss the marriage procedures based on custom (adat) as well as religion.

Procedures of Marriage

In Bugis adat (custom), the wedding ceremony (I. *nikah*) is preceded by proposal procedures, which consist of seeking the way (B. *mabbaja laleng*), the preliminary inquiry or acting like a bird (*mammanuq-manuq*), coming forth with the proposal or to delegate (*madduta*), and the acceptance of the proposal (*mappettu ada*).[8]

In the initial opening stage, (*mabbaja laleng*, a term consisting of two words: *baja*, which means open, and *laleng*, which means way), the man's family would observe whether or not there appeared to be the possibility of making a proposal to a particular girl. This is then followed by acting like a bird (*mammanuq-manuq*, a term derived from the noun *manuq*, which means bird). It is stated in a manuscript that there are three things which cannot be considered: uncertain news, gossip and feeling (*tellu tempedding riattepperi: anutemmanessa, karéba, kapang ati*) (Machmud 1994:85). Hence, in order to avoid 'bird news' (*karéba manuq-manuq*), the man's family should find out ahead of time, important information concerning the woman's background and whether or not she has been reserved (*ritaro*) by the proposal of another man before coming forth with their proposal. This is because a man cannot propose to a woman who is being proposed to by another man before the former proposal has been decided by the woman's side (KHI, Chapter III,12:3). The woman's family also examines the man's background, including his marital status, before deciding to accept his proposal. The final step in the proposal procedure is to delegate (*madduta*, from the noun *duta*, which means a delegation). To delegate involves the man's family sending delegates to propose formally to the woman. I found in oral circulation and observed that the dialogue during to delegate (*madduta*)

8 While the terms may vary, the meaning is similar. For example, *mabbaja laleng/mabbalao ciciq*; *mammanuq-manuq/mappéseq- péseq*; *madduta/massuro. Mabbalao ciciq* comes from the words *balao* (B. mouse) and *ciciq* (small) which means trying to use a 'small mouse strategy' which is, for example, investigating someone without it being known by the one who is being investigated or by others, particularly if the *bali* (B. prospective in-law) comes from another kinship group. The secret investigation, in addition to the above, also aims to ascertain a woman's descent, character, attitude and family background. In the past, when the groom's side submitted their proposal, the food served by the prospective bride's side indicated the probable outcome of the proposal. Food made from edible tubers indicated the refusal of the proposal. In contrast, food made from brown sugar and coconut, which symbolise sweet and delicious, indicated a positive response from the woman's side (see, for example, Mattulada 1995:45–46; Millar 1989:71–74; A.P. Hamzah et al. 1984: 101–106; Ridwan Borahima et al. 1974:17–30).

is commonly expressed as a word game that both parties play in order to balance the status of both sides. The following dialogue between the one who proposes, TM (*to madduta,* man's party), and the one who is being proposed to, TR (*to riaddutai,* woman's party) is based on *lontaraq* and illustrates this word game (A.P. Hamzah et al. 1984:103–104).

TM:

Dua kuala sappo,	Two things are used as a fence
unganna panasaé	jackfruit flower
bélo kanukué	nail polish

This passage may be interpreted to mean that with honesty and purity, we come to bring happiness, to convey our purpose.

Iaro bunga rositta	The rose
tépu tabbakka toni	has blossomed
engkanaga sampona?	does anything cover it up?

The subsequent sentence is an inquiry if the girl has attained adult status and if anyone else has yet reserved her.

TR:

Dégga pasaq riliputta	There are markets in your country
balanca rikampotta	expenses in your village
mulincoq mabéla.	you go far away.

In this passage, the woman's family points out that there are beautiful girls nearby, why does the prospective groom have to go somewhere else?

TM:

Engka pasaq riliputta	There are markets in our country
balanca rikampotta	expenses in our village
nyawami kusappaq.	we are looking for a soul.

The groom's relatives respond by expressing that though there are beautiful girls nearby, they are looking for a kind-hearted girl with a soul.

TR:

Iganaro éloq ribungataq	Who is interested in our flower
bunga temmaddaungngé	a leafless flower
bunga temmakkétakkéwé.	a branchless flower?

The bride's family, in essence, ask who wants to marry our girl, she is simple and unadorned?

TM:

Taroni temmaqdaung	Although it is leafless
taroni temmattakké	and branchless
bélo-bélo temmalaté.	she is an unfading ornament.

The groom's family then responds that even if she is unadorned, she will become the light of his life.

While the words may vary slightly in such dialogues, the meaning is similar.[9] During the dialogue, the two parties (TM and TR) attempt to balance the conversation in order to protect *siriq* on both sides. At the end of the dialogue, the TR modestly conveys to the TM: 'If that is your purpose, back-up and examine us, and we will also examine you' (B. *komakkoitu adattaq, soroqniq tangngaq kaq, nautangngaq tokkiq*) which indicates that the TR has given a positive hint to the TM that the proposal will be considered. Thus, the TR and the TM respectively investigate each other.

The next step is 'the acceptance of the proposal', a process referred to with the term *mappettu ada. Mappettu,* literally means deciding and *ada* means words. In this step, all matters, including rank price, bridewealth, and the woman's and man's engagement gifts are determined. These procedures are indicated by Millar as the proposal stage to be followed by a number of ceremonies in order to legitimate the marriage, according to custom and law.[10]

Although custom (adat) is different from the required state procedures,[11] there are some similarities between the two. For example, in the initial phase of the state procedures (registration), the applicants (both the man and the woman) or their representatives have to go to the *kelurahan* (that is the Indonesian political district administered by the *lurah*) in Rappang (see Map 1.2) in order to register the marriage, and to receive marriage advice from the official marriage registrar, termed the Pegawai Pencatat Nikah (PPN)[12]

9 See, for example, Mattulada (1995:11–2); Ridwan Borahima et al. (1974:20–22), and in everyday circulation.

10 Millar (1989, Chapter IV) identifies the main stages of Bugis wedding as formal proposal, engagement, marriage, wedding party (I. *pesta*), and formal subsequent meetings.

11 The guide book, *Pedoman Pegawai Pencatat Nikah dan Pembantu Pegawai Pencatat Nikah* (P3N&P3N, 1997/1998).

12 The PPN is appointed by the Ministry of Religion, based on Law No.22/1946 in any Kantor Urusan Agama (KUA) in the *kecamatan* (I. subdistrict).

at least ten days before the marriage contract (I. *akad nikah*) is performed.[13] The procedures of this registration include publicizing the request for marriage, investigating whether the applicants are eligible to marry under the Marriage Law No.1/1974 (for instance, by checking marital status, age of the applicants), announcing the marriage and signing the marriage certificate at the end of the marriage contract (*akad nikah*) ritual.[14] In the process of investigating the marital status of the couple, the man, the woman, and their representatives (*wali*), have to be carefully investigated by the PPN, who is the only official appointed to do this in Islamic marriage procedures. The aim of this investigation is to determine whether or not either of the applicants has ever been married. This procedure is closely related to the stage of 'preliminary inquiry' (*mammanuq-manuq*) of the customary (adat) procedure.

Polygyny

In reference to the requirements of polygyny,[15] a verse in the Qur'an (*An-Nisa*:129) states that a man has to be fair to each of his wives and children from any wife. Otherwise, another verse (*An-Nisa*:2) states that he should only have one wife. In Bugis, these verses are interpreted in light of a popular Bugis saying that a man may take more than a wife: 'as long as a man can feed his wives and children'. The implied meaning of this philosophy is to be fair to any wife and child financially and emotionally. This emphasis on fairness, difficult for any person to practice, reinforces the Bugis commitment to monogamy.

In practice, however, financial matters are strongly emphasized, whereas emotional concerns are neglected. As a result, rich men can easily have more than one wife.[16] Although Millar (1989:28) argues that polygyny is generally

13 Ten days before a marriage, an investigation is required by the PPN as well as a consultation with BP4 (Badan Penasihat Perkawinan, Perselisihan dan Perceraian—Institute for Marriage Disputes and Divorce Counselling) for pre-marital advice. PP No.9/1975 (Chapter II, 3:3), however, states that an exemption can be given for urgent reasons, such as one of the couple will be on duty abroad. The exemption will be given by the subdistrict head (I. *camat*) under the authority of the regent (*bupati*).

14 P3N & P3N (1997/1998).

15 There have been three major reforms challenging polygyny (in the 1930s, 1950s and 1970s) in Indonesia. However, these efforts have always failed because of the symbolic importance of the Qur'anic verse, allowing polygyny (Lev 1996).

16 Millar's (1989:28) further discusses the importance of plural marriage by husband (as the number of dependents constitute proof of his great influence) and wives (as being part of the extensive family networks).

solely practised by powerful and wealthy men, I found that less well-off men are no exception. Regardless of the financial ability to support more than one wife, illegal marriage (I. *kawin liar*) is an alternative, cheaper way for marriage. It is also easier because it is non-procedural and unregulated. Data provided by the Pengadilan Agama in Sidrap indicated that between 2000 and 2014, only two cases of requests for consent of polygyny. All requests were granted because the wives were sick (and therefore could not fulfil their husband's sexual needs). This is one of the circumstances as stated in the Marriage Law of 1974 (article 4:2) that can be used for a husband to take another wife. The judges, however, confirm that the regulation of polygynous marriages through the Marriage Law seldom works, since the consultation of wives and children are not easily obtained.

According to the Marriage Law (Chapter I, 5:1a), a married man who wants to obtain his first wife's consent[17] through the local Pengadilan Agama before taking another wife (see Plate 6.1). One way to successfully marry a second time is by not disclosing the wife's place of residence. In such a case, the second marriage may take place because the first wife would not have been informed of the husband's intention to marry. In addition, there are cases in

PLATE 6.1 *The Pengadilan Agama Sidrap, 2015*

17 See, for example, Butt (2008) and Robinson (2006).

which the existing wife knows of her husband's intentions, but does not object to his second marriage for various reasons, or agrees with it for fear of losing financial support. This circumstance is especially prevalent among dependent wives who have no income of their own and who have young children.

One extreme case handled by the Pengadilan Agama in Sidrap was the case of Anna and her husband, Rasyid. Rasyid intentionally concealed the place of residence of his first wife, Anna, when he filed for divorce. Thus, her permission for the divorce could not be sought, nor could she object and obstruct his plans to take on another wife. As a result, the certificate of divorce was issued by the Pengadilan Agama and Rasyid married another woman, Lina. However, when the former wife, Anna, found out she had been divorced, she reported the case to the court. Subsequently, Rasyid's marriage to Lina was then nullified by the court because it was an offence to divorce one's wife without her knowledge or consent, under the Marriage Law of 1974.[18] Anna's case is exceptional because not every woman has the courage to take such action in order to assert her rights and sustain her marriage.

Pak Amir, a successful middle-aged gold trader well known for his wealth and polygyny, had been married eight times, with only the first two marriages being legal. He justified his polygynous marriages with the philosophy: 'The more often he gets married, the more fortune he will have' because, according to him, every time he married another woman, his fortune grew and he proudly acknowledged his polygynous marriages. In spite of the fact that he enjoyed polygyny, he had never had more than two wives at any one time. Interestingly, he called his second wife (he divorced his first wife and had a daughter from this marriage) 'my permanent wife' (B. *bainé tetteqku*), indicating that she was his favourite, while the rest of his wives were called 'my ladies-in-waiting' (*dayaq-dayakku*). Hence, whenever Pak Amir attended a party or formal occasion (for instance, wedding party, celebration of a circumcision and so on), he was usually accompanied by his 'permanent wife'. He described this marriage as a 'kingdom', and his 'permanent wife' (*bainé tetteq*) as the 'queen' of his kingdom, meaning she and her child could enjoy the property provided by the king (the husband, Pak Amir).

This glamorous play-acting was, in fact, intended to persuade his wife to 'tolerate' his polygynous life style. Thus, money had become the primary factor supporting his behaviour. Whenever he intended to marry another woman, he would get divorced—by desertion or illegal divorce—from the previous wife, while retaining his 'permanent' one.

18 The Marriage Law (Chapter III:13–22): marriage prevention.

Among rich men, taking on additional wives has become a sign of prestige, a symbol of high status, and can be socially 'tolerated'.[19] In contrast, people will often criticise a lower class polygynous man for his financial incompetence. There was a joke related to polygyny among the judges in the Pengadilan Agama that the reason for polygyny is not because the husband does not like his wife, but because he wants to 'taste' another woman. This relates to another joke I frequently heard from the judges that all women have the same vagina shape, so a novel sensation is what men seek. Thus, the incentive for polygyny is solely related to sexual desire.

In line with the above thinking, the customary Bugis text *lontaraq* or manuscripts *Fikhi/Nikah* (p. 3). states: 'Get married to a woman who is legal for you, two or three or four' (B. *Nikkai mennang makkunrai hallalaq é riko mennang dua iaréqga tellu iaréqga eppaq*). Even though this manuscript refers to the verse of the Qur'an (*An-Nisa*:2 and 129),[20] there is no discussion of the responsibilities involved in polygyny, and this omission may be evidence of tolerance of unofficial polygyny. In fact, one verse in the Qur'an (*An-Nisa*:3) states:

> If ye fear that ye shall not be able to deal justly with the orphans, marry women of your choice, two or three or four. But if ye fear that ye shall not be able to deal justly (with them), then only one, or (a captive) that your right hand possess. That will be more suitable to prevent you from doing injustice.

In this verse from the Qur'an, justice is considered the right for both parties, the husband and the wife. While the statement from the *lontaraq* mentioned above is incomplete, it implies that a husband has the authority to have four wives in any circumstance. My interviews with many men and some women reinforced the understanding that polygyny was regarded as permissible if one could be fair in providing for each wife and all children. However, the general view of most scholars is that fairness (for example, to treat all wives and children equally) was beyond human capability. In many cases, fairness would be subjected to the husband's exercise of his own discretion in this matter (Nurul Ilmi Idrus 2006a). Therefore, fairness is subjective and realistically difficult to practise in a polygynous marriage (Mernissi 1985), and has become a source of injustice towards women and children (Nina Nurmila 2009).[21]

19 Polygynous marriage among noble people has been extensively described in the Bugis classic story of *La Galigo* (Muhammad Salim and Fachruddin Ambo Enre 1995, Kern 1989, Fachruddin Ambo Enre 1999, and Muhammad Salim and Fachruddin Ambo Enre 2000).

20 This is also stated in KHI (Chapter IX, 55: 2–3).

21 A number of recent studies on polygyny has been published in Indonesia which criticizes the practice of polygyny. For example, Nurul Ilmi Idrus (2006) examines polygyny on the

In contrast to the above line of argument, people often commented: 'How can he be fair to each of his wives?' This view indicates that while polygynous marriage was accepted by some, others were sceptical in regard to fairness. While most women did not accept polygyny themselves, they believed that men could marry up to four wives. Such an unquestioning disposition could lead to emotional disturbances and anxieties about the possibility of them becoming co-wives themselves at some points in their lives. The fear itself often has more to do with economic factors than jealousy, since a husband's income would inevitably have to be shared among the multiple families. Robinson points out that taking on a second wife in Soroako, Sulawesi, had become a common 'male fantasy', while women had 'female fear'—of the contender (Robinson 1986:228). Such fear was verbalized by the wife of *Pak* Bakri (my host in Sidrap), who had struggled not to get divorced from her adulterous husband in order to be able to survive economically, particularly for the sake of her children's education, as discussed in Chapter 4.

In another case I observed in the Pengadilan Agama in Sidrap, a woman named Rosna had reported her husband Arman's plans for a second marriage.

PLATE 6.2 *With the judges, clerks and staff in the Pengadilan Agama, 2015*

basis of public debate from the perspective of both, legal and local norms; Sri Purwatiningsih (2005) on the practice of polygyny among civil servant; Abdul Halim Soebahar et al. (2005) on the debate among Muslim leaders as to whether or not polygyny is an emergency 'door' for Muslims to take more than one wife; Siti Musdah Mulia (2004), a feminist scholar, tries to redefine texts of Islamic teaching from gender perspective.

She and the police came to the court to discuss the case and were told the second marriage could not proceed because Rosna did not give her consent and there was no justification for Arman to take another wife. The police were ordered to prevent the marriage.[22] In spite of this, the marriage eventually took place. Rosna finally accepted her husband's second marriage for the sake of their children.

The question is why was the court successful in preventing Rasyid's second marriage, but not Armand's? In Rasyid's case, he was willing to accept the regulation of the Marriage Law, whilst in Armand's case, Rosna believed that the police had been bribed by Arman in exchange for facilitating the procedures of his unlawful second marriage. In such circumstances, judges in the courts find it frustrating to apply the existing Marriage Law on formalized marital unions since some people are able to secure their own wants even if they contravene the law. This is seen, for example, in the practice of forced marriage (*kawin paksa*) and illegal marriage (*kawin liar*), both of which are against the Marriage Law. Under the civil law, one could marry with the consent of both parties and including that of the existing wife if a polygynous marriage is to be contracted in accordance with legal procedures. The following section discusses types of socially offensive and unofficial marriages.

Kawin Paksa, Terpaksa Kawin and *Kawin Liar*

> Marriage, in adat [customary] law, is to varying degrees, a matter of kinship group, family, community and personal concern.
>
> TER HAAR 1948:163

Kawin Paksa *and* Terpaksa Kawin

Forced marriage (I. *kawin paksa*) is an offence according to Marriage Law No.1/1974. The consent is the basic principle of marriage (the Marriage Law, Chapter II: 6), either because the marital pair gets married out of mutual love, or they have both agreed to an arranged marriage. The law notwithstanding,

22 See KHI (Chapter XI) for marriage cancellation. According to Pak Sama, the grounds for cancellation of marriage vary, among others are forced marriage, *kawin liar*, non-consensual polygyny, and so on (Personal interview with Pak Sama, the head of the Pengadilan Agama Sidrap, 4-8-2010). Data provided by the Pengadilan Agama in Sidrap indicated that within thirteen years (between 2000 and 2013), there were seven cases of requests for marriage cancellation, one case in 2000, 2001, and 2007 respectively, and four cases in 2009.

forced marriage is culturally legitimated to some extent. This reveals a paradox, but does not necessarily mean that the community is unaware of the Marriage Law.

Despite the fact that forced marriage could not usually be detected from the commencement of marriage contract, it would usually surface during the court hearing. However, forced marriage has become one of the ways to enhance the parents' reputation since those who are able to force their children into marriage are socially considered to be 'successful parents' who still wield control over their children, particularly daughters. For example, if a daughter is considered to be 'mature enough' to get married, but remains unmarried, a forced marriage is then considered a socially acceptable option. Romantic attachment following marriage is idealized, as elders say: 'You will like each other after marriage', which indicates that love is only expected to blossom after marriage. This idealism, however, is not always translated into reality.

I observed during my fieldwork that acceptance of a proposal can be based on a silent response since in Bugis culture, the silence of a woman is interpreted as a sign of her agreement.[23] Silence, however, may have various meanings. A focus group discussion with young women in the village clarified their views on this issue. For instance, they considered that a silent-act was a risky response for a girl who received a proposal from someone who was not her sweetheart because, whatever her silence meant to her, it would be understood as an agreement by other people. Indeed, silence was considered a modest response, whereas answering with words, such as 'yes, I accept the proposal', or some similar phrase, was regarded as aggressive. On the other hand, silence could indicate disagreement because the girl was afraid of family disappointment or anger, particularly on the part of her parents, or was afraid of being sinful.

In forced marriages within well off families in Makassar, I frequently observed the mother of the bride trying to persuade her crying daughter to accept the undesired proposal by promising to give her daughter a new car or a set of diamonds, as long as she accepted the marriage and stopped crying, because such a resistant attitude shamed the family. A similar circumstance is captured in the epic La Galigo in the account of the marriage between Batara Lattuq and Wé Datu Sengngeng. In the following passage, Wé Adiluwuq, Wé Datu Sengngeng's twin sister, persuades Wé Datu Sengngeng to stop crying (Muhammad Salim and Fachruddin Ambo Enre 2000).[24]

23 KHI (Chapter IV, 16:2) states that the forms of agreement of the girl can be a written, verbal or a signal.

24 Wé Datu Sengngeng and Wé Adiluwuq are twins of 'white blood' descent. They are the daughters of La Urung Mpessi from the upper world and and Wé Pada Uleng from the

Yet Wé Datu Sengngeng shrank from showing [her] face
She just bowed her head and wept
her tears flowed down.
Wé Adiluwuq [her elder sister] herself wiped away
the flowing tears of her royal younger sister.
In tears, Wé Adiluwuq said,
'Why, dear Highness,
do you not want to turn and show
the full oval of [your] face to the mighty man?
Do not wail, dear Highness, in your trouble.
even if our self-respect [*siriq*] be lost,
even if our word lie lifeless and in tatters,
the wise judgement of To Palanroé [the Creator] has to be accepted.
People in the future will say,
[See how she was not greedy for bridal gifts,
for only little lords care about their possessions]'.[25]

Ala wedding ga Wé Datu Sengngeng *paleppang rupa.*
Cukkuq i sia pariléq-kiléq
uaé mata mabbalobona.
Watanna muna Wé Adiluwuq *sapuiang ngi*
uaé mata mabbalobona datu anrinna.
Terri makkeda Wé Adiluwuq,
'Magi ro waé, Anri Ponratu,
mutéa giling paléppangi wi
rupa mabboja to marajaé.
Ajaq naua, Anri Ponratu, raju-rajummu
teddeng aré ni sia siriqta, Anri Ponratu,
maté aré ni caré adatta
risékuana pagguligana To Palanroé
Lé makkeddai matuq taué,
[Pépa gi waé temmakékélla ri tampaq é
nadatuq kasiq tenreq anunna]' (pp. 174 and 176).

lower world who were sent to inhabit the middle world just about the same time as Batara Lattuq. But they died just after insulting their descents who originated from the upper world. Then, Wé Datu Sengngeng and Wé Adiluwuq became orphans (Muhammad Salim and Fachruddin Ambo Enre 1995:20).

25 Loosely transliterated by Campbell Macknight (17-5-2003).

The above prose indicates the effort of Adiluwuq to persuade her twin sister to accept the marriage arranged by the creator (B. *risékuana pagguligana* To Palanroé). Refusing this marriage would cause shame (*teddeng aré ni sia siriqta*), especially because the other party is the grandson of the creator. Significantly, elders usually comment that '*iko tommitu pakasiriq i alému nakko silorimukko matu lakkaimmu*' (you shame yourself if you come to like/love your husband in the future). A crying girl who refuses such a marriage proposal is not given any respect.

I was told of a case of suicide because of a forced marriage in Kulo in 1994, which involved a 25-year-old woman, Radiah. This age was considered quite old for a woman to remain unmarried in the village and was seen as transgressing her parents' *siriq* (honour or shame). Afraid of being sinful towards her parents, Radiah responded to the proposal of a middle-aged bachelor of 48 years old with silence, which was regarded as agreement by her parents. Her parents' acceptance, however, was followed by her suicide. Suicide itself is not just an atypical reaction for people in the village, but is also against Islamic principles.

Another instance of forced marriage I observed in the Pengadilan Agama was the case of a young girl named Hartati who was uncertain whether she should divorce her husband to marry another man (see her earlier story in Chapter 3). Hartati seemed to be confused, as she stated:

> I did not know what I wanted, my mother wanted me to get a divorce because there was someone who wanted to propose to me, I was not sure if he was going to be better than my former husband.
>
> HARTATI, 17 years, Junior High School graduate, 'housewife', divorced, no children, interviewed on 2 March 2000

After her testimony in court, Hartati's mother was asked by the judge to give Hartati more time since her daughter was doubtful about making a decision and was under stress. Hartati's mother, however, urged the judge to grant the divorce immediately. This was because she definitely intended to marry off her daughter to another man to whom she had already given a 'positive hint' without her daughter's consent.

During the court hearing, I heard Hartati's uncle and other family members argue loudly over her divorce outside the courtroom. Instead of delaying the court hearing because of Hartati's uncertainty, the judges decided to grant the divorce. In this case, the family pressure was based on two considerations: Hartati and her former husband were considered incompatible and, at the same time, someone else had already approached Hartati's mother and announced his intention to marry her as soon as she obtained a divorce certificate, regardless of her wishes. In this case, Hartati's family felt ashamed because of the first unsuccessful marriage and believed that marrying her to another man would balance the *siriq* of the family caused by Hartati's failed first marriage. The approach of the prospective husband indicated that she was still a 'saleable' girl, especially because the first marriage remained unconsummated.

Hartati was not only an example of a victim of a forced marriage and the marriage of a minor (she was fifteen at the time of the first marriage),[26] but also the victim of the hasty decision of the court. I argued with the judges outside the courtroom as I felt they had granted the divorce too hastily. I assumed that the marriage itself could still work out if the judges tried to understand the situation between Hartati and her husband, both of whom were too shy to talk about their marriage. However, the judges argued that even if the case were prolonged, it would still end in divorce because of the strong family pressure. Hence, delaying was considered a waste of the court's time. This indicates that the court does not see marriage as a sole and principal between two individuals, but also as a bond which involves the interlocking interests of the extended family.

In regard to unconsummated marriage (A. *qabla-al-dhukhul*), the Qur'an (*Al-Baqarah*:236–237) states that divorce prior to consummation is lawful and that the wife is entitled to keep half of her rank price (B. *sompa*, I. *mahar*) paid by a husband to a wife with agreement of both sides.[27] However, the return of half the rankprice rarely occurs in Sidrap.[28] If return is demanded by the groom's side, the elders state 'according to *lontaraq*, half of the rankprice should be returned if the marriage is unconsummated' (*makkeddai lontaraq é, lisuitu sompaé, nakko déqna éngka musitinroang lakkaimmu*). Sharing the same bed (*sitinroang*) in this case literally means sexual intercourse. This is in line with a statement in *lontaraq* which states that only if a bride has not been

26 According to the Marriage Law, the age of marriage for a girl is 16 years old. But according to the judge, other reason may be used to allow marriage of a minor, such as she is considered to be capable enough to serve her husband, is already menstruating, is physically well developed (I. *bongsor*).

27 There is some controversy about whether or not a wife is entitled to retain half the *mahar* after divorce prior to consummation, see for example Abu Hanifah et al. (in 'Uwaidah, 1998:458–459).

28 Even though the demand of returning rankprice is very rare, I was told by the judges in the Religious Court that when the man's side demands to return the rankprice (*sompa*), they actually ask for spending money (*duiq ménréq*). In fact, spending money is the money which is used for the wedding ceremony and is not to be returned.

touched by the groom (*tenrirapiq i makkunraié ri oroanéna*)—excluding the touch after the marriage contract (*mappasikarawa*)—should her rankprice (*sompa*),[29] as well as wedding gifts (*pabbéré*)[30] be returned in full. If the bride has been touched by the groom, but the marriage has not yet been consummated (*narapiq sala-salai makkunraié ri oroanéna*), half of her rankprice along with the entirety of the wedding gifts should be returned.[31] This Bugis text not only legitimates divorce prior to consummation, but also determines the circumstances in which rankprice and wedding gifts must be returned.

In Hartati's case, her first husband did not demand the return of the rankprice, even though Hartati told the judges that she had been touched without sexual intercourse by her husband during her short marriage. Thus, I assumed that her 'touch acknowledgment' was an attempt to prevent the divorce, as she stated above. Elders told me that in the old days, if the marriage had not been consummated, both rankprice (B. *sompa*) and wedding gifts (*pabbéré*) were returned in full.

In another case I observed in the Pengadilan Agama , the father of the groom from a low status group—in terms of both traditional Bugis classification and modern socioeconomic classification—who became one of the witnesses for his son's case in court—demanded that the bride return all the bride wealth (rankprice and spending money, *duiq ménré*), including wedding gift given by him and his son. However, the wife, Isa (then aged 20), responded to this demand by saying, 'I was a virgin when I got married with your son, so I will return all your gifts if you return my virginity'. Such a statement indicates that she did not consider that her husband (Udin, 21) and his family were deserving of return of any wedding gifts since the marriage was consummated (A. *ba'da-dhukhul*). According to a judge in the Pengadilan Agama in Sidrap:

> Whether or not the touch is by the bride's consent, it is considered that she has accepted the groom (*ba'da-dukhul*), and therefore when divorce is granted, the waiting period (*iddah*) is applied. By contrast, when the bride has not been touched by the groom, it is perceived that the groom

29 It is implicitly stated in the manuscript edition of *Ritumpanna Wélenrénngé* that *sompa* functions as *mahar*, *pengikat/bukti* (B. *pappasiarekeng*: tying the knot) and *pembendung lamaran* (*teppoq duta*, stemming any forthcoming proposal) (Fachruddin Ambo Enre 1999:492).

30 *Pabbéré* are wedding gifts presented to a newly married couple by the groom's family during the visit to the groom (*marola*).

31 *Lontaraq Membicarakan Tentang Berlaki-Bini*, MAK No.74, pp. 77–78 (Macknight 1972: reel 5, microfilm).

> is not accepted. Therefore, rankprice is returned, but wedding gifts are not (*lisu sompa, tellisu pabbéré*), except when there is an agreement prior to marriage that both *sompa* and *pabbéré* are to be returned, as stated in article 35 of KHI[32].
>
> PAK SAMA, Judge, interviewed on 4 August 2010

During my fieldwork, however, I had never heard anyone mentioning the return rankprice because of divorce, unless it was part of common or matrimonial property (I. *harta gono-gini*),[33] which usually resulted in further conflict. It is considered shameful to insist on the return of things that have been given to the bride, especially for well off or noble families. In spite of the fact that Islam does not specifically encode common or matrimonial property, such property has been affirmed by Indonesian civil courts as fundamental to the local culture in many parts of the archipelago and it has been incorporated in KHI (Robinson 2001:29).[34] However, Pak Sama told me that in the case of marital violence, women don't mind to return both *sompa* and *pabbéré* as long as the divorce can be granted immediately.[35]

Although other factors, such as education and employment, might contribute to the current preference for self-choice of marriage partners in the village (see Jones 1994), and the influence of popular culture—television is the most popular source of new information in the village—these have not stop the practice of forced marriage in Kulo, although they have at least reduced it.[36] A community leader noted that parents in Kulo now think carefully before forcing their children into marry as they consider that circumstances have changed

32 Article 35 of KHI states that (1) a husband, who divorced his wife before the marriage is consummated (*qabla-al-dhukhul*), is obliged to pay half of rankprice determined during the marriage contract (*akad nikah*); (2) If a husband died before the marriage is consummated (*qabla-al-dhukhul*), the wife has the full right towards the whole rankprice; (3) If a divorce is granted before the marriage is consummated (*qabla-al-dhukhul*) and the amount of rankprice has not been determined, the husband is obliged to pay the rankprice (*mahar mitsil*).

33 See, for example, Bowen (nd:14) who discusses equal property rights for husband and wife in the Religious Court Sumatra.

34 See KHI (Chapter XIII): common property in marriage.

35 Personal interview with *Pak* Sama, the head of the Pengadilan Agama Sidrap (4-8-2010).

36 My interviews with youth, *ibu-ibu* (I. mothers) and *tokoh masyarakat* (community leaders) in regard to forced marriage in Kulo indicate that the practice of forced marriage has decreased significantly since the suicide of Radiah in 1994. Thus, they see the suicide as important in reducing the practice of forced marriage.

compared to previous years; children socialize more openly in school or in the workplace where they might find their own marriage partners. In addition, unsuccessful forced marriage may not only cause shame (*siriq*) for both families, but also financial losses on marriage expenses.

In reference to one of the prerequisites (*syarat*) for a man—that he is not forced to marry the bride—mentioned previously, I observed a case in the court in which a man claimed to have been forced to marry (*terpaksa kawin*) a woman whom he was filing for divorce. The following dialogue (in Buginese)[37] during the court hearing illustrates the case:

> JUDGE: 'Why did you get married with Fatma if you didn't want to take responsibility as a husband?'
> *Magimu pubainéi I*[38] *Fatma nakko téako tanggunjawa' ribainému?*
>
> BAHAR: 'I was caught, I did not want to get married, but I was forced to marry her.'
> *Itikkemmaq, déqpa uéloq botting, tapi natikkéngnga makkunraié.*
>
> FATMA: 'What is the evidence that you were caught? I was not pregnant, we did not have children, there was no reason for me to force you to marry me.'
> *Aga buttinna utikkekko, déqkumattampu, déggaga anaq ilolongeng, déggaga alasang upassako kkawingikaq.*
>
> COURT HEARING, 20 April 2000

During the court hearing, Bahar used the word *tikkeng* (B. catch, literally meaning 'force')—which is highly criticised by the judges—to accuse Fatma. Even though the judges did not directly judge Fatma based on Bahar's accusation of 'force' (*tikkeng*), it was evident that the judges ignored Fatmah's allegation of

37 *Bahasa* Bugis is used to make it easy for the clients to better understand the dialogue during the court hearing. This is due to the fact that in the village, as in the regency, people usually speak the local language in their everyday encounters.

38 'I' is an article which accompanies a Bugis woman's name, such as I Fatma. While 'La' is used for a Bugis men's names such as La Bahar. These articles are rarely used by urban people. Mattulada (1995:50) identifies that while *Baco* and *Beccé* are two terms to be used as subtitute names for boys and girls, the terms Wé (for women) and La (for men) are commonly used in front of the names of people in relation to their social status. This is best illustrated in the *I La Galigo* manuscript, for example the names La Tenrisinrang and Wé Majang.

violence in the marriage. Fatma unrelentingly accused her husband of irresponsible and abusive during their marriage.

If Fatma had calmly responded to questioning during the court hearing, she might have received sympathy from the judges. However, her 'aggressive' behaviour was considered too unbecoming of a Bugis wife, as I heard from the judges when I discussed the case with them after the court hearing. This cause of disharmony in their marriage was attributed to her excessive aggressiveness towards her husband in verbal disputes. Her behaviour was considered inappropriate in regard to the ideal behaviour of a modest Bugis wife (*déqna malebbiq*). One judge assumed that this marriage was a result of emotional decision (*botting emosi*), which means that the couple were not mature enough to get married (Fatma and Bahar were 21 and 22 respectively at the time of the court hearing) and that they believed that marriage was only about love without consideration the responsibilities that come with it.[39]

Even though one of the prerequisites (*syarat*) of marriage for the groom is that 'he is not forced to marry the bride', there are cases in which the accusation of forced to marry (*terpaksa kawin*) are put forth by couples after the marriage does not work out, as in the case of Fatma and Bahar. They were finally granted the divorce on the grounds of incompatibility, after almost three years of marriage, including four months of separation (*mallawangeng*).[40]

Through my daily encounters and court observations, I discovered that a man is often forced to marry a woman because of an unwanted pregnancy, usually when he refuses to take responsibility for having engaged in premarital sex. Despite the absence of specific statistical data on hasty divorces soon after marriage (I. *kawin-cerai*), I observed in a number of court hearings that many cases of hasty divorce in Sidrap were the result of premarital pregnancy. Subsequently, the couple divorced soon after the marriage or after the baby's birth. In one case, a man refused to marry a woman he had impregnated, and someone else married her in order to save her and her family from shame, and in doing so, saved the man who impregnated her and his family from shame too (B. *massampo siriq*).

---

39 Millar (1989:27), for example, notes that marriage at a young age in Soppeng frequently ended with a divorce.

40 Some literature indicates the importance of separation prior to divorce in Indonesia (see, for example, McDonald and Edeng Abdurahman 1974; Ter Haar 1948; Budi S. Mortokoesoemo 1979; Jones et al. 1994). Separation is not documented by the Religious Court, even though it is stated in reports, and mentioned in court hearings. This seems to be pragmatic in view of the fact that the status of separation is not used as a legal term in Indonesia (Budi S. Mortokoesoemo, 1979:90).

Kawin Liar

In Indonesia, terms such as *kawin sirih, nikah sirri,* and *kawin bawah tangan,*[41] are used to describe marriage based on religion (*nikah secara agama*) which are socially legitimate, but unregistered by the state. However, this unregulated practice may vary from one place to another. In the rural area of Sidrap and elsewhere throughout the regency, a specific term, *kawin liar,* is used.[42] This term indicates that the marriage is 'wild' or not according to the state's legal strictures. However, it is still considered as 'marriage based on religion' in practice. *Kawin liar* is not specific to people in rural areas since it is also practised in the city of Makassar—the capital city of South Sulawesi—and elsewhere throughout in the province.[43]

With or without their parents' consent, *kawin sirih* is increasingly practised among urban university students, particularly for those who live in boarding houses during the period of their study,[44] and it is considered different from 'living together like water buffalo' (I. *kumpul kebo'*) in which the union is non-marital.[45] Masyiatul Maula terms such marriage as *nikah sirri* and defines it as 'secret marriage', among people in Central Java such marriage is called *nikah agama,* a term that means 'marriage based on religion' or unofficial marriage. Even though *nikah sirri* follows the requirements of marriage according to Islam, thus it is legal according to marriage principles (*fikhi pernikahan*), Masyiatul Maula argues that its secrecy contravenes the notion that a marriage must be publicly announced (A. *walimah al'Ursy*)[46] and is illegal because it is not registered by the state. Her argument concerning the importance of state registration is based on a verse in the Qur'an (*An-Nisa*:59) which states that 'Muslims must adhere to Allah, the Prophet, and political leadership or authority'. Therefore, she argues that unofficial marriage (*nikah sirri*) should be eliminated (Masyiatul Maula 2002:1–2).

---

41 Instead of mentioning the whole term and avoid long repetition, I will only use the term *kawin sirih* for the rest of the chapter, as this is the most commonly used term in Indonesia.

42 Nurul Huda Haem (2007) in his book *Awas Illegal Wedding: Dari Penghulu Liar Hingga Perselingkuhan,* used the term *pernikahan liar* and *penghulu liar* for 'wild' marriage and 'wild' *imam* respectively.

43 For example, the head office of the Department of Religion—Tsabit Najamuddin—expressed his concern about the practice of *kawin liar* in Polmas. Among 186 cases of divorce in Polmas between 1998 and 1999, 5 percent resulted from illegal marriages (*kawin liar*) (*Fajar,* 1-3-2000)

44 See, for instance, Iwu D. Utomo (1997:175) and Dadi Nurhaedi (2003).

45 See, for example, Chapon (1976:10); Hull and Hull (1987:108).

46 See, for example, 'Uwaidah (1996:406–407); Rahmat Sudirman (1997:113–114).

Whilst *kawin sirih* is based on religion, except for marriage registration and/or public announcement required by the state, *kawin liar* is exceptionally flexible and may be unique in the archipelago. The uniqueness of *kawin liar* is not just related to the term, it also indicates that the marriage is 'wild' in the sense that even though it is considered as a 'marriage based on religion', in practice it is not, because some of the religious and legal requirements are not fulfilled.

While other forms of 'marriage based on religion' require a representative (*wali*) and witnesses (*saksi*), and are implemented by a legal *imam*, *kawin liar* in South Sulawesi is implemented by an illegal *imam* (*imam liar*) with the presence of either a representative (*wali*) or witness (*saksi*), or sometimes neither of them, and with or without public announcement (*walimah*) and registration. Therefore, *kawin liar* is illegal according to both the religion and the state, not just because it does not fulfil the marriage requirements based on Islamic law, but it also does not have legal status. Unquestionably, *kawin sirih* and *kawin liar* are other forms of cohabitation that are not legalised by the state.[47]

Muhammad Salim—a Bugis scholar—maintains that most Bugis who live in villages still practice custom (I. *adat-istiadat*), which they consider lofty (I. *luhur*) and sacred (*keramat*) (1978:36). In relation to marriage, even though the state has regulated marriage procedures, *kawin liar* is considered by many as an alternative way to get married. Even though *kawin liar* itself cannot be considered part of Bugis norms (*pangngadereng*),[48] community acceptance is possible if it has been publicised through a customary ritual. Since *kawin liar* unions are not registered, the prevalence of these marriages is unknown. In fact, in every day life *kawin liar* cannot be differentiated from legal marriages. My observations indicate that the number of *kawin liar* is not comparable to the number of legal marriages. For example, I observed during my fieldwork that of the weddings I attended, none were *kawin liar* although I interviewed two women who had married illegally in the village of Maddenra (Kecamatan Kulo) where I stayed. When I revisited the village in January 2002, I heard that there was another case of *kawin liar* between a married man, Hasan, and a woman, Mega who became pregnant to him outside of marriage.

---

47 See Chapter III for the story of Ramlah who was abducted by Bahar and forced to marry him by illegal marriage (*kawin liar*) in Makassar.

48 Mattulada (1998:85–89;1995:54–55; 1971:275–277) defines *pangngadereng* as a holistic norm, including how people act among themselves and the relationship between people and institutions which result in community dynamics. *Pangngadereng* consists of *adeq* (B. ethical norms), *bicara* (justice system), *rapang* (guidelines for the conduct of kinship and political relationships), *wari* (classified and ordered society) and *saraq* (Islamic law).

Hisako Nakamura states that 'Muslims must marry lawfully' (Nakamura 1981:41). In Kulo, however, as I have noted, *kawin liar* is not a new phenomenon. While the majority of people considered *kawin liar* to be illegal, others were ambivalent regarding its legitimation. When they talked about *kawin liar*, they said it was an illegitimate marriage (I. *kawin tidak sah*), but that there were ways to legitimate such marriages according local custom, such as Qur'anic chanting.

In a regular marriage, though *akad nikah* is regarded as the legalization of marriage under state law, the wedding ceremony (B. *pesta botting*)[49] that follows the *akad nikah* is regarded as more significant for the legitimation of the marriage than *nikah* itself (Robinson 2001:21). This is similar to *duduk bersanding,* a term used generally in Indonesia to refer to the bride and the groom sitting together on a throne in the wedding ritual.[50] The wedding ceremony for Bugis is the centre of the celebration, that is, a formal sitting of the newlyweds through which the status of wedding sponsors is affirmed.[51]

In reference to legalization of marriage, Natzir Said points out that the normative value of custom, not only includes values of worldly of accomplishment (I. *nilai-nilai lahiriah*), but also values of inner experience (*nilai-nilai batiniah*), which are regarded as sacred. The 1974 Marriage Law, in his view, takes account only of worldly values, that confirm that one has married legally according to state law (Natzir Said 1984:27). From this point of view, Natzir Said perceives that while customary law contains social and spiritual values, the secular Marriage Law legalizes marriage only according to the state.

When I revisited my field site briefly in 2002, I interviewed a man in a neighbouring village, who has been an illegal imam (*imam liar*) since 1980.[52] He had been a legal *imam* between 1971 and 1973 in a neighbouring subdistrict,[53] but stopped this work because he opposed the government, although he did not explain in detail his precise objections. He assumed I had come to him to get married since I was accompanied by a man, my host. My first questions to him were to inquire how and why he had become an *imam*. He stated that he had become an illegal *imam* (I. *imam liar*)[54] based on 'social demand' in relation to fornication (*zinah*). As he said: 'How can I neglect people engaging in sex outside marriage, while there is another way to marry them off?'

49 See Millar's discussion on Bugis marriage (1989:81).

50 See, for example, Robinson (1986:235) in her discussion on Soroakan marriage.

51 See Millar (1989) for the display of social location in Bugis weddings.

52 In Desa Mario, Kecamatan Kulo, Kabupaten Sidrap.

53 In Desa Dengeng-Dengeng Wanua BelawaE, Kecamatan Dua PituE, Kabupaten Sidrap.

54 During the interview, he accepted *imam liar* as the term for his illegal status.

This interview confirmed to me the rumour surrounding his response towards inquiries regarding his illegal job. He showed no guilt, saying that he acted only in response to requests from a man and a woman to marry them. If he does not grant their request, they would stay unmarried and in a state of fornication. Therefore, it was better to marry them off rather than to 'let' them engage in illicit sex. Otherwise, they would be committing a sin. When I asked who was responsible for such a marriage, he explained by showing examples of marriage certificates he had produced for both parties. On the right hand side of the certificate, it was stated that 'we [husband and wife] fully acknowledge any risk resulting from this marriage', followed by their signatures and the photos of both parties. The signature of the *imam liar* was situated on the left hand side of the certificate as the person who carried out the marriage (see the certificate of an illegal marriage or *kawin liar*, in Appendix 6.1, and the certificate of a legal marriage in Appendix 6.2). The marriage certificate, indeed, is designed to protect the *imam liar* from prosecution and any complaints from the relatives of the couple and the state. As he said:

> It is true that I marry them, but they are the ones who get married, not me. I only 'help' them to avoid fornication. If the government considers this is wrong, arrest me if they can prove it is wrong.
>
> PAK UMMARENG, imam liar, interviewed on 4 August 2002

His slogan, which is expressed in an Indonesian saying: 'Daring to do, daring to be responsible' indicate that he is a responsible man and is contradicted by his disavowal of responsibility for the marriage. The illegal marriage certificate (I. *surat nikah*) states that he 'implements' the marriage, however, 'implementing' according to him means 'helping'. 'Helping', in his own words, is to 'prevent' them from fornicating (*perzinahan*). This seems to be his strategy when arguing with the police whenever he is arrested. He has been arrested twelve times since he became an *imam liar*. Indeed, he said he will stop acting as an *imam liar* if the government will provide a pension for him. This indicates, to some extent, that his financial considerations were more significant than his social responsibility to help couples avoid fornication, as he did not want his children to get married illegally.[55]

The contract stage (*akad nikah*), of an illegal marriage is commonly performed without a subsequent wedding feast as a form of public announcement (A. *walimah*) and only the man and a woman concerned and the *imam liar* are

55 Interview with Pak Ummareng (4-8-2002), Desa Mario, Kecamatan Kulo, Sidrap, South Sulawesi.

present. But, the *imam liar* confirmed that some 'couples' come with their wedding clothes, food, traditional cookies, camera and relatives, with or without spending money (*duiq menreq*), which is part of Bugis bridewealth. Such a marriage contract is regarded by the *imam liar* as a lively marriage (*kawin ramai*). In many cases, however, the 'couples' come only to perform the marriage contract without any ritual. In any case, the couple has to pay the cost of the illegal marriage, which ranges between Rp 100,000 (US$10 at current exchange rates) and Rp 500,000 (US$50), depending on how much they can afford. I was told by village residents in Kulo that the standard cost is Rp 300,000 (US$30). The cost of *kawin liar* is usually not discussed openly by the couple and the *imam liar* except if the couple do not have enough money to pay the 'standard amount.' *Kawin liar* is far more expensive than the cost of a legal marriage which is Rp 150,000,- or about US$15.

For a widow or female divorcee who intends to get married through *kawin liar*, the *imam liar* insists on seeing a divorce certificate. This is not the case, however, for a widower or a divorced man. This distinction is related to the *imam liar*'s belief that a man may marry up to five wives, even more than the number of polygynous unions allowed by Islamic law, as he considers five to be a 'sacred number', whether or not the groom has a letter of consent from his wife. If the first wife happens to claim her husband, the *imam liar* suggests he divorce her in order to stop her from claiming her marriage rights.

Another factor which is usually required for a man and a woman to get married legally is attainment of legal age of marriage. In *kawin liar*, the age of marriage, according to the *imam liar*, is 18 for both a woman and a man. Proof of age is solely based on the individual's word; so, one does not necessarily have to prove age through the presentation of a birth certificate. The *imam liar* considers a girl who is married younger than 18 as having 'died in girlhood' (B. *maté gadis*) or 'died in childhood' (*maté colliq*), which means that a girl is married when she is too young.

My interviewee claimed the marriages he performs are legitimate according to religion (I. *sah secara agama*), even though they are illegal according to the state. In fact, in *kawin liar* some elements of essential principles (A. *rukun*) and prerequisites (*syarat*), such as the presence of the representative (*wali*) of the bride and witnesses (*saksi*), are not necessarily fulfilled. The *imam liar* believes that the *wali* is simply a representative of the bride's family (*wali nasab*). If her family does not agree with the marriage, there is no point in having a representative. The *imam liar* may act as both *imam* and *wali hakim*[56] of the bride. In addition to this, witnesses (*saksi*) are not necessary in *kawin liar*; people are

56 See footnote 3.

reluctant to be witnesses to *kawin liar* because they are afraid of future risk, especially in regard to elopement (*silariang*) and polygyny. Thus, the 'validity' of *kawin liar* is not affirmed by the presence of *wali* or *saksi*.

Grounds for *Kawin Liar*

Kawin liar occurs for various reasons. The most common reason is to circumvent legal requirement for taking another wife polygynously, as stipulated in the 1974 Marriage Law.[57] Many of these marriages are practised by male civil servants, who are discouraged by the state from practising polygyny.[58] In reference to PP No.10/1983, I often heard from male civil servants that this regulation is a state law to approve unofficial marriage. As they said: 'PP10 makes it difficult for a male civil servant to have more than one wife, while [in law] a polygynous marriage is approved as long as the former wife does not object'. There was a rumour regarding polygyny among civil servants in South Sulawesi that 'according to the governor,[59] as long as a husband still supports his wife and children financially, it is not necessary for the wife to complain. If she does, the wife will be divorced without any financial support'. Adulterous polygyny has become the marital culture of government officials (see Julia I. Suryakusuma 1996:108). Adultery is accepted as long as it is not publicly exposed.[60] According to PP No. 10/1983, a wife will lose her right to financial support if she demands a divorce (article 8:4), unless she has initiated the divorce because of her husband's polygyny (article 8:5). In many cases, the wife usually gets no such resource. This is because, since *kawin liar* is illegal, no legal proof can be used to report this misdemeanour to her husband's superior, and therefore, using it as the basis for legal complains would be a waste of time.

In regard to legislation on polygyny, the *imam liar* suggested that PP No.10/1983 is a regulation to destroy the nation because it makes it difficult for a man to marry more than once. In other words, he agrees with polygynous marriage no matter how it is accomplished and whatever the reasons. Many of his clients were state officials. One of them was the head of police who was illegally married (*kawin liar*) in 1990. At the time, the *imam liar* was arrested

57 The Marriage Law 1974 (Chapter I, 5:1a) states that a man who wants to take on another wife has to have his former wife's consent.

58 See, for example, Sri Purwatiningsih (2005) on polygynous marriage among civil servant.

59 The statement was made in 2000 when Zainal Basri Palaguna was the governor of South Sulawesi.

60 A public case of adultery of a senior official in Makassar will be discussed later in Chapter 7.

because of a complaint by the policeman's wife and also by the representative (*wali*) of the bride and the members of the state-sponsored women's organization of military wives, Dharma Wanita Bhayangkari. The *imam liar* was finally released after five days in jail because, he said, no one could prove that what he had done was wrong.

Lack of parental consent is another motive for couples to enter into legally unrecognized marriage. I interviewed a married couple that already had two children as a result of their *kawin liar*.[61] Despite the fact that they are happy, this marriage does not have legal status. Another case I was told about by the *imam liar* was the case of Tija and her boyfriend Hamid. Hamid abducted Tija because her parents did not consent to their marriage. She finally agreed to get married because she was under Hamid's threat. When the girl's parents came to the *imam liar*, complaining about the illegal marriage of their daughter, the *imam* defended himself by showing the statement in the marriage certificate that placed all responsibility for the marriage on the couple themselves and told them to complain directly to the couple instead.

Another reason for *kawin liar* is inability to pay the requested 'spending money' (*duiq ménréq*).[62] In many cases, the woman is already pregnant when the couple goes to the *imam liar* for marriage. Usually, the couple is married twice by the *imam liar*, first for the sake of the unborn baby, and then soon after the baby is born a second marriage is performed in order to further legitimize the marriage. This repeat marriage is socially puzzling as to its necessity. But in legal marriage, this has been resolved in KHI (Chapter VIII, 53:3), which states that the marriage of a pregnant woman does not have to be repeated after the baby is born.

The acceptance of *kawin liar*, as an alternative to legal marriage, may also be based on the idea that marriage is a private business that should fall outside of state jurisdiction. Before the coming of Islam, marriage was considered legitimate without any formal documentation, if the families of the couple had given their consent, accompanied by their witnesses. Such marriages were legitimated through rituals witnessed by the families of the bride and the groom and surrounding communities (Natzir Said 1984:27). In the early seventies there was a debate between Muslim organizations and the state regarding

61 This is also a motivation for elopement among other ethnic groups, such as Sasak (see, for example, Bennett 2002, Chapter V).

62 See Millar's (1989:69–71) discussion on customary principles of Bugis weddings. I was told by the head of Religious Court Sidrap that the standard *duiq ménréq* for *to tebbeq* (B. commoners) in 2000 was Rp 7,000,000 (US$700 at current exchange rates).

the perceived secularising of marriage and divorce by giving civil courts extended jurisdiction.[63] In fact, the Marriage Law was one of the fundamental agendas demanded by Indonesian Women's Organizations in their first congress in 1928 (Robinson 2001:28). The right of the state to regulate marriage, established in the 1974 Marriage Law, has been accepted by the majority of people in Indonesia.

Since the enactment of the Marriage Law in 1975, however, the implementation of marriage outside this regulation (such as *kawin liar*) has led to debate about whether or not this form of marriage is legitimate according to religion (I. *sah secara agama*) and/or legitimate according to custom (*sah secara adat*), but illegal according to the law (*sah secara hukum*). If a marriage is considered legitimate according to religion, in theory it should include principles (*rukun*) and prerequisites (*syarat*), as should marriage legitimated through custom and that recognized by the law, because, as noted previously, religion, custom, and law are interrelated. But many argue that whether such marriage is legal (I. *sah*) depends on an individual's beliefs. Thus, one may say that if the couple only requires the legitimacy (*keabsahan*) of the marriage without legal status, *kawin liar* is sufficient.

PP No.9/1975 of the 1974 Marriage Law stipulates that a marriage should be solemnized before the PPN (official marriage registrar or *Pegawai Pencatat Nikah*) and in the presence of two witnesses (article 10:3). In addition, a marriage is officially registered only when a marriage certificate provided by the official registrar is signed by both the bride and the groom, both witnesses (*saksi*), and the bride representative (*wali*) (article 11:1–3). These procedures indicate that marriage not only includes an act of law, but must also carry proof of legal status. In regard to the implementation of unofficial marriages in the name of religious legitimacy (*sah secara agama*), M. Yudhi R. Haryono—a young socio-religious observer—claims that the implementation of such marriages, including illegal plural marriage (particularly polygyny among religious figures), *kawin sirih*, *kawin liar* and *kawin mut'ah* (contract marriage) are 'crimes in the name of religion' (M. Yudhi R. Haryono 2000:93). Despite the fact that these kinds of marriages are illegal according to the state, his moral judgement neglected the fact that such marriages are socially acceptable and are not forbidden by religious rules (*haram*).

Cerai Liar, Isbath Nikah, *Remarrying*

Cerai liar, literally 'wild divorce', as an alternative to obtaining a divorce from a legal marriage or *kawin liar*, but conducted by an *imam liar*. Two common

63 See, for example, Bowen (nd.: 5); Blackburn and Bessell (1997)

reasons for *cerai liar* are neglect of a wife by her husband and the husband desire to take another wife. But, most people asking for this kind of divorce were women whose marriages were also illegal (*liar*). There were, however, some cases in which women from legal marriages came to the *imam liar* for a divorce in order to avoid the legal procedures of the Pengadilan Agama or official religious court. A woman from *kawin liar* has no legal status to request a divorce through the Pengadilan Agama unless her marriage is first validated through a process termed *isbath nikah* in Arabic. *Isbath nikah* is the validation of a marriage requested in the Pengadilan Agama and which is required in the following cases: to finalize the process of divorce; when the marriage certificate is missing; when there is doubt about the validity of the marriage; for marriages implemented prior to the enactment of the Marriage Law of 1974; and for marriages implemented outside of the Marriage Law of 1974 (KHI, Chapter II, 7:3). Such validation, however, can only be granted when the kawin liar confirms to the essential principles (*rukun*) and prerequisites (*syarat*) as required by Islam. This reflects women's vulnerability in regard to *kawin liar*.

To get an illegal divorce (*cerai liar*), the presence of both parties is not required and when a wife initiate the divorce, she simply tells the *imam liar* that she has been deprived of economic maintenance (I. *lahir*) and of emotional and sexual fulfilment (*bathin*) by her husband for over 100 days.[64] In this case she is not even required to provide a witness (*saksi*) to attest the validity of her complaints. This 100-day period is similar to the waiting period (A. *iddah*) of a divorcee from legal marriage. The *imam liar* considers that a divorce (A. *talak*) is automatically granted after this period. This means that if a husband has been neglecting his wife for 100 days the *imam liar* assumes the husband would also want a divorce. The *imam liar* believes, in the name of religion, that it is a husband who has the right to divorce his wife and not the reverse, no matter what the circumstances, but this same *imam liar* can contradict his own belief by granting a divorce to a woman even without the explicit consent from his wife or *talak* by the husband. The authenticity of her signature is not an issue in this matter.

A divorce initiated by the husband is even easier. He only needs to provide a letter of consent from his wife—whether or not the signature is really his wife's. In either case, the initiator should pay the standard cost for *cerai liar*, that is, Rp1,000,000 (US$100 at current exchange rates), consisting of

64 A number of recent studies on polygyny in Indonesia highlights the economic and emotional negligence it causes among women and show the various constraints inherent in such relationships (Nurmila 2009; Robinson 2006; Blackburn 2004; Jennaway 1996; Krulfeld 1986).

Rp 500,000 (US$50) for the cost of *cerai liar* and another Rp 500,000 which is considered to be a fine for the divorce, received by the *imam liar*. This is designed to caution the initiator—whether the husband or the wife—to think carefully before getting a divorce (see certificate of *cerai liar* in Appendix 6.3 and legal divorce in Appendix 6.4).

An example of a case of *cerai liar* and *kawin liar* in Kulo is Rahmatiah, a 28 year old woman with three children who had become a 'divorcee who was not divorced' (B. *janda tenri telleq*)[65] for almost three years after leaving her husband in Malaysia in order to see her sick mother and deliver her baby in Kulo. Her husband married to another woman in Malaysia without her consent only months after she had left Malaysia.

Despite her denial of having a relationship with a married man (Rahman) during the period of my initial fieldwork in 2000, she was pregnant as a result of this non-marital relationship when I revisited the village early in 2002. I wondered how she was coping with her 'uncertain' status (I. *status tergantung*)[66] as she was still not legally divorced from her first husband. The Qur'an (*Al-Baqarah*: 231) states that a husband should not keep his wife in a state of uncertainty and without financial support as this would cause her suffering in a manner similar to torture. In addition, the father of her unborn child was still married to someone else. She told me: 'My husband got married without my consent and without divorcing me, so why couldn't I?' This comment indicates her disappointment and anger at her husband's infidelity.

While Sundanese culture encourages remarriage soon after divorce (Zuidberg 1978:87) because it testifies to a woman's attractiveness to men (Yasmine Al-Hadar 1977:72; Zuidberg 1978:88), the Bugis culture is quite different. A widow or divorcee is expected to remain unmarried for some time to indicate her loyalty to her late husband; and for a divorcee, this is aimed to show her honour (B. *alebbireng*) as a divorcee.

However, there were a number of cases in the Pengadilan Agama in Sidrap in which a woman finally filed for a divorce when there was another man who intended to marry her. If a married woman wants to marry a man, the Pengadilan Agama stipulates a certificate of divorce as a requirement. In such

---

65 *De facto*, *janda tenri telleq* automatically becomes the household head, whether or not she lives with her children or lives with her parents as a joint family in which *de jure* her father becomes head of the household. See Jones (2002:220–4) in his analysis of the demographic aspects of *de jure* and *de facto* of female-headed households.

66 *Status tergantung* is the term I use to describe a woman's status who has been living separately from her husband without emotional and financial support, but has not divorced yet.

cases, *kawin liar* may become an alternative method to legal marriage due to the lack of official divorce papers. In fact—in Rahmatiah's case—she went through *kawin liar* as soon as the *cerai liar* was granted by the *imam liar*. In addition, an *iddah*, the Islamic 'waiting period' was not required of her, as it would have been required under a legal marriage.

In line with this, most cases of marriage validation (A. *isbath nikah*) filed in the Pengadilan Agama were the result of *kawin liar*. Since 2006, despite the variation, there has been a significant increase in cases of *isbath nikah* filed in the Pengadilan Agama Sidrap,[67] possibly because the administrative requirement has become stricter than ever.[68]

In Kulo, for instance, a number of women had uncertain status (I. *status tergantung*), like Rahmatiah. This is not to say that women are reluctant to get divorced, but that they are unable to pay for the divorce costs in the formal court system because of their poverty.[69] In Rahmatiah's case, her *cerai liar* and her *kawin liar* were both paid for by Rahmat, her second husband. Therefore her first husband would not be able to claim anything against her as her second marriage was not legally recognized. Nevertheless, the trend of getting illegal marriages validated is increasing, as evident in the Pengadilan Agama Sidrap over the last 10 years. The judges maintained that there was a significant correlation between harvest time (April-May and October-November) and the number of cases filed in the court, including validation cases. This trend is somewhat evident in the Pengadilan Agama Sidrap in the last 16 years.

Fortunately, Rahmatiah did not have any difficulty related to the custody of her children. If women need help with divorce or child custody, the Pengadilan Agama is the sole institution to deal with these matters. Legal Aid Services, such as Lembaga Bantuan Hukum untuk Pemberdayaan Perempuan

---

67 In Sidrap, the number of *isbath nikah* between 2000 and 2005 is between 3 and 13 cases, then the number is higher and fluctuates between 2006 and 2014; 26 (2006), 61 (2007), 69 (2008), 43 (2009), 32 (2010 and 2011), 34 (2012), 31 (2013), and 32 (2014)(Statistics of the Pengadilan Agama Sidrap).

68 For example, children has to have birth certificate as one of the requirement for school enrolment, while birth certificate is made based on marriage certificate. Those whose marriage implemented outside of the Marriage Law of 1974 have to legalize their marriage by *isbath nikah*.

69 The cost of a legal divorce case varies between Rp 270,000 and Rp 450,000 (US$27 and US$45 at current exchange rates). Costs vary based on the distance of residence. For instance, when the residence is situated around the Religious Court, the cost will be Rp.270.000,-. When it is in a different subdistrict Rp 350,000 (US$35). (interview with one of the officials in the Religious Court Sidrap, 31-7-2002). Thus, *cerai liar* is more expensive than legal divorce.

(Legal Service for Indonesian Women Empowerment, LBH-P2I) and Lembaga Bantuan Hukum-Assosiasi Perempuan untuk Keadilan (Legal Service-Indonesian Women Association for Justice, LBH-APIK), are accessible only in the capital city of Makassar and one office in Bone[70] named Lembaga Pemberdayaan Perempuan (Organization for Women Empowerment, LPP, see Chapter 7). However, in a bilateral society like Bugis in which the notion of the right of a father toward children is not strong, the custody of children is often in the hands of their mother. This contrasts with a patrilineal society like Bali in which there is a strong notion of father's right, so children belong to their father (Robinson, 2000b:143–144).

In Rahmatiah's case, it was not only that her second marriage was illegal, but also that this marriage was without the consent of either her parents with whom she and her children from her first husband still lived, or from Rahmat's first wife, Haji Asma. Unfortunately, I was not able to talk to Haji Asma, but I was told that she had said: 'As long as he still financially supports us, I do not really care'. People said Haji Asma was not angry because her husband had paid for her pilgrimage to Mecca (hajj), a personal achievement which also enhanced her social status and which could be seen as recompense for her husband's polygynous marriage. This suggests that economic considerations are often more significant than personal attachment. In fact, Rahmat always spent the night in *Haji* Asma's house, while he visited Rahmatiah once in a while during the day, which indicates that he belonged to *Haji* Asma's house rather than to Rahmatiah's. Most importantly, as *Haji* Asma's children were grown enough to be independent, she wanted to enjoy her life with her new status, as a hajj. I was told not only by Rahmatiah, but also the neighbours that she was given rice (Indonesia staple food) from *Haji* Asma once in a while. This indicates that *Haji* Asma, who lives in a moderate style, cares about Rahmatia and her children (from her first husband) lives—an unusual attitude to adopt toward a co-wife.

There are two reasons why Rahmatiah and Rahmat did not get married legally. First, Rahmat did not have any legitimate reason to take another wife. The Marriage Law (Chapter I, 4:2) states that a husband may marry more than one wife only if his wife cannot perform her duty as a wife, is physically handicapped or suffers from an incurable disease, and has no children. Second, Rahmatiah was not divorced. Regardless of her financial difficulties, she was already pregnant and needed to be married immediately, while the process of a legal divorce would take a long time, especially because her first husband was in Malaysia. It is forbidden to propose to a woman who has not been divorced

70 Bone is one of the regencies in South Sulawesi to the southeast of Sidrap.

by her husband, let alone to marry her (the Marriage Law, Chapter III, 12:2). By resorting to *kawin liar*, however, all these requirements can be neglected, which makes it easier for a woman like Rahmatiah to remarry.

Another exceptional case in Kulo was that of Nadirah (23 years), a village girl of a lower class family. Revisiting her in the village in 2002 was a surprise, since she had had another baby as a result of a second non-marital pregnancy. In the beginning, I did not think that her first marriage with her supposed father-in-law was illegal since she told me that she had a marriage certificate (I. *surat nikah*), and divorced immediately afterwards (*kawing pura*).[71] This practice occurs to provide a social father for a baby. In fact, Nadirah's first and second marriages to different men were both problematic and illegal (see the earlier story of Nadirah in Chapter 2). This is in violation of the 1974 Marriage Law (Chapter I:1) which states that marriage is aimed to create a happy and everlasting family life. Hence, *kawing pura* is regarded as illegal and never happens through legal procedures in the court; rather, *kawing pura* is, in many cases, a solution to *kawin liar*.

While I was waiting for her to return from the wet rice fields, I talked to Nadirah's grandmother who was babysitting both of Nadirah's sons. Nadirah's grandmother commented on Nadirah's marriage before I even asked her a question, by saying: 'All this has happened due to her fate because we do not think that they will ever be legally united since that man is still with his former wife'. Hence, Nadirah's second marriage was understood as her 'fate'. For Nadirah, however, the fact that her husband had not divorced his former wife was irrelevant. Nadirah was happy to be a wife and a mother of her two children from the same father, instead of being a single mother, regardless of whether or not financial support was given. Since Nadirah's marriage was illegal, the first wife could not make a claim against her husband's polygyny through the Pengadilan Agama. In fact, a legal marriage can be cancelled if a husband practises polygyny without permission from the Pengadilan Agama (KHI, Chapter XI: 71a).

Nadirah's grandmother's comment indicates her anxiety in regard to community gossip about Nadirah's problematic marriage, on the one hand, and her acceptance of her status on the other. What had happened with Nadirah was a case of *siriq* (shame) conduct. However, I observed in a number of cases of *siriq* during my fieldwork that the response of the community towards lower class' *siriq* was different from that associated with the middle class. *Siriq* for the

71 *Kawing pura*—which consists of two words: *kawing*—marriage and *pura* – ending—is the local term that is used to describe a divorce right after marriage.

middle class got more social attention and pressure from the community than it did for lower class.

Although *kawin liar* is regarded as illegal marriage, as mentioned earlier, there is a way to make it socially acceptable through an adat ceremony, such as a small party with a number of people invited to publicise that the couple have been married. On this account, the social legitimation of *kawin liar* is a matter of public announcement. In such a ceremony, it is usually women who prepare food in the kitchen, while men are the guests and perform a chant recounting the Prophet Muhammad's life (B. *mabbarazanji*). In Islamic legal weddings, the ceremony is related to the concept of the wedding feast for public announcement (A. *walimah*). Rahmat Sudirman argues that the *walimah* is not only a public announcement to show approval of the marriage, but also a ceremony to thank God and to express the happiness of the families of both the husband and wife (Rahmat Sudirman 1999:113).

In both Rahmatiah and Nadirah's cases, their marriages were legitimated through this ritual. However, their marriages did not have legal marriage status according to the 1974 Marriage Law because these marriages were not conducted by an official marriage registrar (KHI, Chapter II:62). But legal status is not important for ordinary people like Rahmatiah and Nadirah. What is more significant for them is that they have a piece of paper which indicates that they are married, whether or not it is a legal marriage certificate. As Nadirah said:

> I do not want to worry about whether or not this marriage is legal. The most important thing is that I have a marriage certificate that indicates that I am married, I am his wife and he is my husband.
>
> NADIRAH, 25 years, 'married', two children, wedding decorator, graduated from high school, interviewed on 13 January 2002

Women who recognize their *kawin liar* tend not to report their case to the court. Nevertheless, this is not the case for women who have been deceived in their *kawin liar.* Nati, a woman I met in the Pengadilan Agama in Sidrap while I was waiting to observe the court hearing, is an example of a victim of *kawin liar.* Despite her husband having divorced his first wife before marrying Nati, she was married to Hamid illegally. When Nati got pregnant, her husband left her without any explanation and returned to his former wife because, in fact, he had never divorced her. In such a case, the procedure of legal divorce is even more complicated because one is not solely dealing with the divorce, but also with the validation of marriage (A. *isbath nikah*).

To obtain an acknowledgment from the court, Nati's marriage had first to be validated in terms of Islamic law. Then, when a marriage certificate was issued, divorce could be processed. Nati was not aware of her illegal marriage status. As she stated:

> I did not know that my marriage was illegal, not until I went to the Pengadilan Agama to file for divorce and was told that I was not registered. I was really shocked to discover that my marriage was not registered because I had my 'marriage certificate', I did not know that this certificate was issued illegally. If I had known that my marriage was illegal, I would not have come to the Pengadilan Agama. I felt that I had been deceived by my husband.
>
> NATI, 25 years, 'married', housewife, first pregnancy, graduated from junior high school, interviewed on 10 May 2000

This statement reflects Nati's status as ignorant of the law. The marriage certificate she had was an illegal one, issued by an *imam liar.* Nati did not know the difference between legal and illegal marriage. Telling Nati that the marriage was illegal (*kawin liar*) is similar to questioning Hamid's divorce status, whether or not he truly divorced his first wife. After experiencing this illegal marriage, she realized that her marriage was a 'game marriage', created by her husband to deny responsibility for his wife and his unborn child, Nati's case was an unusual one because she had been deceived by her husband even though she was not pregnant when he married her.

I observed both in the village and in the court hearings that women are not always the victims of *kawin liar* because it is also a situation in which women can exercise agency, as demonstrated in Rahmatiah's story above. In many cases, women are reluctant to report to the Pengadilan Agama, and so leave themselves vulnerable. They continue to practice *kawin liar* when remarriage is an alternative, particularly because of poverty. Getting married is a way to ensure financial support from a husband, as t is assumed that once she marries, the husband is financially responsible for his wife's support. Such an assumption corresponds to the notion of marriage discussed in Chapter 3.

The Court Hearing: *Cerai Talak, Cerai Gugat* and *Silisuang*

According to the Marriage Law, there are three grounds which may legally discontinue a marriage: death, divorce and decision of the court (the Marriage

Law, Chapter VIII: 38). Divorce will be the focus of discussion here, as this is controlled by the Pengadilan Agama (Robinson 2000b:146–147 and 2001:27–28). While marriage is viewed as a 'legal contract', divorce is regarded as 'breaking the marriage contract' (Robinson 2001, Nakamura 1981). There are three grounds which may legally discontinue a marriage: death, divorce and decision of the court, and in the case of divorce for Muslims, this is the Religious Court or the Pengadilan Agama (Robinson 2000:146–147 and 2001:27–28).

In Islamic law, divorce is severance of the marriage bond and is allowed because marriage is regarded as a contract which can be broken by either one or both parties. However, one cannot divorce without a legitimate reason.[72] A Hadith (Ahmad, Abud Daud, Ibnu Majah and Tarmidzi) states 'any woman who asks her husband for divorce without some strong reason, the odour of paradise will be forbidden for her' (in 'Uwaidah 1998:427). The husband should have a good reason to pronounce the *talak*, and a divorce can only be granted through Religious Court (Pengadilan Agama) after trying to reconcile the husband and wife (KHI, Chapter XVI:115). This reflects the position stated in a Hadith that 'divorce is lawful, but deeply dispised by Allah' (Zaini A. Noeh 1980:5).[73] Therefore, the Indonesian legal system encodes the principle that divorce should be avoided if there is still a way to work out the marriage.

In the local context, the Bugis term for divorce is *sipurang*,[74] a term that carries the meaning of terminating (*pura*). Thus *sipurang* means terminating the marriage. Either spouse may request a divorce; which is known as *cerai gugat* when the divorce is demanded by the wife and *cerai talak* when the request comes from the husband, and both of them are shameful occurrences.

For the Bugis, *sipurang* is a tabooed word (B. *pémmali*). If a husband or a wife states 'I do not want to see your back' (*déqna uélo mitai pungkuqmu*) because the partner is reluctant to see her/his back (*pungkuq*), not to mention her/his face; or 'return to your parents' (I. *pulanglah ke rumah orang tuamu*) since the partner does not want to see her/him. Such statements are already considered as the 'language of divorce' (I. *bahasa cerai*). Regardless of the legality, she/he has been customarily divorced (*ritelleq adeq*) given that it has been pronounced. Despite the fact that women can divorce their husbands, when

72 See *Peraturan Pemerintah* No.9/1975 (Chapter V:19): reasons for divorce.

73 Zaini A. Noeh (1980) freely translated this Hadith and considered 'lawful' to be an appropriate word to explain '*halal*' in this Hadith.

74 Another Bugis term for divorce is *massarang*, derived from the word *sara* (troublesome). *Massarang* carries the sense of being apart from each other, and is popularly used by the Bugis in Makassar. The term *sipurang*, however, is frequently used by the people in Sidrap, including in the court hearing.

PLATE 6.3 *A Court hearing in the Pengadilan Agama Sidrap, 2015*

the judges talked about divorce, instead of using the genderless term—*cerai*—they used the term *talak*, which is the term for divorce initiated by the husband. To me, this implies an assumption that it is the husband who is entitled to divorce his wife rather than the reverse.

In the Pengadilan Agama Sidrap, when the judges dealt with cases of divorce in the court hearings (see Plate 6.3), they commonly gave the following advice when they tried to mediate the problems in couples' marriages:

> If you can't carry it in your hand, carry it on your shoulder.
> If you can't carry it on your shoulder, carry it above your head.
>
> *Nakko déqmullé wiccangngi, lémpaq i.*
> *Nakko déqmullé lémpaq i, jujungngi.*

Analysing this piece of advice, *wiccang* (B. carrying) refers to 'lower' (hand), *lémpaq* (carrying on shoulder) refers to 'middle' (shoulder), and *jujung* (carrying above your head) refers to 'upper' (head). It thus begins with the easiest way to carry, *wiccang*; then moves to the more difficult, *lémpaq*; and ends with the most difficult, *jujung*. This advice does not just delineate the steps to follow, but also reflects the cosmological problem-solving methods of handling marital problems in Bugis. If this method, which corresponds to the teaching in *lontaraq,* cannot solve the problem, then the marriage will end with divorce (*sipurang*).[75] In Tikka's case above, *sipurang* is considered as the problem-solving because she cannot carry the burden of ongoing violence in her marriage.

The advice describes how one should handle problems in marriage in stages, by carrying in the hand (*mawwiccang*), on the shoulder (*mallémpaq*) and on the head (*majjujung*), indicate that one should stay in a marriage, as patiently as possible, no matter what the problems are. Although such advice can be directed at both husband and wife, I observed in a number of court hearings that such advice is usually given to the wife, especially when the husband apologised for his behaviour. Nevertheless, such efforts might raise questions such as how can a woman stay in a marriage when her life is in danger? Should the cultural considerations be so significant that a woman should not leave her house even when her life is at risk?[76]

The Bugis consider divorce to be shameful, not only for women, but also for men. This is not the case in all of the Muslim people of the archipelago: see for example discussion of divorce among the Sundanese of west Java (McDonald and Abdurahman 1974:6; Jones et al. 1994). However, the stigma is greater for women, especially if a woman is divorced by her husband because of his infidelity, not to mention her infidelity. The infidelity of the husband may lead to gossip which pushes a woman into a corner, since it is assumed that such a wife did not 'serve' her husband properly, which is expressed in Bugis and is usually uttered by elders as 'she is not capable of meeting her husband's needs' (B. *déqna issengngi duppaiwi éloqna oroanéna*).[77] In general, the advice given by the judges in court hearings sided with the men. A man was asked to compromise only if he still wanted to reconcile the marriage, regardless of the reasons for divorce, by persuading his wife to withdraw from the case. The following case study, of Tikka's divorce, exemplifies the complex interaction of law, religion and custom in cases brought to the Pengadilan Agama in Sidrap.

Tikka was a victim of domestic violence throughout her marriage who I met her when I observed her court hearing. Tikka married Kadere in 1975, and had

---

75 *Lontaraq Membicarakan Tentang Berlaki-bini* indicates the steps for handling marital conflict, MAK No. 74: pp. 77–78 (Macknight 1972: reel 5, microfilm).

76 At the end of 2000, *Fajar*—a local newspaper—reported a murder case in which a husband had killed his wife in Pare-Pare, a neighbouring regency of Sidrap. It was suspected that the wife had been continuously abused during her marriage, see Chapter 7 for details.

77 The term *duppaiwi* is equivalent to the term *moloi,* discussed in Chapter 3.

lived separately from him since March 1999. Tikka had finally left her husband when she could no longer tolerate her husband's abusive behaviour. She had been hit until she bled and was hospitalized. Since this separation, Kadere had been having an extramarital relationship with another woman and had never let Tikka see their children.

Despite the fact that the cruel treatment experienced by Tikka was reasonable grounds for divorce based on the 1974 Marriage Law,[78] Tikka was criticised in the court hearing because she had left the house. In Bugis culture, it is tabooed by elders for a wife to leave the house during a marriage dispute. This is considered similar to 'slapping her husband's face in public' since it is seen as violating her husband's authority, regardless of the reason for her departure. Using an analogy of a human body, the husband is regarded as the head and the wife is the body. The body without a head is blind and a head falls over without the body. This notion illustrates that one without the other, husband without wife or visa versa, will unbalance family life, as husband and wife are considered to be 'two-in-one' (discussed in Chapter 4). In fact, Kadere used to leave the house whenever they had marital disputes. In regard to marriage disputes, a piece of advice frequently uttered by elders to young couples is:

> If for any reason you or both of you get angry with each other, do not ever leave the house because such behaviour is tabooed by elders.
>
> *Nakko engka sabaq-sabaq namumacai ri lakkaimmu, iaréqga musicairi, ajaq lalo musalai bolamu, nasabaq iaro gauq é, nappémmaliangngi tomatoaé.*

The above statement is directed at both husband and wife, but this advice is, in fact, usually given to wives. Indeed, the advice aims to prevent outside interference as well as indicating the couple is capable of solving the problem as a private matter. Tikka stated:

> I had been married for over 24 years and I had experienced violence since the early phase of our marriage. My husband was a violent man. He liked to utter bad words to me as well as hit me. Whenever he got angry, I was the one to be blamed. He was not just angry at ease, but also a batterer. He said I was a misfortune, a worthless wife, stupid and many other words directed at me and he would spend the nights in someone else's house. I felt my life with him was useless, except for my children. Whatever I did

78 See KHI (Chapter XVII:116d): reasons for divorce.

> he never appreciated it. Finally, he hit me on the head and I was bleeding, I was taken to the hospital by my neighbour and my head had to be stitched. I thought I was going to die. After that we separated. What made me really sad was that he took all the children and did not allow them to see me or me to see them. Then, I tried to negotiate with him by asking him to work out our marriage. But he came to me and hit me again.
>
> TIKKA, 40, housewife, 3 children, divorced, primary school, interviewed on 10 May 2000

The attitude of judges in the Pengadilan Agama in dealing with violence against women in conjugal relations seemed to be ambivalent. Although violence in marriage was adredded in Tika's case, the consideration of custom (*adat*) surrounding conduct during disputes became critical in the process of the court hearing. Tikka was criticised by both the judges and her husband during the court hearing. The judges asked, 'Why did you leave your husband when you were angry?' 'I was chased away', she said. Violence in the home, on the other hand, was the reason stated in a formal letter. Tikka and Kadere finally divorced in the middle of 2000 after 24 years of marriage, including one year of separation (B. *mallawangeng*).

Ter Haar (cited Nakamura 1981:37) points out that separation before granting a divorce is common in Indonesian. This is evident in a number of cases I observed in the court hearings. Separation in Bugis is encouraged to give the couple time to have second thoughts about whether they want to continue with the divorce or to reconcile the marriage.

Nakamura, in a study of divorce in Kotagede, Central Java suggested that separation is also designed to discontinue sexual intercourse and thus avoid pregnancy preceding the divorce based on Islamic law (Nakamura 1981:37). This is particularly to avoid pregnancy prior to divorce. During the separation (*mallawangeng*) period and after the divorce, Tikka lived with her parents, and her children—one of them married and had a child—lived in the house where Tikka and her husband used to live together, while her husband lived with his family. Since Tikka had an arranged marriage, the psychological burden to return to her parents because of divorce was insignificant, as her family still welcomed her. It is common in an arranged marriage that any subsequent marriage break-up becomes, to a great extent, the parents' responsibility. If Tikka's marriage had been by free-choice, the consequence might have been different.[79]

79 See, for example, Robinson (1986:224–225 and 1999:258) in her discussion of Soroakan's romantic love.

Another instance is the case of *Ibu* Kasmawati and her husband *Pak* Yunus, who were both teachers in a local school is an instance of the outrageous case of divorce and polygyny. They filed for divorce in the Pengadilan Agama, but only a few weeks after the first stage of divorce (*talak* 1) (see below) was granted, *Pak* Yunus get married with another woman. According to the Marriage Law, only a wife has to wait for the waiting period (*iddah*) after the divorce. On the grounds of this, *Pak* Yunus may marry another woman during the *iddah* of *Ibu* Kasmawati or he may return to her before the end of her *iddah*.

Talak, or divorce, has three steps, which helps to prevent arbitrary divorce since a couple may still be reunited before coming to the final stage (*talak* 3: *talak ba'in*). As stated in the Qur'an (*Al-Baqarah*:229), a divorce is only permissible twice: after that, the parties should either hold together on equitable terms, or separate with kindness. If *talak ba'in* has already been granted, a wife has to marry another man, then get a divorce after that marriage is consummated (A. *ba'da dukhul*) and pass her *iddah*,[80] if she wishes to remarry her original spouse. Each of them, however, cannot marry someone else for the purpose of remarry his/her original spouse.

However, a few days before *Ibu* Kasmawati's waiting period (*iddah*) ended, *Pak* Yunus was urged by his male and female colleagues during a school camp to take his 'portion' (B. *malai tawana*), which carries the sense in English of making love. *Ibu* Kasmawati was intentionally left alone by her female colleagues in a tent, while male teachers provoked her husband to approach her. This meeting finally ended in their making love, confirmed by a female colleague the following day. The drama was designed to be an expression of the Bugis feeling of social solidarity (*pessé*) among teachers, who pitied *Ibu* Kasmawati given that she still expected her husband back. It was understood that through this plan they would be able to reunite without remarrying, given that a husband and a wife may still return as a married couple if they happen to change their minds before the wife has passed her *iddah,* that is, three menstrual periods, according to the Islamic Law.[81] However, can the incident of sexual intercourse be accepted as a mutually consensual reconciliation (B. *silisuang*)? *Silisuang* is derived from the words *si* (mutual) and *lisu* (to return), so *silisuang* carries the meaning of reconciliation on the ground of mutual consent (husband and wife), regardless of who initiates it. An article in

80 Only after all these steps can a woman remarry her previous husband. A marriage for the purpose of returning to her former husband (A. *muhallil* marriage) is unlawful (see, for example, 'Uwaidah 1998:385–386 and Rahmat Sudirman 1999:87–88). In fact, I did not see any single case of *muhallil* marriage handled by Sidrap Religious Court.

81 This is also stated in KHI (Chapter XVIII,163:1): reconciliation.

KHI (Chapter XVIII:165) states that *rujuk* (I. reconciliation) without the wife's consent can be regarded as illegal by the Religious Court.

Given that there was no complaint from *Ibu* Kasmawati, her silence was seen as her agreement. As the Qur'an (*Al-Baqarah*:231) states, a husband may divorce his wife as well as reconcile with her before the end of her *iddah*. It was assumed that because *Pak* Yunus had gotten his 'portion' (B. *purani naala tawana*) before the end of Ibu Kasmawati's *iddah* period, he was still legally her husband. In other words, he had given his wife a co-wife (*mappammarué*). Nevertheless, he spent most of his time with his second wife.

In contrast, *Ibu* Kasmawati never accepted that she had been given a co-wife (*ripammarué,* passive verb of *mappammarué*), as shown by the fact she would never let *Pak* Yunus spend the night in her house to avoid being *ripammarué*. Hence, there are two different perceptions of *mappammarue* between *Pak* Yunus and *Ibu* Kasmawati in this case. Since the sexual intercourse before the end of *Ibu* Kasmawati's *iddah* period was regarded as reconciliation (*silisuang*), *Ibu* Kasmawati was still his legal wife as far as *Pak* Yunus was concerned. On the other hand, not staying or spending the nights with *Ibu* Kasmawati indicated that she did not consider full reconciliation to have occurred. She seemed ambivalent in view of the fact that they had had sexual intercourse, both in the tent and in her house during the day once in a while. She insisted that in order to be reunited as a couple, however, *Pak* Yunus had to divorce his second wife and to perform a remedial marriage (B. *kawing pabbura*; I. *kawin obat*). According to Bugis custom, a remedial marriage (*kawing pabbura*) is a ceremony of reconciliation to re-establish a couple as married after the first or second stage of divorce (A. *talak raj'i*), or for those who have a shaky marriage, in order to recuperate from any marriage disputes.

Subsequently, *Pak* Yunus liked to talk about his second wife's positive points, such as 'she always accompanies me when I am eating or watching TV, and welcomes me home from work' to compare her with *Ibu* Kasmawati. This then led to gossip about *Ibu* Kasmawati's negative behaviour towards her husband. People said: 'She does not know how to fulfil her husband's needs' (B. *Déqna issengngi moloi éloqna lakkainna*). The violence experienced by *Ibu* Kasmawati was no longer a hot issue, as it had been when they were still a married couple (*sikalaibiné*) and about to divorce. However, I was told by a female colleague of *Ibu* Kasmawati, that she felt *Pak* Yunus was trying to justify the situation in his former marriage, so he would not shoulder all the blame and could still enjoy his polygynous marriage.

The legal situation in this case not only had reference to the 1974 Marriage Law, but also to a special regulation further restricting rights to polygamous marriage for civil servants (PP No.10/1983:article 4). The latter regulation determines that a male civil servant should have the permission of his superior before divorcing his wife or acquiring another. In many instances, this regulation is ignored. *Ibu* Kasmawati and *Pak* Yunus, both were teachers in a local school at the same government school (see Chapter 4). Officially, Ibu Kasmawati could file for divorce because of her husband's infidelity and violence. Under this Presidential Decree, she was entitled to submit a complaint through her husband's superior. In practice, the complaint begins through the head of PKK and Dharma Wanita at the village level (see Chapter 1), in this case, the wife of the principal of the school where *Ibu* Kasmawati and her husband both worked as teachers. However, since the principal, *Pak* Bakri, had also had an extramarital relationship, followed by practising illegal polygyny, such a complaint seemed pointless. Another female teacher in the same school criticised the principal's attitude, asking how a superior could reprimand his staff if he himself practiced polygynous marriage and take another wife without his first wife's consent? One could not admonish others if one played a similar game in one's own marriage. Despite the fact that polygyny for civil servants is restricted under the requirements mentioned earlier, this case was considered 'mutual agreement' (I. *tahu sama tahu*) between *Pak* Yunus and his superior, *Pak* Bakri, in a mutually advantageous (illegal) deal with the plausible excuse that 'his wife did not complain about her husband's second marriage'. Such argument is logical to some extent, but it encourages others to continue to manipulate the regulations.

According to Julia I. Suryakusuma, PP No.10/1983, which was supposed to protect civil servants' wives from polygyny and divorce, has rebounded on them (Julia I. Suryakusuma 1996:109). This led the former Minister of Women's Empowerment, Khofifah Indar Parawangsa, to question the usefulness and the continuity of PP No.10/1983, as it has not prevented the occurrence of adultery and polygyny. While rumours regarding the revocation of PP No.10/1983 have created anxiety among some wives of civil servants, others may not be concerned. For example, some commented that adultery and polygyny would worsen if the PP No.10/1983 were revoked. Others argued that the PP No.10/1983 has no power to control the sexual and marital life of civil servants, as many high government officials were and are involved in adultery as well as polygyny without adverse consequences.[82]

Divorce Registration

I now return to the subject of divorce registration. In Sidrap as well as in Makassar the records divided divorce by dividing divorce registration into two categories, *cerai gugat* (wife-initiated divorce) and *cerai talak* (husband-initiated divorce).[83] However, there is no category to indicate the mutual initiation of both husband

82 Interview with a number of wives of civil servants in Sidrap and Makassar in 2000.

83 See, for example, Nakamura (1981) and Jones (1994:402).

and wife. In fact, I found during the court hearing that when both parties wanted to get a divorce, the registration was typically initiated by the husband. Hence, it was categorized as *cerai talak*. In such a case, he is identified as the plaintiff (I. *penggugat*) and the wife become the accused (*tergugat*) in the official report.

In Sidrap, the records of the initiation of a divorce is associated with the one who pays for the divorce. All cases of *cerai gugat* were paid by women, unless there had been prior agreement that the husband would pay the divorce costs before registering the case in the court. Such an agreement usually occurred if the man was eager to get divorced quickly. In other cases, wives had to live with uncertain status (*status tergantung*) until they could afford to pay the divorce costs, especially women without their own incomes. In contrast, the cost of cases of *cerai talak* was automatically paid by men.

Data provided by the Pengadilan Agama Sidrap indicates that the number of *cerai gugat* is always higher than *cerai talak*. In the last 16 years (2000–2013), in spite of some variation, the data shows the significant increase of divorce cases, and *cerai gugat* is approximately 3 to 5 times as many as *cerai talak*, as can be seen in Table 6.1.

TABLE 6.1 *The Number of* Cerai Gugat *and* Cerai Talak (*2000-2015*)

No.	Year	*Cerai Gugat*	*Cerai Talak*	
1.	2000	227	60	287
2.	2001	261	66	327
3.	2002	287	70	357
4.	2003	240	67	307
5.	2004	270	53	323
6.	2005	261	83	344
7.	2006	273	95	368
8.	2007	387	82	469
9.	2008	394	100	494
10.	2009	478	125	603
11.	2010	417	130	547
12.	2011	483	126	609
13.	2012	570	138	708
14.	2013	517	162	679
15.	2014	584	149	733
16.	2015	575	183	758

SOURCE: CALCULATED FROM DOCUMENTED CASES IN THE PENGADILAN AGAMA SIDRAP (2016).

This higher number of women demanding divorce (*cerai gugat*) relates to the reasons for divorce and leads one to assume that more women suffer in marriage and that their suffering is more severe. It may also reflect that divorce can be less important for men because they also have the option of polygyny which women do not have. This figure indicates that the primary clients of the courts were women. However, a study of divorce in West Java indicates a number of ways wives can obtain divorces. Rather than simply initiating a divorce, one way for a wife to obtain a divorce is by persuading her husband to pronounce the *talak*. In this sense, the case is registered as a husband-initiated divorce (Jones et al. 1994:402). This method was also noted in Nakamura's study of dissolution of marriage in Kotagede, Yogyakarta (Nakamura 1981:140).

Grounds for Divorce and Marriage Counselling

Grounds for divorce, in this sense, refer to the reasons for legal divorce requested through the Pengadilan Agama. However, my observations of court proceedings, and interviews with petitioners provide further information. The reasons for divorce which can be inferred from several concrete situations commonly leading to divorce filed by the court and observed during the court hearings were reminiscent of those found by Nakamura and Jones et al. in Kotagede and West Java respectively.[84] The reasons cited in the Pengadilan Agama Sidrap were economic problems (I. *masalah ekonomi*), moral crisis (*krisis moral*), usually indicating male infidelity,[85] irresponsibility (*tidak ada tanggungjawab*), fertility problems (*masalah biologis*), usually referring to male impotence, interference by a third party (*gangguan pihak ketiga*), polygyny (*dimadu*), jealousy (*cemburu*), incompatibility (*tidak ada kecocokan*), usually implying tension between the couple or conflict between affinal relatives, physical abuse (*penganiayaan*), forced marriage (*kawin paksa*), political problems (*masalah politik*), referring to different political ideology between husband and wife, and conviction of a crime (*dipenjara*).[86] Indeed, incompatibility

84 See Nakamura (1981:95–98) and Jones et al. (1994:403–404).

85 The category of male infidelity is according to wife who files for divorce. This contrasts with the marriage records in Soppeng (South Sulawesi) which indicate that moral crisis refers to female infidelity (Millar 1989:27).

86 When I revisited the Pengadilan Agama Sidrap (4-8-2010), I found that some terms in the list of legal reasons for divorce have changed, such as economic problems (*masalah ekonomi*) becomes *ekonomi*, fertility problems (*masalah biologis*) becomes *cacat biologis*,

was the most dominant reason for divorce in Sidrap in 2000, followed by irresponsibility. Wife beating and forced marriage are also among dominant reasons for divorce. When I revisited Pengadilan Agama in 2010, polygyny and incompatibility are the two most common reasons for divorce. Interestingly, *masalah biologis* and *masalah politik* have recently become more common reasons for divorce.[87]

Nakamura claims that irresponsibility leading to unhappiness is the most common reason stated in the court reports in Kotagede, Yogyakarta (1981:115). Forced marriage and beating were not mentioned by Nakamura which might be because these reasons were not relevant in Kotagede, or because they were included under 'other', or the appropriate questions were not asked. H. Geertz concluded in her findings of Modjokuto that divorce was largely a result of abbreviated courtship, economic irresponsibility, conflict between affinal relatives and arranged marriages (1961:139–42). Even though my interviews with the judges in the Pengadilan Agama Sidrap indicate that conflict between affinal relatives is in many cases a cause of marriage disputes, it is not registered as one of the reasons for divorce, but such cases are included under incompatibility. In line with this, my male and female informants in Kulo told me that the most common reasons for divorce were irresponsibility which meant that the husband neglected to provide living necessities to his wife and children, usually because of leaving the village in search of fortune (B. *massompeq*), and infidelity related to polygyny, not to mention *kawin liar*.

Millar's finding in Soppeng, another regency in South Sulawesi, indicated that the dominant reason for divorce listed in the Pengadilan Agama was failure to satisfy the obligations of the contract (Millar 1989:27 and 1983:485). However, the explanation of this ground for divorce is similar to incompatibility (the dominant ground for divorce in Sidrap) between the couple or between their families. This fortifies Millar's account that marriage is related to kin ties, affiliation to important leaders and social location (Millar 1983:486), aspects which I have discussed in Chapter 3. Therefore, there is confusion on how to

---

polygyny (*dimadu*) becomes *poligami, tidak sehat*, incompatibility (*tidak ada kecocokan*) becomes *tidak ada keharmonisan*, political problems (*masalah politik*) becomes *politis*, conviction of crime (*dipenjara*) becomes *dihukum*, and moral crisis (*krisis moral*) becomes *krisis akhlak*. Marriage of the minor (*kawin di bawah umur*) appears to be an additional term under the list of reason for divorce. Despite the fact that birth certificate is one of the prerequisite for prospective bride and groom for marriage registration, only recently (since 2009), it has become an obligatory requirement, in respond to the fact that many cases of marriage under the legal age of marriage.

87 Personal interview with Pak Sama, the head of the Pengadilan Agama Sidrap (4-8-2010).

classify the grounds for divorce as irresponsibility or incompatibility because both of them are interrelated. The narrative explanation, however, clarifies that a husband's failure to satisfy the obligations of a marriage contract leads to tension and unhappiness between the couple. In that sense, when such a case is filed, it is registered under incompatibility by the divorce registrar in the Pengadilan Agama.

Counselling Processes and Reconciliation

The 1974 Marriage Law requires the Pengadilan Agama to attempt reconciliation of the parties and this is formally done through the BP4 which is attached to Balai Nikah (taken literally *balai* means place, *nikah* means legalisation of marriage) the local office which registers marriages, gives information and advice to Muslims who are planning to marry (B. *kawing*), but also to those considering divorce (*sipurang*) or reconciliation (*silisuang*). My Sidrap informants were more familiar with the term Balai Nikah than BP4. For people in the village, Balai Nikah was only known as an office for marriage registration, no one understood that this institution could also provide marriage counselling. Marriage disputes were either solved internally within the family and/or couples directly filed for divorce at the Pengadilan Agama. As people did not seek divorce at BP4, no one filed for divorce through Balai Nikah. Thus, the Pengadilan Agama was also involved in marriage counselling. No matter who initiated the divorce, the marriage counselling or advising took place during the court hearing, usually in the first court sitting when husband and wife were present at the same time. One case hearing usually consisted of at least three court sittings (see also Jones et al. 1994:409).

However, the circumstance is quite different in Sidrap. No matter who initiates the divorce, whatever the reasons for divorce and whether or not the husband agrees to divorce, all cases are brought to the Pengadilan Agama. Balai Nikah did not function as it did in Kotagede where Nakamura conducted her research. This might be because the role of the Balai Nikah was not widely known in Sidrap and people seemed to be ignorant of how it could be used for divorce (B. *sipurang*) and reconciliation (*silisuang*). According to the judges, when a case turned from divorce to reconciliation without the intervention of the court, the case became uncertain (I. *tergantung*), which meant that the couples did not report reconciliation cases to the court. Information regarding reconciliation was later found from people talking about the delicate reconciliation of the couple. This reconciliation might be because of the intervention of the family or solely between the couples themselves, and such an event might easily become widely known, as one's business easily becomes everybody's business in the village as well as in the regency. However, there are also rare cases in which the couple or the husband or the wife come to the court and ask to terminate the case because they have already reconciled the marriage. In such circumstances, the case is closed on demand by either the husband or the wife or both. But even though the court in Sidrap endeavoured to provide counselling and reconciliation, the people saw the court mainly as a place for divorce. Every time I wanted to visit the Pengadilan Agama, *Ibu* Bakri (my hostess) said: '*Ibu* Ilmi is going to the place of divorce'. Local mini bus (*pété'-pété'*) drivers always greeted me: 'Are you going to deal with the divorce people again, *Ibu* Ilmi?' The tricycle driver (I. *tukang beca*) in Pangkajene once told me: 'Are you going to divorce?' because he had seen me several times visiting the Pengadilan Agama.[88]

In contrast, in the city of Makassar, although not all people who experienced marriage disputes sought advice at BP4,[89] it was used as one of the marriage counselling alternatives by the urban community. Nevertheless, there were also cases in which people came directly to the Pengadilan Agama to register a divorce officially. In such case, the Pengadilan Agama at the same time acted as BP4 because what was considered best procedure by the state was not always ideal for the community.[90] In the words of my informants, seeking advice at BP4 was more likely to complicate the problem because, for instance, men were reluctant to come for marriage counselling because they considered themselves shamed (B. *ripakasiriq*) by discussing their marriage problems with outsiders.[91] It was too public, a place for what was considered a private matter. On top of this, BP4 was seen as a formal institution where people could not express their problems confidentially with complete strangers.

The situation is quite different in the province of West Java, where a divorce can be officially registered only after counselling is implemented through BP4 (Jones et al. 1994: 401–402). This is similar to Nakamura's finding that people in Kotagede (Yogyakarta) usually proceeded to BP4 for marriage counselling before coming to the Pengadilan Agama (Nakamura 1981:59).[92] In Sidrap,

88 To get to the Religious Court in Pangkajene, I had to take *pété'-pété'* to Rappang, then took another *pété'-pété'* to the terminal in Pangkajene, and from there I took a tricycle to the Religious Court.

89 See footnote 13.

90 Personal interview with Ibu Husnang, a staff member of BP4 who deals with counselling and marriage registration, Makassar (14-2-2000).

91 For example, BP4 Makassar does not provide a specific room for counselling. Clients discuss their marriage problems in an open room, where they can be witnessed and overheard by others.

92 The ideal procedure of counselling starts from BP4 where the couple is advised in regard to their marriage disputes. If the marriage can no longer be continued after the counselling process, the case will be continued in Religious Court.

although the Balai Nikah could provide marriage counselling before marriage disputes escalated toward the court, it was considered shameful to seek marriage advice. Consequently, the Balai Nikah was predominantly, if not solely, an institution involved in marriage registration. Indeed, Balai Nikah can also be utilized as a marriage venue. For the Bugis, however, marriage in Balai Nikah would be considered shameful, it would be assumed that this marriage was a result of premarital pregnancy (I. *kawin kecelakaan*), or the parents could not afford marriage expenses, or other negative situations.

There are other differences between the situation I found in 2000 and in Nakamura's (1981) study in Kotagede in the late 1970s. In Kotagede, a wife would come to the Pengadilan Agama if her husband agreed to proclaim the dissolution of marriage. Also, as long as a wife had reasons based on Islamic law, whether or not her husband wanted to divorce her, a marriage can be dissolved through the Pengadilan Agama. Nakamura (1981:70) further adds that through Balai Nikah, a wife will not be divorced if her husband refuses to divorce her. While through the Pengadilan Agama, as long as a wife has reasons based on Islamic law, whether or not her husband wants to divorce her, a marriage can be dissolved through the Pengadilan Agama. No matter which institution one should go to for the dissolution of marriage, whether Balai Nikah or the Pengadilan Agama, Nakamura argues that the dissolution of marriage is not based on who initiates it or the reasons for divorce. It is merely on the grounds of whether or not disputes exist according to Islamic law and the agreement of the husband to divorce has been determined by the related institution (Nakamura 1981:59).

In Nakamura's study, however, none of the cases analysed was from outside the court. In my study, in addition to the court, I also looked at cases in the community. This gave a more complete picture. Although in Nakamura's study people usually proceeded through BP4 before the court, she found that the office of BP4 had never been officially used for divorce counselling sessions. People usually came to the counsellors outside office hours, usually at night since they were already familiar with the counsellors. This made it easier for people to consult them about their marriage problems in informal and confidential circumstances (Nakamura 1981:69). Jones' study of divorce in West Java indicates that despite the state requirement to address marital problem through BP4 prior to divorce, the BP4 did not have enough staff to deal with approximately 30–40 cases per day (Jones 1994:411). Thus, the encouragement to consult BP4 prior to divorce is not compatible with the number of counsellors provided by the government, and that causes insufficient consultation for the clients, resulting in the reluctance of clients to consult BP4.

Since the establishment of a woman's crisis centre LBH-P2I (see Chapter 7) in 1995 in Makassar, this has become an alternative marriage counselling centre, particularly for women who are the victims of violence. Even though this centre offers counselling for men and women, all clients are women. Despite the fact that the statistics on violence against women from LBH-P2I are small, they grow every year.

Conclusion

In examining Bugis marriage, its form and practice cannot be separate from Islamic dictates, as the majority of the Bugis are Muslims. The adoption of requirements and procedures of marriage as part of local custom and civil laws are all influenced by Islamic stipulations. Despite the fact that local customs closely follow one another, people contravene or circumvent the rules within them. People do so not because they are ignorant of the law, but in order to find alternative means (such as the falsifying age at first marriage, breaching the need for marital consent, neglecting the *iddah*, or performing marriage and divorce outside of state strictures) so as to get around a difficult or prohibitive situation for marriage and divorce.

The effort of religious officials to enact the 1974 Marriage Law in conjunction with the local culture—which has been incorporated in KHI—have been well illustrated in the court hearings. This may lead one to assume that the process of handling cases related to marriage, divorce and reconciliation vary throughout Indonesia. Comparison with the findings of other researchers bear this out.

The general view of polygynous marriage is inconsistent. Fairness to wives and children is usually only understood in terms of a husband's financial capability to provide for his wife and children. Thus, it is acceptable for richer man to enter into polygynous marriage even if they neglect the emotional concerns, views and well-being of wives and children. This contravenes the Marriage Law.

In spite of the fact that the majority of people accept the implementation of the Marriage Law of 1974, which was designed to standardise the process of marriage and divorce, some people ignore the law or still lack awareness regarding the law and follow other procedures which contravene religion and the Marriage Law of 1974. This is obvious in the practice of marriage of minors, forced marriage (*kawin paksa*), illegal marriage (*kawin liar*), illegal divorce (*cerai liar*).

The prevalence of forced marriage, which commonly occurs because of parents' need to marry off their children (*terpaksa kawin*) in times of social embarrassment, such as in a situation of unwanted premarital pregnancy or sex prior to marriage (as in the case of Bahar and Fatma).

Another finding in this chapter is the occurrence of *kawin liar*. While *kawin siri* and other kinds of illegal marriages are legitimated according to religion (Islam) and therefore have religious status, *kawin liar* is not, it is illegal according to the state, but, to some extend, is not socially forbidden. Those who enter into *kawin liar* do so to avoid having to fulfil legal and customary requirements and procedures involved in a marriage, particularly in the following circumstances: civil servant prohibitions, lack of parental consent, inability to pay for spending money (bride wealth), and premarital pregnancy. Similar to *kawin liar*, *cerai liar* is conducted to avoid procedures and requirements of legal divorce. This would include avoidance of the waiting period (*iddah*) before a re-marriage can take place, or to do away with witnesses to testify to an allegation that a wife has been neglected by her husband, or to circumvent the rules when a husband seek to marry another wife.

These illegal practices also serve as a means for men to avoid bearing the financial responsibility to wives and children. Divorce or marriage outside the tenets of the law leaves women with no legal recourse to implicate errant husbands. Thus, while the mother has the right to custody (and burden of care) of her children, she can in fact be cut-off from financial support from her husband. Children born in marriages that are not legally recognized will likely face difficulties in establishing their rightful claims to maintenance from their fathers.

Although women are commonly assumed to be the victim of marital conflict, as in forced marriage (Hartati's case) and polygynous marriage (Rosna's case), my social encounters and observations in the court hearings indicate that women can also exercise agency. This could be seen in the case of Isa, who refuse to return her wedding gifts after the divorce as her marriage was consummated; in the case of Anna, who successfully prevented her husband from having a second marriage; and in the case of Rahmatiah, who terminated her first marriage illegally because her husband's infidelity and went on to pursue an illegal second marriage. Thus, even though there are cases in which women are married by *kawin liar* without their consent (Nati's case), other cases indicate that women are also willing participants in the process of *kawin liar* and *cerai liar*. Eventually, in spite of the state imposing its regulations on marriage and divorce, regulations are breached because there is a constant invocation of adat, state law and local practice in a selective way, at times in consonance, and at other times in contradiction with one another. Consequently, the findings of this research show the institution of marriage is not yet within the control of the modern state.

The legal institutions for marriage, divorce and reconciliation in practice do not function as intended. For example in the Sidrap case, the Balai Nikah (incorporating BP4), which were established not only for marriage registration, but also for marriage counselling is only used by the local community as an institution at which to register one's marriage. In order to seek marital conflict-resolution, all cases are brought to the Pengadilan Agama, or the problem is handled internally, amongst family members. Using Balai Nikah/BP4 as marriage counselling is shameful for village people.

The study shows the limitation of national standardize procedure for dealing with marriage and divorce which are firmly grounded in local customary practices and local accommodations to Islam. While the protocols established in the KHI, and the ways these are implemented by local Islamic courts, show flexibility, there is more to be done, especially in providing to protect rights in marriage.

In the subsequent chapter, I will talk about family dynamic in the context of urban life, by examining media coverage on violence and domestic violence from different institutions with a number of case studies.

CHAPTER 7

Family Dynamics in Urban Life: Violence, Media and the State

Introduction

I have extensively discussed the marital life of the Bugis in the context of rural village life in the previous chapters. This chapter will look at issues of marital life in urban settings. Central to this chapter are marriage and violence in urban households and the positive and negative aspects of bringing family problems into the courts.

I start with a discussion of how violence in the home is increasingly no longer considered solely 'private', as it has attracted media and political attention. I present two public cases covered by local media as part of this discussion in order to understand how violence occurs and how victims deal with the problem. I consider further cases from LBH-P2I—an agency to assist women with legal advice—the Religious Court (Pengadilan Agama) Makassar, and Detention Centre (Lembaga Pemasyarakatan, LP) Maros and to contrast cases from different institutions.[1] In the subsequent section, I discuss an incident involving a high ranking official in order to examine PP No.10/1983 (see Chapter 1) as a regulation of marriage, divorce and sexual attitudes for civil servants in addition to the Marriage Law of 1974.

'Break the Silence': Local Media Coverage on Violence in the Household

Violence in the household is commonly regarded as a personal matter in the village as well as in the city. As a result, many cases of such violence are not exposed, as victims are afraid of being shamed or experiencing more violence from the perpetrators. However, some women are confident enough to report cases to the police or related institutions. Reporting such cases does not always benefit women because, for example, family matters are not regarded as the concern of the police or the police themselves are not trained to deal with such

1 See Footnote 11 in Chapter 2 for details.

 | DOI 10.1163/9789004311947_008

problems (see Stanko 1985, Stets 1988).[2] Women often become the targets of harassment from police (I. *bulan-bulanan polisi*) who blame women as the cause of anger of their husband, say such things as they do not serve their husband properly and cause him angry, so 'the problem is you not your husband', or they ask the women to go home and solve the problem themselves.

I will present two extreme cases of violence in the household which were publicised by three local newspapers—*Fajar* and *Berita Kota Makassar* and *Pare Post*. One case was in Makassar and the other was in Pare-Pare municipality (see map 1.2).[3]

The first case was the severe burning of a woman by her husband early in 2000 in Makassar. The hearing I observed in the High Court (I. Pengadilan Tinggi) illustrates ambivalence in the wife's attitude towards the case. After the burning, the wife reported the case to the police, then the case was processed (see Appendix 7.1). In the initial court hearing, the following facts emerged. The couple (Agustina and Armansyah) had married by elopement (B. *silariang*) in October 1999 because of the opposition of Agustina's parents. Agustina was in her third month of pregnancy with her first child when she was badly burned by her husband on 23 January 2000 at 8.00 o'clock in the evening. During their marriage (October 1999–January 2000), she had been physically abused by her husband, who threatened to divorce her every time they had an argument. On the day of the incident, Agustina had written a passionate letter to her former boyfriend which caused her husband's anger. He scolded her and threatened to divorce her. Agustina said:

> I don't want you to divorce me because I am in my third month of pregnancy, I am willing to die if you divorce me.
>
> High Court, 10 May 2000; *Fajar*, 11 May and 20 June 2000

Instead of pitying her, Armansyah further hit and kicked her until she fell on the floor. Then Armansyah poured petroleum over Agustina's body, set fire to her, and then pushed her out of the house. Agustina plunged into a drainage

2 In fact, Regional Police of South Sulawesi (Polda Sulsel) in collaboration with Lembaga Bantuan Perlindungan Perempuan (LBP2, Women Protection Service, a woman's NGO) Warapsari conducted training for the police to provide a Ruang Pelayanan Khusus (RPK, Special Investigation Service) for women who are victims of violence, an innovation of the former Minister of Women Empowerment under Abdurrahman Wahid presidency—Khofifah Indar Parawansa—to eliminate violence against women, on 9–10 October 2000 at Quality Inn, Makassar.

3 While I could observe Agustina's court hearings, this was not the case for Satirah's because the case had not been convened at the time of my fieldwork in 2000.

ditch to put out the fire but still suffered permanent physical damage; her belly, vagina, thighs, calves, and back were badly burned. She was taken to the hospital by her neighbours (*Berita Kota Makassar*, 11 May 2000 and 20 June 2000).

Agustina expected that by reporting her husband to the police with proof from a doctor attesting to her permanent physical damage, her husband would be punished by the court. But what happened later was that Agustina regretted her report. Before the prosecution, she sat in close proximity to her husband in the waiting room as if they were in harmony and she had forgotten the tragedy she had experienced a few months before. Likewise, Armansyah's family who attended the court hearing explained that the two families were now on good terms with each other, while the family of the wife stayed quiet, as if they agreed the case should not continue. At the end of the third court hearing, both Agustina and Armansyah's sister (Yulianti) demanded leniency for Armansyah, who was, however, pronounced guilty of a crime, for which the maximum penalty was a seven year sentence. Yulianti then fainted and Agustina threw herself on her mother's lap. Agustina was hysterical and screamed:

> I don't want my husband [to be sentenced]. [The sentence] is too long. I want justice.
>
> High Court, 1 June 2000 and FAJAR, 2 June 2000

The senior female judge advised Agustina to try to endure the trial her husband had to face and asked her to be patient (*Berita Kota Makassar*, 2 June 2000). The judge's comment reflects the view Agustina had to face the reality that her husband would be jailed for quite some time. In fear of being a single mother without financial support from her husband, Agustina demanded the judge lessen her husband's punishment, as if what he had done to her could be easily tolerated because of her financial incapability.

Despite Agustina's mother's earlier opposition to the marriage and the shame (B. *siriq*) which had resulted from the elopement (*silariang*), her presence in the court hearing and the testimony of Agustina's younger sibling indicated their emotional support for Agustina. This did not necessarily mean that the marriage was approved, but their support showed that Agustina was no longer at risk of being killed by her own family because of shame resulting from her marriage.

But, Agustina's attitude during the court hearing shows the conflicts inherent in her situation. She was afraid that she would not be able to support herself or her as yet unborn-child. Despite the fact that Agustina had been physically and psychologically abused by her husband during her marriage, she could not see a future life without her husband. This is because they both came from poor families. This was reflected in the words of Armansyah's mother when she responded to the testimony of Agustina's younger sibling who said that Armansyah neglected to pay the cost of Agustina's treatment in the hospital. It could also be seen from the appearance of both families. Armansyah's mother said: 'The cost of the hospital treatment was paid by Yulianti by selling her goods, including her kitchen utensils' (*Berita Kota Makassar*, 2 June 2000). However, in spite of the fact that Agustina' attitude during the court hearing was intended to show the judge that they were once again in harmony, it could not prevent her husband from being sentenced. Armansyah was finally given a five and a half year sentence (*Berita Kota Makassar,* 20 June 2000).

The second notorious case was the murder of a woman named Satirah by her husband, Rahman, in Pare-Pare at the end of 2000 (see Appendix 7.2). The case was known as *Pembunuhan Bidan Satirah* (I. The Murder of Midwife Satirah). Even though there were suspicious signs on Bidan Satirah's body (e.g., broken neck, bruises on her head, congealed blood in her stomach, and other injuries around her legs, back, chest, and thighs), her body was not medically examined before she was buried. Her family reported the case to the police a few days after the funeral.

Having been pressured by Satirah's family for physical evidence to reveal the circumstances of her death, Satirah's body was exhumed for autopsy two weeks after the murder. The autopsy was conducted a few weeks after the local media (*Fajar*) reported the case. When I read the report a day after the autopsy, I was shocked by the fact that Satirah's naked corpse was examined in an open area (near her recently-opened grave) and witnessed by over two hundred people. The picture published in *Fajar* showed her genitals facing the camera (*Fajar*, 16 October 2000). I asked myself: Why should her genitals become the focus of the image of the autopsy? Wasn't there a hospital in Pare-Pare that could be used for the autopsy? Was the autopsy in an open space aimed to demonstrate to society that the body was visibly examined? Didn't the body of Satirah become a pornographic display for people who witnessed the autopsy and who read the newspaper? Might not the family of Satirah feel shamed because Satirah's body had been subjected to public display?

From the forensic point of view, examining Satirah's body in an open space was unethical. Furthermore, from a journalistic perspective, displaying Satirah's naked body with her genitals facing the camera was equivalent to exploiting women's bodies through the media. The media did not consider how Satirah's family felt about the public display of her body (Nurul Ilmi Idrus 2002).

In spite of the fact that the result of the autopsy had not been released by the forensic team, *Fajar* reported that there were indications that Satirah had been abused by her husband based on the testimony of her neighbours, the last patients of Satirah, her son, and other family members, including her mother (*Fajar*, 16 December 2000).

There was a story behind this. Before the murder, Satirah had told her mother about the consistent abusive behaviour of her husband. It was reported that her mother had suggested to her:

> If your husband hits you, you should leave the house because if you were outside there, people would see and help you.
>
> FAJAR, 20 October 2000

Even though Rahman denied all accusations, he was finally arrested based on these testimonies (*Fajar*, 16 December 2000). This arrest not only comforted the family, but also the surrounding community in Pare-Pare who condemned the murder.

In both cases, neither woman reported the violence against them. Even though in Makassar, Agustina might have recourse to institutions other than the police (such as LBH-P2I or FPMP, both women's crisis centres in Makassar),[4] to which she could have reported the violence, and Satirah might have reported to the police in Pare-Pare, neither woman did so. Even if Agustina and Satirah were aware of the possibility of reporting their cases, I would assume that they would feel ashamed to expose their marital problems, presumably not just because Agustina had married by *silariang* and Satirah was a local midwife. They were also afraid that reporting their cases might result in more violence. This was indicated by the statement of Satirah's mother mentioned above, that instead of reporting the case to the police, Satirah should get help from her neighbours. Agustina's unwillingness to divorce had resulted in more violence from her husband, so we can assume that he would also react violently if she reported the case to the police.

These two extreme cases reported in the media show the important role the media has in informing the public about violence in the household. The

4 LBH-P2I and Forum Pemerhati Masalah Perempuan Sulawesi Selatan (FPMP, Women's Forum)—two women's crises centres in South Sulawesi—were established in 1998 and 2002 respectively. In practice, both institutions cooperate with each other. In addition to these women's crises centres, a number of local media (*Fajar, Bina Baru* and *Pedoman Rakyat*) and local radio (e.g. Telstar FM, Sentosa FM, Bharata FM, Smart FM and Mercurius FM) raise awareness of women's rights, including discussion on domestic violence. For details, see Baso and Idrus (2002).

display of Satirah's naked body with her genitals facing the camera reflects the insensitivity of the local newspaper on this account, however. In other words, the media does not act just as an agent to expose information on violence against women, but can also act as an agent of further violence against women.[5]

These reports indicate that such cases are not just private, but also public matters. This can be seen from the enthusiasm of the community response to the cases. For example, Agustina's neighbours directly helped her by taking her to the hospital without thinking of the possibility of violence they might themselves experience from Agustina's husband for interfering in a family problem. The willingness of Satirah's neighbours to inform the police about the violence Satirah experienced can also be regarded as a positive sign that communities are willing to testify before the courts about violence in the household.

No one connected with either case, however, took steps to protect the women from further violence, not even the families who witnessed persistent violence in these marriages. The cases were finally reported only after it was too late, that is, after Agustina's injury and Satirah's murder.

Both Agustina and Satirah were trapped in violent marriages. Both media coverage and my own observations in the court hearings indicate that Agustina's economic dependence was a major factor keeping her in a violent marriage. Gelles (1976) asserts that the fewer the resources a woman has, the less power she has, the more she is entrapped in a violent marriage, and the more she suffers at the hand of her husband. But Gelles' theory does not fit in Satirah's case, given that she was an employed woman, a midwife. From the media coverage, it can be assumed that Satirah's status as a well-known midwife in Pare-Pare (*Pare Post*, 16 December 2000) underpinned her acceptance of her violent marriage.

The two cases presented correspond to Walker's theory of 'learned helplessness' which may help us to explain why these two women stayed in violent marriage. Walker states:

---

5 Ana Nadya Abrar's (1997) study of sexual harassment and sexual violence examines articles on violence against women published in Indonesian national newspapers—*Kompas, Republika* and *Pos Kota*—she shows how the media has become an agent of information and violence by blaming the victims as the cause of the incidents. Saraswati Sunidyo (1996) analyses the media and public discourse on three public cases of wife and mistress murder in Indonesia. She analyses the cases based on the dichotomy of sexualised victims and desexualised aggressors to explain how the victims have been blamed because they are considered 'bad women', while the aggressors' attitude is regarded as 'men's nature.'

> Once the women are operating from a belief of helplessness, the perception becomes reality and they become passive, submissive, 'helpless'.
>
> WALKER 1979:46

When applied to Agustina and Satirah's cases, Walker's theory is logically acceptable because neither of them sought help. Further, Walker's definition of a battered wife fits the pattern of violence experienced by these two women.[6] Thus, Walker's theory of 'learning helplessness' is useful for understanding women who, despite repeated experiences of violence, stay without any help.

The Many Faces of Violence in the Household

When discussing the family in Indonesia, the first image that comes to mind is a nuclear family, particularly given the celebration of the notion that a 'small family is a happy and prosperous family' (I. *keluarga kecil, bahagia and sejahtera*) by the Family Planning Program of the New Order.[7] In this context, a family consisting of a husband, a wife and two children is idealised with the slogan two children are enough (*dua anak cukup*).[8] This modern image of family has transformed the customary ideal of 'many children, much fortune' (*banyak anak banyak rejeki*) into the new idea that having many children entails great risk (*banyak anak banyak resiko*), a sentiment employed to emphasise the importance of the family planning program (see Gerke 1993; Hull and Sri Moertiningsih Adioetomo 2002).

A detailed discussion of family planning is beyond the scope of the present work. I also do not mean to suggest that having children causes problems. But violence in marriage is difficult to solve through divorce because women fear

6 Walker defines a battered woman as 'a woman who is repeatedly subjected to any forceful physical or psychological behaviour by a man in order to coerce her to do something he wants her to do without any concern for her rights…in order to be classified as a battered woman, the couple must go through the battering cycle at least twice. Any women may find herself in an abusive relationship with a man once. If it occurs a second time, and she remains in the situation, she is defined as a battered woman' (Walker 1979:xv).

7 See Pausacker's (2001:92–4) criticism of the advertisements for the New Order family planning program.

8 Robinson (2000a:40) displays a photo of a poster from Ujung Pandang (now Makassar) which shows a lively picture of an ideal family, a group of two parents with two children of opposite sex.

losing custody of their children, or being unable to support their children, or the unwillingness of the children for their parents to divorce.

In this section, I discuss seven cases of women who have acted on their marital problems. They have been recorded in three different sites: LBH-P2I, the religious courts in Makassar (Pengadilan Agama) and the Detention Centre in Maros (Lembaga Pemasyarakatan), the neighbouring regency to the South of Makassar.

LBH-P2I:[9] *Consulting Women's Crisis Centre*

Nurasmi*:* A Secondary Wife

I first met Nurasmi at Sedona Hotel in Makassar at a seminar entitled 'Regional Consultation and Socialisation for the National Action Plan on the Elimination of Violence against Women (RAN-PKTP),' funded and organised by local government agencies, the Ford Foundation, and local NGOs (7–8 August 2000). Nurasmi was one of the victims of domestic violence who had contacted LBH-P2I to discuss her marital problems. She had been told about the refuge by a friend. She was invited by this women's crisis centre to attend the seminar. When I approached her during a break, she enthusiastically invited me to come to her house.

Nurasmi was the fourth wife of a Javanese man, named Parto. They married in 1988 with neither his first wife's nor both their parents' consent. His wife and both their parents refused to agree to this marriage because of Parto's existing polygynous marriages. He had divorced his second and third wives before marrying Nurasmi; his first wife lived with her mother-in-law. By 2000, he had fourteen children altogether, seven from his first wife, three from the second wife, one from the third wife, and three from Nurasmi.

Nurasmi, then 34, never dreamed she would be Parto's fourth wife. But she said: 'He was my pre-destined marriage partner (I. *jodoh*)'. Drawing from her experience, she believes that if one meets one's *jodoh*, one cannot avoid marriage (see Chapter 2). To clarify what she meant, she told me that when she was introduced to Parto by her college mate, she started to shake, not because she

---

9 Statistics on violence against women in Indonesia is difficult to obtain. However, it is possible to obtain statistics on the number of cases of violence reported to women's crisis centres or to the legal services in South Sulawesi. The establishment of the Law Service for Indonesian Women's Empowerment (LBH-P2I) in 1995 in Makassar was followed by the opening of a Women's Crisis Centre, under the same umbrella three years later. The centre keeps files on reported cases of violence. While data collected by this centre does not represent the number of cases of violence against women in South Sulawesi, it at least indicates an escalating number of reported cases.

was scared, but because she felt an 'electric reaction' in her body and had a feeling that she wanted to completely surrender herself to him. I have heard this idea expressed before from a woman who was married to a polygynous man. Nurasmi recognised that Parto was her *jodoh* even though she was unwilling to marry him because she knew he was already married.

Nurasmi knew Parto was married by his age (Parto was 40 and Nurasmi was 22 at the time of marriage), a wedding ring on his right hand, and his acknowledgment of his other marriages. But the more she tried to get away from him, the more he came to her. He usually came to pick her up at her college to avoid her parents' surveillance. Even though he had not proposed to Nurasmi, her parents objected to him as a prospective husband for a number of reasons: his marital status, the age difference, his unemployment, and the fact that he was ethnically Javanese. Her parents were afraid that Nurasmi would be neglected by her Javanese husband. But, as she suggested, it was her recognition of him as her *jodoh* that made their union possible. Knowing that Parto intended to abduct (B. *rilariang*) her, Nurasmi's parents threatened to throw her out (I. *dibuang*), consider her a lost daughter, and make an official statement that Nurasmi had been disowned. Parto, at the same time, was at risk of being killed by Nurasmi's family because of their suspicion of his intent to marry her through abduction (*rilariang*).

Nurasmi was in a difficult situation. To save Parto from being killed by her family, she reported herself as a lost girl, so she could be free to act without family interference and they would be under police guard. This procedure was unusual because such problem is usually taken care of by the families of both sides. It was not clear what was the legal status from Nurasmi's parents' part, but in the side of Nurasmi, it was taken to protect her from family anger. The couple were finally married without either family's consent under *wali hakim* (I. person who acts on behalf of the father of the bride), and Nurasmi discontinued her studies at the insistence of her husband.

Nurasmi, then, lived in a boarding house owned by Parto's parents. She occupied one room initially, then two rooms after having children. The other five rooms were occupied by other tenants. She refused to live in the same house with her in-laws and her husband's first wife. As noted in the previous chapter, a Bugis wife is usually the one who manages the family income. But, in Nurasmi's case, this was almost impossible for several reasons. Parto had a first wife (also Javanese) who was recognised by his parents and regarded as his primary wife and he had eleven children from his previous marriages to support, and he also had no income of his own. He only helped his parents in their restaurant which meant that all of his expenses were paid from this family business. As a secondary wife, Nurasmi was only given financial support after the needs of the primary wife were met (see Palmier 1960), a practice that followed Javanese custom and was an arrangement of primary-secondary wife instead of following Islamic prescriptions for polygynous marriages under which each wife has to be treated equally.

Nurasmi was only given daily cash for meals (Rp3000/day equal to US$0.30 at current exchange rates), increasing to Rp5000/day (US$0.50) after the monetary crisis hit Indonesia in 1997. This was not even enough to buy basic food for Nurasmi and her children. To survive, Nurasmi opened a food stall (I. *warung*) selling cheap cooked food, particularly for tenants of the boarding house, assisted by her eldest son (12 years). Parto, however, did not appreciate her self-sufficiency and became suspicious that she would make contact with other men at her food stall. Nurasmi also used to work at a restaurant, a real estate business and an insurance company, but her husband always terrorised her in her workplace because of his jealousy towards her male workmates. Despite the fact that Parto was jealous of her opening the food stand (*warung*), he took advantage of her ingenuity and stopped offering her any financial support at all.

Every time she asked for money for expenses, such as school fees for the children or money for food, tension between Nurasmi and her husband arose, particularly if she asked for additional daily expenses. If Nurasmi ran away, Parto would come and pick her up, and if she asked for a divorce, he would ask for forgiveness and promise that he would change his behaviour. But he never changed. Rather, he became more jealous. Anywhere Nurasmi went, Parto suspected her of meeting other men. If he found out where she went, he would come and force her to go home, no matter what she did. When Nurasmi and Parto argued, he very often hit her, kicked her, slapped her, or pulled her hair. This situation continued for over ten years.

Nurasmi had nowhere to go. Despite the fact that her parents had already forgiven her (B. *maddéceng*) after having three children, she had never told them the real circumstances of her marriage, afraid of her family's anger. But Nurasmi's mother suspected that Nurasmi's marriage was troubled and challenged Parto to divorce Nurasmi saying she was willing to take her daughter back, an overture to which Parto did not respond.

Nurasmi had tried to negotiate with her husband, expecting that he would change his attitude, but he could not be urged to compromise. Nurasmi and her mother did not understand what he wanted. Nurasmi had tried to work out the marriage with her husband peacefully. Thinking that there was no response or change from him, however, she decided to find another way to solve her marital conflict.

Nurasmi had tried several times to report her husband to the police, but unfortunately the case was never processed. She was asked to go home by the police and work out her problems with her husband, a typical response on the part of the police (Stets 1988). Another time when she went to the police, Nurasmi was told that she had no proof against her husband because the bruises on her face and her back were already gone. Subsequently, she went to the police with a bruised face and thigh to convince the police and told them: 'Are you waiting for my corpse to prove that I have been violated by my husband?' Her husband had never been arrested, but she was advised to threaten her husband that she would report him to the police if the violence continued, a threat that finally persuaded him to stop his abuse.

With the money she earned from her food stall, Nurasmi took tailoring lessons. She wanted to become a seamstress in order to support her children without her husband finding out. Her eldest son took care of his younger brothers and instructed them not to tell their father where she went, otherwise Parto would come and take her home. Nurasmi wanted to be independent. Thinking that there was no future by staying married with Parto, she planned for a divorce. She consulted the LBH-P2I about the possibility of using violence as the grounds for divorce, gaining legal custody of the children, and obtaining child support from Parto.

It would have been very difficult for Nurasmi to get child support from her husband after a divorce because Parto did not have a job. Furthermore, she would probably have had to leave the house because it was owned by her mother-in-law who had tried twice to chase Nurasmi from the house during the marriage.

When I left Makassar, Nurasmi was still consulting LBH-P2I about her problems. She expected that the LBH-P2I could mediate between her and her husband to negotiate the custody of the children and for child support before taking the case to the Pengadilan Agama in Makassar for a divorce. This reflects the vulnerable position of woman in relation to divorce. But it is interesting that in the end she had her parents' support.

Hasniah*:* A Neglected Wife

During the same seminar mentioned above, I also met Hasniah. Hasniah was a 35 year old seamstress with four children, two in primary school and another two in high school. During the course of ten years, from 1981 to 1991, Hasniah's marriage was a happy one. Her husband, Idam, who was a military police officer, was not only a good husband, but also a good father to their children. This happy marriage changed when Idam had an extramarital relationship with someone he met in a bar when he was on duty as a security guard. After this, Idam changed and moved from one woman to another. Tension between Hasniah and Idam increased, reaching a peak when Idam brought his girlfriend to the house on his son's birthday. Hasniah's son poured a glass of tea on his father's girlfriend's body and the girlfriend ran away from the house, pursued by Idam. Hasniah and Idam lived separately after this incident, beginning in 1997. Hasniah, Adam and their children used to live in an official residence (I. *rumah dinas*) for military police, but finally left because of social pressure over Idam's infidelities. Then, Hasniah and her first daughter lived with Hasniah's sister's family. Hasniah's three other children lived with her parents. Idam, by this point, lived with his second wife, who he had married in an illegal marriage (I. *kawin liar*). Military police are supposed to notify a divorce to the military unit (*kesatuan militer*) before taking the case to the Pengadilan Agama. As a result, Idam did not report his second marriage to his office, as he was afraid that it would be rejected by his superior because of his reported infidelities. Through this strategy, Idam sought to avoid the legal procedures and requirements regarding taking a second wife. Idam no longer supports his first wife, Hasniah, and their children. Although her marriage was not an arranged marriage, Hasniah receives support from her parents and siblings, who have threatened to throw her out (*dibuang*) if she were to return to her husband.

Hasniah did not report her case to her husband's superior initially because she learned from other members of the *Dharma Pertiwi*—the women's organization for the wives of military police—whose husbands worked in the same office, that in previous cases of marriage conflict, the wronged wife was usually blamed by her husbands superior or by the wife of the superior, the Chair of Dharma Pertiwi. The complaining wife was accused of not being able 'to serve' her husband so her attitude must have caused her husband to leave or to have an affair. The interference of *Dharma Pertiwi* in marital conflict illustrates how this state-sponsored women's organization intervenes in domestic life. Nonetheless, the intervention itself usually does not benefit women. Thus, learning from previous cases, women face a dilemma; they must choose between reporting their cases to their husband's superior and accepting the blame or staying in a conflicted marriage.

Hasniah told me that there was a case in which a wife had reported her husband's infidelity to his military unit (*kesatuan militer*). There was never any official action from the superior, though the case had been going on for years. I was told of another case in which a man had reported to his *kesatuan militer* that his wife had been found in a Karaoke Club. In fact, she happened to be there with other female friends; the women had sought to entertain themselves and to forget their marital problems for a while. Such places are considered to be places for 'bad women', however, and this piece of evidence had been used by her husband to blame his wife for marital conflict. The man was able to convince his superior to cover up his marital infidelities. There was also the case of a military wife whose case was processed for seven years before she was finally able to get a divorce. Once a wife registers a request for a divorce with her husband's *kesatuan militer*, she has to monitor how the request is proceeding on a weekly, if not daily, basis. Otherwise, she would have to start from the beginning again because her inattention would mean it was considered a discontinued case. Hasniah learned this lesson and realised that she should find another strategy to address her problem. Soon after she found out about LBH-P2I from a friend, she hoped that this institution would help her in dealing with her marriage conflict.

A local newspaper—*Berita Kota Makassar* (3 and 5 June 2000) in an article entitled 'A Scream from the Heart of a Military Wife' (I. *Jeritan Hati Istri Polisi Militer*)—reported a case of repeated violence and adultery by a military police officer in Makassar.[10] The officer's wife was admonished by her husband's *kesatuan militer* because it was considered that such news shamed the *kesatuan militer* as a whole. Following this case, there was a significant change in dealing with marital conflict amongst the military police after pressure from LBH-P2I Makassar which threatened publicly to expose cases through the newspapers if cases were not taken seriously and dealt with in a proper fashion.

Hasniah's case shows evidence of this change, at least in that her husband's salary was passed on to her every month. However, Hasniah faced a dilemma. On one hand, she could forgive her husband if he changed his bad behaviours. But, this would not be accepted by her parents. She would be thrown out (*dibuang*) if she reunited with her husband. Besides, Hasniah herself was not sure whether or not her husband would change his behaviour. On the other hand, if she divorced, her husband would be fired from his office as a result of his infidelity (as had been threatened by his superior), which meant that Hasniah would lose financial support for her children. She was, in effect, 'leaving the tiger's mouth for the mouth of a crocodile' (*keluar dari mulut harimau, masuk ke mulut buaya*).

In her discussion of marriage in Soroako, South Sulawesi, Robinson found that marital conflict and divorce mostly arose because the husband marries another woman, seeking romantic involvement that has diminished in the first

10 A similar case reported by *Fajar*, entitled '*Dimaki dan Digiring ke Kantor Polisi*' (I. [She] was Abused by Words and Brought to the Police Station) involved a police officer's wife who was neglected by her husband and reported her case to her husband's office. After repeated reports, she was finally responded to by her husband's superior. But he and his other two inferiors crudely brought her to the police station, and negligently left her there (*Fajar*, 19 June 2000).

marriage whether or not the union is based on 'two romantically involved individuals' or 'a pack between two families' (Robinson 1986:226). In Hasniah's case, despite the fact that she was married to an outsider (B. *to laing*), the marriage was based on romantic love and a pact between two families. Therefore, her marital problem was also her family's problem. This at least gave her moral support from her family.

In both cases, financial difficulties and the expectation that the husbands would change their behaviour explained why these women did not break off their relationships. Some of the factors discovered by Truninger (1971), in her study of violence against wives, support this finding.[11] But they did not engage in 'learned helplessness' as did Agustina and Satirah. Rather, Nurasmi and Hasniah sought ways to deal with their problems, but they demurred from acting assertively because of fear of losing financial support for their children.

The Pengadilan Agama: Divorce in the Court Hearings

The following discussion deals with two cases of domestic violence—Sartiah and Imah—processed in the Pengadilan Agama Makassar for divorce. I interviewed Imah before the court hearings, and Sartiah was introduced by a friend. She invited me to meet her in her friend's house to avoid her husband's suspicion.

Sartiah*:* An Independent Woman

Sartiah was a 35 year old, middle class woman who worked as a civil servant and had a five year-old-son. She had married Hasan, a 38 year-old Bugis from Luwu in 1993. Hasan had grown up in a noble family and was used to being served based on his royal status (I. *keturunan opu*). When he married, he expected such service to continue within his marriage. Sartiah, however, was not a noble woman, though she came from a middle class, educated, democratic family. Both Hasan and Sartiah recognised their respective social locations (B. *onro*). Hasan identified himself according to ascribed status, while Sartiah assessed herself based on achieved status. Sartiah refused to serve him as a king (I. *raja*) in the home because in her estimation they were equal, though in different areas of attainment.

11 Truninger (1971) identifies seven factors which explain why women stay in violent marriages: women's negative self-concepts, the expectation that husbands will reform their attitudes, economic hardship, economic support for the children, marriage reconciliation, stigmatisation of divorcees, the difficulties of getting work for women with children.

Before Sartiah married Hasan, her parents set the condition that Hasan should allow Sartiah to work after marriage as all her siblings had, and this was agreed to by Hasan. Hasan, however, was a jealous man, a characteristic that had been evident since they were first dating. Sartiah enjoyed this at first, assuming that it was a sign of Hasan's attachment, caring, and loving, and Hasan assured her that he would not behave like this once they got married. Sartiah was convinced that she was with 'Mr Right'.

Unfortunately, Hasan's jealousy became more pronounced after marriage. Hasan did not want Sartiah to be actively involved in her office activities outside of official office hours, as he was afraid she would attract sexual attention in the work place. He suspected her of playing around with another man whenever she came home later than usual. He asked searching questions as soon she got home, such as: what did she do in her office? who was there? how did she get home? In fact, Sartiah was a very active woman both in her office and in the neighbourhood social organization, activities that were disapproved by her husband. In contrast, Sartiah's involvement in *Dharma Wanita* (see Chapter 1) in his work place was greatly appreciated by her husband as it allowed his position of power to become visible. In her own office, she was an independent person and not her husband's companion, indicated by the Indonesian term *pendamping suami*, a term used to articulate the notion that a wife's existence is attached to her husband.

In the house, Hasan complained about the food his wife served; he had 'expensive tastes', which contrasted with his parsimonious attitude. In this double-income couple, money management is often a problem. In spite of the fact that Hasan gave his salary to Sartiah every month, he maintained control of his own and Sartiah's salaries by, for example, interrogating her about how she spent the money. To give the details of the household expenditures, Sartiah provided a monthly financial report to her husband. Many of the expenses were related to his family, such as for transportation or presents (I. *oleh-oleh*) whenever they came to visit. In addition, Sartiah had to feed another four members of her husband's family—a couple with two children—who lived with them. Sartiah had agreed that Hasan's relatives could live in the house, expecting that they would help with domestic activities while Sartiah concentrated on her work in the office. In fact, all of them only lived as parasites (*benalu*, to describe one who lives in someone's house without any contribution), and expected to be served like her husband. Instead of serving only three people (herself, her husband and her son), Sartiah had also to be a servant to four others. When she got home from work, she had to cook for all of them and wash all the dishes from lunch. Whenever she complained to her husband, she was the one blamed, told that she did not have any respect for his family, or she was not sincere in her wish (*tidak ikhlas*) to have them in the house. Even though the house belonged to Sartiah, given by her parents, she could not exercise her own will in the house.

In addition, Hasan liked to play around behind her back—*suka main belakang*—a phrase she used to describe her husband's tendency to give money to his family without her consent. For instance, his family came to her husband's office and asked for money. Whenever she complained to her husband, she would be scolded as a woman with eyes for money alone (*perempuan mata duitan*). In fact, they had agreed that whoever from his family came to ask for money or goods, such gifts should be given by Sartiah. Hasan, in turn, would deal with requests from her family. Such an 'intersecting duty' is typical in Bugis families (see discussion in Chapter 4).

With regard to this 'intersecting duty', sharing is intended to ensure that what has been achieved by a family can also be enjoyed by other members of the family on both sides. Such sharing and integrating can elicit a closeness between a wife and her husband's family, and vice versa, especially for people who marry outsiders (B. *to laing*). Through this arrangement, each party may control what has been given to the family of the other in order to achieve equality. This agreement between Hasan and Sartiah, however, was broken by Hasan through 'playing behind her back' (I. *main belakang*).

When Sartiah became pregnant with her second child, her husband suspected that her pregnancy was a result of adultery with her office colleague. His accusation arose from suspicions aroused by her colleague calling her at home on official matters. As a result, Hasan's and Sartiah's quarrelling became more intense during her pregnancy. The climax of their quarrel was when she asked her husband to help to prepare the room for the twin babies she expected would be born prematurely. Hasan refused to help and even told her that the babies were not his. Sartiah denied the accusation and they began fighting. Hasan slapped and hit Sartiah during their argument and she miscarried as a result. Ironically, her mother-in-law who was in the house when they were fighting blamed her for the quarrel and also suspected that her pregnancy was the result of adultery.

In critical condition, Sartiah went to the hospital along with her five-year-old son. She refused to be visited by her husband in the hospital and later asked for a divorce. Sartiah felt that if her twin babies had lived, her husband would not have acknowledged them and would have considered them, instead, to be illegitimate (I. *anak haram*). That was why God took them, she said.

Sartiah tried to file for divorce afterwards. According to PP No. 10/1983 (Article 3:1, see Chapter 1), as a civil servant, Sartiah had to get a letter of consent for divorce from her superior. However, to get this letter was not simple.

Her male superior did not give his consent since the reason for divorce stated in the letter was marital disputes with an emphasis on economic issues, though everybody in her office, except her superior, knew that she was also physically abused by her husband. She was advised by her superior that as a wife she should be patient and know how to act properly as a wife (*pandai menempatkan diri sebagai seorang istri*), particularly as everybody in her office knew that her husband was a jealous man due to Sartiah's beauty. She told me that her male and female colleagues commented on her husband's jealousy by asserting:

> If you already know that your husband is a jealous man, you should be well mannered, do not make him jealous. You are beautiful and attractive. That is why he always gets jealous.
>
> SARTIAH, 22 December 2000

This statement implies that Sartiah's beauty and attractiveness were the cause of Hasan's jealousy. Even though Sartiah had never stated that she was also physically abused by her husband, she eventually received a letter of consent from her superior after repeated requests. Then, she proceeded to seek a divorce in the Pengadilan Agama Makassar. After two attempts, she had not succeeded because her husband and her son said in the court hearing that they did not want her to get divorced. Although the Marriage Law of 1974 (Article 39) allows violence as grounds for divorce, Sartiah was not confident enough to state violence as the ground for divorce for three reasons: she had no physical evidence, no witness to the physical violence, and she was ashamed to tell the truth. Instead, she claimed economic problems as the reason in court. Unfortunately, it is not easy to get a divorce on these grounds alone, especially because her husband stated he still wanted to work out the marriage.

In Sartiah's case, the wishes of her son were used by her husband and supported by the judges to deny her request for divorce. She was criticised for not being a 'good mother', not only by her husband, but also by the judges who said: 'If you get divorced because of money, how will you feel about yourself as a mother?' (I. *Masa' gara-gara uang anda mau cerai, bagaimana perasaan anda sebagai ibu*?). Her husband dramatised the situation in the court hearing by asking her forgiveness, reading a verse in the Qur'an and promising to change his behaviour. Sartiah was not just criticised on her performance of womanhood, but the judges stressed that a human being should accept another's apology, regardless of the actual problem.

In Sartiah's court hearing, violence in marriage was not a matter of concern because she stated consistent marital disputes about money as the grounds for divorce, and there was no further questioning to elicit other reasons for her request for divorce. Even though marital disputation is a legal reason to terminate the marriage (PP No.9/1975, Chapter 5:19f), it was not convincing enough to justify divorce, especially given her husband's apology and her child's refusal to accept divorce. The case was closed.

A number of studies have shown that sexual jealousy and financial problems are the precipitating factors for marital violence (see, for example, Carlson 1977; Dobash and Dobash 1979). In Sartiah's case, marital problems involved both sexual jealousy and financial problems. The financial problems were more about control of money—rather than inadequate support.

Imah*:* A Victim of Forced Marriage and Sex

An extreme case I observed in the Pengadilan Agama Makassar was the case of a lower class young woman age 17, named Imah, who was forced to marry Radi, 35, in the middle of 1999. Imah was extremely unhappy, traumatised, and fearful whenever she met her husband outside or in the court room. Accordingly, she was always accompanied by a policeman—a member of her family—and her father during the court hearings.

Imah stated that marrying Radi was a nightmare because it was a forced marriage, not to mention having sex with him. Imah never stated that she had been raped by her husband, since the term 'rape in marriage' is still alien in Indonesia, but she insisted that he had 'forced her to sleep with him '(I. *dipaksa tidur*).[12] As Finkelhorf points out 'rape is traumatic not because it is with someone you don't know, but it is with someone you don't want—whether stranger, friend or husband' (cited in Pagelow 1988:208). Radi defended himself by claiming that she refused to have sex, which caused him to force her, implying that Imah's behavior provoked his violence. This reflects the 'politics of language' in which the language gives her the blame (see Marcus 1992).

In the beginning, Imah's parents did not agree to the divorce. She was even bound (*diikat*) by her husband in her grandmother's house with the support of her family to prevent her from running away from the house because they felt ashamed that Imah was unwilling to sleep with her husband. Her parents then realised that her husband was coarse (*kasar*), reflected in the way he talked to Imah after their marriage, but they advised her to be patient.

Imah did not have the courage to divorce without her parents' consent, not just because she was afraid of being sinful (*berdosa*) to her parents, but also

12 In Indonesia, it is very sensitive to connect rape with violence against wives, since rape is understood only between strangers and is considered as a western concept that is incompatible with Indonesian culture, for details see Nurul Ilmi Idrus (2001:43–4).

because she did not know how to seek a divorce and did not have the money to initiate it. Her parents finally agreed she should file for divorce when they saw her bleeding as a consequence of forced sex and her struggle to resist. In this case, physical evidence became a significant indicator of violence in her marriage, even though she had been psychologically, sexually and physically abused during six months of marriage.

Despite the fact that State Regulation states that violence is a valid reason for divorce (PP No. 9/1975, Chapter 5:19d), it was not easy for Imah to get a divorce on this ground alone since her husband still wanted to work out their marriage. When I discussed Imah's case with the judges, they said it was their task to offer the couple a second chance to reconcile their marriage before granting them a divorce,[13] even though Imah had experienced repeated violence in her marriage.

After Radi repeated his request for reconciliation and Imah repeated her refusal, she was finally granted a divorce. But the divorce did not put an end to her fear. She was afraid Radi's unwillingness to divorce might lead him to seek revenge, especially because he was a police officer. Her fear was also caused by her past experience of sexual violence. In such a case, Finkelhorf claims that victims of sexual violence in marriage encounter greater and longer trauma than victims of other types of sexual violence because of feelings of disloyalty, imprisonment, and repeated sexual violence, leading to a long term fear (in Pagelow 1988:208). Russell emphasised that women who were sexually abused by their husbands experience more serious trauma than those raped by strangers (Russell 1980:193).

In both Pengadilan Agama Makassar and Sidrap, I observed a number of cases in which the husband used apology as a strategy to terminate the divorce process. If the husbands were attempting reconciliation, the wives were persuaded to accept it, regardless of the problem. In both courts, the judges clarified that the law requires marital advice (I. *penasehatan perkawinan*) as an attempt to work out the marriage prior to dissolution, as one of the pre-requisites before divorce is granted.

Women in the Detention Centre: The Power of the In-Laws

In this section, I will discuss three cases of women who were jailed for murder and drug offences.[14] One morning in the first week of December 2000, I went

---

13 Interview with a female judge—Ibu Syarifah Nuraini—in the Pengadilan Agama Makassar (27 December 1999).

14 See Footnote 11 in Chapter 2 for details of crimes the women involved in this detention centre had committed.

to the Detention Centre (I. Lembaga Pemasyarakatan, LP) in Maros to interview women prisoners.

Three cases—those of Sairah, Ratna, and Arti—are discussed in detail below not just because they were Bugis and/or married to Bugis men, but also because their cases were related to marital violence. The case of *siriq* (Sahariah) has already been discussed in Chapter 2.

Sairah: Stereotyping Stepmother

One of the murder cases was the case of Sairah, then 37 years. Sairah was accused of killing her stepson, Gani (18). She was the first prisoner the prison official suggested I interview. I was quite scared when I first met her, but my fear went away as we talked, and I was not the first researcher who had interviewed her since she had been sentenced.

Sairah was a divorcee with one child when she married Ramli, a divorced man with six children. Only the youngest of Ramli's children was in the custody of his former wife. The rest of his children were taken care of by Sairah, who was Ramli's second wife. Sairah described her relationship with her stepchildren as similar to the relationship between a mother and her own children. She married Ramli two years after she divorced her first husband and she did not receive any financial support for the child born from that marriage. Her first husband had been a drunkard and a violent man. Sairah described that marriage as hell, and violence had become part of her daily life, physically and psychologically. Her first husband was not just incapable of maintaining the family. He also spent his wife's income which she earned as a shopkeeper to buy alcoholic drinks for himself. Whenever she refused to give him money, he hit her, even in front of her child. His frustration resulted from losing his job after the first few months of their marriage. He enacted his frustration through drinking and violent behaviour.

A number of studies have considered the relationship between violence and drunkenness. The findings vary from one study to another. The study of Hotaling and Sugarman (cited in Buzawa 1990) in the Unites States indicates that men's drunkenness and men's power and control in marriage are considered the best predictors of violence towards their wives. There is a possibility that violence against a wife is a consequence of a husband's drunkenness. However, it may also be the case that a husband intentionally gets drunk in order to hurt his wife. Thus, he can use his drunkenness to avoid blame. In such a circumstances, Alberta (1995) argues that the relationship between drugs or alcohol and violence of the husband is ambiguous because substance-use is treated as a 'mask' which is compatible with the concept of diffusion of responsibility. Nonetheless, Hopkins provides a counter argument that if men become intoxicated by choice in order to beat their wives, they are responsible for their behaviour (Hopkins 1991:116). In other words, being intoxicated cannot be used as a justification for abusive behaviour.

In Sairah's case, her first husband's violent behaviour was a problem-solving device to compensate for economic incompetence. That is, his inability to 'surround the kitchen seven times' (I. *mattuliling dapureng wékka pétu*). She had never reported his violence until she sued for divorce. Indeed, she had no idea that she could report this violence within their marriage. In addition, she claimed she felt too ashamed to tell others that she was being violated by her husband. In fact, under the Marriage Law of 1974 (Chapter 5:19d), she had the right to divorce her husband. He never showed up in the court hearings, until the judges decided to grant for a divorce a few months after the registration of divorce.

Sairah had a daughter from her marriage to Ramli and was a housewife who spent most of her time at home in the city of Makassar. This happy marriage, however, changed dramatically after the death of her stepson, Gani. She told me the story with resignation. A day before the murder, there was a quarrel in the house. Ramli, Gani's father, was angry at Gani because Sairah had told Ramli that Gani had broken his father's motorcycle. As a result, Gani was angry with Sairah and scolded her calling her a bitch mother (I. *mama sundala*). Sairah did not reply, assuming that it would make the situation worse, but Pak Ramli yelled at Gani saying: 'If I were your stepmother, I would poison you, so you would die.

Not long before the incident the following day, she was sure that she had seen Gani watching TV before she went down to the well to wash the family's clothes. She was washing with her husband's brother's wife (B. *lago*), Aminah, when her stepdaughter, Tati, came down from the house and screamed. Then Sairah, Aminah, and Tati saw Gani descending the steps with his sarong on fire. He threw himself down to the ground close to the well. Sairah and Aminah splashed him with water to put out the fire. Sairah panicked and was afraid to touch Gani. Instead of taking him to the hospital immediately, Sairah went to a public telephone to call her husband at work. She left Gani by the well in agony and he died without any further help. There were two witnesses at the time—Tati, her stepdaughter, and Aminah, her *lago*.[15] Neither Tati nor Aminah, however, appeared at the court hearing to support Sairah because, according to Sairah, they were pressured by Ramli's family and the family of Pak Ramli's former wife (Gani's mother). Instead of standing up for Sairah, Pak

15 *Lago* is a Bugis kinship term for a woman's husband's brother's wife or a man's wife's sister's husband.

Ramli supported the accusation that she was the one who was responsible for Gani's death, though he was on Sairah's side in the initial part of the court hearing. During the interview, Sairah said she always questioned herself:

> Who was the killer of my stepson or did he kill himself because of what his father had said to him and because he felt ignored?
>
> SAIRAH, 6 December 2000

She has not found the answers to these questions, though it happened seven years ago. In Sairah's case, apart from whether or not she killed her stepson, it was very easy to accuse her. First, because she was a stepmother, a position stigmatised by society as an evil mother (I. *ibu tiri kejam*) for stepchildren. Secondly, Sairah had quarrelled with her stepson the day before the incident. Finally, she did not take Gani to the hospital immediately after the incident. All of these factors were used to incriminate her in the court hearing. Besides, Sairah told me that she was not well-behaved during the court hearing, partly because she had been forced to confess to the murder. In the interrogation process, Sairah was threatened by a police officer with a gun to her head to confess the murder. She stated that the case could be manipulated as long as one had money, referring to the absence of the two sole witnesses who could have defended her in the court hearing.

Since her arrest on the day of the incident, she had only been visited by her husband once, and never saw her daughter from her marriage to Ramli. Her other daughter from her first marriage was taken care of by her aunt. She thought that her husband had punished her by taking her daughter away from her and marrying another woman without her consent when the case was still being processed in court. When asked whether or not she resented this, she responded by saying:

> I did not kill Gani. If I killed him, he would haunt my mind throughout my life. I will get through this sentence not because I admit to the murder, but simply because I will think that I probably sinned in the past and this is the retribution.
>
> SAIRAH, 6 December 2000

Sairah considered that this event was a way of redeeming sin (I. *penebus dosa*), of cleansing the dirt from her inner and outer aspects (*lahir* dan *bathin*). For the Bugis, *lahir* and *bathin* have to be balanced.[16] A person who

16 See Millar (1983), Errington (1989) and Acciaioli (1989).

has unbalanced *lahir* and *bathin*, will also have an unbalanced life. In the early years of sentence, Sairah's life was meaningless, dark and without a future (B. *déqna masumangeq*). Then she realised that she had to have her *sumangéq* back (I. *mengembalikan semangat hidupnya*) at least for herself and her two daughters. Thinking this way, she had gotten back her spirit (B. *sumangéq*) after four years in the detention centre.

Sairah was sentenced to seventeen years and she had served a period of seven years in 2000 at the time of interview. Although, she still had a long time (10 years, unless she received a commutation of her sentence) to stay in the detention centre, Sairah already had plans for her future, quite unconnected with her husband, though she worried about her daughter who was under her husband's custody.

Based on the Marriage Law 1974 (Chapter 1, 4:2) a husband may take another wife only if the first wife cannot perform her wifely duties, is handicapped, suffers from a disease that cannot be cured, or cannot give birth. In Sairah's case, none of these legal reasons existed. But, a marriage can also be terminated if one of the parties is sentenced to jail for five years or more (PP No.9/1975, Chapter 5:19c). In fact, her husband married another woman before divorcing her. If her husband married because of this and assumed that she could not perform her responsibilities, this constitutes neglect of Sairah's rights as a wife, since the marital union includes both responsibilities and rights. Is it because she was in jail that she could be treated arbitrarily by her husband? It is also clearly stated in the Marriage Law (Chapter VI, 34:1) that the husband is responsible for protecting his wife and fulfilling her needs based on his capacity. However, such a situation is very common: when a wife does not fulfil her responsibilities, her rights are not the matters of concern.

Sairah had never complained about her husband because she had been neglected for more than six months[17] and he had married another woman without her consent. In spite of the fact she is an urban resident of Makassar, the Marriage Law is irrelevant for a woman who is ignorant of the law (I. *buta hukum*) like Sairah. She knew nothing but her own responsibilities as a wife. In Sairah's circumstance, it was very difficult to be reunited with her husband because his family and his former wife considered her a potential killer of *Pak* Ramli's other children. Returning to her husband would be impossible because the stigma of stepmother had been combined with that of murderer. Sairah said:

17 *Sighat ta'lik* (A. marital agreement) is pronounced by the husband after the *akad nikah* states that a wife can claim a divorce from her husband if she has been neglected for six months.

> Whatever I do or say, I am a stepmother, and a stepmother is always thought to be a bad mother, even if I did not kill anybody.
>
> SAIRAH, 6 December 2000

Even though as a wife of *Pak* Ramli, she is supposed to be considered part of his family and vice versa, as reflected in the term *siala*, meaning 'to take each other', in Bugis marriage, in this instance, her status as a stepmother positioned her as an outsider (*to laing*) in the family. Tati (her step daughter) and Aminah (her *lago*) were prevented from being witnesses in the court hearing, presumably, because they thought it was pointless to defend someone who was *to laing*, an outsider. Sairah ended our interview by saying:

> I am only a stepmother and an outsider, so I am not regarded as a part of the family.
>
> SAIRAH, 6 December 2000

Sairah's statement reflects the stigmatisation towards a stepmother and her lack of hope for her marriage.

Ratna: A Non-virgin Girl and a Hotel Worker

Ratna, eighteen, was already pregnant when she married her boy friend Nasir in 1998. Her in-laws did not respect her, not just because her marriage was precipitated by a premarital pregnancy (I. *kawin kecelakaan*), but also because she was not considered an ideal wife for Nasir for a number of reasons. First, she worked in administration in a hotel in Makassar, a job that was not respectable according to her in-laws. Once her mother-in-law said: 'Only cheap women work at hotels because they can easily meet other men there'. Second, her child was taken care of by a maid, despite the fact that Ratna lived with her in-laws. Her in-laws expected her to be trapped in the domestic realm to make it easier for them to control her. Her mother-in-law as well as her sisters-in-law always controlled her marriage by, for instance, determining what kind of food had to be served, how to take care of her son, or how to manage household finances. Her husband, on the other hand, could not mediate the conflict between Ratna and his mother and sisters. He could not choose on which side to stand. This situation was used by her in-laws to force Nasir to divorce her. Ratna said:

> Everything I did was wrong, and they tried to find anything that could put me in a difficult situation, as if I was supposed to be divorced by Nasir.
>
> RATNA, 6 December 2000

Ratna finally could not withstand the pressure and asked for a divorce on the grounds of incompatibility. Despite the fact that this incompatibility was between her and her in-laws, she accused her husband of not standing on her side. They finally got divorced in 2000 (*talak* 1)[18]—a type of divorce during which the couple can still reconcile the marriage—with the support of Ratna's family, after two years of continuous disputes with her in-laws.

In spite of the fact that she was the one who asked for a divorce, she was not ready to be a divorcee (I. *janda*), especially a young divorcee (*janda kembang*). Becoming a *janda* in her 20s was terrible for Ratna. She became brittle and frustrated. In her tenuous condition, she was introduced to different types of drugs by a friend of hers and became addicted. She was arrested along with other friends when they had a party in her friend's house. She was sentenced to eighteen months in prison. Her child was in the custody of her husband during her incarceration.

Ratna expected to rejoin Nasir after her release, especially because he continued visiting her in prison and their divorce was still in the stage of *talak* 1. She set the condition that she wanted her nuclear family to be together but living apart from her in-laws.

Nasir was the eldest and only son in the family. His mother's expectations for him were very high. He was expected to have a good job, wife and marriage. His mother was extremely disappointed when Nasir told her that he had to marry Ratna because she was already pregnant. Virginity is highly valued in Bugis society, and losing one's virginity prior to marriage is extremely shameful (discussed in Chapter 2). But an Indonesian saying states the rice has already become porridge (*nasi sudah jadi bubur*), meaning that what has happened to Nasir is a reality. Despite Nasir's mother's disappointment, Nasir married Ratna. Nasir's mother dream of a full feast for Nasir's wedding (B. *botting roaq*) was realised instead as a flat marriage (*botting makemmé*). Furthermore, having two money managers (Ratna and her mother-in-law) in the same house always has potential for conflict.

Ratna was stigmatised by her in-laws, not only because of her premarital pregnancy, but also because of her job. The work opportunities open for women to work outside the home do not accord with the readiness of the society to accept this. There are certain places that are stereotypically considered inappropriate for women, regardless of the specific job in question. After the divorce, Ratna had to face the reality of being a young divorcee (*janda kembang*, literally blooming widow), whether or not she was flirtatious, a judgment typically attached to the status *janda*.

18 See Chapter 6 for further discussion *talak* 1, 2 and 3.

Arti: A *Bainé Jawa-jawa*

Arti, a twenty year Javanese woman from Surabaya, married to Basir, whom she met when he was on office duty in 1996 in Surabaya. They married in Surabaya without Basir's parents' presence. His parents did not agree to the marriage, partly because, they said 'his wife, however, is Javanese' (B. *Jawa-jawami bainéna*), a phrase that refers to Javanese as lower status, in the position of a domestic servant or prostitute. In addition, Arti was considered by her mother-in-law to behave like Javanese (B. *massipaq jawa-jawa*) or to behave like an outsider (*massipaq to laing*), which refers to Javanese behaviour of being independent within marriage, evidenced by neglect of the mother-in-law. This assumption is associated with the Javanese notion of marriage, that is, to establish a new autonomous household (H. Geertz 1961), while Bugis marriage is to make two families into one (*siala*). Therefore, the bride has to take her husband's family as hers, and vice versa (see discussion in Chapter 3).

In Arti's case, being a complete stranger in her mother-in-law's house was presumably already a burden for her, made harder by being neglected as a 'Javanese wife' (B. *bainé jawa-jawa*). It was presumably too early to judge if Arti was acting Javanese (*massipaq jawa-jawa*) since the marriage was still very young and she still had to learn about Bugis culture.

Thus, it is obvious that Arti's Javanese identity was the basis of the marriage disputes between Arti and her mother-in-law. Arti finally gave up after two years of conflict and placed her child in her mother's care in Surabaya because she was afraid that she could not support her. Then, she returned to Makassar to live in a boarding house with the consent of her husband. She did not tell her own mother that her marriage was shaky. She expected her husband to join her to live with her as a normal couple, but he never did. He only visited her once in a while in the boarding house and he provided irregular financial support. She said:

> I was frustrated by my marriage. This was a living hell. I had married status, but I was separated from my husband because of the conflict.
>
> ARTI, 6 December 2000

In this uncertain situation, Arti was introduced to drugs by her friends and became addicted. Unfortunately, she was arrested by the police after weeks of secret investigation around the area of her boarding house.

In both of the above-described cases, Ratna and Arti lived in their parents-in-laws' houses which, though not prohibited, is culturally unacceptable in Bugis marriage. In spite of the fact that their husbands might have been able to stand on their own feet (B. *nalaoanni aléna*) to support their own families, both Nasir and Basir were the sole income providers in these families. While Ratna's parents had already passed away, Arti's were in Surabaya, so both of them had nowhere to go. Therefore, staying with the in-laws was the only practical arrangement for both women.

There was inter-ethnic tension in Arti's marriage because of her Javanese identity, an aspect which is not just related to the norms of Bugis marriage, but also to the social status of the family. If Arti had been a Bugis, the circumstances would probably have been different. Both cases involve women's drug use after a failed marriage.

Sexual Adventurism: A Case of a High-Ranking Official

> Sexual adventurism among high-ranking government officials is rampant. The openness of it reflects a confidence that can only be born of power. It is a public secret that many high officials, whose marriages may or may not be shaky, keep mistresses or have more than one wife.
>
> SURYAKUSUMA 1996:115

Sexual adventurism among civil servants has become common in Indonesia. Despite both high and low ranking officials being involved in this practice, high ranking officials have more control than lower ones because the lives of the former are more visible publicly (Suryakusuma 1996:113). Despite being controversial, there is no doubt that this sexual adventurism happens across the archipelago. Many wives know that their husbands are involved in such affairs, but they act as if it is not happening.[19] Suryakusuma indicates four types of marital patterns among government officials: dominant husband, overpowered husband, hypocritical husband, and understanding couple, and the first and the third are the most common types (Suryakusuma 1996:111).

In 2000, there was a very public case involving a high-ranking official in Makassar. Despite the controversy as to whether this was a business relationship or a love affair between *Pak* Dahlan and *Nyonya* Rahmi[20]—a high-class, married, business woman—the case was considered to be the hottest court hearing in Makassar in 2000. The newspaper *Fajar* (26 December 2000)

---

19 Personal interview with a number of female civil servants and the wives of civil servants in Makassar at different times during my fieldwork in 2000.

20 *Nyonya* is a term of address similar to Mrs in English, but it is usually used as the title for middle class married women.

highlighted the case in a news story that carried the headline 'The Pleasure that Ended in Misery' (I. *Nikmat Itu Akhirnya Membawa Sengsara*).

Drawing on Suryakusuma's theory of marital patterns, *Pak* Dahlan was regarded as a hypocritical husband by people who witnessed the court hearings and people who talked about the case when it became heated. He maintained the welfare of his family, treated his wife well, but secretly had a business affair with another woman. Some people pitied him because such situations are common, but his behaviour became public knowledge.

The affair was revealed when *Pak* Dahlan reported his business partner, *Nyonya* Rahmi, to the police on the grounds of business deception. Despite this, the jealousy of *Pak* Dahlan towards *Nyonya* Rahmi's relationship with a male inferior—*Nyonya* Rahmi's assistant in her business office—was as heated as the report of her professional deception. He displayed his jealousy when he found *Nyonya* Rahmi was chauffeured by her assistant. In response, *Nyonya* Rahmi stated that she had been physically abused by *Pak* Dahlan because of his jealousy, and that he had tainted her name as a successful business woman (*Fajar*, 2 June 2000 and *Berita Kota Makassar*, 3 June 2000).

There was much gossip about this affair. *Nyonya* Dahlan—*Pak* Dahlan's wife—was an 'old fashioned' Bugis woman who enjoyed social status as the wife of a high ranking official and as a hajj, an additional achieved status. *Pak* Dahlan was a successful Bugis man who was at the peak of his career (I. *puncak karir*), but more importantly, he was in the stage of his second puberty (*puber kedua*) and received too 'little attention' from his wife. During the court hearing, people commented on *Nyonya* Rahmi's appearance: 'Look at her, she is beautiful, it is understandable that *Pak* Dahlan is interested in her' (*Lihat, dia cantik, pantas Pak* Dahlan *tertarik*). Beauty is considered crucial for a business woman for the smooth operation of the business. Thus, the adultery of *Pak* Dahlan was considered by many as a 'reasonable act,' given his wife's unremarkable appearance. What really mattered, however, was the notion that his wife was no longer 'compatible' with *Pak* Dahlan's sexual needs given his *puber kedua*. Since taking another wife was 'restricted' according to PP10/1983, *Pak* Dahlan's secret affair could be understood by society at large as the expression of male human nature. *Pak* Dahlan needed more than one woman to satisfy his sexual desires (see Sunindyo 1996), especially because a man of his age (around 50) is regarded as having a second youth (*puber kedua*).

As a Bugis man with a high-ranking position, however, many criticisms were directed at *Pak* Dahlan not just by people who attended the court hearings, but also by other people who talked about the case, such as he was not grateful to God (I. *kurang bersyukur*), he did not achieve balance between this world and the hereafter (*tidak menyeimbangkan antara kehidupan dunia and akhirat*), or he did not balance his inner and outer aspects (*Pak* Dahlan *tidak menyeimbangkan antara kehidupan lahir and batinnya*).

From these points of view, it is assumed that *Pak* Dahlan reached high social standing in society as a high-ranking official, but his inner life had been neglected. The case which resulted in him losing his social status, was a warning for him that he should have a balanced life. Similarly *Nyonya* Rahmi had gained social status because of her successful business, but later lost it because of the disclosure of the affair. A Bugis aphorism states that 'the biggest enemy is desire' (B. *musu pong maraja ianaritu napesué*) to which people often replied that was 'because she/he follows her/his desires and passions' (*nasaba' cinna manisa sibawa napesunna naturusi*). This implies that both *Pak* Dahlan and *Nyonya* Rahmi fell into misery as a result of being unable to control *cinna* and *napesu*, two Bugis terms for desire.[21]

It is interesting to note that while *Pak* Dahlan denied the affair, *Nyonya* Rahmi admitted it, and it was attested to by three witnesses in court: a maid, a female cook in the rented house they used for their rendezvous, and a security guard in *Nyonya* Rahmi's business office. All these witnesses were from *Nyonya* Rahmi's side and all of their testimony attested to the affair between *Pak* Dahlan and *Nyonya* Rahmi (*Fajar*, 17 November 2000). More than that, *Nyonya* Rahmi claimed that the money given to her by *Pak* Dahlan was not for her business, but constituted a gift in the context of their love affair (*Fajar*, 4 January 2001). *Pak* Dahlan's denial resulted in commotion in the court hearing with the audience screaming and expressing cynicism in the local expression: [*Pak* Dahlan] forgot that he had fallen in love at first sight [with *Nyonya* Rahmi] (I. *lupa mi sedeng jatuh cinta pada pandangan pertama*) (*Fajar*, 15 September 2000).

Despite the fact that people blamed *Pak* Dahlan for his attitude, people felt pity for him because the case risked his reputation and position, blame was also apportioned to the women, a theme we have seen recur with civil servant's wives. Both *Nyonya* Dahlan and *Nyonya* Rahmi were regarded as 'bad wives' (see Sunindyo 1996:137–138). While *Nyonya* Dahlan was considered as lacking in her attention to her husband (*kurang servis*), *Nyonya* Rahmi was seen as a sinful wife who used her beauty to 'cheat' on her husband in the name of business.

Such an affair was not unique. What made the case special was that it attracted media fascination on the basis of a high class business affair, and the case blew up because of *Pak* Dahlan's report to the police and his jealousy. Thus, many argued that many other cases of adultery among high-ranking civil

21 *Cinna* and *napesu* are inseparable, as if because *cinna* exists, *napesu* is activated.

servants in Makassar were protected by this affair, and that *Pak* Dahlan was a protective agent (*tumbal*) who was victimised (*yang dikorbankan*). This argument was based on the assumption that if he had not become the protective agent (*tumbal*) in this case, many other cases might have been made public.

The governor of South Sulawesi commented in this case that he would not defend an inferior who was found guilty, and that administrative sanctions would be imposed (*Fajar*, 26 December 2000), though he did not clarify what he meant by guilty or sanction. According to one source, there was a deal between *Pak* Dahlan and his superior that if the court proved he was guilty, *Pak* Dahlan would leave his position or he would work out the case with *Nyonya* Rahmi by peaceful means (*jalan damai*) in order to close the case and save himself from more shame. *Pak* Dahlan attempted to secure a resolution (*jalan damai*) through a delegate when *Nyonya* Rahmi was in the hospital after being arrested for the deception, but she refused (*Fajar*, 19 July 2000). According to the protocols for PP No. 10 (Article 15:1), *Pak* Dahlan's behaviour warranted that he should be admonished (*ditegur*) by his superior when he was found guilty because of his no-longer-secret infidelity, and subject to administrative sanction, and asked to leave his position.

In addition, the governor intended to show the public that such affairs were not 'tolerated' among respected high class officials who were to be the model for the rest of the society. What is unclear in this case is whether or not *Pak* Dahlan and *Nyonya* Rahmi continued the affair. But according to one source, the resolution (I. *jalan damai*) that was suggested by his superior was actually used by *Pak* Dahlan as a way to continue the affair 'behind the scenes' and to muzzle public opinion (*meredam opini publik*) on the case.

When the case was heated, the only response from *Nyonya* Dahlan was that she—along with others, probably members of her family—came to the rendezvous rented house and ran amuck (*mengamuk*), by stoning it. I never heard whether she reported the case to her husband's superior to save her marriage, or sought the intervention of *Dharma Wanita*. PP No.10/1983, which was aimed to protect the wives of civil servants against legal divorce and polygynous marriage. In fact, PP10 does not regulate sexual infidelity (Suryakusuma 1996:113). The only sanction for such behaviour stated in the PP No.10/1983 is by admonition, whether or not the governor acted under the PP10, it can be assumed that his suggestion for resolution was an admonition for *Pak* Dahlan. Therefore, *Pak* Dahlan would not be affected by the PP No.10/1983 in this case because he did not marry *Nyonya* Rahmi. Ironically, *Nyonya* Dahlan was socially criticised that she was not able to serve her husband and that her inadequacy caused his affair.

There is a euphemism frequently uttered in response to adultery in Makassar—*asal kembali botol*—which roughly means let him go to another woman, as long as he brings his bottle home. The 'bottle' is the husband's penis, which indicates that he is still the husband when he is at home. Even though reference to the penis may suggest that it is the wife's 'sexual property,' this phrase actually has more to do with economic considerations than sexual desire. In that sense, returning the 'bottle' home may not threaten the wife's social status or welfare, as she is officially a legal wife, compared with if the husband taking a second wife (see Suryakusuma 1996:115). This 'silent understanding' is, to some extent, a way 'to tolerate' the sexual adventurism of the husband.[22]

One can see a sexual double standard in the case of *Pak* Dahlan and *Nyonya* Rahmi. Despite the fact that a sexual relationship outside marriage is considered bad, as long as it is covered up, it can be tolerated. Once it becomes public, however, the man usually denies his involvement (Suryakusuma 1996:117), or if he admits involvement, claims it was because of his male nature that he became involved in such relations (Suryakusuma 1996:135). Therefore, it is excusable for men to have extramarital relations. Even though *Nyonya* Rahmi initially denied the affair (*Fajar*, 3 June 2000), in the end she bravely acknowledged it, which meant she risked her marriage and her reputation as a high class business woman. This is because she thought nothing more could be done (I.: *terlanjur basah*) (*Fajar*, 26 December 2000). People joked about her admission that 'instead of paying the money back to *Pak* Dahlan, it is better to accept the love affair' (*dari pada disuruh bayar, lebih baik mengakui kisah cinta*). Thus, admitting the affair is a way of avoiding return of the money which was approximately Rp450.000.000,- (US$45,000 at current exchange rates). In contrast, people commented in Bugis of *Pak* Dahlan: 'Greed makes people have nothing' (B. *Ngowa kékéla sapu ripale' acappurenna*) because he was not grateful to God (*dé'na mappasikua*).

Conclusion

Violence against women has attracted more media attention, in local as well as national newspapers, as well as research–based publication, especially after the fall of Suharto in 1998.[23] Furthermore, the willingness of the society to deal

22 Similar finding from the study of Thai society on extramarital behaviour of Thai men. Thai women prefer their husbands to have extramarital relations with prostitutes than take another wife, and act as if nothing is wrong in their marriages (Saengtienchai et al. 1999).

23 See, for example, Nurul Ilmi Idrus and Bennett (2003), Zohra A. Baso and Nurul Ilmi Idrus (2002) and Blackburn (1999a).

with such violence has become more common, even though it is still far from ideal and has not necessarily led to high levels of community awareness to report violence in the household.

Women who are the victims of violence in the home cannot easily get away from their violent husbands, because of, for example, economic dependence. From the cases I presented in this chapter, we can see variations in how women, families and communities deal with such violence. Some find themselves in violent situations without any help, like Agustina's burning and Satirah's death. Other cases are brought to the Pengadilan Agama, but they do not always end in divorce. The custody of children, child support, or the apologies of husbands in court are among the considerations taken into account, as I observed in courts.

Cases from the Pengadilan Agama in Makassar, specifically those of Sartiah and Imah, are also distinct. Even though Sartiah wanted a divorce, she had to accept reconciliation because her husband was contrite. I observed in both the Pengadilan Agama in Sidrap and in Makassar, that if a husband expresses contrition regarding the divorce, judges will 'turn a blind eye' to the reasons for divorce in order to reunite the couple, even if the wife still wants a divorce. Imah had to deal with her problem alone before getting moral support from her parents. She had to attend repeated court hearings because the apologies of her husband were taken more seriously than her complaints of ill-treatment. While in Imah's case, the divorce was granted, this was not the case for Sartiah because of the objections of her child.

For lower class women, like Nurasmi and Hasniah selected from LBH-P2I, the support for their children has become their primary concern since Nurasmi's home food stall or Hasniah's work as a seamstress was not enough for their basic needs. Thus, they avoided acting assertively in order to get financial support for their children.

The three lower class female prisoners, Sairah, Ratna, and Arti, were similar in terms of stigmatization by their in-laws. Even though Sairah stayed in the nuclear family residence, her status as a stepmother, the interference of her in-laws, and her husband's wife from his first marriage, were the sources of conflict in her marriage. Ratna who was not a virgin at marriage and worked in a hotel and Arti who was a 'Javanese wife' (B. *bainé jawa-jawa*), stayed with their in-laws in virilocal residence, which is not prohibited but is considered unusual and undesirable in Bugis marriage.

The importance of kinship ties in Bugis marriage, as reflected in the term *siala* (to take each other) makes marriage with non-Bugis (*tennia to ugiq*) potentially unstable. Even though marrying out is not forbidden, it may raise ethnic suspicion in regard to outsiders family values, as discussed in the case of

Nurasmi marrying a Javanese man (Parto) and Basir marrying a Javanese woman (Arti). Regardless of how the couple get married (such as *silariang* or marriage by proposal), when the couple have marital conflict, women received at least moral support from their family, reinforcing the view that marriage is about kin ties.

Employment may be a potential conflict between the couple, as discussed for Nurasmi, Sartiah and Ratna. While Nurasmi's and Sartiah's employment resulted in on-going conflict with their husbands, Ratna's case is quite different from that of Nurasmi and Sartiah because her in-laws were the ones who problematised her employment in a hotel, rather than her husband. In fact, the objections of her mother-in-law became the impetus for divorce.

Women's lack of awareness of their rights often makes them vulnerable to violence in the household. This vulnerability is particularly acute for illiterate women. Even when women have some familiarity with the Marriage Law and the PP10 (for civil servants), they do not really understand what is included in these laws. Thus, for women who are legally illiterate, rights are not a focus of concern; women's personal rights come after their wifely duties.

In rural areas, many women are not aware that they may object to a husband's polygynous marriage if there is no legal reason to take a second wife. The widespread 'textual interpretation' of the Qur'an that a man may marry up to four wives, regardless of the pre-requisites of plural marriage based on Islamic law, makes polygynous marriage permissible, though never idealised even for rich men, as I discussed in the previous chapter. In urban Makassar, taking a second wife or engaging in sexual infidelity is not a new phenomenon, but is often 'invisible'. Sexual infidelity amongst high-ranking officials is easily 'tolerated' by the society at large because of these officials' power, male sexual drive, and the view that such behaviour is a consequence of modernity. It is almost as if they are not powerful, machismo or modern if they do not cheat.

CHAPTER 8

The Ethnography of Marriage: Understanding Bugis Domestic Life

My initial inspiration to do an ethnography of marriage came from my previous study which dealt with sexual violence in marriage among the Bugis (Nurul Ilmi Idrus 1999 and 2001). I concluded that I needed an understanding of how gender relations among the Bugis is operated. My aim is to present an interpretation of Bugis social and sexual experience by examining gendered values, the notion of marriage and divorce, and marital violence using a well established tradition of analysis in order to provide an understanding of gender relations of contemporary Bugis society through an ethnography of marriage.

In Bugis, given that 'who you are' is more important than 'what your gender is,' the individual has to know her/his own 'place' (B. *naisseng onrona*). In other words, men and women are, first and foremost, stratified based on social location and personal achievement. Gender, however, makes a difference when it comes to political claims in public arenas.

The Bugis are socialised according to gender in relation to *siriq* (shame or honour). Single men and women realise that women are expected to remain close to the house, while men are free to move in an extensive radius. Women should be easily controlled by their families, so outside the home they may be unprotected and, most importantly, their behaviour can threaten family honour.

For the Bugis, sexuality is regulated by Islam and local values, based on written manuscripts (*lontaraq*) and oral traditions (many derived from *lontaraq*) revealed by elders. Male and female sexuality is understood in terms of the expression and repression of desire respectively, a central theme in sex-related *lontaraq*, like *Lontaraq Assikalaibinéngeng*. This manuscript describes the passivity of women in sexual intercourse and dictates that women should not express more desire than men; this dichotomy is expressed in everyday life amongst the Bugis.

In addition, the epic poem La Galigo illustrates the desire of Batara Lattuq in contrast to the desire of his wife, Wé Datu Sengngeng, to 'sell herself dear' (I. *jual mahal*). It is not that the desiring attitude of Batara Lattuq is the concern of this epic, but it is the self control of his wife in relation to Batara Lattuq, which at the same time provokes his sexual desire. This dynamic reflects the notion that women are expected to be passive though they can be active agents

 | DOI 10.1163/9789004311947_009

in controlling men's expression of sexual desire, while paradoxically repressing their own. For single women, expressing sexuality is dangerous whether or not it is expressed openly. Even though marriage is the culturally and religiously legitimated context for heterosexual cohabitation, wives have to behave according to 'appropriate' manners, that is, they must be modest (*malebbiq*), even with their husbands.

The dangerous character of women's sexuality is reflected in a number of symbols, sayings, aphorisms, and also in the social surveillance that women are subjected to from childhood through puberty and during courtship. Despite the fact that men's sexuality is also regarded as dangerous, it is often attributed to men's nature; it is women who have to avoid contact with men as much as possible to control the inherent danger of men's sexuality.

In rural areas, the social surveillance of courtship is very strong, though courtship is permitted following a marriage proposal. In other cases, it is a source of conflict between parents and children. While courtship can thus be negotiated, single women who are never courted are regarded as more virtuous than women who have had courtship experience, though in urban areas attitudes to courtship are more flexible.

Sexuality and gender relations in marriage are influenced by Islamic teaching and local values, including how men and women should relate to each other, and the rights and duties of husbands and wives. This is illustrated in a *lontaraq* with a theme of marital relations, called *Daramatasia*. This narrative strongly emphasises the obedience of a wife to her husband and pronounces such obedience as religious duty. Such values circulate in the everyday lives of the Bugis and in texts, but are more common in popular idioms and everyday practices.

The fundamental objective of marriage for men and women is based on 'local Islamic values' that emphasise the importance of reproduction. In spite of the importance of reproduction for both men and women, the aspirations for marriage vary between the sexes. Single men and women have their own ideal characteristics for prospective spouses. In spite of the fact that the most important quality for an ideal spouse is piety (B. *pagama*) for both men and women, single women in Kulo emphasise men's financial competence, expressed in the phrase: 'as long as he has a job' (*assalaq engka jama-jamanna*); men's ideals for prospective wives is expressed in terms of obedience in the sense that 'she understands me' (I. *dia mengerti saya*). Even though both sexes do not express strong preferences in regard to the prospective spouse's level of education, single women expect to have a spouse who is better educated than themselves. A desire for physical attractiveness in a prospective wife is openly expressed by men, which explains why women guard their beauty. In contrast, single women have a negative view of men's physical attractiveness, fearing that it may result in sexual infidelity after marriage.

However, given that social status is so important for the Bugis, the match has to be considered in terms of whether the prospective bride and groom are 'proper' (B. *sekapuq*) or 'improper' (*tessikapuq*) according to measures of descent and/or social achievement.

Marriage for the Bugis is understood to be a union between two families, as a united family, termed *siala*. The importance of kinship prior to marriage is demonstrated in the way that the whole family considers the prospective spouses and the timing of marriage. While marriage to non-Bugis is not prohibited, the fear of bringing alien values into the family explains why marriage with non-Bugis (*tennia to ugiq*) is not favoured by elders. When marriages experience conflict, differences in ethnic identity are used as a 'scapegoat', as illustrated in the stories of Nurasmi's violent husband and Arti's conflict with female in-laws discussed in Chapter 7. In marriage, the family plays an important role in guiding couples efforts to manage marital life, including their expected behaviours in marriage, and how to deal with conflict, divorce and reconciliation.

The burden of 'taking care' of daughters reveals why parents have to 'hold their breath' if there are still unmarried daughters in the house and reflects the justification for early marriage, especially in rural areas. On the other hand, the opportunity to attend school and participate in wage labour explains why later age at marriage is becoming more common, particularly in urban areas. Even though the opportunity for education is not gendered, depending on the capabilities of children and parents' financial capacity, women often discontinue their studies after marriage, especially in rural areas.

Age difference is important in marital relations of the Bugis. The ideal of an older man and a younger woman is not just related to the view that women age more quickly than men, but also reflects social hierarchy between a husband and wife, which is understood as akin to the relationship between big brother (B. *kakaq oroané*) and little sister (*anri makkunrai*) (the terms *kakaq* and *anri* are used to address older and younger siblings).

The complementarity of gender differences is reflected in marriage in the identification of wives with the house (*to ri bola*) and husbands with the public domain as income providers and protectors of the family (*pangngulu bola*) from the dangers of the outside world. Even though this indicates a clear-cut division of labour between husband and wife, it is by no means expressed as a superior/inferior positioning in conjugal relations. The relationship between husband and wife is complementary: men and women play their respective roles in the domestic as well as public domains. However, the influence of the New Order development ideology, identifying the husband as head of the family (I. *kepala keluarga*) and the wife as mother of the household (*ibu rumah tangga*) has led to a rigidity in the dichotomous association of men with the public sphere and women with the domestic sphere. In the socialization of the children, the father trains his son to be the head of the household and the mother plays the role of agent in the reproduction of gendered structural inequality.

The local ideology of gender relations, which emphasises women's motherhood, seems to be enjoyed by women in the village. Bugis women have their own ways of expressing their power by maintaining their husbands' social prestige and the social status of their families. While men's incomes go to maintain the family, women's incomes are used for their own expenses, which is expressed in a phrase: 'your money is my money, my money is mine', and for enhancing family status. This reflects that a wife is a money manager in the household, though both income is combined as family income.

Even though women are idealised as passive, they exercise agency in many situations. They can act in *siriq* situations, arrangement of marriage, divorce and remarrying, money management, or in violent situations. In a *siriq* situation, if no man acts as a *to masiriq*, a woman can substitute for a male defender, as discussed in Sahariah's story in Chapter 2. In divorce cases, women sometimes act as if they do not want a divorce in order to slow down the process and to inhibit their husband's remarriages. Women can also sue for divorce. 'Bringing herself' (B. *Najjuluang aléna*) is another example of how women exercise agency; a woman can also bring herself to a man in order to be married, usually through illegal marriage (I. *kawin liar*) if the consent of her family is difficult to obtain.

In their roles as money managers in the household, women control not just the husbands' salary, but they can also take loans through banks which are paid through the husband's salary. In a violent household, when a woman is sick of her husband's abusive behaviour, she can strategise to keep her husband away from her and prevent him from returning to the home, so she can peacefully enjoy her life with her children. But such action can only occur when women are not financially dependent on their husbands.

Bugis couples retain individual ownership of property brought to the marriage. Property acquired during the marriage is considered common property (*harta bersama* or *harta gono-gini*). In the case of divorce, the couple may claim property rights through the Religious Court (I. Pengadilan Agama) at the time of divorce or they can make a separate claim afterwards. Otherwise, property is divided by mutual agreement. While in law, common property is shared equally following the divorce (KHI, Chapter 13: 97), the practice is more complicated, as I observed a number of times in the Religious Court.

Apart from marriage, inheritance for men and women is based on the ratio 'two to one' (2:1) which is identical with the local custom (adat), expressed in a euphemism: 'men are carrying on the shoulders, women are carrying above their heads' (B. *mallémpaq oroané, majjujung makkunrai*). While carrying on the shoulders (B. *mallémpaq*) contains the connotation of 'two parts', the 'left' and the 'right' shoulders, carrying above the head (*majjujung*) indicates 'one' thing on her head. In practice, inheritance is shared equally, or the sharing is decided on a case-by-case basis.

Women's lack of awareness about their marital rights underscores their vulnerability in conjugal relations related to polygyny, divorce, and/or violence. Many women involved in this study have been subjected to their husbands' polygynous marriages without their consent and also denied ongoing financial support.

Since an ideal marriage is a monogamous lifelong union, no matter how capable a man is of maintaining a polygynous marriage, it can never be comparable to the ideal of monogamous marriage. The Bugis philosophy that 'as long as a man can feed each of his wives and children' (*sampang naullé mui panréi anaq binéna*), which emphasises economic needs, it never works in reality.

There is on-going debate about the religious legitimation of marriage across the archipelago, and the debate in South Sulawesi deals with whether or not marriage is legitimated with or without principles (I. *rukun*) and prerequisites (*syarat*). Marriage without *rukun* and *syarat* is what people in South Sulawesi generally call 'wild marriage' (*kawin liar*).

The majority of people realised that *kawin liar* is illegal because it is not registered by the state. However, some people use this type of marriage as an alternative to legitimate cohabitation in order to avoid the legal requirements surrounding polygynous marriages, especially for government officials. Others use it as an easier way to get divorced (*cerai liar*) and to remarry illegally (*kawin liar*) in order to re-establish their marital status after a long period of separation (*status tergantung*). In such cases, there is no legal way for a previous wife or husband officially to claim their rights because the marriage is unregistered. A woman who is married by *kawin liar*, as opposed to state-recognised forms of legal marriage, without her knowledge and consent eventually recognises that she has been deceived by her husband when she files for divorce. In *kawin liar*, whether or not marriages are implemented with their consent, women are not always the victims because it is also a condition in which women can exercise agency, as I demonstrated in Chapter 6.

Divorce is officially regulated by Islam through the 1974 Marriage Law based on the principle quoted from a Hadith that 'divorce is legal, but is hated by Allah.' Therefore, divorce is prevented as much as possible. The lengthy procedure of legal divorce, however, can be facilitated by *imam liar*, through illegal divorce (*cerai liar*), which is just as easy as *kawin liar*. The simplicity of *kawin liar* allows husbands to leave their wives without even going through illegal divorce (*cerai liar*). In any case, *cerai liar* is implemented either if a neglected wife intends to marry another man or if she wants to have a socially recognised divorce to clarify her marital status. In other words, she has written proof (*hitam di atas putih*) of divorce, regardless of its legality.

For the Bugis, patterns of residence after marriage can vary for a number of reasons: financial capability, childcare, or personal attachment of a wife to her mother and siblings. In spite of the fact that the couple can live uxorilocally or virilocally, uxorilocal residence is the most common type. The usual explanation for uxorilocal residence is that it avoids conflict between daughters-in-law and mothers-in-law.

Female virginity at marriage is highly valued by the Bugis, and it is one of the most important pre-requirements of a prospective bride. Her virginity has to be ascertained before she is proposed to, that is, during the phase of preliminary inquiry (B. *mammanuq-manuq*). Premarital pregnancy leading to marriage may become a source of conflict between a wife and her in-laws, as in the case of Ratna in Chapter 7, and such marriages sometimes end in divorce. Women who experience premarital pregnancy are subject to social stigma as if the pregnancy is solely her own responsibility, as reflected in the story of Nadirah in Chapter 2. In this case, Nadirah's talent as a wedding decorator and the other skills she used to earn money made her an independent woman and not fully isolated from society.

Growth in opportunities for women in the labour force have not been accompanied by social acceptance of all the types of employment women are involved in. Certain jobs, such as working in a hotel, are evaluated negatively and women who work in such places have a continuing dilemma, as to whether to continue work, to find another job, or just quit.

Wives who work outside the home have to be 'super mums' if they do not want to be called 'bad wives'. However, an overly powerful wife can result in the stigmatization of her 'weak husband' because of his inability to control his wife's behaviour in public. Thus, a working wife not only has to make sure that her domestic 'duties' are properly managed, but also has to maintain her reputation as a 'good wife'. Even a domestically dominant wife like *Ibu* Farida, illustrated in Chapter 4, depends on the assistance of her domestic helper in the house to ensure the balance of her domestic and public roles as a middle class female trader (B. *pajjakarta*), to protect her reputation as a 'good wife'. In other words, women have to maintain an equilibrium in their 'dual role', which is nationally termed *peran ganda*.

One of the key contributions of this ethnography has been to continue to disrupt the silence that surrounds violence against Indonesian women in the private sphere. At the national level, the public attention given to gender-based violence has increased following the May riots in 1998. For instance, a public campaign for equality between the sexes was advertised on one of the private TV channels by the Ministry of Women's Empowerment under Khofifah Indar Parawansa (during the Abdurrahman Wahid presidency) with the popular slogan: 'Women and men are different, but it does not mean that they can be treated differently' (I. *laki-laki dan perempuan memang beda, tapi bukan berarti dapat dibeda-bedakan*). Khofifah Indar Parawansa, in collaboration with Women's NGOs, declared a 'Zero Tolerance Policy' towards violence against women in January 1999, as an initial collaboration between government and civil society.

However, the growing visibility of violence against women, and the increased political attention to the issue, has largely been due to the very public nature of the attacks on ethnically Chinese Indonesian women during the May riots in 1998 and other similar politically motivated attacks on women. While the visibility of such violence has created greater political will to address violence against women at a legislative level, the process of establishing a national board to combat violence against women is slow and on-going.

In 2004, during the presidency of Megawaty Sukarno Putri, the fifth president of Indonesia, after 11 years of effort, UU No. 23/2004 on Domestic Violence was finally out. In the beginning of the implementation of this regulation, however, many understood that this regulation is aimed to divorce marital couple as domestic violence was understood to only happen between husband and wife, neglecting other members of the family, including children and domestic helpers.

What is also needed to combat gender-based violence is an understanding of how such violence operates at the local level and is promoted by multiple ideologies and sectors of society. The silence that surrounds the most prevalent violence to which women are routinely subjected, that is violence in their families and intimate relationships, remains virtually unbroken in Indonesia (Manderson and Bennett 2003). My thesis has explored marriage in-depth to reveal how and why violence occurs against Bugis women, and to provide a convincing understanding of this violence that cannot simply be dismissed as unrepresentative of Bugis society in general.

By exploring Bugis notions of sexuality, gender and social location, and how these interact with *siriq*, I have revealed the complex role of custom (I. *adat*) in producing gender status and legitimating violence against women within some marriages. My discussion of Islam and its local meanings and practices for the Bugis has also demonstrated how gender biased interpretations of Islam can be used against married women, particularly in relation to their sexual autonomy in marriage. As both marital relations and marital violence in Bugis society are a product of how state ideology, religion and adat are interpreted at the family level, the solutions to combat such violence against women must also address each of these overlapping spheres of influence.

Bugis practices of gender, sexuality and marriage embody the tensions between adat, Islam, and the state. Thus, we cannot view adat and/or Islamic values simply as the enemies of modernising state ideology. As Boellstorff suggests, 'tradition' isn't the enemy: the modern gender ideologies set forth by contemporary nation-states can be just as oppressive as 'tradition' (2001:2). As a final point, this thesis has great potential value for the development of practical gender policies.

Appendix 4.1*

Lontaraq Daramatasia

Makkedani Nabitta, nigi-nigi makkunrai giling gandong nakana maélo' nanré lakkainna riwéréngngi décéng ri Allataala sitebbe' bilanna gandong nagilingngé. Makkeddai toi Nabitta, ***nigi-nigi makkunrai mannasuangngi lakkainna inanré ripabélaiangngi ri Allataala apinna ranaka.*** *Makkeda toi Nabitta, nigi-nigi tennungangngi nenia jaikangngi pakéng lakkainna ripappakéangettoi matti paké-pakéang malebbi'na risuruga. Makkeda toi Nabitta,* ***nigi-nigi makkunrai sessakengngi pakéanna lakkainna riaddampengangngi ri Allataala dosana padatoha paccinna pakéanna lakkaina nasessa'é.*** *Makkeda toi Nabitta, nigi-nigi makkunrai sara'-sarakangngi gemme'na lakkinna riwéréngngi appalang ri Allataala sitebbe' gemme'na lakkainna. Makkeda toi Nabitta, nigi-nigi makkunrai tuling mallauangngi décéng lakkainna, ripasiwolongpolongngi matti lakkainna ri suruga. Makkeda toi Nabitta, nigi-nigi makkunrai tuling cabberu-beru mitai lakkainna engkai matti micawa-cawa muttama suruga. Makkeda toi Nabitta, nigi-nigi makkunrai tuling mario pulana mitai lakkainna ripura saraiangngi ri Allataala onronna rilalenna surugaé. Makkeda toi Nabitta, nigi-nigi makkunrai masero mamaséiwi lakkainna sibawa natumaninginna tungke'-tungke' passuronna ripasiwollompollongngi matti lakkainna rilalenna surugaé sibawa ritumaningi toi ri ana' bidadarié.* ***Makkeda toi Nabitta, nigi-nigi makkunrai tuling mellauangngi décéne lakkainna ri esso ri wenni ritimpakengngi babanna surugaé.***

* The first numeral of the appendix refers to the chapter in which the topic is discussed.

 | DOI 10.1163/9789004311947_010

Appendix 4.2

Lontaraq Daramatasia

Makkeda toi ***Nabitta, nigi-nigi makkunrai maja' atinna ri lakkainna engkani matu' terri-terri muttama' ri naraka.*** *Makkeda toi Nabitta,* ***nigi-nigi makkunrai tuling macai'na rilakkainna riadémperangngi matti ri malaéka' muttama' riranaka.*** *Makkeda toi Nabitta, nigi-nigi makkunrai tuling majjamerru' dé'na madécéng nyawana mitai lakkainna ripasibokorengngi matti rupanna. Makkeda toi Nabitta,* ***nigi-nigi makkunrai mappolori lakkainna bettuanna pégau'i riséuaé gau' natennaisseng lakkainna ricallai matti rilalenna ranakaé*** *pada paccallana patappuloé tellolang.*

 | DOI 10.1163/9789004311947_011

Appendix 6.1

Certificate of Illegal Marriage (*Kawin Liar*) for Man

بسم الله الرحمن الرحيم

MARRIAGE CERTIFICATE

Day :
Date :
Time :

The akad nikah of a man has been implemented

Name :
Age :
Religion :
Occupation
Date of Birth

Akad nikah was implemented by the former Imam Dengeng - Dengeng Wanua BelawaE, Kecamatan Dug PituE

(UMMARAENG)

We fully acknowledge any risk resulting from this mariage

Stated by

(______________)

Photo 3 x 4 — MAN

Photo 3 x 4 — WOMAN

بسم الله الرحمن الرحيم

KUTIPANAKTA NIKAH

Pada hari :
Tgl./Bln. Thn. :
Pukul :

Telah dilangsungkan Akad Nikah Seorang :
Laki-Laki
Nama
Umur
Agama
Pekerjaan
T. Tgl. Lahir

Yang melaksanakan Akad Nikah bekas Imam Dengeng - dengeng Wanua BelawaE Kecamatan Dua PituE

(UMMARENG)

Benar - benar menanggung resiko, bertanggung jawab segala sesuatunya atas perkawinan mereka

Yang membuat pernyataan

(______________)

Foto 3 x 4 — PRIA

Foto 3 x 4 — WANITA

FIGURE 6.1A *English translation (above) and original in Bahasa Indonesia (below)*

 | DOI 10.1163/9789004311947_012

Certificate of Illegal Marriage (*Kawin Liar*) for Woman

بسم الله الرحمن الرحيم

MARRIAGE CERTIFICATE

Day :
Date :
Time :

The akad nikah of a **woman** has been implemented

Name :
Age :
Religion :
Occupation :
Date of Birth :

Akad nikah was implemented by the former Imam Dengeng - Dengeng Wanua BelawaE, Kecamatan Dug PituE

(**UMMARAENG**)

We fully acknowledge any risk resulting from this mariage

Stated by

( )

Photo 3 x 4 — MAN

Photo 3 x 4 — WOMAN

بسم الله الرحمن الرحيم

KUTIPAN AKTA NIKAH

Pada hari :
Tgl./Bln. Thn. :
Pukul :

Telah dilangsungkan Akad Nikah Seorang :
Perempuan
Nama :
Umur :
Agama :
Pekerjaan :
T. Tgl. Lahir :

Yang melaksanakan Akad Nikah bekas Imam Dengeng - Dengeng Wanua BelawaE Kecamatan Dua PituE

UMMARAENG)

Benar - benar menanggung resiko, bertanggung jawab segala sesuatunya atas perkawinan mereka

Yang membuat pernyataan

( )

Foto 3 x 4 — PRIA

Foto 3 x 4 — WANITA

FIGURE 6.1B *English translation (above) and original in Bahasa Indonesia (below)*

Appendix 6.2

Certificate of Legal Marriage for Husband

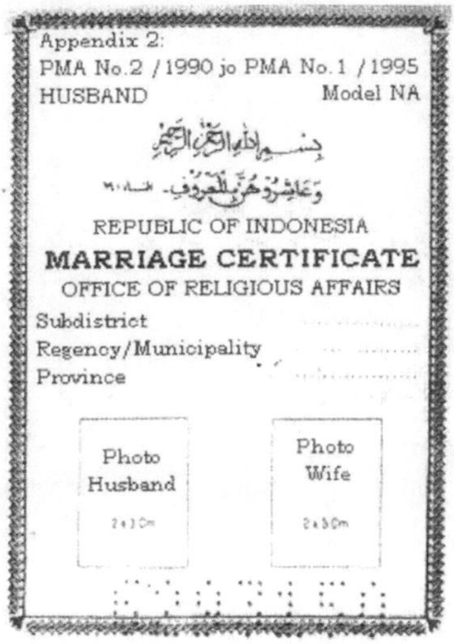
Appendix 2:
PMA No.2 / 1990 jo PMA No.1 / 1995
HUSBAND Model NA

بسم الله الرحمن الرحيم

وعاشروهن بالمعروف

REPUBLIC OF INDONESIA
MARRIAGE CERTIFICATE
OFFICE OF RELIGIOUS AFFAIRS
Subdistrict
Regency/Municipality
Province

Photo Husband

Photo Wife

SERI: MH

MARRIAGE CERTIFICATE

No: ..../........../........../

HUSBAND

Day : ....

Date : .... M

: .... H

The akad nikah of a man has been implemented

1 Name : ....
2 Family Name : ....
3 Date of Birth : ....
4 Citizenship : ....
5 Religion : ....
6 Address : ....
7 Status : ....
8 Occupation : ....

with a woman:

1 Name : ....
2 Family name : ....
3 Date of Birth : ....
4 Citizenship : ....
5 Religion : ....
6 Address : ....
7 Status : ....
8 Occupation : ....

with a wali nikah

1 Name : ....
2 Date of Birth : ....
3 Citizenship : ....
4 Religion : ....
5 Address : ....
6 Occupation : ....

As wali nasab / nakion
with a bridewealth which consist of:
....

in full / credit; with agreement = yes / no

after the akad nikah, the husband recites and signs taklik talak = yes / no

....
(date)
Quoted in accord with its original
KUA Kecamatan

....
Marriage Registrar

....
MP

FIGURE 6.2A *English Translation*

 | DOI 10.1163/9789004311947_013

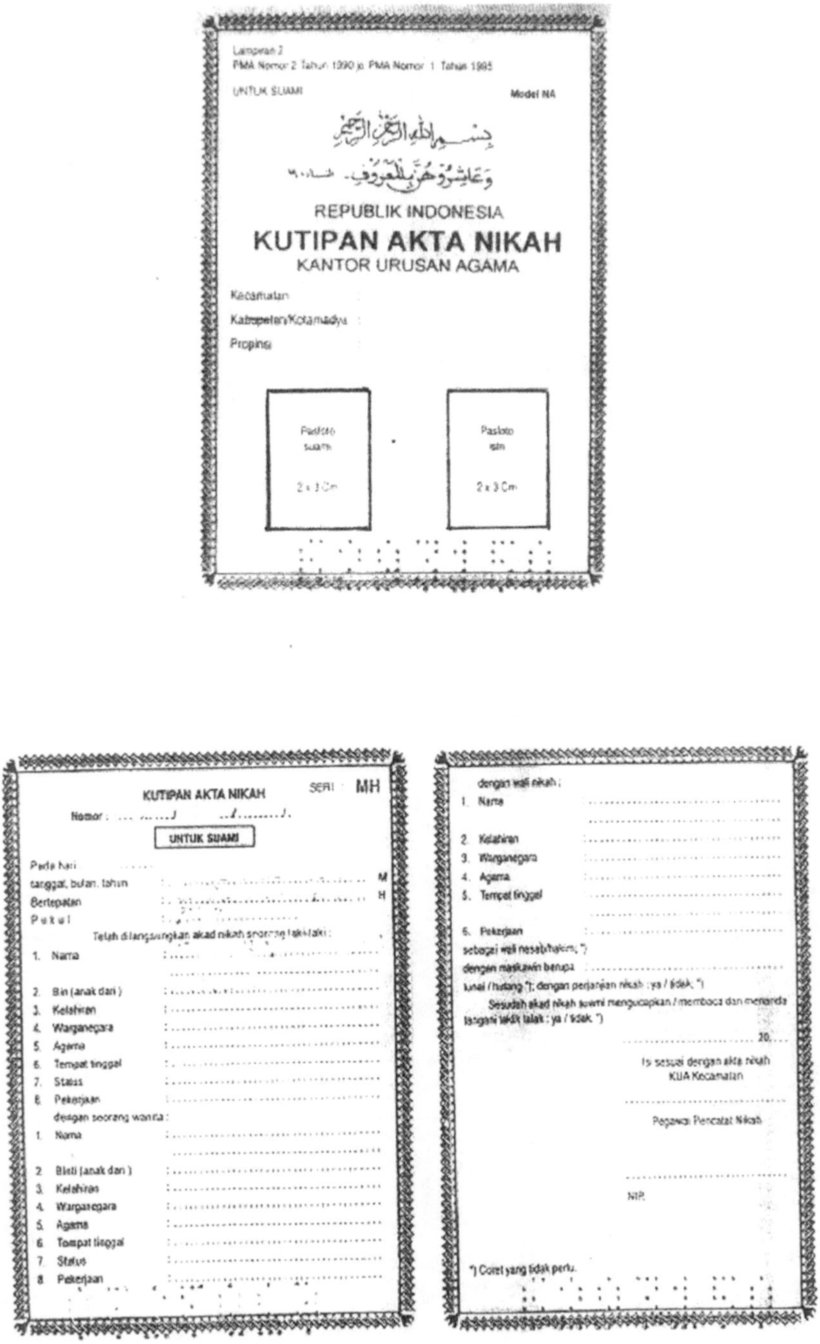

Lampiran 2
PMA Nomor 2 Tahun 1990 jo. PMA Nomor 1 Tahun 1995

UNTUK SUAMI Model NA

بسم الله الرحمن الرحيم

وعاشروهن بالمعروف - النساء ١٩

REPUBLIK INDONESIA

KUTIPAN AKTA NIKAH

KANTOR URUSAN AGAMA

Kecamatan

Kabupaten/Kotamadya :

Propinsi

Pasfoto suami 2 x 3 Cm

Pasfoto isteri 2 x 3 Cm

KUTIPAN AKTA NIKAH SERI : MH

Nomor : ..../........./.........

UNTUK SUAMI

Pada hari ....
tanggal, bulan, tahun : .... M
Bertepatan : .... H
P u k u l : ....

Telah dilangsungkan akad nikah seorang laki-laki :

1. Nama : ....
2. Bin (anak dari) : ....
3. Kelahiran : ....
4. Warganegara : ....
5. Agama : ....
6. Tempat tinggal : ....
7. Status : ....
8. Pekerjaan : ....

dengan seorang wanita :

1. Nama : ....
2. Binti (anak dari) : ....
3. Kelahiran : ....
4. Warganegara : ....
5. Agama : ....
6. Tempat tinggal : ....
7. Status : ....
8. Pekerjaan : ....

dengan wali nikah :

1. Nama ....
2. Kelahiran ....
3. Warganegara ....
4. Agama ....
5. Tempat tinggal ....
6. Pekerjaan : ....

sebagai wali nasab/hakim; *)
dengan maskawin berupa ....
tunai / hutang *); dengan perjanjian nikah : ya / tidak. *)

Sesudah akad nikah suami mengucapkan / membaca dan menanda tangani taklik talak : ya / tidak. *)

.... 20....

Isi sesuai dengan akta nikah
KUA Kecamatan

....

Pegawai Pencatat Nikah

....

NIP.

*) Coret yang tidak perlu.

FIGURE 6.2B *Original in Bahasa Indonesia*

Certificate of Legal Marriage for Wife

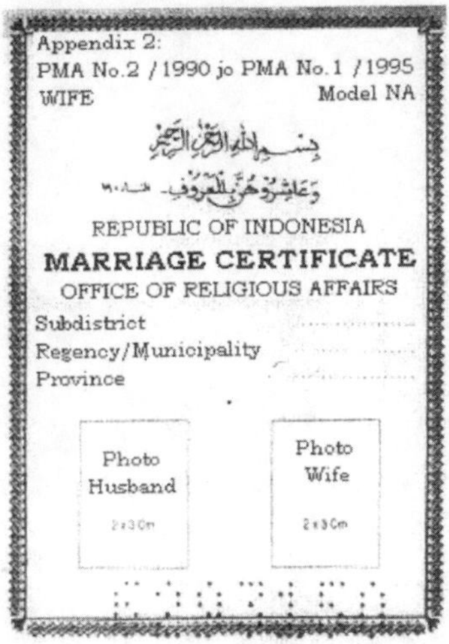

Appendix 2:
PMA No.2 / 1990 jo PMA No.1 / 1995
WIFE Model NA

بسم الله الرحمن الرحيم

وعاشروهن بالمعروف

REPUBLIC OF INDONESIA
MARRIAGE CERTIFICATE
OFFICE OF RELIGIOUS AFFAIRS
Subdistrict
Regency/Municipality
Province

Photo Husband 2x3Cm
Photo Wife 2x3Cm

SERI: MH

MARRIAGE CERTIFICATE
No: ..../........./........./
WIFE

Day :..................................
Date :.................................. M
:.................................. H

The akad nikah of a man has been implemented
1 Name :..................................
2 Family Name :..................................
3 Date of Birth :..................................
4 Citizenship :..................................
5 Religion :..................................
6 Address :..................................
7 Status :..................................
8 Occupation :..................................
with a man:
1 Name :..................................
2 Family name :..................................
3 Date of Birth :..................................
4 Citizenship :..................................
5 Religion :..................................
6 Address :..................................
7 Status :..................................
8 Occupation :..................................

with a wali nikah
1 Name :..................................
2 Date of Birth :..................................
3 Citizenship :..................................
4 Religion :..................................
5 Address :..................................
6 Occupation :..................................

As wali nasab / nakion
with a bridewealth which consist of:
....

in full / credit; with agreement = yes / no

after the akad nikah, the husband recites and signs
taklik talak = yes / no

....
(date)
Quoted in accord with its original
KUA Kecamatan

....
Marriage Registrar

....
MP

FIGURE 6.2C *English Translation*

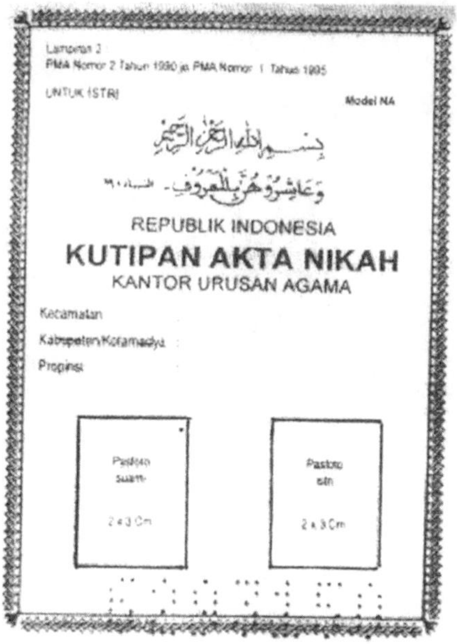

Lampiran 2 :
PMA Nomor 2 Tahun 1990 jo. PMA Nomor 1 Tahun 1995

UNTUK ISTRI

Model NA

بسم الله الرحمن الرحيم

وعاشروهن بالمعروف - النساء ١٩

REPUBLIK INDONESIA

KUTIPAN AKTA NIKAH

KANTOR URUSAN AGAMA

Kecamatan

Kabupaten/Kotamadya :

Propinsi

Pasfoto suami 2 x 3 Cm

Pasfoto istri 2 x 3 Cm

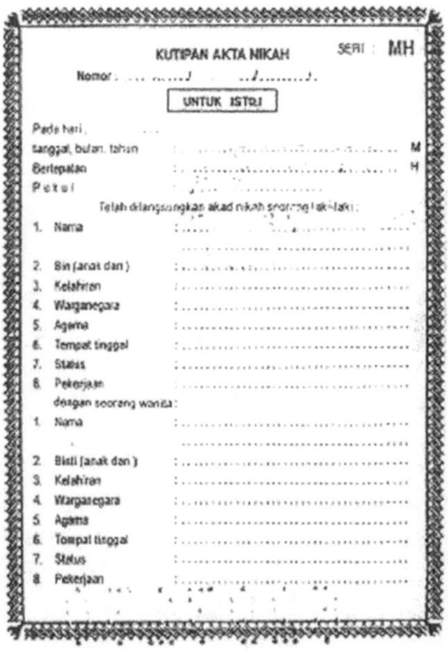

KUTIPAN AKTA NIKAH SERI : MH

Nomor : ..../........./.........

UNTUK ISTRI

Pada hari, ...

tanggal, bulan, tahun : .... M

Bertepatan : .... H

P u k u l : ....

Telah dilangsungkan akad nikah seorang laki-laki :

1. Nama : ....
2. Bin (anak dari) : ....
3. Kelahiran : ....
4. Warganegara : ....
5. Agama : ....
6. Tempat tinggal : ....
7. Status : ....
8. Pekerjaan ....

dengan seorang wanita :

1. Nama : ....
2. Bisti (anak dari) : ....
3. Kelahiran : ....
4. Warganegara : ....
5. Agama : ....
6. Tempat tinggal : ....
7. Status : ....
8. Pekerjaan : ....

dengan wali nikah :

1. Nama ....
2. Kelahiran : ....
3. Warganegara ....
4. Agama ....
5. Tempat tinggal ....
6. Pekerjaan : ....

sebagai wali nasab/hakim; *)

dengan maskawin berupa : ....

tunai / hutang *); dengan perjanjian nikah : ya / tidak; *)

Sesudah akad nikah suami mengucapkan / membaca dan menandatangani taklik talak : ya / tidak. *)

.... 20...

Isi sesuai dengan akta nikah
KUA Kecamatan

....

Pegawai Pencatat Nikah

....

NIP.

*) Coret yang tidak perlu.

FIGURE 6.2D *Original in Bahasa Indonesia*

Appendix 6.3

Certificate of Illegal Divorce (*Cerai Liar*) for Man

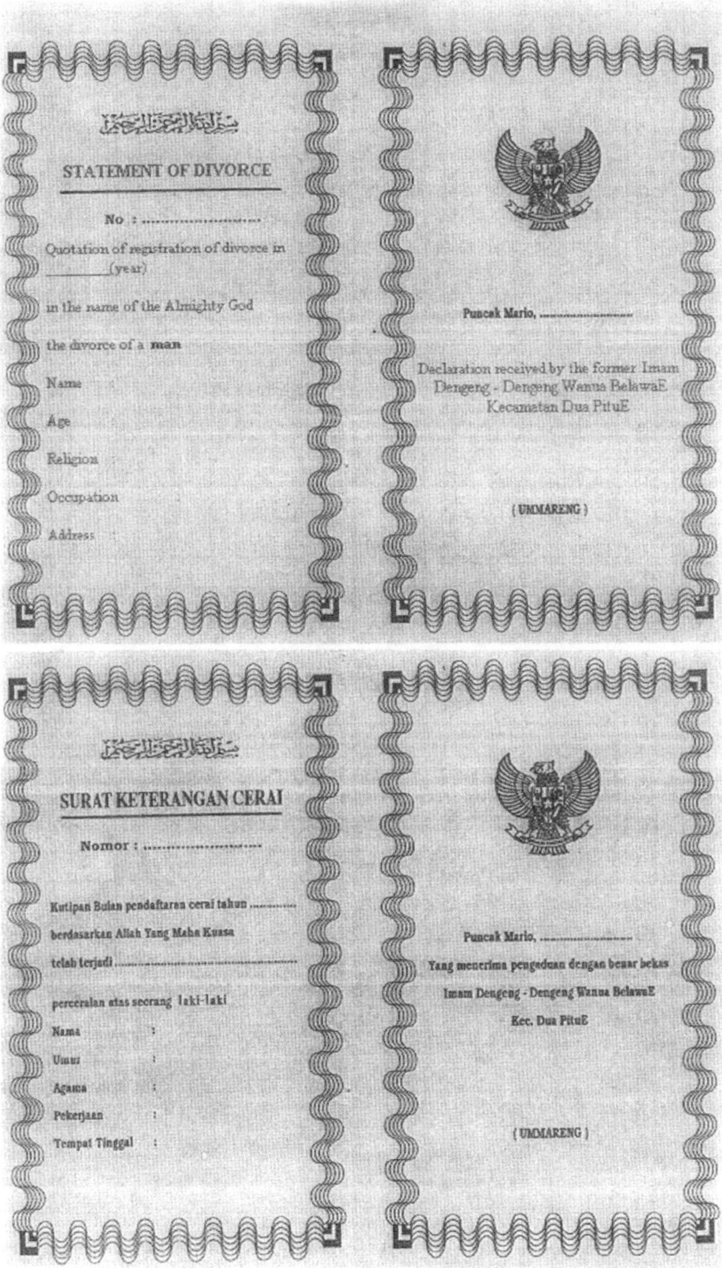

بسم الله الرحمن الرحيم

STATEMENT OF DIVORCE

No : ....

Quotation of registration of divorce in ________(year)

in the name of the Almighty God

the divorce of a **man**

Name

Age

Religion

Occupation

Address

Puncak Mario, ...

Declaration received by the former Imam Dengeng - Dengeng Wanua BelawaE Kecamatan Dua PituE

(UMMARENG)

بسم الله الرحمن الرحيم

SURAT KETERANGAN CERAI

Nomor : ....

Kutipan Bulan pendaftaran cerai tahun ....

berdasarkan Allah Yang Maha Kuasa

telah terjadi ....

perceraian atas seorang laki-laki

Nama :

Umur :

Agama :

Pekerjaan :

Tempat Tinggal :

Puncak Mario, ...

Yang menerima pengaduan dengan benar bekas Imam Dengeng - Dengeng Wanua BelawaE Kec. Dua PituE

(UMMARENG)

FIGURE 6.3A *English translation (above) and original in Bahasa Indonesia (below)*

 | DOI 10.1163/9789004311947_014

Certificate of Illegal Divorce (*Cerai Liar*) for Woman

بسم الله الرحمن الرحيم

STATEMENT OF DIVORCE

No : ....

Quotation of registration of divorce in ________(year)

in the name of the Almighty God

the divorce of a **woman**

Name :

Age :

Religion :

Occupation

Address

Puncak Mario, ...

Declaration received by the former Imam Dengeng - Dengeng Wanua BelawaE Kecamatan Dua PituE

(UMMARENG)

بسم الله الرحمن الرحيم

SURAT KETERANGAN CERAI

Nomor : ....

Kutipan Bulan pendaftaran cerai tahun ....

berdasarkan Allah Yang Maha Kuasa

telah terjadi ....

perceraian atas seorang perempuan

Nama :

Umur :

Agama :

Pekerjaan :

Tempat Tinggal :

Puncak Mario, ...

Yang menerima pengaduan dengan benar bekas Imam Dengeng - Dengeng Wanua BelawaE Kec. Dua PituE

(UMMARENG)

FIGURE 6.3B *English translation (above) and original in Bahasa Indonesia (below)*

Appendix 6.4

Certificate of Legal Divorce

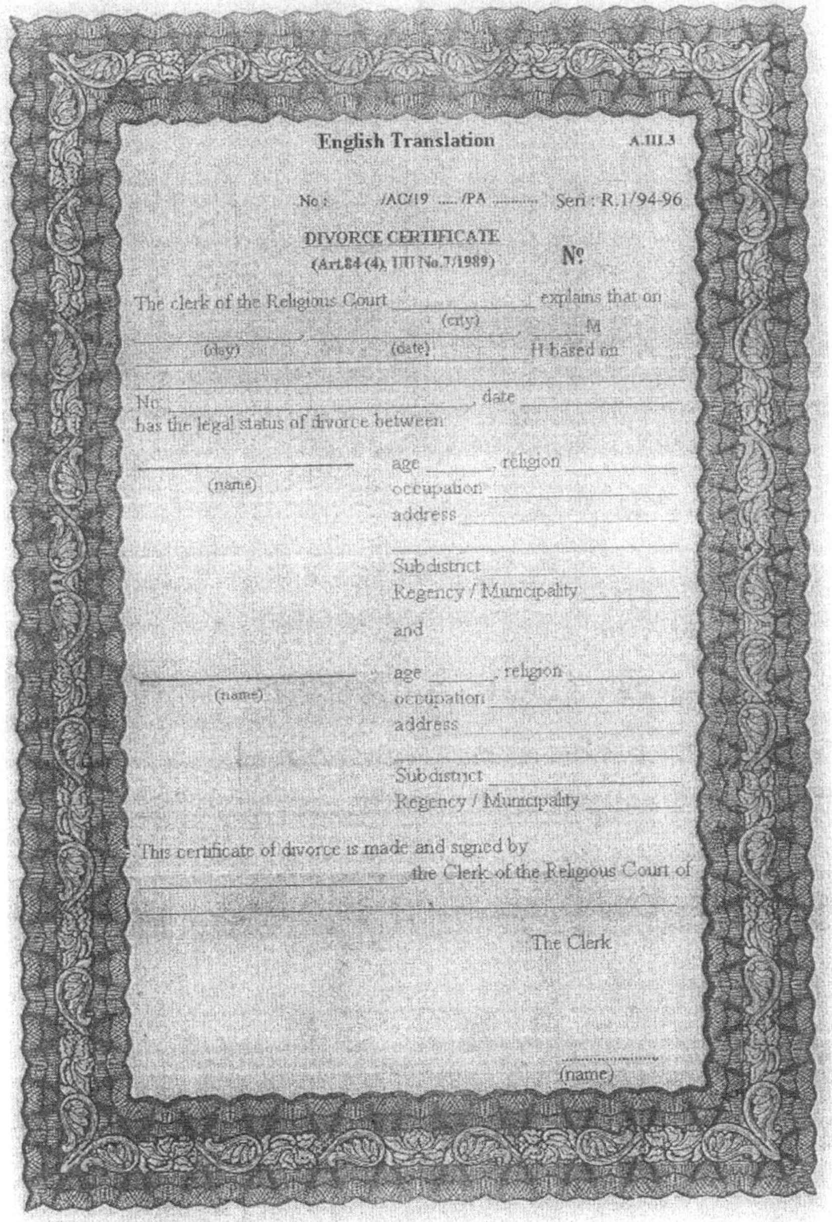

English Translation A.III.3

No : /AC/19 ..... /PA .... Seri : R.1/94-96

DIVORCE CERTIFICATE
(Art.84 (4), UU No.7/1989) №

The clerk of the Religious Court ______________ explains that on
(city)
______________, ______________, ______ M
(day) (date) H based on
____
No ______________________, date ______________
has the legal status of divorce between

______________ age ______, religion ______________
(name) occupation ______________
address ______________
____
Subdistrict ______________
Regency / Municipality ______________

and

______________ age ______, religion ______________
(name) occupation ______________
address ______________
____
Subdistrict ______________
Regency / Municipality ______________

This certificate of divorce is made and signed by
______________ the Clerk of the Religious Court of
____

The Clerk

....
(name)

FIGURE 6.4A *English Translation*

 | DOI 10.1163/9789004311947_015

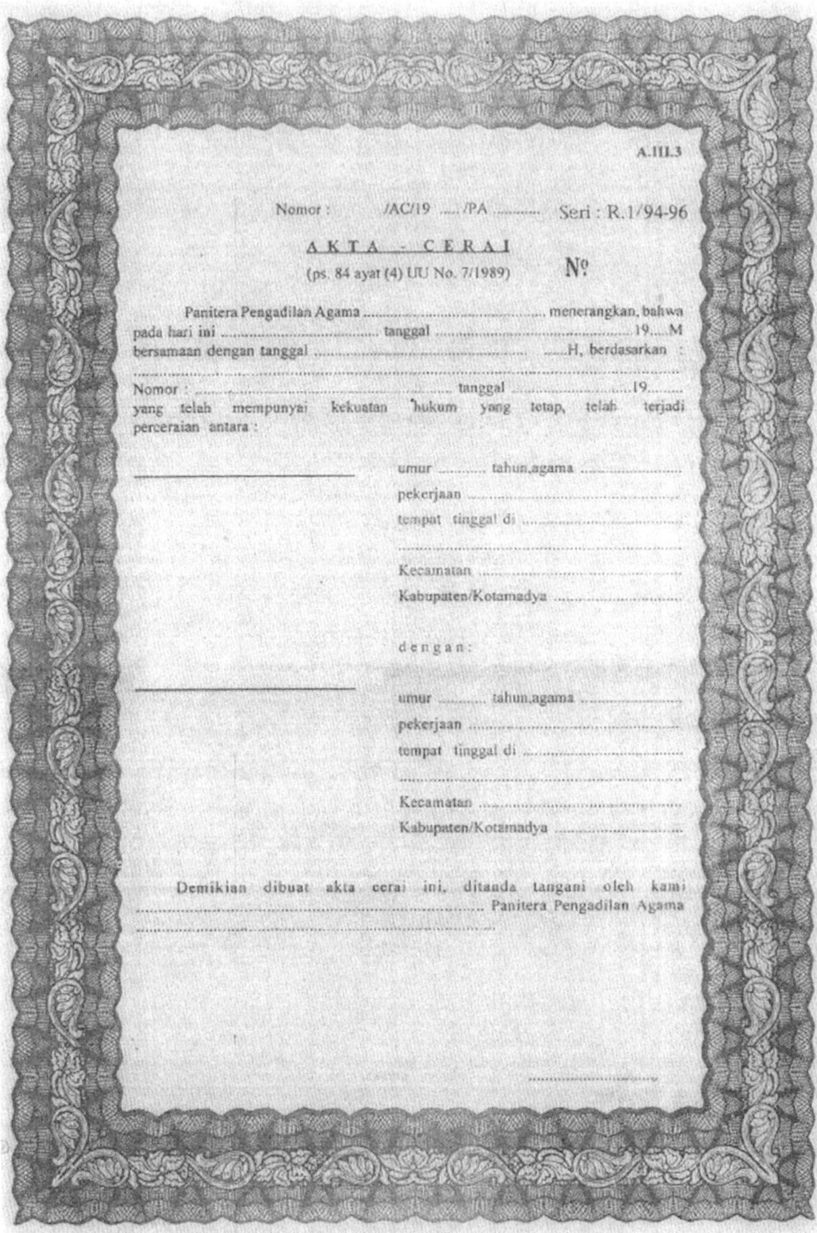

A.III.3

Nomor : ..../AC/19 ...../PA .... Seri : R.1/94-96

AKTA - CERAI

(ps. 84 ayat (4) UU No. 7/1989) №

Panitera Pengadilan Agama .... menerangkan, bahwa pada hari ini .... tanggal .... 19.....M bersamaan dengan tanggal ....H, berdasarkan : ....

Nomor : .... tanggal .... 19........ yang telah mempunyai kekuatan hukum yang tetap, telah terjadi perceraian antara :

________________________ umur .... tahun,agama ....

pekerjaan ....

tempat tinggal di ....

....

Kecamatan ....

Kabupaten/Kotamadya ....

d e n g a n :

________________________ umur .... tahun,agama ....

pekerjaan ....

tempat tinggal di ....

....

Kecamatan ....

Kabupaten/Kotamadya ....

Demikian dibuat akta cerai ini, ditanda tangani oleh kami .... Panitera Pengadilan Agama ....

....

FIGURE 6.4B *Original in Bahasa Indonesia*

Appendix 7.1

Fajar 11 May 2000

SUAMI DIDAKWA MEMBAKAR ISTRI

-Sidang Kasus di Perumahan Telkomas Jl Telegram Mulai Digelar

MAKASSAR-BKM.

Sepasang suami istri, Armansyah (21) dan Agustina Marlina akhirnya berlanjut ke Pengadilan. Sang suami didakwa telah menganiaya dengan membakar istrinya sendiri. Akibatnya, Agustina yang lagi hamil 3 bulan mengalami luka-luka di bagian perut, alat vital, paha, betis, daerah punggung dan kedua pahanya. Fakta itu terungkap dalam sidang yang berlangsung di PN Makassar, Rabu kemarin.

Sidang kasus penganiayaan dan pembakaran istri sudah mulai digelar dengan mendudukan Armansyah bin Arsyad (21), sebagai terdakwa. Jaksa John Parindingan L membacakan dakwaannya dihadapan ketua majelis hakim yang dipimpin Mozimah didampingi Ny Rukimni dan Tangkepadang di PN Makassar, pekan kemarin, mengatakan bahwa terdakwa telah menganiayaan dan membakar istrinya yang mengakibatkan menderita luka-luka sekujur tubuhnya.

Peristiwa tragis yang terjadi di Jl Telegram (Perumahan Bangsal Telkomas, sekitar pukul 20.00 Wita, Minggu (2) Jaksa Jhon Parindingan mengungkapkan kejadiannya bermula dari kehadiran terdakwa dan dan istrinya Agustina Marlina. Terdakwa nekat memperistri Agustina Marlina meski tanpa restu dari keluarga istrinya itu. Mereka nekat kawin lari, sejak Oktober tahun lalu.

Sejak mereka hidup seatap, sering terjadi pertengkaran dan bahkan tidak jarang korban dipukuli. Padahal, saat itu Agustina lagi hamil 3 bulan. Bukan itu saja, dalam dakwaan jaksa juga disebutkan terdakwa sering mengancam korban akan diceraikan.

Puncak hubungan mereka, saat korban sedang menulis lagu yang penuh dengan kata-kata puitis. Dari kata itu, ditemukan ada kata sayang yang ditujukan korban kepada mantan pacarnya Kadek. Terdakwa melihat kata-kata itu, jadi penasaran. "Surat siapa," tanyanya mendesak. Karena korban tidak menanggapi pertanyaan itu, akhirnya terdakwa pun naik pitam dan melampiaskan kekesalannya. Dari situlah, terdakwa kembali mengeluarkan kata-kata akan menceraikan korban.

"Saya tidak mau dicerai, karena saya terlanjur hamil 3 bulan dan bahkan saya siap mati bila dicerai," teriak korban. Mendengar ucapan korban, terdakwa makin beringas. Dia layangkan pukulan ke arah korban yang disusul dengan tendangan. Akibatnya, korban pun tak berdaya dan terjatuh ke lantai.

Terdakwa yang melihat istrinya dalam keadaan tergeletak malah tidak merasa iba. Yang terjadi justru semakin beringas dengan menyiramkan minyak tanah ke tubuh korban. Setelah itu, terdakwa lalu mengambil korek api dan korban pun terbakar. Dalam keadaan api mulai menjalar di tubuh sang korban ini, terdakwa mendorong tubuh korban keluar dari rumah. Akibatnya, korban yang lagi kesakitan menjerit dan mencari jalan penyelamatan dengan terjun masuk ke selokan.

"Saya dibakar suami saya," teriak korban meminta pertolongan. Dan saat itu juga tetangganya, A Tenrioji dan Kamisa Dg Kebo turun tangan dan melarikan ke ke Rumah Sakit Umum Pusat DR Wahidin Sudirhusodo. Luka-luka yang diderita korban dilengkapi hasil visum dari dr Muhammad Nuralim. Sidang akan dilanjutkan Rabu mendatang untuk mendengarkan keterangan saksi. (B19/A3/A)

Terdakwa Armansyah dengan memakai kopiah duduk di kursi pesakitan sembari mendengarkan kesaksian istrinya Agustina Marlina dan ipama sendiri. (Foto:man)

FIGURE 7.1 *Suami Didakwa Membakar Istri*

 | DOI 10.1163/9789004311947_016

Appendix 7.2

Fajar 16 October 2000

Masih Soal Kematian Bidan Satirah yang Misterius

Kuburan Bidan Satirah Akhirnya Digali

Parepere, Fajar

Memenuhi desakan keluarga almarhumah bidan Satirah yang meminta agar kuburan Satirah digali kembali guna diotopsi, maka tim medis forensik Universitas Hasanuddin (Unhas) Makassar kerjasama tim Dik Dokkes Polda Sulsel; melakukan penggalian dan pembedahan terhadap jenazah almarhumah guna kepetingan otopsi, Sabtu, (14/10).

Seperti pernah diberitakan sebelumnya, sejumlah keluarga almarhumah merasa keberatan dan melaporkan ke Polisi agar ditelusuri penyebab kematian bidan Satirah, mengingat kematiannya dianggap tidak wajar. Para keluarga bidan Satirah, tidak yakin kalau korban yang ditemukan suaminya, Rahman, meninggal karena terbentur di kamar mandi, Rabu (27/9) lalu, sekitar pukul 16:00 Wita, di rumahnya di Jalan masuk Terminal Induk LumupuE, Kecamatan Bacukiki, Kodya Parepare.

Penggalian kuburan bidan Satirah untuk diotopsi ini, dipimpin langsung dr Randanan Bandaso DSf (Unhas), dan Asisten Superintendent (Ass Supt) Pol dr Maparape B. Nonchi (Dokpol) yang berlangsung, mulai pukul 11:25 Wita hingga pukul 13:27 Wita.

Proses pembedahan sendiri, begitu mayat diangkat dari liang lahat dan diletakkan di atas meja altar otopsi, Maparape langsung meminta dan memberikan isyarat kepada sejumlah tim medis koast Unhas yang mengenakan baju praktikum putih-putih untuk segera membuka kain kapan pembalut bidan Satirah.

Begitu kain kapan dibuka, tampak jelas mayat bidan Satirah yang berada di atas bale-bale sedang diamati dan diperiksa oleh tim medis. Maparape, setelah mengamati kondisi mayat langsung memegang kepala bidan Satirah sambil mencambut rambut pada batok kepala yang terlihat hitam. Dilanjutkannya pemeriksaan sekitar bagian leher bidan Satirah, dimana telah diperkirakan sebelumnya sebagai penyebab kematian karena patah leher.

Pemantauan *Fajar* sendiri terhadap mayat tersebut, terlihat jelas adanya bagian memar menghitam pada bagia leher kiri, dan pada sekitar dada juga terlihat bekas kucuran darah.

Tim medis yang melakukan pemeriksaan, selanjutnya melakukan pembedahan mayat, dengan menggergaji bagian kepala bidan Satirah. Karena batok kepala keras, maka tim medis mengganti dengan menggunakan pahat untuk membuka isi kepala ibu bidan Satirah. Dan setelah berhasil membuka tengkorak kepala, selanjutnya tim medis juga membuka bagian perut korban dan dada korban demi untuk mengetahui penyebab kematian tersebut.

Menyaksikan jalannya otopsi dari gabungan tim medis ini, diperkirakan sekitar 200 orang yang berjubel di atas pekuburan di belakang Terminal Induk LumpuE tersebut. Bahkan rata-rata pelayat tersebut adalah keluarga dekat bidang Satirah sendiri. "Kami datang untuk melihat sepupu kami, dan sekaligus ingin membuktikan apakah Satirah benar-benar meninggal karena kecelakaan ataukah memang sengaja dibunuh suaminya, Rahman," ujar salah seorang keluarga Satirah.

Sementara itu, masyarakat yang semula menyaksikan dari jarak dekat, dan berusaha membobol pagar penghalang, di samping ada yang memanjat pohon guna menyaksikan jalannya otopsi, begitu kain kafan dibuka, langsung bubar dan menjauh karena tidak tahan bau busuk.

Membusuknya mayat bidan Satirah, karena memang sudah memakan waktu selama dua minggu sejak dikuburkan-nya hingga penggalian kembali.

Sedangkan sebagian yang masih bertahan dan mau menyaksikan dari dekat, terheran-heran anak koast dan dokter yang tidak memakai masker penutup hidung, yang bekerja santai mengotopsi bidan Satirah. Bahkan beberapa di antara para tim medis ini, masih sempat minum dan makan permen.

Begitu pelaksanaan otopsi selesai, jenazah bidan Satirah dibersihkan dan dikuburkan kembali. Sedang Maparape sendiri, termasuk Radanan Bandoso, belum bisa memberi penjelasan lebih lanjut mengenai hasil otopsi yang dilakukan bersama timnya.

"Kami masih melakukan penyelidikan dan mencari bukti-bukti autentik. Di samping itu, pemeriksaan lebih lanjut, akan dilakukan di Fakultas Kedokteran Unhas, guna menemukan fakta-fakta lebih jelas. Makanya, hasil otopsi ini, baru kami bisa berikan sekitar seminggu ke depan," tandas Maparape (lis/ull/d)

—mukhlis—

Tim medis ketika melakukan pembedahan guna otopsi terhadap mayat bidan Satirah yang baru saja digali dari kuburannya.

FIGURE 7.2 *Kuburan Bidan Satirah Akhirnya Digali*

 | DOI 10.1163/9789004311947_017

Glossary

A. = Arabic B. = Bugis I. = Indonesian

A

Adanna to matoaé	(B.) Elders words
Adat	(I.) Custom
Ade'	(B.) Custom
Agaga makebbong	(B.) Flabby stuff
Agustusan	(I.) Independence day celebration
Aju mamata	(B.) Green wood
Aju tubi	(B.) Prohibited fruits
Akad nikah	(I.) Marriage contract
Alaikummussalam ya sadikul mu'minin	(A.) Peace be upon you, the faithful friend
Alé Bola	(B.) Body of the house
Alebbireng	(B.) Honour
Alhamdulillah	(A.) Praise the God
Ambo'	(B.) Father
Ana' dara wélang pélang	(B.) Single girl
Ana' daraé	(B.) Young girl
Anak zinah	(I.) Offspring as a result of premarital pregnancy
Anakarung	(B.) Noble people
Anréna	(B.) Her/his food
Anyamengngeng	(B.) Pleasantness
Api	(B.) Fire
Api masua	(B.) Burn
Arapo-rapong	(B.) In a state of vulnerable
Arung	(B.) Noble
Asabbarakeng	(B.) Patience
Asénéng	(B.) Monday
Aséra	(B.) Nine
Assalamu alaikum ya baburrahmati	(A.) Peace be upon you, the merciful door
Asséajingeng	(B.) Kinship
Assellengeng	(B.) Islam
Assialang marola	(B.) Suitable matrimony
Assialanna mémeng	(B.) Coherent matrimony
Assikalaibinéngeng	(B.) Marital life

Ata	(B.) Slave
Aurat	(A.) Private body
Awa bola	(B.) Beneath the house
Awa sao	(B.) Beneath the house

B

Ba'da dukhul	(A.) Consummated marriage
Bahasa	(I.) Language
Bahasa gado-gado	(I.) Mixed languages
Bainé	(B.) Woman, wife
Bainé tette'ku	(B.) My permanent wife
Bainéna	(B.) His wife
Balai Nikah	(I.) Institution for marriage registration, marriage venue
Balancana	(B.) Her/his money, expenses
Bantu-bantu istri	(I.) Helping the wife
Bantu-bantu suami	(I.) Helping the husband
Bapak pembangunan	(I.) The father of development
Bapak-ibuism	(I.) Father-motherism
Bathin	(I.) Inner self
Bendahara	(I.) Treasurer
Bidan	(I.) Midwife
Bismillahirrahmanirrahim	(A.) In the name of Allah, Most Gracious, Most Merciful
Bokoro' sebbo'	(B.) Leaky washbasin
Bola	(B.) House
Bola riase'	(B.) Stilt-house
Boting Langi'	(B.) Upper world
Botting makemmé	(B.) Flat marriage
Buah ranum	(I.) Ripe fruit
Bulan madu	(I.) Honeymoon
Bunga sibollo	(B.) Rose
Bupati	(I.) Regent
Buta hukum	(I.) Ignorant of the law

C

Calabai	(B.) Cross-gender
Camat	(I.) Subdistrict head
Camming	(B.) Mirror

Canggoréng	(B.) Fried peanut
Canring	(B.) Sweetheart
Carido'	(B.) Adam's apple
Cemburu	(I.) Jealousy
Cerai gugat	(I.) Divorce initiated by the wife
Cerai talak	(I.) Divorce initiated by the husband
Cinna	(B.) Desire

D

Dangdut	(I.) Contemporary Indonesian music form
Dari Laki-laki	(I.) From man
Dauppacci	(B.) Betel leaves
Daya'dayakku'	(B.) My ladies-in-waiting
Dé'na sijodo	(B.) Incompatible as a couple
Dé'na tettong lasona	(B.) His penis does not 'turn on', impotent man
Desa	(I.) Village
Dharma Wanita	(I.) Women's Duties
Diapelin	(I.) Home courtship
Dibuang	(I.) Thrown out
Diikat	(I.) Tied up
Dimadu	(I.) Given a co-wife, polygamy, polygyny
Dipaksa tidur	(I.) Forced to sleep, sexually abused
Dipenjara	(I.) Conviction of crime
Dispensasi kawin	(I.) Dispensation of marriage
Ditegur	(I.) Admonished
Dosa	(I.) Sin
Dua anak cukup	(I.) Two children are enough
Duda bercerai	(I.) Divorcee
Duda ditinggal mati	(I.) Widower
Dui' ménré	(B.) Spending money
Dukun aborsi	(I.) Abortion specialist

E

Élo'na agamaé	(B.) Based on religion
Emma'	(B.) Mother
Engngalang	(B.) Harvest time
Esso maja'	(B.) Bad day
Esso makessing	(B.) Good day

F

Fikhi Nikah	(A.) Marriage principles
Foya-foya	(I.) Extravagant with money

G

Gangguan pihak ketiga	(I.) Interference by third party
Gau madéćeng	(B.) Good behaviour
Gau' maja'	(B.) Bad behaviour
Getteng	(B.) Firm

H

Hadith	(A.) The Traditions of Prophet Muhammad
Halal	(A.) Permitted
Hallakiangngi	(B.) Allow, welcome
Haram	(A.) Forbidden
Hubungan darah	(I.) Genealogical relation

I

Ibadah	(I.) Religious duty
Ibu	(I.) Mother
Ibu pembangunan	(I.) The mother of development
Ibu rumah tangga	(I.) Housewife
Ibu rumah tangga	(I.) Mother of the household
Ibu-ibu	(I.) Mothers
Iddah	(A.) Waiting period of widow or divorcee
Ijab kabul	(I.) Bride's family consent at wedding ceremony
Imam liar	(I.) 'Wild imam,' illegal imam
Ipa' makkunrai	(B.) Sister-in-law
Isbath nikah	(A.) Validation of marriage
Isyani	(B.) Time for evening prayer
Itamukki'	(B.) Please browse

J

Janda bercerai	(I.) Divorced woman
Janda calléda'	(B.) Flirtatious divorcee
Janda dé'na mangngure'	(B.) Unflirtatious divorcee
Janda ditinggal mati	(I.) Widow
Janda kembang	(I.) Young divorcee

Janda tenri telle'	(B.) Separated, but not divorced
Jappi-jappi	(B.) Magic formulae, incantations
Jodoh	(I.) Predestined marriage partner
Jual mahal	(I.) 'Sell herself dear'
Jujung, majjujung	(B.) Carrying above head

K

Kabupaten	(I.) Regency
Kaca	(B.) Glass
Kallolo campéngnga'	(B.) Handsome boy
Kamar pengantin	(I.) Wedding bedroom
Kasar	(I.) Coarse
Kawin cerai	(I.) Divorce right after marriage, serial divorce
Kawin kecelakaan	(I.) Marriage as a result of premarital pregnancy
Kawin liar	(I.) 'Wild marriage,' illegal marriage
Kawin obat	(I.) Remedy marriage
Kawin paksa	(I.) Forced marriage
Kawin ramai	(I.) Lively marriage
Kawing pabbura	(B.) Remedy marriage
Kawing pura	(B.) Divorce right after marriage
Kawissoro'	(B.) Marriage beforehand
Keabsahan	(I.) Legitimacy
Kebbi'-kebbi'	(B.) To steal at glance
Kecamatan	(I.) Subdistrict
Kekeluargaan	(I.) Family principle
Kelakuan baik	(I.) Good behaviour
Kelambu	(I.) Mosquito net
Kelurahan	(I.) Political district
Kemauan masyarakat	(I.) Social demand
Kemitrasejajaran	(I.) Equal gender partnership
Kencan malam minggu	(I.) Saturday night rendezvous
Kepala keluarga	(I.) Head of the household
Kepala sekolah	(I.) Principal
Keperawanan	(I.) Virginity
Kesatuan militer	(I.) Military unit
Kitangnga' mui	(B.) Please look
Kodrat wanita	(I.) Women's destiny
Kotamadya	(I.) Municipality

Krisis moral	(I.) Moral crisis
Kualat	(I.) Damned
Kumpul kebo'	(I.) Living together like water buffalo

L

La Ilaha Illallah	(A.) There is no God except Allah
Lago	(B.)The husband's brother's wife
Lahir	(I.) Outer world
Laki-laki punya	(I.) Man's
Lakkai macukkéréng	(B.) Inquisitive husband
Lakkai matunreng	(B.) Parsimonious husband
Lakkainna	(B.) Her husband
Lamming	(B.) Wedding throne
Langganan	(I.) Customer
Lase'	(B.) Penis
Laso	(B.) Penis
Layu	(I.) Withered
Lemah	(I.) Weak
Lembaga Pemasyarakatan	(I.) Detention Centre
Lémpa,' mallémpa'	(B.) Carrying on shoulder
Lempu'	(B.) Honest
Léppakki' mai	(B.) Please stop by
Li'an	(A.) Cursed
Lino	(B.) World
Lipa'	(B.) Sarong
Lobbang	(B.) Hole, circle
Lontara'	(B.) Bugis manuscript

M

Mabbainé/Mallakkai	(B.) Getting married
Mabbaja laleng	(B.) Seeking a way of
Mabbarazanji	(B.) A chant recounting the Prophet Muhammad's life
Macawa cabbéru'	(B.) Smiling
Macca	(B.) Clever
Maccanring	(B.) Courtship
Maccéia	(B.) Become luminous
Maddara	(B.) Menstruation
Maddécéng	(B.) Reconciliation after [elopement]
Madderos	(B.) Harvesting

Madduta	(B.) Coming forth with the proposal
Madécéng	(B.) Good
Magrib	(I.) Sunset prayer
Mahar	(I.) Dowry
Mahasiswa	(I.) College student
Makan gratis	(I.) Eat for free
Makelléni	(B.) Withered
Makkalépu'ni	(B.) Complete, to have achieved adulthood
Makkeddai lontara'é	(B.) *Lontara'* said
Makkeddai to matoaé	(B.) Elders stated
Makkobbi	(B.) Squeezing
Makkunrai	(B.) Woman
Makkunrai calléda'	(B.) Flirtatious woman
Makkunrai dé'na tarala	(B.) Unsaleable maiden
Makkunrai deggaga siri'na	(B.) Shameless woman
Makkunrai lado'	(B.) Old maid
Makkunrai macilaka	(B.) Unlucky woman
Makkunrai mangngure'	(B.) Flirtatious woman
Makkunrai marota'	(B.) Dirty woman
Makkunrai masémpo	(B.) Cheap woman
Makkunrai masolang	(B.) Damaged woman
Makkunrai nawélai pasa'	(B.) Maiden who is left by the market
Makkunrai sétang	(B.) Devil woman
Malaéka'	(B.) Angel
Malam pertama	(I.) 'First night' of newlyweds
Malaweng Pangkaukeng	(B.) Deviant behaviour
Malebbi'	(B.) Modest
Maléda'	(B.) Flirtatious
Mallaibiné	(B.) Conjugal pair, husband-wife
Mallawangeng	(B.) Separation
Mallegga	(B.) Abortion
Mallellung	(B.) Skipping over
Maloga	(B.) Loose
Malopponi	(B.) Grown-up
Mammanu'-manu'	(B.) Acting like a bird, preliminary inquiry
Mancaji baliperri'	(B.) To become one in all circumstances
Mancaji I Mattaro	(B.) To become a household manager
Mancaji makkunrai	(B.) To become a woman
Mancaji misseng dapureng	(B.) To become aware of domestic responsibilities

Mandi junub	(I.) A bath after sexual intercourse
Mangkalinga ada to matoa	(B.) Listen to elders
Mangngaribini	(B.) Time for sunset prayer
Mangngure'	(B.) Flirtatious
Manni	(B.) Semen
Mannippi	(B.) Dream, wet dream
Manyameng	(B.) Pleasant feeling
Mapato	(B.) Obedient
Maperreng	(B.) To hold steady
Mappaccicil	(B.) Selling on credit
Mappakasiri'-siri'	(B.) Caused shame
Mappangngéwang	(B.) Verbal disputes, arguing
Mappasikarawa	(B.) Touching each other
Mappettu ada	(B.) The acceptance of the proposal
Marilaleng	(B.) Deep
Maringngerrang	(B.) Conscious
Marisaliweng	(B.) Outside, visible, open
Masalah biologis	(I.) Biological problem
Masalah economy	(I.) Economic problem
Masalah politik	(I.) Political problem
Masiri'	(B.) In a state of *siri'*
Massala-salang	(B.) Be disarray
Massampo siri'	(B.) Save face from shame
Massanro	(B.) Use witchcraft
Masséddi siri'	(B.) Sharing one *siri'*
Massipa' jawa-jawa	(B.) Behave like Javanese
Massipa' to laing	(B.) Behave like outsider
Massompe'	(B.) Migrating in search of fortune
Maté colli'	(B.) Die in childhood
Maté gadis	(B.) Die in girlhood
Maté ri siri'na	(B.) To die because of *siri'*
Maté siri'	(B.) Alive without dignity
Mattonang oto toa	(B.) Driving an old car
Mattuliling dapureng wékka pétu	(B.) Surround the kitchen seven times
Matuang makkunrai	(B.) Mother-in-law
Mawaddah	(A.) Safe
Mengamuk	(I.) Run amuck
Mens	(I.) Menstruation
Meredam opini publik	(I.) To muzzle public opinion
Mimpi basah	(I.) Wet dream

Mitzaq al-ghaliz	(A.) Firm contract
Moloi lakkainna	(B.) Facing her husband
Mu'asyarah Bil-ma'ruf	(A.) Act in good manners
Muhrim	(A.) Guardian
Murtad	(A.) Converting religion

N

Najis	(A.) Dirt
Najjuluang aléna	(B.) Bring herself
Nalaoanni aléna	(B.) Able to stand maintain his family
Napeddiri bainéna	(B.) Abuse his wife
Nappémmaliangngi to matoaé	(B.) Tabooed by elders
Nasihat perkawinan	(I.) Marital advice
Nikah	(I.) Legalisation of marriage
Nilai-nilai bathiniah	(I.) Values of inner experience
Nilai-nilai lahiriah	(I.) Values of worldly accomplishment
Nyameng	(B.) Pleasure

O

Onro	(B.) Social status
Onro sikalabinéng	(B.) Household
Oroané	(B.) Man

P

Pabbau seppulodua	(B.) Twelve kissings
Pabbéré	(B.) Wedding gifts
Pacaran bekstrit	(I.) Clandestine courtship
Pacaran moderen	(I.) Modern courtship
Pacaran pas foto	(I.) physical contact between partners that is restricted to above the waist
Pacilakai	(B.) Carrier of misfortune
Pada sicinta	(B.) Like each other
Pada silori	(B.) Like each other
Padderos	(B.) Paddy huller
Pagama	(B.) Pious
Pajaga bili'	(B.) Housekeeper
Pajjakarta	(B.) Middle class traders
Pakéanna	(B.) Her/his clothing
Panca Dharma Wanita	(I.) Five Women's Duties
Pangngadereng	(B.) Customary law

Pangngonro bola	(B.) Housekeeper
Pangngulu bola	(B.) 'Head of the house', the husband
Panrita	(B.) Religious leader
Panter	(I.) Inter-regency transportation
Papasenna to matoaé	(B.) Message of elders
Paseng	(B.) Aphorism
Passampo siri'	(B.) Protector of someone else's shame
Passilessurengeng	(B.) To regard as kin
Passompe'	(B.) Migrant, wanderer
Patémba'na urané	(B.) Man's gun, penis
Pattanra esso	(B.) Day decider
Pélloreng	(B.) Timid
Pemberdayaan	(I.) Empowerment
Pembinaan	(I.) Guidance from above
Penebus dosa	(I.) Sin redemption
Pengadilan Agama	(I.) Religious Court
Penganiayaan	(I.) Physical Abuse
Penggugat	(I.) The plaintiff
Pénné pinceng	(B.) Porcelain plate
Percobaan pembunuhan	(I.) Attempted murder
Perkawinan yang dirahasiakan	(I.) Secret marriage
Permainan	(I.) Game
Permusyawaratan	(I.) Deliberation
Perreng	(B.) To hold
Perrengngi aléna	(B.) To hold his/herself
Perumahan mertua indah	(I.) 'Beautiful housing complex of the in-laws'
Perzinahan	(I.) Fornication
Pessé	(B.) Social solidarity
Pesta botting	(B.) Wedding party
Pété'-Pété'	(I.) Local minibus
Piaraéngngi bainéna	(B.) Taking care of his wife
Pintu baruga	(I.) Wedding entrance
Pos ronda	(I.) Guard station
Posi' bola	(B.) House's navel
Potong gaji	(I.) Paying through salary
Puber kedua	(I.) Second puberty
Puncak karir	(I.) Peak of [one's] career
Purani botting	(B.) Have married
Puskesmas	(I.) Community health centre

Q

Qabla al-dukhul	(A.) Unconsummated marriage

R

Rahmah	(A.) Merciful
Rakkéang	(B.) Rafter
Reppa'	(B.) Broken
Rilariang	(B.) Abducted
Ripaddeppé' mabélaé	(B.) Bring close
Ripakasiri'	(B.) Shamed
Ripammarué	(B.) Sharing husband with another wife, polygyny
Ripatunru' rilakkainna	(B.) Obedient to her husband
Risanroi	(B.) Bewitched
Risunna'	(B.) Circumcision
Ritaro	(B.) Reserved
Rukun	(I.) Principles
Rumah dinas	(I.) Official house
Rumah makan	(I.) Restaurant
Rumah panggung	(B.) Stilt-house

S

Sah	(I.) Legal, legitimate
Sah secara adat	(I.) Legitimate according to custom
Sah secara agama	(I.) Legitimate according to religion
Sakinah	(A.) Harmonious
Saksi	(I.) Witness
Salasa	(B.) Tuesday
Saling percaya	(I.) Trust each other
Sappokkadua	(B.) Second cousin
Sappokkatellu	(B.) Third cousins
Sapposiseng	(B.) First cousin
Saraddasi mallino	(B.) Strong magic
Sawah	(I.) Rice field
Séajing	(B.) Kin, family
Seddi	(B.) One
Segar	(I.) Fresh
Sejodoh	(I.) Two of a kind
Sekapu'	(B.) Proper
Seks bebas	(I.) Free sex

Senjata pamungkas	(I.) Ultimate fatal weapon
Siala	(B.) To take each other
Sighat ta'lik	(A.) Marital agreement
Sikalaibiné	(B.) Conjugal pair, husband-wife
Silariang	(B.) Elopement
Silisuang	(B.) Reconciliation
Sipakatau	(B.) Mutual respect
Sipakkuruseng	(B.) Two of a kind
Sipubainé	(B.) Conjugal pair, husband-wife
Sipurang	(B.) Divorce
Siri'	(B.) Honour, shame
Sitinroang	(B.) Sharing one bed
Sombéré'	(B.) Friendly
Sompa	(B.) Rankprice
Sopir pété'-pété'	(I.) Minibus driver
Status hukum	(I.) Legal Status
Status tergantung	(I.) Uncertain status
Subuni	(B.) Time for early morning prayer
Sugi'	(B.) Wealthy
Suka sama suka	(I.) Like each other
Sulapa' eppa'	(B.) Four sides, square
Sumange'	(B.) Spirit
Surat nikah	(I.) Marriage certificate
Sure' nikka	(B.) Marriage certificate
Suruga	(B.) Heaven
Syarat	(I.) Prerequisites

T

Talak	(A.) Divorce
Talak ba'in (talak 3)	(A.) Final divorce
Talak Raj'i (Talak 1 & 2)	(A.) Divorce which can still be reconciled
Talinge'	(B.) Conscious
Tangngasso	(B.) Noon
Tanra	(B.) Sign
Tarawé	(B.) Non-obligatory evening prayer during fasting month
Tarimai	(B.) Received
Tello'	(B.) Egg
Tello' kannasa'	(B.) Salted egg
Tennia to laing	(B.) Not outsider

Tergugat	(I.) The accused
Terpaksa kawin	(I.) Forced to marry
Tessikapu'	(B.) Improper
Tidak ada kecocokan	(I.) Incompatibility [as a couple]
Tidak ada tanggung jawab	(I.) Neglecting responsibility
Tidak dihargai	(I.) Disrespected
Tikkeng	(B.) Catch
Timung bunga sibollo	(B.) Door of the rose, vagina
Tinro	(B.) Sleep
To Décéng	(B.) Good people
To laing	(B.) Outsider
To madduta	(B.) The one who proposes, male party
To Malebbi'	(B.) Big or better people
To Mangkasa'	(B.) Makassarese
To Maradéka	(B.) Freemen
To masiri'	(B.) *Siri'* defender
To matoa	(B.) Old person, respected elder, a generational layer, two senior to the speaker, spiritually potent person
To Menre'	(B.) Mandarnese
To polé	(B.) The one who comes, guest
To ri bola	(B.) The one who is in the house, the wife
To riaddutai	(B.) The one who is being proposed to, female party
To Sama'	(B.) Regular people
To Tebbe'	(B.) Commoners
To Ugi'	(B.) Buginese
Toddang Toja	(B.) Lower world
Tokoh masyarakat	(I.) Community leader
Toraja	(B.) Torajanese
Tukang beca	(I.) Tricycle driver

U

Uaé	(B.) Water

W

Waju	(B.) Blouse
Wali	(A.) Representative of the bride
Walimah	(A.) Wedding party
Walimah al-Ursy	(A.) Public announcement of marriage

Wara api	(B.) Ember
Warani	(B.) Brave
Warani	(B.) Brave
Warung	(I.) Food stall
Wasiat	(I.) Testament
Wettu pasa'	(B.) Market days
Wiccang, mawwiccang	(B.) Carrying
Wudhu	(A.) Ritual ablution before praying

Bibliography

Abdullah, A. Gani (1994). *Pengantar kompilasi hukum Islam dalam tata hukum Indonesia.* Jakarta: Gema Insani Press.

Abdullah, Hamid (1985). *Manusia Bugis Makassar; Suatu tinjauan historis terhadap pola tingkah laku dan pandangan hidup manusia Bugis Makassar.* Jakarta: Inti Idayu Press.

Abdurrahman (1992). *Kompilasi hukum Islam di Indonesia.* Jakarta: Akademika.

Abidin, A. Zainal (1983). *Persepsi orang Bugis-Makassar tentang hukum, negara dan dunia luar.* Bandung: Penerbit Alumni.

——— (1999). *Capital selecta kebudayaan Sulawesi Selatan.* Ujung Pandang: Hasanuddin University Press.

Abrar, Ana Nadya (1997). *Pelecehan seksual dan kekerasan seksual; Analisis isi surat kabar Indonesia.* Yogyakarta: PPK-UGM and the Ford Foundation.

Abu-Lughod, Lila (1991). 'Writing against culture', in: Richard G. Fox (ed), *Recapturing anthropology: Working in the present,* pp. 137–162. Sante Fe: School of American Research Press.

Acciaioli, Gregory (1989). *Searching for a good fortune; The making of a Bugis shore community at Lake Lindu, Central Sulawesi.* Canberra: PhD Thesis, the Australian National University.

——— (2000). 'Kinship and debt; The social organization of Bugis migration and fish marketing at Lake Lindu, Central Sulawesi', in: Roger Tol, Kees van Dijk and Greg Acciaioli (eds), *Authority and enterprise among the peoples of South Sulawesi,* pp. 211–240. Leiden: KITLV Press.

Adriana, Purwandari, Kristi, Triwijati, Nike, and Sabaroedin Sjarifah (1998). *Hak-hak reproduksi perempuan yang terpasung.* Jakarta: Pustaka Sinar Harapan.

Alberta (1995). 'Wife abuse', *Family violence,* 10 April.

Al-Gazali, Imam (1995). *Tentang perkawinan sakinah.* Translated by Kholila Marhijanto. Surabaya: Tiga Dua.

Al-Hadar, Yasmine (1977). *Perkawinan and perceraian di Indonesia; Sebuah studi antar kebudayaan.* Jakarta: Lembaga Demografi – Fakultas Ekonomi, Universitas Indonesia.

Ambo Enre, Fachruddin (1999). *Ritumpanna wélenrénngé; Sebuah episoda sastra Bugis klasik Galigo.* Jakarta: Yayasan Obor Indonesia, Ecole francaise d'Extreme-Orient & Fakultas Sastra Universitas Indonesia.

Andaya, Leonard Y. (1979). 'A village perception of Arung Palakka and the Makassar war 1666–1669', in: Anthony Reid and David Maar (eds), *Perception of the past in Southeast Asia,* pp. 365–398. Kuala Lumpur-Hongkong: Heineman Educational Book (Asia) Ltd.

——— (2000). 'The bissu; study of a third gender in Indonesia, in: Barbara Watson Andaya (ed), Other Pasts; women, gender and history in early modern Southeast Asia, pp. 27–46. Honolulu: Center for Southeast Asian Studies.

Bangun, Masliana (1991). 'Sensitive social relationships; Fieldwork in a Javanese village', in: M.N. Panini (eds), *From the female eye; Accounts of women fieldworkers studying their own communities*, pp. 81–87. Delhi: Hindustan Publishing Corporation.

Baroja, Julio Caro (1965). 'Honour and shame; A historical account of several conflict', in: J.G. Peristiany (eds), *Honour and shame; The values of Mediterranean society*, pp. 79–95. London: Weidenfeld and Nicolson.

Baso, Zohra A. and Idrus, Nurul Ilmi (2002). 'Women's activism against violence in South Sulawesi', in: Kathryn Robinson and Sharon Bessell (eds), *Women in Indonesia; Gender, equity and development*, pp. 198–208. Singapore: Institute of Southeast Asian Studies (ISEAS).

Beazley, Harriot (1998). *The sexual life of street children in Yogyakarta, Indonesia.* Paper, The Ninth National Conference of the Australian Population Association, 'Population matters; Global, regional, local', University of Queensland, Brisbane, 29 September–2 October 1998.

——— (1999). *'A little but enough'; Street children's subcultures in Yogyakarta, Indonesia.* PhD Thesis, the Australian National University, Canberra.

Behar, Ruth and Deborah A. Gordon (eds) (1995). *Women writing culture.* Berkeley, Los Angeles and London: University California Press.

Bellows, Laura J. (2003) 'New sexual practices and modern threats to Balinese-ness', *Review of Indonesia Malaysia affairs,* in: A special issue on 'youth, gender, and sexuality in Indonesia,' 37-1:71–105.

Bennett, Linda R. (2000). *Sex, power and magic; Constructing and contesting love magic and premarital sex in Lombok.* Working Paper Series 6. Gender Relations Project, RSPAS, the Australian National University, Canberra.

——— (2001). 'Single women's experiences of premarital pregnancy and induced bortion in Lombok, Eastern Indonesia', *Reproductive Health Matters* 19–17:37–43.

——— (2002). *Dialectic of desire and danger; Maidenhood, sexuality and modernity in Mataram, Eastern Indonesia.* PhD Thesis, University of Queensland, Brisbane.

——— (2005a). 'Pattern of resistance and transgression in Eastern Indonesia; Single women's practices of clandestine courtship and cohabitation', *Culture, health and sexuality* 7-2:101–112

——— (2005b). *Women, Islam and modernity; Single women, sexuality and reproductive health in contemporary Indonesia.* London and New York: Routledge Curzon.

——— (2008). 'Poverty, opportunity and purity in paradise', in: Michele Ford and Lyn Parker (eds), *Women and Work in Indonesia*, pp. 82–103. London and New York: Routledge.

Berita Kota Makassar
11 May 2000 *Suami didakwa membakar istri.*
2 June 2000 *Istri terdakwa histeris, kakak terkapar di lantai.*
3 June 2000 *Mengaku dianiaya oknum Kadis pertambangan.*
3 June 2000 *Jeritan hati istri polisi militer.*
5 June 2000 *Jeritan hati istri polisi militer.*
19 June 2000 *Dimaki dan digiring ke kantor Polisi.*
20 June 2000 *Cemburu, istri dibakar.*
19 July 2000 *Tiap malam saya diteror.*

Bhachu, Parminder (1991). 'The re-socialisation of an Anthropologist; Fieldwork within one's own community', in: M.N. Panini (eds), *From the female eye; Accounts of women fieldworkers studying their own communities*, pp. 66–73. Delhi: Hindustan Publishing Corporation.

Blackburn, Susan (2004). *Women and the state in the modern Indonesia.* Cambridge: Cambridge University Press.

——— (1999a). 'Gender violence and the Indonesian political transition', *Asian Studies Review* 23-4:433–448.

——— (1999b). 'Women and citizenship in Indonesia', *Australian Journal of Political Science* 35-2:189–284.

Blackburn, Susan and Sharon Bessell (1997). 'Marriageable age; Political debates on early marriage in twentieth-century Indonesia', pp. 107–142. *Indonesia*, 63, April.

Blackwood, Evelyn (1995). Senior women, model mothers, and dutiful wives; Managing gender contradictions in a Minangkabau village', in: Aihwa Ong and Michael G. Pelletz (eds), *Bewitching women, pious men; Gender and body politics in Southeast Asia*, pp. 124–158. Berkeley: University of California Press.

——— (2000). *Webs of power; women, kin and community in a Sumatran village.* Lanham Boulder, New York and Oxford: Rowman and Littlefield Publishers, Inc.

Boellstorff, Tom (2001). *HIV, sexuality and gender in the Pacific and Asia.* Observation paper, The 6th International Congress on AIDS in Asia and the Pacific, Melbourne, 5–8 October.

——— (2002). 'Ethnolocality'. *The Asia Pacific Journal of Anthropology* 3 (1):24–48.

——— (2004a). 'Playing back the nation; Waria Indonesia transvestite', *Cultural Anthropology* 19-2:159–195.

——— (2004b). 'The emergence of political homophobia in Indonesia; Masculining and national belonging', *Ethnos* 69-4(December):465–486.

——— (2004c). 'Gay and lesbian Indonesians and the idea of the nation', *Social Analysis*, 50-1(Spring):158–163.

——— (2005). *The Gay Archipelago; sexuality and nations.* Princeton and Oxford: Princeton University Press.

——— (2007). *A coincidence of desires; Anthropology, queer studies, Indonesia.* Durham and London: Duke University Press.

Boon, James A. (1977). *The anthropological of romance of Bali 1957–1972; Dynamic perspectives in marriage and caste, politics and religion.* Cambridge: Cambridge University Press.

Borahima, Ridwan, P. Wajong, and Djenen (1974). *Adat dan upacara perkawinan sukubangsa Bugis dan Makassar di Desa Baju Bodoa, Sulawesi Selatan.* Makassar: Lembaga Sejarah dan Antropologi.

Bouhdiba, Abdelwahab (1985). *Sexuality in Islam.* Translated from French by Alan Sheridan. London: Routledge & Kegan.

Bowen, John R. (n.d.). *Contextual interpretation and legal pluralism in Indonesian Islamic jurisprudence* [Manuscript].

——— (1993). *Religion and ritual in Gayo society.* New Jersey: Princeton University Press.

BPS (2000). *Social indicators on women in Indonesia (1999).* Jakarta: Badan Pusat Statistik Jakarta, Indonesia.

——— (2011). *Social indicators on women in Indonesia (2010).* Jakarta: Badan Pusat Statistik Jakarta, Indonesia.

——— (2013). *Women and Men in Indonesia (2013).* Jakarta: Badan Pusat Statistik Jakarta, Indonesia.

BPS Provinsi Sulawesi Selatan (2002). *Karakteristik Penduduk Sulawesi Selatan; Hasil Sensus Penduduk 2000.* Makassar: Badan Pusat Statistik Propinsi Sulawesi Selatan.

Brakel, L.F. (1975). *The hikayat Muhammad Hanafiyyah.* Leiden: The Hague.

Brawn, David M. (1993). *Immanent domain: Ways of living in bone, Indonesia.* PhD Dissertation. Bell & Howell Company, Michigan.

Brenner, Suzanne A. (1995). 'Why women rule the roots; Rethinking Javanese ideologies of gender and self-control', in: Aihwa Ong and Michael G. Peletz (eds), *Bewitching women, pious men; Gender and body politics in Southeast Asia*, pp. 19–50. Berkeley and Los Angeles: University of California Press.

——— (1998). *Domestication of women; Women, health and modernity in Java.* Princeton: Princeton University Press.

Brook, Geraldine (1995). *Nine parts of desire; The hidden world of Islamic women.* Sydney: Anchor Books.

Browne, Susan (2000). *Gender implication of dangdut kampungan; Indonesia 'low-class' popular music.* Monash Working Paper Series no. 109. Melbourne: Monash Asia Institute.

Budhisantoso, S., Ambo Gani, Husnah, G.S., Baco, B. and Ahmad Yunus (1990). *Wasiat-wasiat dalam lontarak Bugis.* Jakarta: Departemen P&K, Dirjen Kebudayaan, Direktorat Sejarah dan Nilai Tradisional, Proyek Penelitian dan Pengkajian Kebudayaan Nusantara.

Bulbeck, F. David (1996). 'The politics of marriage and the marriage of polities in Gowa, South Sulawesi, during the 16th and 17th centuries', in: James J. Fox and Clifford Sather (eds), *Origins, ancestry and alliance*, pp. 280–315. Canberra: Department of Anthropology, RSPAS, the Australian National University.

Bunzl, Matti (2005). 'Anthropology beyond crisis: Toward an intellectual history of the extended present', *Anthropology of humanism* 30:2, 187–195.

Butt, Simon (2008). 'Polygamy and mixed marriage in Indonesia; Islam and the marriage law in the courts', in: Tom Lindsey (eds), *Indonesia; Law and society*, second edition. Annandale: The Federation Press.

Buzawa, Eve S. and Carl G. Buzawa (1990). *Domestic violence; The criminal justice response*. California: Sage Publications.

Caldwell, Ian (1988). *South Sulawesi A.D. 1300–1600; Ten Bugis texts*. PhD Thesis, the Australian National University, Canberra.

Carlson, B.E. (1997). 'Battered women and their assailants', *Social Work* 22-4:455–460.

Chabot, Hendrik T. (1990). 'Changing patterns of marriage and household formation in Peninsular Malaysia', *Sojourn* 5-2:163–193

——— (1996). *Kinship, status and gender in South Celebes*. Leiden: KITLV.

Chapon, D. (1976). *Divorce and fertility; A study in rural Java*. Population Institute Report series no. 40. Yogyakarta: University of Gadjah Mada.

Connell, R.W. (2000). *The men and the boys*. Sydney: Allen & Unwin.

Daud, Ma'mur (1983). *Terjemah Hadis shahih muslim*. Jakarta: Penerbit Widjaya.

Davies, Sharyn Graham (2006). 'Gender and status', in: Stephen J. Epstein (ed). *Understanding Indonesia*, pp. 93–101. New Zealand: Asian Studies Institute, Vicyoria University of Wellington.

——— (2007). *Challenging gender norms; Five genders among the Bugis in Indonesia*. Belmont: Thomson Wadsworth.

——— (2009). 'Hunting down love; Female masculinities in Bugis, South Sulawesi', in: Saskia E. Wierega, Evelyn Blackwood, and Abha Bhaiye (eds). *Women's sexualities and masculinities in globalizing Asia*, pp. 139–158. New York: Palgrave Macmillan.

——— (2010). *Gender Diversity in Indonesia; sexuality, Islam and queer selves*. London and New York: Routledge.

Djajadiningrat-Nieuwenhuis, Madelon (1987). 'Ibuism and privatization: Path to power', in: Elsbeth Locher-Scholten and Anke Niehof (eds), *Indonesian women in focus*, pp. 43–51. Holland: Foris Publication.

Djamaris, Edwar (1983). *Hikayat Nabi mikraj, hikayat Nur Muhammad, dan hikayat darma tasiya*. Jakarta: Proyek Penerbitan Buku Sastra Indonesia and Daerah.

Djuher (1983). *Hukum perkawinan Islam and relevansinya dengan kesadaran hukum masyarakat;* Islamic marriage law and its relevance with the law awareness of society. Jakarta: Dewaruci Press.

Dobash, R.E. and R.P. Dobash (1979). *Violence against wives; A case against patriarchy.* New York: Free Press.

Van Doorn-Harder (2013). 'Polygamy and harmonious Families; Indonesian debates on gender and marriage', in: Susanne Schröter (ed), *Gender and Islam in Southeast Asia; Women's rights movements, religious resurgence and local traditions*, pp. 55–72. Leiden and Boston: Brill.

Douglas, Mary (1978). Purity and Danger. London: Routldge and Kegan Paul.

Echols, John M. and Hassan Shadily (1989). *Kamus Indonesia-Inggris.* Jakarta: P.T. Gramedia. Third edition.

Ellen, Roy F. (1984). *Ethnographic research; A guide to general conduct.* London: Academic Press.

Emerson, Robert M., Rachel I. Fretz, and Linda L. Shaw (2011). *Writing ethnographic fieldnotes*. Second edition. Chicago and London: The University of Chicago Press.

Errington, Shelly (1977). *Siriq, darah dan kekuasaan politik di dalam kerajaan Luwu' zaman dulu.* Seminar on the '*Siriq* and Its Problems in South Sulawesi', Ujung Pandang, 11–13 July.

——— (1979). The cosmic house of the Buginese', *Asia* 8-14(January–February).

——— (1983). 'Embodied sumange' in Luwu. *Journal of Asian Studies* 42-3:545–570.

——— (1989). *Meaning and power in a Southeast Asian realm.* Princeton: Princeton University Press.

——— (1990). 'Recasting sex, gender and power; A theoretical and regional overview', in: Jane M. Atkinson and Shelly Errington (eds), *Power and difference; Gender in islands Southeast Asia*, pp. 1–58. California: Standford University Press.

Fajar

4 January 2001	*Terdakwa Dahlia resmi jadi DPO.*
9 January 2002	*Pernikahan dini, 'buah' trauma warga.*
15 January 2002	*Kasus silariang mencolok.*
1 March 2000	*'Kawin liar' masih sering terjadi.*
14 May 2000	*Kekerasan dalam rumah tangga*, Jendela.
2 June 2000	*Perseteruan Dahlia-Azis makin tajam.*
9 June 2000	*Kisah pasangan silariang dari desa Bune, Libureng.*
1 November 1999	*Anak habisi ibu dan kakak kandung.*
10 November 1999	*Karena siriq, bunuh saudara dan ibu kandung.*
11 November 1999	*Perbuatan kedua korban telah lama diketahui.*
17 November 2000	*Perselingkuhan Azis-Dahlia terkuak di pengadilan.*
15 November 2000	*Sidang Dahlia Narra diwarnai keributan.*
26 December 2000	*Nikmat itu akhirnya membawa sengsara.*

Fakih, Mansour (1996). *Analisis gender and transformasi sosial.* Yogyakarta: Pustaka Pelajar.

Federspiel, Howard M. (1995). *A dictionary of Indonesian Islam.* Southeast Asia Series no. 94. Ohio: Athens.

Fetterman, David M. (1989). *Ethnography; Step-by-step*. Newbury Park: Sage Publication.

——— (2010). *Ethnography; Step-by-step*. London: Sage Publication.

Fox, James J. (1993). 'Memories of Ridge-Poles and Cross-Beams; The Categorical Foundation of a Rotinese Cultural Design', in: James J. Fox (eds), *Inside Austronesian house; Perspectives on domestic design for living*, pp. 141–179. Canberra: Department of Anthropology, RSPAS, the Australian National University.

Frieberg, Timothy and Barbara Frieberg (1985). 'Geografi dialek bahasa Bugis' *Lontara'* 8:20–47.

Friedericy, H.J. (1933). *De standen bij de Boeginezen en Makassaren*. Leiden: 's-Gravenhage.

Geertz, Clifford (1960). *The religion of Java*. New York: Free Press of Glencoe, Inc.

——— (1983). *Local knowledge: Further essays in interpretative anthropology*. New York: Basic Books.

Geertz, Hildred (1961). *The Javanese family; A study of kinship and socialization*. New York: The Free Press of Glencoe, Inc.

Gelles, Richard (1976). *The violent home*. Beverly Hills, California: Sage Publications.

Gennep, Arnold van (1960). *Rites of passage*. Translated by Monika B. Vizedom and Gabrielle L. Caffee. Chicago: University of Chicago Press.

Gerke, Solvay (1993). 'Indonesian national development ideology and the role of women', *Indonesian Cycle* 59–60:45–56.

Gluckman, Max (1969). 'Introduction', In: A.L. Epstein (ed), *The craft of social anthropology*. Delhi: Hindustan Publishing Corporation.

GOI (Government of Indonesia) (1993). *Indonesian criminal code*. Jakarta: GOI.

Grijns, Mies, S. Machfud, P. Sayogyo, I. Smyth, and Anita van Velzen (1992). *Gender, marginalisasi dan industri pedesaan; Pengusaha, pekerja upahan dan pekerja keluarga wanita di Jawa Barat*. Bandung: Yayasan Akatiga.

Grimes, Charles E. and Barbara D. Grimes (1987). *Languages of South Sulawesi*. Pacific Linguistics Series no. 78. Canberra: Department of Linguistics, RSPAS, the Australian National University.

Haar, B. ter (1948). *Adat Law in Indonesia; Customary Law in Indonesia*. New York: Institute of Pacific Relations.

Hadrawi, Muhlis and Anwar Ibrahim (1999). *Mitos and perilaku sexual*. Makassar: Proyek P3T-Unhas.

——— (2009). *Assikalaibineng: kitab persetubuhan Bugis*. Makassar: Ininnawa.

Haem, Nurul Huda (2007). *Awas illegal wedding; Dari penghulu hingga perselingkuhan*. Bandung: Hikmah.

Hamidy, Muammal (1980). *Perkawinan dan persoalannya; Bagaimana pemecahannya dalam Islam*. Surabaya: Penerbit P.T. Bina Ilmu.

Hamka (1982). *Tafsir Al-Azhar, Juz XV*. Surabaya: Yayasan Latimojong.

Hamzah, A.P., Makmun Badaruddin, and Muhammad Salim. (1983). *Monografi kebudayaan Bugis*. Ujung Pandang: Pemerintah Daerah Tingkat I Sulawesi Selatan.

Hancock, Peter (2000). 'The Lived experience of female factory workers in rural West Java', *Labour Management in Development* 1-1:1–18.

Haniff, Nesha Z. (1985). Toward a native Anthropology: Methodological notes on a study of successful Caribbean women by insider.

Haryono, M. Yudhie R. (2000). 'Religion crime', *Gamma* (8–14 November 2000).

Hastrup, Kirsten (1995). *A passage in anthropology*. London: Routledge.

Hatley, Barbara (1990). 'Theatrical imagery and gender ideology in Java', in: Jane M. Atkinson and Shelly Errington (eds), *Power and difference; gender in island Southeast Asia*, pp. 177–208. Stanford: Standford University Press.

Helliwell, Christine (1995). 'Autonomy as natural equality; Inequality in "egalitarian" societies', *Journal of the Royal Anthropological Institutes* 1-2:359–375.

Hoebel, E. Adamson and A. Arthur Schiller (1979). 'Introduction', in: Ter Haar. *Adat Law in Indonesia*. New York: Institute of Pacific Relations.

Hobart, Mark (1980). *Ideas of identity; The interpretation of kinship in Bali*. Denpasar: Jurusan Antropologi Budaya, Fakultas Sastra, Universitas Udayana.

Hooher, M.B. (2002). 'Introduction: Islamic law in South-east Asia'. *The Australian Journal of Asian Law*, 4(3), 213–231.

Hooker, Virginia M. (1994). 'Transmission through practical example; Women and Islam in 1920s Malay fiction', *Journal of the Malaysian Branch of the Royal Asiatic Society* (MBRAS), LXVII-2(December):92–118.

——— (1997). 'Women with a will? Writing female initiative in the Malay novel', *RIMA* 31-2(December):63–100.

Hopkins, Andrew and Heather Mc. Gregor (1991). *Working for change; The Movement against domestic violence*. Sydney: Allen and Unwin.

Hugo, Graeme (2002). 'Women's international labour migration', in: Kathryn Robinson and Sharon Bessell (eds), *Women in Indonesia: gender, equity and development*, pp. 158–178. Singapore: Institute of Southeast Asian Studies (ISEAS).

Hull, Terence H. (1975). *Each child brings its own fortune*. PhD Thesis, RSPAS, the Australian National University, Canberra.

——— (1996). 'Continuing demographic transition in Asia', *Asia-Pacific Economic Literature* 10-1:42–43.

——— (2002). *The marriage revolution in Indonesia*. Paper, Population Association of America, Atlanta, 9–11 May.

Hull, Terence H. and Valerie J. Hull (1987). 'Changing marriage behaviour in Java; The role of timing of consummation', *Southeast Asian Journal of Social Science* 15:104–119.

——— (1997). 'Culture, politics and family planning in Indonesia', in: Gavin Jones R. Douglas and J. Caldwell and R.D. Souza (eds), *The Continuing Demographic Transition*, pp. 383–421. Oxford: Oxford University Press.

Hull, Terence and Sri Moertiningsih Adioetomo (2002). 'Women, family planning and decentralisation; New variations on old themes', in: Kathryn Robinson and Sharon Bessell (eds), *Women in Indonesia; Gender equity and development*, pp. 235–249. Singapore: Institute of Southeast Asian Studies.

Idrus, Nurul Ilmi (1999). *Marital Rape; Kekerasan seksual dalam perkawinan*. Yogyakarta: PPK-UGM and the Ford Foundation.

——— (2001). 'Marriage, sex and violence', in: Susan Blackburn (eds), *Love, sex and power; Women in Southeast Asia*, pp. 43–56. Clayton: Monash Asia Institute.

——— (2002). Pornografi, media dan tubuh perempuan. Paper, one-day seminar on 'Pornografi Ditinjau dari Perspective Jender' (Pornography from Gender Perspectives), Makassar, 16 January.

——— (2006a). 'Poligini; Perdebatan publik, hukum dan budaya', in: Sulistyowati Irianto (eds), *Perempuan dan hukum; Menuju hukum yang berperspektif kesetaraan dan keadilan*, pp. 231–252. Jakarta: Yayasan Obor Indonesia.

——— (2006b). 'It's the matter of one's feeling; gender, desire and identity among female same-sex relationship in globalised South Sulawesi', *Antropologi Indonesia* 30-1:7–20.

——— (2008a). 'Makkunrai Passimokolo'; Bugis migrant women workers in Malaysia, in: Michele Ford and Lyn Parker (eds), *Women and Work in Indonesia*, pp. 155–172. London and New York: Routledge.

——— (2008b). 'Kekerasan dan homofobia', *Fajar* (kolom Suara), 29 Juli, p. 4.

——— (2009a). 'It's the matter of a piece of paper; Between legitimation and legalization of marriage and divorce in Bugis society', *Intersections: Gender and Sexuality in Asia and the Pacific*, http://intersections.anu.edu.au/issue 19/idrus.htm (accessed 19-1-2012)

——— (2009b). *I know I will be sentenced to death; Violence, Homophobia and Media Coverage*. The 7th International Association for the Study of Sexuality, Culture and Society (IASSCS), Hanoi, 15–19 April.

——— (2011). 'Bugis Marriage; state laws, Islam and local practice', in: Gavin W. Jones, Terence H. Hull, and Maznah Mohamad (eds), *Changing marriage patterns in Southeast Asia; economic and socio-cultural dimensions*, pp. 99–116. London and New York: Routledge.

Idrus, Nurul Ilmi and Linda R. Bennett (2002). 'Presumed consent; Marital violence in Bugis Society', in: Lenore Manderson and Linda R. Bennett (eds), *Violence against women in Asian societies*, pp. 41–60. London and New York: Routledge Curzon.

Istiadah (1995). *Muslim women in contemporary Indonesia; Investigating path to resist the patriarchal system*. Working Paper Series 91. Clayton: Centre of Southeast Asian Studies, Monash University,.

Jay, Robert R. (1969). *Javanese villagers; social relations in rural Modjokuto.* Cambridge: MIT Press.

Jennaway, Megan (1996). *Sweet breath and bitter honey; HIV/AIDS and the embodiment of desire among North Balinese Women.* Ph.D. thesis, University of Queensland, Brisbane.

Jolly, Margaret and Lenore Manderson (eds) (1997). *Sites of desire/economies of pleasure; Sexualities in Asia and the Pacific.* Chicago and London: The University of Chicago Press.

Jones, Gavin W. (1994). *Marriage and divorce in Islamic South-East Asia.* Kuala Lumpur: Oxford University Press.

——— (2001). 'Which Indonesian women marry youngest, and why', *Journal of Southeast Asian Studies,* 32-1(February):67–78.

——— (2002). 'The changing Indonesian household', in: Kathryn Robinson and Sharon Bessell (eds), *Women in Indonesia; Gender, equity and development,* pp. 219–234. Singapore: Indonesian Assessment Series, Institute of Southeast Asian Studies.

Jones, Gavin W., Yahya Asari, and Tuti Djuartika (1994). 'Divorce in West Java', *Journal of Comparative Family Studies,* XXV-3(Autumn):395–416.

Keeler, Ward (1987). *Javanese shadow plays, Javanese selves.* Princeton: Princeton University Press.

——— (1989). 'On Javanese interpretation; A scene from a wayang', in: A.L. Becker (eds), *Writing on the tongue,* pp. 139–181. Ann Arbor: Centre for South and Southeast Asian Studies, University of Michigan.

——— (1990). 'Speaking of gender in Java', in: Jane M. Atkinson and Shelly Errington (eds), *Power and difference; Gender in island Southeast Asia,* pp. 127–152. Stanford: Standford University Press.

Kern, R.A. (1989). *I La Galigo.* Yogyakarta: Gadjah Mada University Press.

KHI (*Kompilasi Hukum Islam*) (1999/2000). *Kompilasi hukum Islam di Indonesia.* Jakarta: Direktorat Pembinaan Badan Peradilan Agama, Direktorat Jenderal Pembinaan Kelembagaan Agama Islam, Departemen Agama Republik Indonesia.

Kompas

29 July 2000 *Ny. Sinta Nuriyah; Pemahaman agama yang keliru, timbulkan penderitaan perempuan.*

22 August 2000 *Kajian text perempuan perlu secara kontekstual.*

Koolhof, Sirtjo (1992). *Dutana sawérigading; een scène uit de I La Galigo.* Leiden: Eindscriptie Vakgroep Talen en Culturen van Zuidoost Azië en Oceanië.

Krier, James E. (2000). 'The Marital project; beyond the exchange of men in Minangkabau marriage', *American Ethnologist* 27-4:877–897.

Krulfeld, Ruth (1996). 'Sasak Attitudes towards polygyny and the changing position of women in Sasak peasant villages', in L. Dube, E. Leacock, and S. Ardener (eds),

Visibility and Power; essays on women in society and development. Delhi: Oxford University Press.

Kulo District in Figures (2014). Sulawesi Selatan: Badan Pusat Statistik Kabupaten Sidrap.

Kumar, Ann and John H. McGlynn (1996). *Illuminations; The writing traditions of Indonesia; Featuring manuscripts from the National Library of Indonesia*. Jakarta and Weatherhill, New York and Tokyo: The Lontar Foundation.

Kurnia, Novi (2009). 'Berbagi suami (love to share); discourse of polygamy in a recent Indonesian film', *Intersections*, 19(February).

La Side (1977). *Beberapa Keterangan dan Petunjuk Tentang Pengertian dan Perkembangan Siriq Pada Suku Bugis*. Paper, seminar on '*Siriq* and Its Problems in South Sulawesi', Ujung Pandang, 11–13 July.

Langley, R. and R. Levy (1978). *Wife beating; The silent crisis*. New York: Pocket Book.

Leach, E.R. (1961). *Rethinking anthropology*. London School of Economics Monograph on Social Anthropology, no. 22. London: Athlon Press, University of London.

Lev, Daniel B. (1972). *Islamic courts in Indonesia; A study in the political bases of legal Institutions*, pp. 191–203. Barkeley: University of California Press.

——— (1996). 'On the Other Hand?' in: Laurie J. Sears (eds), *Fantasizing the feminine in Indonesia*, pp. 191–203. London: Duke University Press.

Lewis, B., V.L. Menage, Ch. Pellat, and J. Schacht (eds) (1971). *The encyclopedia of Islam*. London: Luzac & Co.

Lineton, Jacqueline (1975). 'Pasompe' Ugi'; Migrants and Wanderers', *Archipel* 10:173–201.

Locher-Scholten, Elsbeth and Anke Niehof (1987). 'Introduction', in: Elsbeth Locher-Shcholten and Anke Niehof (eds), *Indonesian Women in Focus*, pp. 1–11. Dordrecht-Holland/Providence-USA: Foris Publications.

Lopa, Baharuddin (1984). *Siriq dalam masyarakat Mandar dan pemanfaatannya dalam pembangunan di Sulawesi Selatan*. Ujung Pandang: Pusat Penelitian Pembangunan Pedesaan dan Kawasan, Lembaga Penelitian Unhas.

Machmud, A. Hasan (1976). *Silasa; Setetes Embun di tanah gersang* (first edition). Ujung Pandang: Yayasan Kebudayaan Sulawesi Selatan.

——— (1994). *Silasa; Kumpulan petuah Bugis-Makassar* (second edition). Jakarta: Bhakti Centra Baru.

Macknight, Campbell (1972). *South Celebes manuscripts*. Canberra: Menzies Library, the Australian National University.

——— (1993). *The early history of South Sulawesi; Some recent advances*. Working Paper Series no. 81. Clayton: The Centre for Southeast Asian Studies, Monash University.

Macknight, Campbell and Paeni, Mukhlis (n.d.). *The chronicle of Bone*.

MacMarmack, Carol (1980). 'Nature, culture and gender; A critique', in: Carol MacCormack and Marilyn Strathern (eds), *Nature, culture and gender*, pp. 1–24. Cambridge: Cambridge University Press.

Madden, Raymond (2013). *Being ethnographic; A guide to the theory and practice of ethnography*. Singapore: Sage Publications.

Makassar in Figures (2014). Makassar: Badan Pusat Statistik Makassar.

Manderson, Lenore (eds) (1983). *Women's work and women's roles; Economics and everyday life in Indonesia, Malaysia and Singapore*. Development Studies Centre Monograph, no. 32. Canberra: The Australian National University.

Manderson, Lenore and Pranee L. Rice (eds) (1999). *Maternity and reproductive health in Asian societies*. The Netherlands: Harwood Academic Publisher.

Manderson, Lenore and Linda R. Bennett (eds) (2003). *Violence against women in Asian Societies*. London and New York: Routledge Curzon.

Marcus, Sharon (1992). 'Fighting bodies, fighting words; A theory of politics of rape prevention', in: Judith Butler and Joan W. Scott (eds), *Feminists Theorize the Political*, pp. 385–403. London: Routledge.

Martin, Del (1976). *Battered wives*. California: Glide Publications.

Marzuki, Laica (1995). *Siriq, bagian kesadaran hukum rakyat Bugis-Makassar; Sebuah telaah filsafat hukum*. Ujung Pandang: Hasanuddin University Press.

Mas'udi, Masdar F. (1996). *Islam and hak-hak reproduksi perempuan*. Bandung: Penerbit Mizan.

Matthes, B.F. (1872). *Boeginesche chrestomathie*. Amsterdam: C.A. Spin & Zoon.

——— (1874). *Boegineesch-Hollandsch woordenboek, met Hollandsch-Boeginesche woordenlijst*. M. Nijhoff, 's Gravenhage.

Mattulada (1971). 'Kebudayaan Bugis Makassar', In: Koentjaraningrat (eds), *Manusia dan kebudayaan di Indonesia*, pp. 264–283. Jakarta: Penerbit Djambatan.

——— (1974). 'Bugis-Makassar; Manusia and kebudayaannya', *Berita Antropologi*, 15:12–25. Fakultas Sastra, Universitas Indonesia,

——— (1977). *Pengaruh ulama dan sistem pendidikan agama (Islam) dalam rumah tangga orang Bugis*. Ujung Pandang: Universitas Hasanuddin.

——— (1995). *Latoa; Satu lukisan analitis terhadap antropologi politik orang Bugis*. Second edition. Ujung Pandang: Hasanuddin University Press.

——— (1998). *Sejarah, masyarakat and kebudayaan Sulawesi Selatan*. Ujung Pandang: Hasanuddin University Press.

Maula, Masyiatul (2002). *Menolak mut'ah-sirri, memberdayakan perempuan; Kajian badal Nyai dan Kyai se Jawa Tengah dan Daerah Istimewa Yogyakarta*. Yogyakarta: The Ford Foundation and Rifka Annisa.

McDonald, Peter and Abdurahman, Edeng (1974). *Perkawinan dan perceraian di Jawa Barat*. Jakarta: Lembaga Demografi, Fakultas Ekonomi, Universitas Indonesia.

M.D. Nor, Mohd. Yusof (1989). *Antologi enam hikayat*. Petaling Jaya: Penerbit Fajar Bakti SDN. BHD.

Mernissi, Fatimah (1985). Beyond the veil; Male–female dynamics in modern Muslim society (revised edition). London: Al Saqi Books.

Millar, Susan B. (1983). 'On interpreting gender in Bugis society', *American Ethnologist* 10(August):477–492.

———(1989). *Bugis weddings; Ritual of social location in modern Indonesia.* Monograph Series, no. 29. Barkeley: Center for South and Southeast Asian Studies, University of California.

Mitchell, Winifred L. (1994). 'Women's hierarchies of age and suffering in an Andean community', in: Dickerson-Putman and Judith K. Brown (eds), *Women among women; Anthropological perspectives on female age hierarchies*, pp. 52–64. Urgana and Chicago: University of Illinois Press.

Mohd. Hasan, Abdul Jalil (1993). *Perkahwinan dalam Islam.* Kuala Lumpur: A.S. Noordeen.

Moore, Henrietta (1988). *Feminism and anthropology.* Oxford: Polity Press.

Morell, Elizabeth (1998). 'Symbolism, spatiality, and social order', in: Kathryn Robinson and Mukhlis Paeni (eds), *Living through history: Culture, history and social life in South Sulawesi*, pp. 151–167. Canberra: Department of Anthropology, RSPAS, the Australian National University and the National Archives of Indonesia.

Morgan, David L. (1988). *Focus groups as qualitative research.* London: Sage Publications.

Mortokoesoemo, Budi Soeradji (1979). *Marriage and divorce in Indonesia; A demographic study.* PhD Dissertation, the University of Chicago, Chicago.

Muhammad Sikki, Syamsul Rijal, Nasruddin, and Syamsul Alam (1998). *Nilai and manfaat pappaseng dalam sastra Bugis.* Jakarta: Pusat Pembinaan and Pengembangan Bahasa, Department of Pendidikan and Kebudayaan.

Muhammad, Husein (2001). *Fiqh perempuan; Refleksi kiai atas wacana agama dan gender.* Yogyakarta: LKiS.

Mukherjee, Wendy (1997). 'The love magic of Khatijah Terong of Pulau Penyengat'. *RIMA* 31-2 (December):29–46.

Mukhlis (1994). *Daftar katalog rol 1–82* (Catalogue list roll 1–82). Proyek Naskah Unhas, Sponsored by the Ford Foundation 1991–1994, Introduction.

Mulia, Siti Musdah (2004). *Islam menggugat poligami.* Jakarta: PT Gramedia Pustaka Utama.

Murata, Sachiko (1998). *The tao of Islam.* Bandung: Penerbit Mizan.

Nader, Laura (1969). 'Up-the anthropologist—Perspectives gained from studying up', in: Dell Hymes (ed), *Reinventing Anthropology*, pp. 284–311. New York, Pantheon.

Nakamura, Hisako (1981). *'A study of dissolution of marriage among Javanese muslims'*, M.A. Thesis, the Australian National University, Canberra.

Narayan, Kirin (1993). 'How native is a "native" anthropologist?' *American Anthropological Association*, 95 (3 September):671–686.

Niehof, Anke (1983). *Women and fertility in Madura (Indonesia).* PhD Dissertation, Leiden University.

Nurhaedi, Dadi (2003). *Nikah di bawah tangan; Praktik nikah sirri mahasiswa Jogja*. Jogjakarta: Saujana.

Nurmila, Nina (2009). *Women, Islam and everyday life; Renegotiating polygamy in Indonesia*. London: Routledge.

Noeh, Zaini A. (1980). *Peradilan agama Islam di Indonesia*. Translation. Jakarta: PT. Intermasa (Introduction).

Nyompa, Johan, Abu Hamid, Husain Hafidz, and Daud Limbugau. (1979). *Sistem kekerabatan dan peranan pranata keluarga dalam masyarakat orang Bugis di Sulawesi Selatan*. Ujung Pandang: FIISBUD-Unhas.

Oakley, Ann (1972). *Sex, gender and society*. New York: Harper Colophon.

——— (1996). 'Sexuality', in: Stevi Jackson and Sue Scott (eds), *Feminism and Sexuality*, pp. 35–39. Edinburgh: Edinburgh University Press.

Okely, Judith (1996). *Own or other culture*. London: Routledge.

Ortner, Sherry (1974). 'Is female to male as nature to culture?' in: Michele Z. Rosaldo and Louis Lamphere (eds), *Women, culture and society*, pp. 67–87. California: Standford University Press.

Ortner, Sherry and Harriet Whitehead (1981). 'Introduction; Accounting for sexual meanings', in: Sherry Ortner and Harriet Whitehead (eds), *Sexual Meaning: The Cultural Construction of Gender and Sexuality*, pp. 1–27. Cambridge: Cambridge University Press.

Pagelow, Mildred D. (1997). 'Marital Rape', in: Vincent L. Morrison, Alan S. Bellack and Michel Hersen (eds) *Handbook of Family Violence*, pp. 207–232. New York and London: Plenum Press.

Palisuri, Udhin (2002). *Bulan pagi hari*. Makassar: Pemda Kota Makassar.

Palmier, Leslie H. (1960). *Social status and power in Java*. Athlone Press, University of London.

Panini, M.N. (ed.) (1990). *From the female eye; Accounts of women fieldworkers studying their own communities*. Delhi: Hindustan Publishing Corporation.

Parawansa, Khofifah I. (2002). 'Institution building; An effort to improve Indonesian women's role and status', in: Kathryn Robinson and Sharon Bessell (eds), *Women in Indonesia: Gender equity and developmen*, pp. 68–77. Singapore: Institute of Southeast Asian Studies (ISEAS).

Pare Post 16 December 2000 *Kematian Bidan Satirah di Pare-Pareterungkap*.

Parker, Lynette (1989). *Village and state in 'new order' Bali*. PhD Thesis, Department of Anthropology, RSPAS, the Australian National University, Canberra.

——— (1993). *Gender and school in Bali*. Working Paper Series no. 4. Canberra Gender Relations Project, RSPAS, the Australian National University.

Pausacker, Helen (2001). 'Dalang and family planning propaganda in Indonesia', in: Susan Blackburn (eds), *Love, sex and power; Women in Southeast Asia*, pp. 89–114. Clayton: Monash Asia Institute.

P3N&P3N (1997/1998). *Pedoman pegawai pencatat nikah & pembantu pegawai pencatat nikah*. Proyek Peningkatan Sarana Keagamaan Islam, Zakat dan Wakaf.

Peletz, Michael G. (2009). *Gender pluralism; Southeast Asia since early modern times*. New York and London: Routledge.

Pelras, Christian (1996). The Bugis. Cambridge: Blackwell Publishers.

——— (1998). 'Bugis culture; A tradition of modernity', in: Kathryn Robinson and Mukhlis Paeni (eds), *Living through history; Culture, history and social life in South Sulawesi*, pp. 19–28. Canberra: Department of Anthropology, RSPAS, the Australian National University and the National Archives of Indonesia.

——— (2000). 'Patron client ties among the Bugis and Makassarese of South Sulawesi', in: Roger Tol, Kees van Dijk and Greg Acciaioli (eds), *Authority and enterprise among the peoples of South Sulawesi*, pp. 15–54. Leiden: KITLV Press.

——— (2006). Manusia Bugis. Nalar: Jakarta.

Pitt-Rivers, Julian (1965). 'Honour and social status', in: J.G. Peristiany (ed.), *Honour and Shame: The Values of Mediterranean Society*, pp. 19–77. London: Weidenfeld and Nicolson.

Platt, Maria. (2010). *Patriarchal institutions and women's agency in Indonesian marriages; Sasak women navigating dynamic marital continuums*. Ph.D. thesis, La Trobe University, Victoria.

——— (2012). 'Married men behaving badly; Islam, gender and extramarital relationship in Eastern Indonesia', *Intersections* 28(March).

P_3B (Pusat Pembinaan and Pengembangan Bahasa) (1999). *Budi Istikharah Indar Bustanil Arifin*. Jakarta: Departemen P and K.

PPIH (Panitia Penyelenggara Ibadah Haji) (2001). *Laporan dan evaluasi penyelenggaraan ibadah Haji embarkasi/debarkasi Hasanuddin Makassar*. Makassar: PPIH.

Purwatiningsih, Sri (2005). Gaya PNS berpoligami; Pelanggaran PP No. 10 Tahun 1983. Yogyakarta: Pusat Studi Kependudukan dan Kebijakan.

Qardhawi, Syekh M.Y. (1993). *Halal dan haram dalam Islam*. Translated by Mu'ammal Hamidy. Jakarta: PT. Bina Ilmu.

Rahim, A. Rahman (1982). *Sikap mental Bugis berdasarkan lontarak-lontarak latoa and budi istikharah*. Makassar: Universitas Hasanuddin.

Rahman, Alwy (1998). *Gelas kaca and kayu bakar; Pengalaman perempuan dalam pelaksanaan hak-hak keluarga berencana*. Yogyakarta: Pustaka Pelajar Yogyakarta, YLK-SS and the Ford Foundation.

Ramali, Ahmad (1951). *Peraturan-peraturan untuk memelihara kesehatan dalam hukum sjara'*. Jakarta: Balai Pustaka.

Ramulyo, M. Idris (1996). *Hukum perkawinan Islam; Suatu analisis dari Undang-Undang No.1/1974 dan kompilasi hukum Islam*. Jakarta: Bumi Aksara.

Reid, Anthony (1988). *Southeast Asia in the age of commerce 1450–1680; The lands below the wind*. New Haven and London: Yale University Press.

Republika 11 December 2000 *Khofifah usulkan siswa hamil boleh sekolah usai melahirkan.*

Robinson, Kathryn M. (1983). 'Women and work in an Indonesian mining town', in: Lenore Manderson (eds), *Women's work and women's roles; Economics and everyday life in Indonesia, Malaysia and Singapore,* Development Studies Centre Monograph, no. 32, pp. 111–128. Canberra: The Australian National University.

——— (1985). 'Modernisation and mothering', *Prisma* 37:47–56.

——— (1986). *Stepchildren; The political economy of development in an Indonesian mining town.* Albany: State University of New York Press.

——— (1987). 'Kartini's vision and the position of Indonesian women', *Mankind,* 17-2:104–113.

——— (1989). 'Choosing contraception; Cultural change and the Indonesian family planning programme', in: P. Alexander (eds), *Creating Indonesian culture,* pp. 21–38. Sydney: University of Sydney, Oceania Publications.

——— (1993). 'The platform house; Expression of a regional identity in the modern Indonesian nation, in: Virginia Hooker (eds), *Culture and society in new order Indonesia,* pp. 228–242. Kuala Lumpur: Oxford University Press.

——— (1994). 'Indonesian national identity and citizen mother', *Communal/Plural* 3:65–81.

——— (1996). 'Women, mining and development', in: Richard Howwitt, John Connell and Philip Hirsch (eds), *Resources, nations and indigenous peoples,* pp. 21–38. Melbourne: Oxford University Press.

——— (1998a). 'Love and sex in an Indonesian mining town', in: Khrisna Sen and Maila Stevens (eds), *Gender and power in affluent Asia,* pp. 63–86. New York: Routledge.

——— (1998b). 'Indonesian women's rights, international feminism and democratic change', *Communal/Plural* 6-2:205–223.

——— (1998c). 'Traditions of house-building in South Sulawesi', in: Kathryn Robinson and Mukhlis Paeni (eds), *Living through history; Culture, history and social life in South Sulawesi,* pp. 168–195. Department of Anthropology, RSPAS, the Australian National University and the National Archives of Indonesia.

——— (1999). 'Women; Difference versus diversity', in: Donald K. Emmerson (eds), *Indonesia beyond Soeharto; Polity, economy, society, transitio,* pp. 237–261. New York: M.E. Sharpe.

——— (2000a). 'Government agency, women's agency; Feminism, fertility, and population control', in: Margaret Jolly and Kalpana Ram (eds), *Borders of being; Citizenship, fertility, and sexuality in Asia and the Pacific,* pp. 36–57. Ann Arbour: The University of Michigan Press.

——— (2000b). 'Indonesia women; From orde baru to reformasi', in: Louis Edwards and Mina Roces (eds), *Women in Asia; Tradition, modernity and globalisation,* pp. 139–169. Sydney: Women in Asia Publication Series, Allen and Unwin.

———(2001). 'Gender, Islam and culture in Indonesia', in: Susan Blackburn (eds), *Love, sex and power; Women in Southeast Asia*, pp. 17–30. Clayton: Monash Asia Institute.

———(2006). 'Muslim women political struggle for Marriage Law reform in contemporary Indonesia', in: A. Whiting and C. Evans (eds), *Mixed Blessings; laws, religions, and women's rights in the Asia-Pacific region*, pp. 183–210. Leiden and Boston: Martinus Nijhoff Publishers.

——— (2009). *Gender, Islam and democracy in Indonesia*. London and New York: Routledge.

Robinson, Kathryn and Muhlis Paeni (eds) (1998). *Living through history; culture, history and social life in South Sulawesi*. Canberra: the Department of Anthropology, RSPAS, the Australian National University and the National Archives of Indonesia.

Rosaldo, Michele Z. (1974). 'Women, culture and society; A theoretical overview', in: Michele Z. Rosaldo and Loui Lamphere (eds), *Women, culture and society*, pp. 17–41. California: Stanford University Press.

———(1980). 'The use and abuse of anthropology; Reflections on feminism and cross-cultural understanding', *Sign* 5:389–417.

Röttger-Rössler, Birgitt (2000). 'Shared responsibility; some aspects of gender and authority in Makassar society', in: Roger Tol, Kees van Dijk, and Greg Acciaioli (eds), *Authority and enterprise among the peoples of South Sulawesi*, pp. 161–182. Leiden: KITLV Press.

Rudnyckyj, Daromir (2009). 'Market Islam in Indonesia', *Journal of the Royal Anthropological Institute (NS)*, S183–S201.

Russell, Diana E.H. (1980). *Rape in marriage*. Indianapolis: Indiana University Press.

Saengtienchai, C.; J. Knodel, M. Vanlandingham, and A. Pramualratana. (1999). 'Prostitutes are better than lovers; Wives views on the extramarital sexual behaviour of Thai men', in: Peter A. Jackson and Nerida M. Cook (eds), *Genders and sexualities in modern Thailand*, pp. 78–92. Thailand: Silkworm Books.

Said, Natzir (1997). *Siriq sebagai suatu nilai dasar atau pedoman bertingkah laku (norma-norma) dalam tertib sosial di Sulsel*. Ujung Pandang: Pusat Penelitian Pembangunan Pedesaan dan Kawasan, Lembaga Penelitian Unhas.

Salim, Muhammad (1978). *'Peranan lontarak sebagai sumber pangngaderreng'*. Sarjana Thesis, Universitas Veteran Republik Indonesia, Ujung Pandang.

Salim, Muhammad and Fachruddin Ambo Enre (1995). *I La Galigo*. Vol. I. Jakarta: KITLV and Penerbit Djambatan.

———(2000). *La Galigo*. Vol. II. Makassar: Universitas Hasanuddin.

Salombe, C. (1984). *Siriq dalam hidup kemasyarakatn suku Toraja*. Ujung Pandang: Pusat Penelitian Pembangunan dan pedesaan dan Kawasan, Lembaga Penelitian Unhas.

Sanday, Peggy R. (2002). *Women at the center; life in a modern matriarchy*. Ithaca and London: Cornell.

Segal, Lynne (1994). *Straight sex; The politics of pleasure.* London: Virago Press.

Sen, Krishna (1993). 'Repression and resistance; Interpretations of the feminine in new order cinema', in: Virginia M. Hooker (eds), *Culture and Society in New Order Indonesia*, pp. 116–133. Kuala Lumpur: Oxford University Press.

Sensus Penduduk 2010 (2011a). *Kewarganegaraan, suku bangsa, agama, dan bahasa sehari-hari penduduk Indonesia: Hasil Sensus Penduduk 2010.* Jakarta: Badan Pusat Statistik.

——— (2011b). *Fertilitas penduduk Indonesia: Hasil Sensus Penduduk 2010.* Jakarta: Badan Pusat Statistik.

Seymor, Susan C. (1999). *Women, family, and child care in India; A world in transition.* United Kingdom: Cambridge University Press.

Siapno, Jacqueline A. (1997). *The politics of gender, Islam and nation-state in Aceh, Indonesia; A historical analysis of power, co-optation and resistance.* PhD Dissertation, South and Southeast Asian Studies, University of California, Berkeley.

Siddik, Abdullah (1983). *Hukum perkawinan Islam.* Jakarta: Tintamas Indonesia.

Sidenreng Rappang in Figures (2001). *Sidenreng Rappang in Figures.* Pangkajene: Pemerintah Kabupaten Sidrap.

——— (2014). *Sidenreng Rappang in Figures.* Pangkajene: Pemerintah Kabupaten Sidrap.

Sikki, Muhammad, Syamsul Rijal, Nasruddin, and Syamsul Alam (1998). *Nilai and manfaat pappaseng dalam sastra Bugis.* Jakarta: Departemen Pendidikan and Kebudayaan.

Sila, M. Adlin (2002). *Gender and ethnicity in Sayyid community of Cikoang, South Sulawesi; Kafa'ah, a marriage system among Sayyid females.* Paper, the 3rd International Symposium of the Journal Antropologi Indonesia, Udayana University, Denpasar – Bali, Indonesia, 16–19 July.

Singarimbun, M. and C. Manning (1974). 'Marriage and divorce in Mojolama', *Indonesia* 17(April):67–82.

Situmorang, Augustina (2011). 'Delayed marriage among lower socio-economic groups in an Indonesian industrial city', in: Gavin W. Jones, Terrence H. Hull, and Maznah Mohamad (eds), *Changing Marriage Patterns in Southeast Asia; Economic and socio-cultural dimensions*, pp. 83–98. London and New York: Routledge.

Sjafri, Aida (1991). 'Multiple role performance; An urban professional woman in a village setting', in: M.N. Panini (eds), *From the female eye; Accounts of women fieldworkers studying their own communitie*, pp. 74–80. Delhi: Hindustan Publishing Corporation.

Soebahar, Abdul Halim, Moh. Fadli, Hamdanah, and Rahmad Sa'idah (2005) *Poligami, pintu daruratkah? Debat di kalangan tokoh Islam.* Yogyakarta: PSKK-UGM.

Soekanto, Soejono (1981). *Meninjau hukum adat Indonesia.* Jakarta: Penerbit CV. Rajawali.

Soewondo, Nani (1975). 'The Indonesian marriage law and its implementing regulation', *Archipel* 13:283–294.

Sosroatmojo, Arso and Wasit Aulawi (1978). *Hukum perkawinan di Indonesia*. Jakarta: Bulan Bintang.

Southon, Michael (1995). *The navel of the perahu; Meaning and values in the maritime trading edconomy of a Butonese village*. Canberra: Department of Anthropology, RSPAS, the Australian National University.

Spradley, James P. (1979). *Ethnographic interview*. New York: Holt Rinehart and Winston.

Stanko, Elizabeth (1988). 'Fear of crime and the myth of safe home', in: Kersty Yllo and Michele Bograd (eds), *Feminist perspectives on wife abuse*, pp. 75–88. Newbury Park: Sage Publications.

Stets, Jan E. (1988). *Domestic violence control*. New York: Springer Verlag.

Strathern, Marilyn (1980). 'No nature, no culture; The Hagen case', in: Carol MacCormack and Marilyn Strathern (eds), *Nature, culture and gender*, pp. 174–222. Cambridge: Cambridge University Press.

Sudirman, Rahmat (1999). *Konstruksi seksualitas dalam wacana sosial*. Yogyakarta: Penerbit Media Pressindo.

Suhatmini, Hardyastuti and Bambang Hudayana (1991). *Pekerja wanita di industry rumah tangga sandang di propinsi* DIY. Yogyakarta: Pusat Penelitian Kependudukan, Universitas Gadjah Mada.

Sulawesi Selatan in Figures (2014). Makassar: Badan Pusat Statistik Propinsi Sulawesi Selatan.

Sullivan, Norma (1983). 'Indonesian women in development; State theory and urban kampung practice', in: Lenore Manderson (eds), *Women's work and women's roles; Economics and everyday life in Indonesia, Malaysia and Singapore*, pp. 147–182. Development Studies Centre Monograph, no. 32. Canberra: The Australian National University.

——— (1994). *Masters and managers; A study of gender relations in urban Java*. Sydney: Women in Asia Publication Series, Allen and Unwin.

Sunidyo, Saraswati (1993). 'Gender discourse on television', in: Virginia M. Hooker (eds), *Culture and society in new order Indonesia*, pp. 134–147. Kuala Lumpur: Oxford University Press.

——— (1996). 'Murder, gender and the media', in: Laurie J. Sears (eds), *Fantasizing the feminine in Indonesi*, pp. 120–139. Durkham and London: Duke University Press.

——— (1998). 'When the earth is female and the nation is mother; Gender, the armed forces and nationalism in Indonesia', *Feminist Review* 58:1–21.

Suryakusuma, Julia I. (1987). *State ibuism; The social construction of womenhood in the Indonesian new order*. M.A. Thesis, Institute of Social Studies, the Hague.

——— (1996) 'The state and sexuality in new order Indonesia', in: Sears, Laurie J. (ed), *Fantasizing the Feminine in Indonesia*, pp. 92–119. Duke University Press: Durkham and London.

——— (1998). 'Perkosaan and Negara' (Rape and the State). *Media Indonesia*. 18 July 1998.

——— (2000). *Militerisme dan Kekerasan terhadap Perempuan, Implikasinya terhadap Hak Asasi Manusia dan Demokratisasi* Paper, Program Kampanye Memperingati Hari Internasional Anti-Kekerasan terhadap Perempuan, Universitas Indonesia, Depok, Jakarta, 25 November 2000.

——— (2004). *Sex, power and nation*. Jakarta: Metafor.

——— (2011). *Ibuisme negara; konstruksi social keperempuanan Orde Baru*. Depok: Komunitas Bambu.

Sweeney, Amin (1980). *Authors and audiences in traditional Malay literature. Centre for South and Southeast Asian studies*. Berkeley: University of California.

——— (1987). *A full hearing; Orality and literacy in the Malay world*. Berkeley: University of California Press.

Syekh al-Hadi, Syed (1925–1926). *Faridah Hanom*. Penang: Al-Aminiyyah Press.

Tol, Roger (1996). 'A separate empire; Writings of South Sulawesi', in: Ann Kumar and John H. McGlynn (eds), *Illuminations the writing traditions of Indonesia; Featuring manuscripts from the National Library of Indonesia*, pp. 213–230. New York and Tokyo: The Lontar Foundation, Jakarta and Weatherhill, Inc.

——— (2000). 'Textual Authority; the toloq rumpaqna Boné by I Mallq Daéng Mabéla, Arung Manajéng', in: Roger Tol, Kees van Dijk, and Greg Acciaioli (eds), pp. 121–142. *Authority and enterprise among the peoples of South Sulawesi*. Leiden: KITLV Press.

Tim Peneliti (1988). *Perkawinan and perceraian di Jawa Barat*. Bandung: PSK-LP, Universitas Padjadjaran.

Truninger, Elizabeth (1971). 'Marital violence; The legal solution', *Hasting Law Review* 23:259–276.

Undang-undang pokok perkawinan (1989). *Undang-undang pokok perkawinan beserta peraturan perkawinan khusus untuk anggota ABRI, POLRI, pegawai kejaksaan, pegawai negeri ipil*. Jakarta: Sinar Grafika.

Utomo, Iwu D. (1997). *Sexual attitudes and behaviour of middle-class young people in Jakarta*. PhD Thesis, the Australian National University, Canberra.

——— (1998). *State ideologies and provision of reproductive health education and services; A case study of Indonesian youth*. Paper, Seminar on 'Gender inequalities and reproductive health; Changing priorities in an era of Social transformation and globalization'. Campus de Jordao, Brazil, 16–19 November.

'Uwaidah, Syaikh Kamil M. (1998). *Fiqih wanita*. Translated by M. Abdul Ghoffar E.M. Jakarta: Pustaka Al-Kautsar.

Visweswaran, Kamala (1994). *Fictions of feminist ethnography*. Minnes and London, University of Minnesota Press.

Walker, Lenore E. (1979). *The battered women*. New York: Harper and Row.

——— (1984). *The battered woman* New York: Springer Publishing Company.

Wieringa, Saskia (1992). 'Ibu or the beast'; Gender interests in two Indonesian women's organisations', *Feminist Review* 41(Summer):98–113.

——— (1993). 'Two of Indonesian women's organisations; Gerwani and PKK', *Bulletin of Concerned Asia Scholars* 25-2:17–31.

Yunus, Ahmad, Rosyadi, T. Kartikasari, I. Made Purna, and Ambo Gani (1990). *Kajian analisa hikayat budi istiharah.* Jakarta: Department P & K.

Yunus, Ahmad, P. Hamid, T. Kartikasari, Soeloso, and Rosyadi (1991/1992). *Lontarak Luwu daerah Sulawesi Selatan.* Jakarta: Departemen Pendidikan dan Kebudayaan, Direktorat Jenderal Kebudayaan, Direktorat Sejarah dan Nilai Tradisional, Proyek Penelitian dan Pengkajian Kebudayaan Nusantara.

Zuidberg, Lida C.L. (ed) (1978). *Family planning in rural West Java; The Serpong project.* Amsterdam: Nabrink and Son.

Index